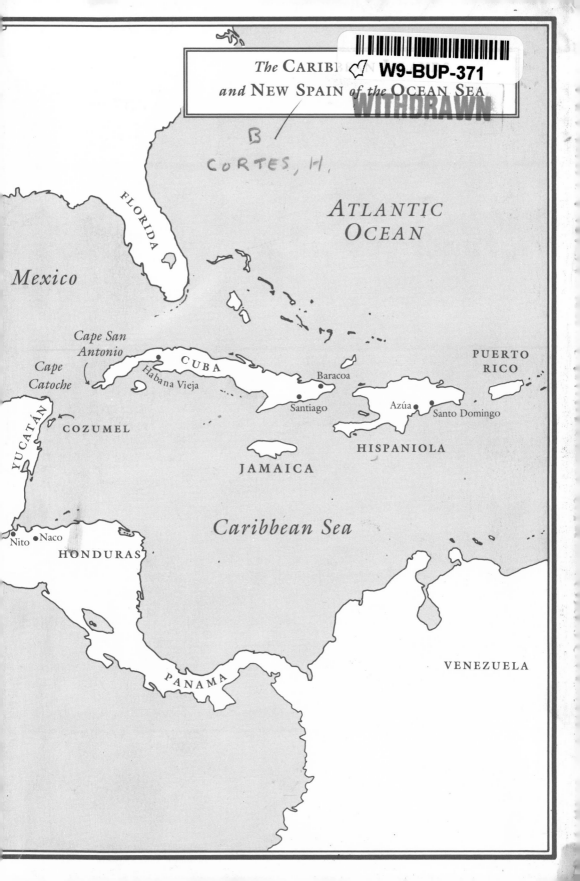

The CARIBBEAN
and NEW SPAIN of the OCEAN SEA

B
CORTES, H.

ATLANTIC
OCEAN

Mexico

FLORIDA

Cape San
Antonio

Cape
Catoche

CUBA

Habana Vieja

Baracoa

Santiago

PUERTO
RICO

Azúa

Santo Domingo

COZUMEL

YUCATÁN

HISPANIOLA

JAMAICA

Caribbean Sea

Nito Naco

HONDURAS

VENEZUELA

PANAMA

RICHARD LEE MARKS

CORTÉS

*The Great Adventurer and
the Fate of Aztec Mexico*

ALFRED A. KNOPF NEW YORK 1993

THIS IS A BORZOI BOOK
PUBLISHED BY ALFRED A. KNOPF, INC.

Copyright © 1993 by Richard Lee Marks
Maps copyright © 1993 by Claudia Carlson
All rights reserved under International and Pan-American Copyright
Conventions. Published in the United States by Alfred A. Knopf, Inc.,
New York, and simultaneously in Canada by Random House of Canada
Limited, Toronto. Distributed by Random House, Inc., New York.

Library of Congress Cataloging-in-Publication Data
Marks, Richard Lee.
Cortés: the great adventurer and the fate of Aztec Mexico/
by Richard Lee Marks.
p. cm.
Includes bibliographical references and index.
ISBN 0-679-40609-3
1. Cortés, Hernán, 1485–1547. 2. Mexico—History—
Conquest, 1519–1540. 3. Indians of Mexico—History—16th century.
4. Aztecs—History—16th century. 5. Conquerors—Mexico—Biography.
I. Title.
F1230.C835M36   1993
972′.02—dc20   92-37170   CIP

Manufactured in the United States of America

First Edition

To Annette

. . . and with a little help from Fortune,
who is blind and favors the bold . . .

—Ricardo Palma

CONTENTS

LIST OF ILLUSTRATIONS

MAPS

ACKNOWLEDGMENTS

———————

I would like to thank for their exceptional helpfulness: Raúl Nuñez of New York City; Dr. Donald F. Danker, professor emeritus of history at Washburn University; Robert B. Marks for advice on all maritime matters; and Steven L. Marks for essential, emergency computer intervention.

R.L.M.

AUTHOR'S NOTE

By chance, I have lived much of my life among American Indians. I think, by nature, I have a Spanish heart. But I don't believe this creates a conflict. On the contrary, I hope that it enables me to tell this story of old glories from fresh viewpoints, candidly yet with compassion. My sources are chiefly the first-hand accounts of participants and the second-hand accounts of chroniclers who interviewed participants, with the accounts of scholarly clerics, who wrote in later years, consulted for comparison and verification. Actually the first-hand accounts vary in many details, and I have consistently chosen the details that seem to me the most credible. I am familiar with most of the places where these events occurred. My speculations are based on sequences of reasonable presumptions, but the attempts to sense the spirit and to fathom the psyche of both Indians and Spaniards are my own.

I
PREDAWN OF CONQUES

THE HOME GROUND

It may come as a surprise to those who bear in their minds a stereotypical impression of Hernán Cortés that when he was a baby he was so puny and sickly that his wet-nurse many times placed lighted candles for him on the altar of the little church in Medellín as she chanted prayers for his survival. Cortés was not suckled by his mother, Doña Catalina Pizarro Altimarano de Cortés, though she was well endowed with milk, because stylish young ladies of lineage in 1485, when Cortés was born, believed that breast-feeding led to excessive enlargement of their bosoms. Consequently Doña Catalina's husband, Martín Cortés de Monroy, found a servant-woman who happened to be fresh, after having lost a child of her own, and hired her to nurse the baby. Martín Cortés owned a few stony acres in Es-tremadura, which is in the interior of the Iberian peninsula not far from the Spanish border with Portugal; often strapped for money, he had cause to grumble over the avoidable expense, yet in deference to his wife's pride and vanity (and perhaps because he liked her figure as it was) he bore the cost; and on the milk from those hired breasts the colicky infant endured.

In the years following 1485, the town of Medellín was like the setting of a carnival for a growing boy. On a hill stood the small castle where the Spaniards had held out against the Moors and from which Spaniards eventually had sallied forth to participate in the reconquest of their own land. The Moors had been expelled from most of Spain, not by a unified national effort, but by local insurgencies in cities and towns all over the peninsula. With the immediate threat of the Moors diminished, the children of Medellín were allowed to play within the castle walls, though the castle remained the residence of the count of Medellín and his family. Up and down the spiral stone steps in the turrets, past the notched battlements and in the courtyards, Hernán Cortés and the friends of his childhood scurried in games of Christians-and-Moors (not unlike cowboys-and-Indians).

At the base of the hill below the castle were the houses and huts of the town, clustered together because Spanish herders and farmers did not choose to live on the land; it was too dangerous, the threat of the Moors was too recent, for Spanish families voluntarily to be far out and by

The castle of Medellín on the hill above the town. In this castle the townsfolk held out against the Moors, and from this castle the Spaniards came forth to join in the reconquest of their own land.

themselves. The castle was the citadel to which they would flee in times of danger, and they wanted to be near it.

In the midst of the town stood the church, not a Gothic edifice aspiring to heaven but a humble building that appeared to be merely a consecrated house. Yet the people profoundly and unwaveringly believed that the church was the source of their spiritual strength; especially the children who attended services in the church—the children who, lisping, chanted and sang in their soprano voices—never had a doubt. The strength of Spanish spirit reposed in the church. The boys of Medellín, including Hernán Cortés, believed this in the depths of their souls. With this strength of spirit Spaniards had been able to drive off the alien Moors, who admittedly were better armed, had better horses, were better organized, and were more knowledgeable and sophisticated than the native people.

All around Medellín, from a boy's point of view, there were plenty of flat fields for kicking around a leather ball—not rubber, because rubber had not yet come from the New World. Spanish boys of the late fifteenth century, however, did not usually play soccer or jai alai: They played war-games, because incessant and often furious war had been the Spanish way of life for at least the preceding seven hundred years. (This town of Medellín in Spain, incidentally, should not be confused with the city of the same name with over a million inhabitants in Colombia where the infamous drug cartel maintains its headquarters, nor with the village of the same name on the island of Cebu in the Philippines. The birthplace of Cortés in Estremadura, however, is the original Medellín for which the others were named.)

A remnant of the glory of Roman Spain. In this reconstructed theatre in Mérida, which is not far from Medellín, the Roman soldiers of the Tenth Legion, having elected to settle in Estremadura, enjoyed performances in praise of their empire.

The Spanish Medellín is in the old Roman section of the country. Early in the Christian era, after Roman legions had conquered Spain, the legionaries had settled in Estremadura and had built for themselves the handsome city of Mérida, where today some of the finest Roman reconstructions outside Rome may be seen. Medellín is only a long day's walk from Mérida, and thousands of Roman soldiers trod that path. Thus the Iberian bloodstream—for Estremadurans in particular, for Spaniards in general—had been supplemented in the dim and distant past both by the rigor of the Romans and by the wildness of the barbarian tribesmen from central Europe who had overthrown Roman rule, and more recently by the invading Moors. Like aphrodisiacs, these supplements made the Spanish pulse prone to spasmodic outbursts when it would race without restraint.

In the late fifteenth century the atmosphere on the European continent was scintillating, but in Spain the atmosphere was different from that in the rest of Europe. Beyond the Pyrenees, the Renaissance was enlivening efforts in science and the arts and was inspiring invention and learning; the Middle Ages had been a time for humanity to catch its breath after the heady glories of ancient Greece and Rome. For Spain, however, the Middle Ages had been no such respite. Ever since the Muslim Moors had crossed the Strait of Gibraltar from North Africa and overrun the Iberian Peninsula early in the eighth century, Spain had been out of step with the rest of Europe. The Moors had even tried to invade France but, repulsed by the Franks, were forced back through the Pyrenees to Spain, where they held onto their conquest for more than seven hundred years. During every one of these years the Spanish people resisted the Moors fiercely and stubbornly. And almost from the outset this civil war was characterized on both sides by religious fervor.

In the ninth century, when Muslim power was at its zenith in Spain, a miracle occurred in Galicia, the remote northwestern corner of the peninsula. The tomb of St. James the Apostle was supernaturally revealed among rocks outside the port village of Padrón. According to Gospel, shortly after the death of Christ, James had been killed by Herod Agrippa in Palestine, and presumably would have been buried there. But in the seventh century a rumor started among the Galicians that the Apostle's body had been brought from Palestine to Spain, where in his wanderings James may have preached. Following the discovery of the tomb, the remains and relics of St. James were moved upriver to the larger town of Santiago de Compostela, which became a magnet for pilgrims in medieval times, while for the Spaniards St. James became the inspiration and champion of the reconquest.

Spain was not then a unified country; it is not an integrated country even now, but a confederation of regions, many of which desire to be autonomous, and the sense of national identity has always been weak. Throughout the Middle Ages the peninsula was called "the Spains" and was composed of separate and distinct realms—Aragon, León, Asturias, Catalonia, Valencia, Saragossa, Castile, Toledo, and more—but the Spaniards were unified in their resentment of the Moors. It was a blurry, bloody, seemingly endless fight, with troops of Spaniards sometimes allied to the Moors, sometimes hired by the Moors, and with Spaniards often fighting Spaniards in internecine quarrels. Yet overall the fighting had a pattern, and the Moors were steadily forced southward as the Spaniards cleared valley after valley, realm after realm.

In the forge of these seven hundred years of fighting, the Spanish character was tempered, and a distinctive Spanish personality emerged that

had two outstanding traits. One trait was that each Spaniard, regardless of his situation or social position, felt a fierce compulsion to assert his own independence—not, in the English style, to assert specific individual rights while remaining deferential; each Spaniard felt in his bones that he should be subservient to no one. This appears to be anomalous, because Spaniards took and take great pride in their bloodlines. But Spaniards, as different from Englishmen, accepted subservience only with pained reluctance. Spaniards were ferociously individualistic, and they cantankerously refused to be deferential—to each other or to anyone. The other trait, formed during the long fight against the Moors, was that Spaniards—while identifying themselves with their native realms as Aragonese, Castilians, Estremadurans, or others, and without pretense of nationhood—all considered themselves Christian and Spanish in contrast to the Moors. And to the Spaniards their victories over the Moors were indisputable proof of Christ's blessing. The Spanish bargain with God was to pay for this blessing with faith.

During the years of Cortés's infancy and early childhood the Moors were reduced to their final landholding in southern Spain, the part of Spain the Moors had always preferred, the Mediterranean subtropical region they called al-Andalus (Hispanicized as Andalucía), which they ruled from their magical capital at Granada. Spain then was being unified following the marriage of Ferdinand of Aragon and Isabella of Castile, "the Catholic kings," as they were dubbed by the Pope. But the unification of Spain by Ferdinand and Isabella was a challenging and complex process. They were trying to meld together a land still divided into age-old realms, with each realm requiring from its inhabitants their sworn allegiance. Also, within Christian territory there remained large communities of Muslims and Jews, many of whom had converted to Christianity. The existence of these separate realms and separate societies slowed and blocked the trend toward nationhood. In fact, Spain was the most intermixed country in all of Europe—linguistically, racially and religiously.

Ferdinand was cynical and clever; Isabella, hopeful and devout; and, acting independently of each other yet in harmony, they moved effectively toward the achievement of their goal. In order to heighten religious fervor as a basis for national unity, Ferdinand and Isabella induced the Pope to grant them the power to make ecclesiastical appointments, which power they promptly exercised to set up the Inquisition. To head the Inquisition, they appointed a cleric, Tomás de Torquemada, who came from a family of converted Jews. With the zeal of a convert Torquemada fanned the flames of fanaticism with his condemnation of both Jews and Muslims.

Under the banner of "the Catholic kings" and with the alliance of Aragon and Castile accomplished, Spanish forces coalesced to a greater degree than ever before. And the fighting effectiveness of the Spanish armies was drastically improved by a tactician of genius, Gonzalo de Córdoba, to whom Ferdinand and Isabella entrusted military command.

By this time the Moors, holding out in Granada, had lost their vigor and their arrogance. They already had paid tribute to the Christians around them in an attempt to maintain peace. But Ferdinand and Isabella again provoked war—to rid Spanish soil, once and for all, of infidel control or influence.

When in 1492 Granada fell, Spain exulted—and celebrated with a frenzy, almost an ecstasy of religious affirmation. Forced mass conversions were ordered for the Moors. Jews who would not obey Torquemada's dictate to convert were sent into exile. There was a saintly Spanish archbishop who argued that conversion should be accomplished only by persuasion and example, but the vast majority of Spaniards had no patience for such a course and concluded that it would be impracticable. In ceremonies, pageants and festivals throughout Spain, battle-hardened Spanish men and their fierce, passionate women gave wholehearted thanks to God for their triumph.

In 1492 Hernán Cortés was seven years old.

THE NETHER WORLD

When Hernán Cortés was born and the baby's name was duly inscribed in the baptismal book kept in the church in Medellín, there existed a whole side of the world totally unknown to Christians, Muslims, Jews, to ancient Romans, Greeks, Persians, to Chinese or Africans, or to any of the peoples who had contributed to the development of what in their known world was considered civilization. That other side of the world had not only never been discovered by any of the people contributing to what they regarded as civilization but, as the result of an error by a famous cartographer/mathematician/astronomer in ancient times, the most knowledgeable people on the known side of the earth were convinced that the unknown portion of the world did not and could not exist.

The cartographer/mathematician/astronomer who made the error was Ptolemy, who worked during the middle of the second Christian century. Whether his family name was Ptolemy or he came from one of the several towns called Ptolemy (there is one in northern Greece, another on the coast of Libya, two or three in Asia Minor), no one knows. The first Ptolemy of importance in history was Alexander the Great's general who in 323 B.C., after Alexander's death, made himself ruler of Egypt and founded a long-lasting dynasty. But the reigning Ptolemies were gone by 30 B.C. So this mapmaker and geographer called Ptolemy, working more than a century after the end of the dynasty, may conceivably have been a descendant of the old royal line. In all likelihood there were many who claimed to be so descended. Ptolemy lived and worked in Alexandria; he spoke Greek and wrote in Greek, his books subsequently being translated into Latin and Arabic. Many of Ptolemy's books were preserved in the great library in Alexandria.

There were a number of ancient thinkers, most of them Greeks, who deduced from the clue of the moon staring at them in the night sky that the planets and stars were globes and the earth likewise was a globe. In fact, those early astronomers made projections of a spherical earth and they divided the circumference of the earth into three hundred sixty degrees of longitude with planes of latitude. Eratosthenes, who lived more than three hundred years before Ptolemy, correctly estimated the circumference of the earth. But Ptolemy, when he recalculated the earth's circumference, made a mistake and came up with an estimate that was 30 percent smaller than we now know the earth to be. Ptolemy envisioned Asia extending farther east than it does and decided that on the small sphere he hypothesized there would be only one ocean separating western Europe from China. Consequently, on his map of the world he made no allowance for the existence of the Americas.

Ptolemy's work in total, however, was substantial and came to be regarded as authoritative. He thought that the sun revolved around the earth, but in many other ways his concepts were sound, and he made the best argument for the earth being round. So until Copernicus in 1543 published his theory that the earth revolved around the sun, Ptolemy's ideas were accepted. Which is why in 1485 the most knowledgeable people in Europe believed that nothing lay to the west between Europe and the Orient.

The human beings then inhabiting the Americas had been wholly out of touch with the rest of the world for a span of time so long that even now we cannot calculate it. Every time human habitation of the Americas is reconsidered, the approximate date is pushed back—the date when hunters and gatherers from Asia trekked across a land bridge from Siberia to Alaska and filtered down through the Americas all the way to Tierra del Fuego where their arrowheads have been found between the ribs of giant prehi toric sloths. These people who crossed the land bridge where the Bering Strait is now were not racially American Indians: They were primitive human beings, early men and women, of a basic racial stock. Then, after the sea rose to cover the land bridge or the land bridge sank beneath the sea, so many years passed that the native inhabitants of the Americas in isolation had time to evolve into a unique race, similar to Oriental sub-races yet distinctive, the race misnamed but generally called American Indians. Fifty thousand years or more seems to be a currently popular estimate for this period of isolation—presuming that is enough time for a race to evolve.

So for fifty thousand years or more, human beings in the Americas developed and progressed on a course unrelated to the development of humankind elsewhere in the world. This is an extraordinary fact.

Granted, there were occasional shipwrecks when vessels from the Orient or the islands of the South Pacific or from Europe and Africa would be driven onto the American coasts. And we know that during the Middle Ages Vikings crossed from Scandinavia via Iceland and landed on Greenland and the northeastern coast of North America. But it is not reasonable to think that these chance contacts were other than rare and random or that they had much significance. The preponderant evidence is that the primitive people in the Americas in nearly utter isolation evolved into the race we call American Indians, and they achieved complex civilizations very different from any other civilizations on earth.

In the year that in Europe was called 1485, in the high valley of Mexico a native American civilization had reached a zenith. According to Europeans, it did not exist, neither the civilization nor its place on earth. Yet it was there—in limbo on a continent in the ocean sea. And this Indian civilization was flourishing with an exultation not unlike that of Spain. Again and again the indigenous population of the high valley of Mexico had been invigorated by infusions of energy from invading tribes, and the Aztecs, who were the currently reigning tribe, were swollen with their own kind of grandiosity.

For better or worse, grandiosity is a common factor among civilizations. Before leaders emerge, when society is composed of family groups independently maintaining themselves (like the simple Yahgans of Tierra del Fuego), the communal life of human beings is not progressive and little in the way of civilization is achieved. But leaders do emerge naturally—this is part of the process of living, as when one gander out of many takes the lead in forming the V when in autumn the geese must fly south (or, in the southern hemisphere, north). Eventually tribal chiefs decide that their family lines must be assured, so the concept of noble blood is concocted.

Then, because the forces of nature keep humans in awe, many of the elements—rain, wind, lightning, thunder, sun, moon, the dark—are personified, are called gods, and there is a strong tendency, once tribal gods have been conceived, for particular humans, usually those of so-called noble blood, to declare that they themselves are divine. This was the tendency among the Mexican Indians, as it was among most peoples in the world.

The complex civilization that the American Indians developed throughout Mexico was amply productive, sustaining millions of people in place without having them wander as nomads in search of sustenance, and there was enough excess production to support nobility, clergy, and an artisan class of builders and artists. The resultant civilization was an original achievement of the native people, and it was flamboyant, ablaze with color, and barbaric only if measured by European notions of delicacy and restraint—notions which, considering many aspects of European history, may be regarded as suspect. The Indian civilization was gorgeous, vital and kinetic, and it was making rapid progress intellectually with considerable material gain.

There are many kinds of calipers which may be used to gauge a civilization. The building of cities is one such measurement; in this the Mexican Indians excelled. In the development of writing, the Indians lagged. In the utilization of metals, they were progressing. In fine jewelry-making, they were masterful.

But this caution must be made clear: Indian civilization should not be regarded as a younger form of our own civilization, a simpler form. This is unjustified condescension on our part. The civilization centered in the valley of Mexico had been building for untold millennia. It should not be compared with our civilization as if the passage of time may be expected to produce similar results. In fact, the Aztec civilization ought not to be compared, aspect by aspect, with European civilization, or Persian, or Chinese, or African, as if children were standing against a wall and marks were being made to see who was taller. Rather, we ought to incline ourselves to view this Indian civilization, this achievement of human beings on the nether side of the earth, as its own unique accomplishment. And it should be respected as such. The civilization of Spain in the late fifteenth century and the Aztec civilization in Mexico at the same time should be viewed as two different ways in which human beings can develop.

What may be said of civilizations, and this should be emphasized, is that they are all constructed by capable, energetic, thoughtful and sophisticated people. And all civilizations result from the application of human ingenuity: Civilizations are the product of genius, hard work, fervor—and cunning;

yet they differ essentially from one another in their emotional context and content and in their evaluation of human conduct. People vary enormously in their response to the conduct of both themselves and others. Each civilization, however, applies to all human conduct its own sense of morality. And each civilization—each separate people—has its own dream of spiritual fulfillment, with the hope and expectation of approbation and reward.

In these critical respects, the civilizations of Spain and of native America—absolutely unknown to each other—were radically different, fundamentally different, each from the other. The Aztecs had conquered Mexico before the coming of Columbus to the New World, so both the Aztecs and the Spaniards may be viewed stereotypically as aggressive, conquering peoples; both of them in their natures were ruthless, yet both had elevating aspects. And each of the two peoples, profoundly, had a capacity for piety (difficult to believe though this may be, especially of the Aztecs). It was the strange working out of their destinies that, blood-enemies at the outset, they were fated to blend, like lovers, to couple and to propagate.

THE GREAT COINCIDENCE

The great coincidence was that in 1492, when Spain was celebrating its ultimate triumph over the Moors and indulging in pageants of piety, feasts of thanksgiving, and banner-waving shows of fighting ability, at that propitious moment—Columbus discovered a new world!

To the Spaniards this discovery seemed clearly God's reward for their faithfulness. Having reconquered their own country, they were now provided with a whole other world to conquer. This delighted and suited the Spanish people; they welcomed the challenge as their destiny.

The Spaniards, however, were slow to appreciate the full significance of Columbus's find. In Spain's mood of jubilation and assertion, the most attractive opportunities for further glory appeared to be in Italy and Africa. In fact, for twenty-five years after Columbus landed in the Bahamas only a trickle of gold and silver came from the western world to Spain. During this quarter-century the Spaniards established settlements on the larger islands in the Caribbean Sea; they discovered Florida and the isthmus of Panama and nibbled at the coasts of Central and South America. But—and this is one of the inexplicable oddities of history—for twenty-five years after Columbus's discovery the Spaniards did not sail due west from the Caribbean islands.

During these years Hernán Cortés was growing up. When he was about fourteen, his father scraped up enough money to send him to Salamanca to attend the university there. This was not easy for Martín Cortés to do. Martín Cortés had not had a brilliant career as a soldier; he had served under the command of a relative and had not fought against the Moors but become embroiled in a factional fight among Spaniards and his faction had been defeated. As a small landholder, according to Bartolomé de las Casas, a monk who knew him well, whenever Martín Cortés would refer to himself as an *hidalgo,* people would shrug. But Martín had a sister who lived in Salamanca, and Hernán was able to stay with his aunt.

Martín hoped that his son might have a career in the law. Martín's experience had led him to believe that there was more to be made from Spanish quarrels than from Spanish conquests. At least, an income from the quarrels would be surer. So Hernán studied law at the university, which was not unlike the thriving, teeming universities, filled with poets and cutpurses, in Paris and elsewhere in Europe.

The law Hernán studied at Salamanca was chiefly embodied in the great Spanish compilation called *Las Siete Partidas,* which dated from the thirteenth century and was a consolidation of all legal procedures and customs, some dating back to the Justinian Code of the Romans, some drawn from the Visigoths, some even from the Moors. The purpose of *Las Siete Partidas* was not to serve the cause of social justice. The purpose was to define the rights of individuals of each social class, to specify the prerogatives that went with each position, to require various appointments in a variety of circumstances, and to prescribe precisely the procedures to be followed by members of any class in order to establish their legal propriety—in other words, to systematize the whole complicated, jumbled, quasi-feudal legal structure and to make definite all its intricacies, and to make this haphazard structure work somehow in the service of the king who was at the top of the social pyramid. The Spaniards had been so busy fighting the Moors and each other that *Siete Partidas* had never been revised, even as Spanish realms coalesced, and it remained the most thorough statement of the Spanish legal code.

Hernán found it fascinating. The maze of the law intrigued him, for he saw all kinds of dodges, loopholes and back passages that reminded him of the games he had played in the castle in Medellín. So he absorbed and retained this legal knowledge, even committing to memory and including in his vocabulary many legal phrases in both Spanish and Latin.

He grew up to be strong, deep-chested and exceptionally nimble, good at all the exercises of war at which Spanish boys spent most of their time (they were intermittent students but diligent warriors). At swordplay and the use of the lance and shield, at riding, at shooting, even at planning strategies for the cannons which were then being put to greater use, he excelled. He was also a fast hand at dice.

But after two years he left the university without becoming a lawyer and without a degree and returned home—because he was insufficiently interested in his studies or because he had simply had enough of a student's life. His parents were vociferous in expressing their disgust, after all they had spent on his education, and, Hernán's response being haughty as well as disrespectful, they were not disinclined to have him set out on his own. (Since these are Cortés's own recollections, as expressed to his secretary who was a practiced diplomat, the description of the family fracas has understandably been muted.)

A young man's choice in those days—this was around 1501 or 1502—was to go east to Italy and join the Spaniards under Gonzalo de Córdoba who were attacking Naples, or to go west to the so-called Indies, from which the trickle of gold was increasing. Hernán opted for the west. His parents, eager to facilitate his departure, believed they could secure for him an appointment in the entourage of Nicolás de Ovando, a nobleman who was being sent to the Indies to assume the governorship.

But Hernán had an accident that made him unable to sail with Ovando. One night, having just left the second-story bedroom of a young wife in Medellín by way of a window, he was walking along the top of a garden wall and the wall collapsed under him. He fell amid a great clatter of sword and shield (if Cortés himself is to be believed, he was fully armed). Out from somewhere ran the young husband who was ready to try to kill him, had Cortés been able to fight. Cortés, however, had sprained his back and could not move. So he was carried home and had to spend several months in bed recuperating, and consequently he missed Ovando's boat. (Cortés loved to tell this tale. In later years, when he was campaigning in Mexico, after he took a *siesta* lying on the ground his back would ache, and he would attribute his discomfort to his fall from the wall—until his soldiers refused to listen to that story again.)

While confined to his bed, and while he was at the university as well, he undoubtedly read the romances that were then wildly popular throughout Spain, as they were throughout most of Europe. These romances—passed about in manuscript, then in cheap printed editions—were Celtic and French in origin; actually the stories were dirty in the Celtic versions, were made elegant but left insinuating in French, and were chaste and nearly holy in Spanish. The tales always dealt with brave knights who clashed with dragons, infidels, evil-doers of all sorts, and the knights were unfailingly faithful in their service to fair ladies. The knights went to wondrous castles that were like the castles of dreamland and attacked impregnable fortresses. The most famous of these romances was *Amadís de Gaula,* a yarn (like an early form of the novel) that had started up in the thirteenth century in Portuguese and was first published in Spanish in 1492; then the text was pirated, and many corrupt versions were printed. These romances were the fullest expression of chivalry, of the medieval spirit—and they were accepted without cynicism until they were so grossly overdone that in 1605 Miguel de Cervantes magnificently parodied them in *Don Quixote* and terminated the romantic efflorescence. But around the turn of the fifteenth into the sixteenth century—one hundred years before *Quixote*—when Cortés and all other young Spaniards were devouring these books, the stories, though not accepted as true, were nonetheless inspiring. Cortés lived during the heyday of these romances, which happened to be the heyday of Spain.

When Hernán was able to travel again, he set off ostensibly for Italy. But he knocked around Spain for most of a year, often cadging meals and living from hand to mouth like many poor wandering students who had left their schools. He never departed for Italy and finally limped home again. Whereupon his father and mother, weary of berating him, gave him money enough to buy passage to the Indies.

Hernán left Medellín, walked to Mérida, and made his way southward, not far, to the port of Huelva. In Moguer, near Huelva on the Tinto River, he found a trader who was taking five ships loaded with merchandise to sell in the Indies, and Hernán booked deck space for himself.

He was nineteen years old and had no position nor any specific expectation in the New World. His departure was hangdog and inauspicious.

II
Dawn of Conquest — and the Nearly Fatal Failure

Ah, the Blitheness and Contrariness of Youth!

A man destined for great accomplishment often displays his mettle at a young age, but this was not true of Hernán Cortés. He went to the New World in 1504, and for thirteen or fourteen years he maintained himself there, hardly distinguishable from all the other young Spaniards who had left their homes and drifted like twigs floating on a tide to the ports of southwestern Spain—Huelva, Sanlúcar de Barrameda, Cádiz—from which they were transported to the New World, where they hung around, sought favors from those in power, and dreamt of grand rewards.

Undoubtedly the expulsion of the unconverted Jews from Spain in 1492 and the expulsion of the unconverted Moors from Andalucía in the years following the fall of Granada (and the disfavor shown the converted Jews and Arabs) contributed to the slowness and inefficiency of Spanish settlement in the New World. The Jews and Moors had directed Spanish trade and finance. In their absence, disorganization ensued. Cortés's initial voyage was an example of it.

The trader from whom Cortés bought his passage to the New World was named Alonso Quintero, and Cortés reasonably assumed that Quintero was in charge. In actuality, each of the five small cargo ships was independently owned and their cargoes in turn were owned by different groups of merchants from Huelva and Palos de Moguer. This was typical of Spanish commercial ventures: They were always financed by many parties vying with each other and there was no agreement on control. Although the first expeditions to the New World had been substantially financed by "the Catholic kings," as time went on, the monarchs came to expect that all funds for exploration and trade would be raised privately. The royal investment was simply the permission to go. Then the task of the royal auditors shifted from overseeing the spending of government money to making sure that the percentage of profit due the Crown—the royal fifth—was properly calculated and turned over (with each auditor off-the-books extracting his own stipend, as do many officials in Latin America today).

On Cortés's voyage, Quintero, after the ships took on provisions in the

Canary Islands, weighed anchor and slipped out of port at night in an effort
to be the first to reach the Indies, where presumably he would be able to
sell his goods before those on the other ships arrived to compete with him.
Quintero, however, with Cortés aboard, was driven back to the Canaries
by a storm so severe that the main mast of his ship was broken. He was
shamed before his fellows on the remaining four ships and they berated
him. But when the westward voyage resumed, Quintero again tried to
outdistance the others. His pilot got lost; all five ships ran out of drinking
water and nearly out of food. All in all, Cortés had not overpaid, considering the quality of his passage.

Disembarking at Santo Domingo on the island of Hispaniola, which is
the island now divided between the Dominican Republic and Haiti, Cortés
promptly called upon Governor Ovando, who was slightly acquainted with
his parents. Ovando had Cortés sign the registry as a newly arrived resident,
granted him some land not far from the coast, land that had on it a few
Indians, and, because Cortés boasted of his legal training, appointed him
notary for the town council of Azúa. Ovando referred him to an *hidalgo*,
Don Diego Velázquez de Cuéllar, who was said to be wealthy, seemed to
be enterprising, and might have use for a young man.

Cortés presented himself to Velázquez—a fat, florid, hearty man—and
accompanied him and a small contingent of Spaniards to quell an Indian
revolt in the interior of the island. The revolt involved little violence. It was
more a refusal of the Indians to work for the Spaniards in the mines and
to bring food from the fields. The disobedience was instigated by the
widow of a chief whom the Spaniards had killed, and compliance was
quickly resumed.

For five or six years Cortés lived and worked patiently and rather
inconspicuously around the town of Azúa, doing a little farming, a little
mining, a little trading, and a lot of gaming, wining, and as much fornicating as he could manage. There were few white women on Hispaniola, but
Cortés did not disdain Indian women. Cortés's detractors claim that during
this time he contracted syphilis from Indian women, though until 1912 it
was presumed that syphilis was brought to America by the Spaniards. But
then in the Peruvian Andes were discovered the ruins of the lost city of
Machu Picchu—an Indian city never found by the Spaniards—and the
undisturbed, desiccated mummies of Indian women buried in hollows
under huge boulders at Machu Picchu bore indisputable signs of syphilis,
proving beyond question the existence of the disease in pre-Columbian
America. Regarding Cortés, it is hard to believe that he ever had syphilis.
In the sixteenth century syphilis was called "the great pox," as different

from many lesser poxes, and it was very difficult to diagnose with certainty. Yet Cortés throughout his life was such a sexual enthusiast—he sired six legitimate children and at least four or five illegitimate children by a variety of women—that it seems illogical to think of him as impeded in any way.

What eventually brought an end to Cortés's easygoing existence on Hispaniola was that Velázquez obtained permission to conquer Cuba. So he sent to Cuba a force under the command of his trusted lieutenant, Pánfilo de Narváez, and Cortés felt obliged to go along. The conquest of Cuba proved to be little more than an occupation. The timid Cuban Indians ran and hid in the woods, as had most of those on Hispaniola; the Spaniards had to lure them back and induce them to serve and to work. When the situation in Cuba was in hand, Velázquez made the crossing and assumed control. As governor of Cuba, Velázquez granted to Cortés a large parcel of land with many Indians on it, and Cortés's holding included several good mines. It was a considerably better set-up than Cortés had had on Hispaniola.

What cemented the friendship of Velázquez and Cortés was their liking of women. This also was the cause of dissension between them. Velázquez, in his official capacity as governor, a responsibility which he took very seriously, was determined to establish in Cuba a mannerly and decent society which would be a reflection of the society of Spain. In pursuit of this aim, he came into conflict with Cortés.

There had come to Hispaniola a family named Suárez, consisting of a widowed mother with four marriageable daughters and a grown son. The mother, eager to marry off her daughters, heard that many Spanish men were moving to Cuba. So she and her family crossed to Cuba and presented themselves to Governor Velázquez. He was pleased with them and gave the son, Juan, a parcel of land and some Indians to be shared with an experienced settler who could serve as his guide, Hernán Cortés.

The Suárez family was by no means noble (they had come to the New World as part of the entourage of the wife of a royal appointee) but they were considered wellborn, and Velázquez hoped they would contribute to the establishment of the society he desired. With very few marriageable white women in the islands, the handsome, lively and headstrong Suárez sisters were quickly in demand and, giddy from the attention of many men, they pouted and pirouetted and were choosy.

The oldest of the sisters was named Catalina, but she was called *La Marcaida*, Marcaida being her mother's maiden name. That she was called *La* Marcaida, in Spanish usage, implied that she resembled her mother, like-mother-like-daughter, and suggested more specifically that they both had big mouths. Catalina announced loudly and publicly that Cortés was her choice.

Velázquez himself, though he was married or about to be married to the niece of the bishop of Burgos, favored the youngest Suárez sister, who was the wildest of the lot and whose reputation quickly became sullied (whether as a result of her relationship with Governor Velázquez or another is not known). The men in Cuba were all talking about the Suárez sisters because there was nothing else of this sort that they had to talk about.

Cortés, for his part, liked two of these sisters, Catalina and another, and was carrying on with both of them. This was what exasperated Velázquez: How could he fit into his scheme for a decent Cuban society the fact that Cortés should have two of the sisters? (Part of the charm of the Spaniards is their frankness in amatory affairs and also in financial dealings. They don't cover up and withhold, like English and Americans. And when Cortés's own account or the favorable account given by his secretary and biographer, Francisco López de Gómara, is compared with the account of Bernal Díaz del Castillo, who was a soldier in the subsequent campaign of Cortés in Mexico and who heard plenty, and when a further comparison is made with the account of Fray Bartolomé de las Casas, who never had a favorable word to say about Cortés, the result is probably not far from the truth.)

Velázquez earnestly implored Cortés to marry Catalina. Velázquez cajoled and threatened, but Cortés was adamant in his refusal. So Catalina sued Cortés for, according to her, breaking his promise of marriage; Governor Velázquez sympathized with her suit; and no fewer than five men, including Catalina's brother, joined in the suit against Cortés, attesting to the validity of Catalina's accusation.

Velázquez became so angry with Cortés that, after public scolding did no good, the governor had him arrested and put in the stocks. But Cortés escaped, either by prying open the lock on the stocks or by promising a bribe to the guard, and he sought sanctuary in a church. This kind of rumpus was dangerous, because a governor in a place as remote from Spain as Cuba could enforce his own concept of justice — and Cortés feared that Velázquez would either send him in chains to Hispaniola for trial or else try him in Cuba and hang him. The nights in Cuba, though, are often so windless and humid that Cortés could not bear to remain in the church. Velázquez had anticipated this and with foresight had sent an armed man to hide in the bushes outside the church and to watch for Cortés. So when Cortés in the middle of a hot night while no one seemed to be around stepped out of the church for a breath of fresh air, he was captured.

Velázquez's man who captured him was Juan Escudero—and Juan Escudero lived to regret it.

Imprisoned again, Cortés escaped again (this time almost surely by bribery) and by this time, as with all Spanish disputes, even amatory ones, legalistic and financial ramifications were growing by leaps and bounds. While in prison, Cortés had written out an indictment of Velázquez, revealing incriminating details Cortés had picked up during his years in Velázquez's service. Word had leaked out about this indictment, and a party of Spaniards was forming to support Cortés, who was popular. Many Spaniards had grudges against Velázquez because they felt he had not granted them enough land or Indians.

On the run, Cortés armed himself—and late at night he sought out Velázquez, who was staying in a farmhouse in the country, attended by only a few servants, while the soldiers of his escort stayed in a village nearby. Velázquez was astonished to be confronted by Cortés and perhaps was frightened. Yet the upshot was that he invited Cortés to sup with him; the two old friends were reunited; and, incredible though it may seem, according to all extant accounts, Velázquez and Cortés slept together that night in the same bed.

And then, after holding out against marriage for nearly a year in spite of the lawsuit and pressure from Velázquez, Cortés finally married Catalina. Cortés built her a house, said to be the first house in Baracoa, and he lived with her, he said, "with as much satisfaction as if she were the daughter of a duchess." Thus, with this lie, and at this early stage in his career, Cortés made clear that his true ambition was to sleep with the daughter of a duchess.

Cortés had a long, frolicsome youth, which lasted into his early thirties. In Hispaniola, then in Cuba, he was liked by those who knew him but was viewed without envy, as sassy, flighty, mischievous, ever ready for a romp—a merry man and a good talker.

There is a further incongruity in the character of Cortés, another facet of him which may not be expected in the make-up of a conqueror. While most Spaniards in the Indies were driving the Indians under their control to overwork the mines in a feverish and wasteful effort to extract what little gold there was, Cortés opted for patience. He tried not to overwork his own mines but to trace the veins as far as possible, to make the ore last. He argued that sound utilization of the land was essential for lasting settlement. He farmed carefully, even scientifically according to the knowledge of the day, and used his Indians efficiently to clear fields and to plant and harvest food-crops. He imported cattle, sheep and horses and was among the first settlers in Cuba to maintain herds. In acknowledgment of this constructive side of Cortés, Velázquez commissioned him to build a smelter and a medical dispensary. Twice Velázquez appointed him *alcalde* (mayor or chief official) of Santiago. Though liberal with money, Cortés saved enough so that he was able to invest two thousand castellanos in a partnership with a trader named Andrés de Duero.

Cortés as a young man revealed a strange mixture of traits and talents and showed little that predicted his future—until the clouds of circumstance around him cleared and he saw his opportunity.

NEW SPAIN OF THE OCEAN SEA

In 1517, twenty-five years after Columbus discovered the New World, the Spaniards on the Caribbean islands finally came to realize that land of importance—probably, they thought, a large island—lay to their west. The realization came about in this way:

Diego Velázquez in Cuba wanted more Indians to work his mines and fields, all the Cuban Indians not already put to his use having been allotted to resident Spaniards. So a business deal was concocted, and a plan was made to send a small force in three ships to some nearby islands, to obtain Indians there by capturing them or perhaps by trading for them, and to bring these Indians back to Cuba. The plan was duly approved by Columbus's son, Diego Colón, who was still clinging to his dubious authority as inheritor of his father's domain. Upon delivery of the Indians Velázquez would pay so much per head. Technically, these Indians would not be slaves because Crown policy sternly forbade slavery. Rather, these Indians would be regarded as part of an *encomienda* or *repartimiento,* the two terms at this time being used synonymously; like other island Indians, these Indians would be entrusted to a Spanish citizen, to wit, Velázquez, who would be responsible for their religious instruction and protection while he put the Indians to work. By this devious course Crown policy was evaded.

As usual with Spanish commercial ventures, several partners, in this instance three, financed the foray (it's doubtful that Velázquez contributed anything since he was to be the ultimate purchaser). One of the partners, Francisco Hernández de Córdoba, was named captain-in-charge. More than a hundred Spanish fighting men were enlisted, and in the company— fortunately for the cause of history—was Bernal Díaz del Castillo, who fifty years later was able to write down his recollections in amazing detail.

Shortly after departing from Cuba, the little fleet was caught in the whirlwind of a hurricane, and the ships were tossed and spun about until, twenty-one days out of port, the Spaniards found themselves off the cape at the tip of the Yucatán peninsula, which extends northward from the mainland of southern Mexico. Peering at the strange low-lying coast, the Spaniards could see the white walls of a large town that appeared to be a few miles inland. On Cuba and Hispaniola, when the Spaniards first came, there were no stone-walled or limed buildings, only thatched wattle huts. So in their two ships with the shallowest draft the Spaniards approached the coast.

Out to them then came a flotilla of long dugouts made from the trunks of huge trees, and in each dugout were about forty Indians vigorously paddling. The Spaniards made gestures of welcome and held up goods for trade. The Indians agreeably brought their dugouts alongside the ships and many of them at the Spaniards' invitation came aboard.

These Indians were wearing embroidered cotton jackets and breech-clouts, unlike Indians in the islands, where the men went naked and the women wore only wrappers from waist to mid-thigh. These Indians were armed with bows and arrows, lances and clubs, but they did not appear to be aggressive or warlike. The one who seemed to be their chief kept saying something that sounded like *"Cones catoche,"* which in Mayan meant "Come to our houses." Consequently the Spaniards—with the age-old reflex of explorers all over the world—promptly named the place Cape Catoche, a name that has stuck to this day. Through gestures the chief conveyed that in the morning he would come with more dugouts to bring the Spaniards ashore.

And the next morning the chief returned with twelve dugouts that were empty except for the oarsmen, and he waved the Spaniards to come on. After some hesitation the Spaniards decided to accept the chief's invitation, and, leaving their ships at anchor with the sailors aboard, they lowered one of their boats so that in the dugouts and the ship's boat all the Spanish fighting men, heavily armed, could go ashore. Once ashore, the Spaniards left a couple of men to guard their boat, and the chief led the Spanish force toward the town along a path between brushy hills.

At a signal from the chief, warriors who had been in hiding attacked the Spaniards from all sides. These Indians were not like the timid and placid islanders. Screaming, blowing whistles and conches, racing to the attack, they rained arrows on the Spaniards, whipped stones from their slings, and in hand-to-hand battle deftly used their bats and copper-tipped lances and shields. As armor they wore lightweight quilted cotton from their necks to their knees, and the quilted cotton afforded them good protection without impeding their movement. The Spaniards responded with fifteen crossbows and ten shooting-pieces. These shooting-pieces were harquebuses, long-barreled, unrifled firearms in which the powder was ignited by a lighted match at the tip of a serpentine, a curved piece of metal that was lowered to the pan at the moment of firing; the resulting blast would send a lead ball about 150 yards. Although translators often refer to Spanish "mus-kets," the musket had not yet been invented. In close fighting the Span-iards used their hard-edged iron pikes and swords to shatter the flint and obsidian blades of the Indians and to blunt their copper lances, and after a fierce engagement the Indians withdrew.

Assisting their wounded, bleeding, the Spaniards limped uphill to seek refuge in a cluster of low stone buildings that were prayer-houses. But inside the houses they came upon idols of baked clay—hideous, monster-faced figures, some figures obviously female and some male figures in the act of sodomy. Shocked and terrified, the Spaniards were about to abandon the prayer-houses when some chests were discovered to be filled with small gold objects, offerings to the idols. Scooping up the gold, the Spaniards, with two Indians they had captured, hobbled back to the beach. The sound of the firing had attracted other boats from their ships offshore, and the battered Spaniards piled in and pushed off.

Setting sail quickly, they followed the coastline to the west, then to the south. They were afraid to land and anchored each night; they were afraid to sail at night because they couldn't see rocks and shoals. As their wounded died, they dropped the bodies overboard. For fifteen days they sailed on—until their drinking water ran out. During this time the two captured Indians were baptized by a priest aboard and were named Julian and Melchior.

The Spaniards were desperate for drinking water and, when they sighted another large town, they presumed there would be a creek or spring to supply water for the town, so they tried to approach the place. But this was difficult because the sea was shallow, the Yucatán peninsula being an upraised part of the ocean floor, and the incline from the coastline is very gradual. Anchoring their ships more than three miles from shore, they put all their casks into the ships' boats and, when they landed from the boats, they saw some Indian women carrying filled jugs and they hastened to a *cenote* (a round hole in the limestone of the Yucatán in which water collects; the whole peninsula is pocked with these holes, which are like the holes in Swiss cheese; the limestone soil is so porous that the heavy rainfall drains right through it).

Before the Spaniards could fill their casks, a delegation of about fifty Indians, dressed in fine cotton cloaks and wearing feathered crests, approached them, walking slowly, and, when the Spaniards through mime explained that they only wanted to take water and would go, the Indians, who seemed to be chiefs, through gestures and their guttural babble asked if the Spaniards came from the east. The Spaniards could not comprehend the sense of the question. Then when the Indians gestured for the Spaniards to come with them to their town, the Spaniards after a brief council did so very reluctantly.

The Indian chiefs led them to the town, which was very well laid out and had stone-walled buildings like the previous town. This was the town of Campeche, and the chiefs led the way toward their prayer-houses on the central square. In the prayer-houses that the Spaniards reconnoitered, there were not only monster-faced idols in human form but also idols that were fanged serpents. Most alarming to the Spaniards was that the altars in these prayer-houses were sticky with clotted blood; blood was spattered all over the walls; the air reeked of blood.

In the square, troops of Indian warriors were assembling—archers, slingers, lancers, and the most muscular Indians who carried hardwood bats studded with razor-sharp obsidian blades, bats that they brandished like two-handed swords. The chiefs had slaves (their own slaves, dirty and thin Indians who wore only twists of rag) bring sheaves of dry reeds that they placed on the ground before the Spaniards. Indian priests appeared, who wore their hair so long that it sometimes touched the ground, hair that was stiff with dried blood from the sacrifices. Then the chiefs and the priests with elaborate gestures made clear to the Spaniards that, if the Spaniards were not gone before the reeds turned to ashes, the Indians would kill all the Spaniards and sacrifice them to the gods. The reeds were then duly set afire, and the Indian warriors in the square stepped up the beat of their drums and heightened the intensity of their whistle-blowing and shrieking.

Hastily the Spaniards retreated toward their boats, with the Indians following them. At the shore the Spaniards were afraid to embark for fear they would be attacked while boarding. So they moved along the beach, warily, while Spanish sailors in the boats on the water moved with them, until in the lee of a huge rock the Spaniards on the beach were able to clamber aboard the boats quickly and escape. They had even succeeded in bringing with them a few casks they had filled from the *cenote*.

Sailing on, the Spaniards soon ran out of drinking water again. (With typical Spanish candor Bernal Díaz explained that they hadn't been able to

This small prayer-house, now set up in the garden of the Museum of Anthropology in Mexico City, was originally located in the province of Campeche. Such temples were brilliantly painted on the outside to accentuate the high relief of the weird, intricate, segmented designs; all the figures and symbols, like the curled proboscis and the eyes above the doorway, had meaning and were intended to terrify. In the small stuffy interior room under a corbel arch were the idols, and the whole place reeked of blood. The paints that were used were made from inorganic dyes found in the mountains—a bright purplish blue, a strong yellow, a bright red and a jet black, against glowing limestone white.

afford good casks and the cheap casks they had bought in Cuba leaked.) So they landed once more near a town where there was bound to be a *cenote*. They found the *cenote*, but this time armed Indians, prepared to fight, came at them, with faces painted in white, black and rust-red (the colors of the natural dyes found in the area). These Indians, likewise, asked the Spaniards through gestures if the Spaniards came from the east.

This repeated question from the Indians about coming from the east has suggested the possibility that the Indians may have expected that gods would be coming from the east. The Indians in the islands had told the

Spaniards of an ancient prophecy that a white-skinned, bearded god called Quetzalcoatl, who once had lived among the Indians and had sailed away to the east, would one day return from the east to resume his rule. So the Spaniards were aware of this myth and wanted to believe that this myth was what the Indians had in mind. Yet it seems more reasonable that these Indians on the coast of mainland Mexico had learned from island Indians that invaders had come from the east, invaders who were oppressing them. This explanation seems more likely because, had the mainland Indians been expecting the return of a god or gods, they would have behaved in a way that was awed, fearful and respectful. If, on the other hand, their thought was that the oppressors from the islands were coming now to try to oppress them, then their behavior naturally would be as it was.

While at night the Spaniards busily filled their casks, the Indians surrounded them. And at dawn the Indians attacked ferociously, killing more than fifty Spaniards and capturing two of them alive. Hernández de Córdoba was hit by ten arrows, Bernal Díaz by three. Many Spaniards suffered throat wounds from the lances. Fresh troops of Indian warriors were coming from the town, bringing with them food and drink in preparation for a celebration to follow this battle of extermination.

Abandoning their casks, the anguished Spaniards, carrying their wounded and dying, fought their way back to the beach and tried to climb aboard their boats to escape. But the overloaded boats began to founder. Some Spaniards had to swim holding onto the gunwales, while the pursuing Indians stoned them, shot arrows at them, or hurled javelins from the shore, and those with the obsidian-studded bats waded into the water and smashed the skulls of the Spaniards who were clinging to the sterns. This was at the town of Champotón.

Now there were not enough Spaniards left to man the three ships, so one of the ships was stripped and the hull set afire and abandoned. In the remaining two ships the Spaniards turned away from this coast. They had no water to drink, and deliriously, while their lips and tongues cracked, uncertain of their direction, they made their way—cursing their pilots—to Florida, where again they were attacked by Indians when they landed and sought water.

More than half the men who had set out were dead and gone by the time the two ships straggled back to Cuba. Hernández de Córdoba died shortly after the ships returned. The expedition, which was the first Spanish experience with the mainland of Mexico, was a disaster.

· · ·

But when Diego Velázquez saw the gold the Hernández expedition brought back to Cuba, brought by those few who came back, he was very interested. Some of the gold was mixed with copper, some was low-grade, most of it was light, but it was gold—some in the form of fish and ducks, some disks, a few pendants and diadems. Velázquez had expended nothing on the expedition, and the only Indians for him to buy were the cross-eyed pair named Julian and Melchior. Many Mayans have crossed eyes; the Mayans are also the roundest-headed people on earth; in other respects, they are short, squat and strong. Julian and Melchior had picked up a little Spanish, and Velázquez questioned them himself. On the basis of the gold in hand—a promising show, though not in total of great value—Velázquez concluded that another expedition should be organized, to see if more gold could be obtained, which seemed likely.

This was late in the year 1517—and conditions in Spain had changed even since Hernández de Córdoba had set out. Spain was in flux.

Queen Isabella having died in 1504, Ferdinand as the sole Catholic king had ruled until his death in 1516. Juana, the eldest surviving child and daughter of Ferdinand and Isabella, was insane. All her life Juana had been unstable and, after her arranged marriage for dynastic purposes to Philip the Handsome of Habsburg, she had been broken down completely by her husband, an Austrian, not a Spaniard, who flaunted before her his flagrant infidelities. But Philip had died, and the Spanish Crown, following Ferdinand's death, was shared by Juana, who was incompetent, and her son, who was a boy living with his aunt in Flanders, now a part of Belgium, on which Spain had a dynastic claim. The boy was King Carlos the First (*Primero*) of Spain, and after the death of his paternal grandfather he became Emperor Carlos the Fifth (*Quinto*) of the Holy Roman Empire, which was the imperial role his relatives had intended and designed for him. While Carlos was absent from Spain, the cardinal who had been Isabella's confessor had ruled as regent, but then he had died while the boy-king was en route to meet him.

So Velázquez in Cuba could not be sure just what the situation in Spain was or would be—especially since communication between Spain and the Indies was uncertain and slow—and he had to move carefully to obtain authorization for his exploration of the newly found land, authorization that would be more impressive than the approval of Diego Colón, which he already had. In Spain a Council of the Indies supervised overseas development, and this council had sent to Hispaniola three monks of St. Jerome to investigate the atrocities against the Indians, as reported by Fray Bartolomé de las Casas, who was already on the scene. From these Jeronymites on the nearby island Velázquez sought and obtained permission to proceed with a trading venture that might also lead to settlement.

It was doubtful whether the Jeronymites were empowered to grant such permission, so Velázquez, an adroit politician, pursued yet another course to assure the legitimacy of his position. His wife being the niece of Juan de Fonseca, the bishop of Burgos, who was president of the Council of the Indies and advisor to the boy-king, Velázquez wrote a letter to Bishop Fonseca in Spain and had it taken by a messenger aboard ship, a letter in which Velázquez reported that at great expense to himself he had discovered new lands and asked his uncle to obtain for him from the king the right to settle these new lands in the king's name.

Thus Velázquez buttered his bread on both sides and had some left over. He even borrowed Crown policy in that, since he was the one officially licensed to explore, he expected that the next expedition should be financed to the greatest extent possible by others who wanted to participate.

Four ships were assembled, the two that had come back with Hernández de Córdoba and two others, and two hundred forty men responded to Velázquez's call. Among these two hundred forty—as evidence of Spanish grit—were many of those who had been with Hernández, including Bernal Díaz. It was Velázquez's proposition to these men that they were to arm themselves at their own expense if they could afford to do so, and each man would be allowed to bring his own stock of trade-goods to exchange for gold. Velázquez provided a large quantity of glass beads, made loans, and obtained supplies on credit.

Velázquez, who did not choose to go himself, appointed as captain-in-charge his own nephew Juan de Grijalva, an ardent spirit who, like Velázquez, came from Cuéllar (a rutted little town, not in Estremadura, but north of Segovia in Spain). To captain the other three ships, Velázquez appointed three already battle-seasoned adventurers who were destined to play major roles in the campaigns of the New World—Pedro de Alvarado, Francisco de Montejo, and Alonso de Ávila.

In May 1518 the ships left Cuba and, guided by pilots who had been with Hernández, sailed to Cape Catoche, where they were caught by the current and carried around to the island of Cozumel in the lee of the Yucatán on the east. On Cozumel the Spaniards found that the natives, like the timid Indians on other islands, had fled from their villages and were hiding in the woods. Reembarking, the Spaniards successfully rounded the cape against the current and sailed down the western coast of the Yucatán to Champotón.

On the shore at Champotón, as expected, Indian warriors were lined up in battle formation, brandishing their arms and with drums beating and conches sounding. This time, however, the Spaniards had brought several small cannons which they lowered into their boats, and they were well supplied with crossbows and shooting-pieces. As the Spaniards in their boats neared the beach, the Indians sent volleys of arrows, darts and javelins at them. But the Spaniards fired their cannons, which momentarily startled the Indians but did not terrify them, and the Spaniards landed behind the barrage. In the fierce fight that ensued, the Spaniards prevailed, although seven soldiers were killed and Grijalva was hit by three arrows and suffered two broken teeth. When the Indians retreated into a swamp, the Spaniards occupied the deserted town.

For three days the Spaniards held Champotón. They were prepared for another attack but, when the Indians did not resume the fight, Grijalva decided that the defeat of Hernández had been avenged. So the Spaniards reboarded their ships and proceeded along the coast.

Occasionally they sighted prayer-houses on shore and, thinking villages would be close by, landed to investigate. But this was a sparsely settled region, and the prayer-houses were for the use of hunters or traders who, while passing through, would make sacrifices and offer up prayers. (Many such temples were built by the ancient Greeks around the Mediterranean.) Once, while ashore, the Spaniards lost a greyhound bitch that, excited by the scents of deer and rabbit, ran away.

When the Spaniards in their ships came to the wide mouth of the Tabasco River, they again saw Indian warriors in battlelines on the beach. Determined to oppose any defiance from the Indians, Grijalva had the ships anchored outside the sandbar, and the Spaniards in their boats sailed the few miles to shore, with cannons in the prows, crossbowmen and har-quebusiers at the gunwales. They evaded the Indian troops on the beach and went upriver, where they disembarked on a headland near a large town.

In their dugouts the Indians followed the Spaniards and, when the Indians were within earshot, Grijalva had Julian and Melchior call out in Mayan that the Spaniards came in peace and had presents for them, that the Spaniards wanted to trade for gold if they had any or, at the least, for fresh food, and that there was no cause for fear.

Startled to be addressed in their own language—and intrigued by the green-glass beads Grijalva held up, which looked like the jade the Indians prized—a befeathered chief and a long-haired priest had their dugout brought in close and replied that they knew of the strangers' victory at Champotón but that here at Tabasco they commanded more than twenty thousand warriors.

Through Julian and Melchior, Grijalva tried to preach to the Indians about his king and his God—and the Indian chief and the priest may have replied in kind, telling about their leaders and their gods (Bernal Díaz said they did so). But considering the limited Spanish of Julian and Melchior and the difficulty of translating thoughts in a Spanish context into forms comprehensible to the Mayans and vice versa, it seems reasonable to assume that only the basic fact of the situation was understood: that the choice was to trade or fight.

The chief and the priest retired to consult with other chiefs and priests, while the Spaniards set up a fortified camp on the headland. After a couple of hours a dugout filled with Indians again came close to the Spaniards, and the Indians announced that they were willing to trade and would collect some gold since Julian and Melchior had told them that gold was what the strangers valued most highly.

On the next day thousands of Indians came to the headland both by dugout on the water and by paths across a swamp from the land, bringing roast turkey and fish, the unleavened cornmeal pancakes the Spaniards called *tortillas* (which fluff up if prepared fresh with a heated flat rock as a griddle), and a tropical fruit called *mamey* (small and brown like a sweet avocado, and not bad). The relieved and delighted Spaniards responded by giving the Indians glass beads, articles of clothing, and small instruments made of iron.

Then the Indians spread mats on the ground and laid out a variety of things made of gold. Chiefs and priests sat cross-legged on one side of the row of laden mats; Spanish captains sat opposite them. With Julian and Melchior translating, as well as through gestures, the Indians made clear to the Spaniards that the gold was a gift—and that the Spaniards should go.

This Indian procedure of giving the Spaniards a present, usually of gold, along with a wish for the Spaniards to go away and never come back has, I believe, been generally misunderstood. The Indian leaders were not showing weakness or fear. These Indians, within the framework of their own lives, were thoughtful and deliberate people. What they were doing was customary for them under the circumstances: When a fight was not desired by either party, the Indian custom was to make a gift of whatever would be most pleasing to the other side with the expectation that the other side, in accepting the gift, would accede to the wish of the givers. This was the Indians' assumption and expectation. But the Spaniards didn't understand what was going on; the Indians' conception simply did not occur to the Spaniards. They saw the gold—and they wanted more because obviously there was more where this had come from—and they wouldn't think now of going away and not returning. To the Indians the Spaniards' acceptance of the gold and rejection of the Indians' wish was almost inconceivably rude.

When the Spaniards asked for more gold, the Indian chiefs shook their heads and, waving toward the northwest, said, "Mexico, Mexico," which meant nothing to the Spaniards or to Julian and Melchior.

In the late afternoon a north wind rose that endangered the anchored ships. If a gale developed, as was not uncommon, the ships could be driven onto the sandbar. So the Spaniards packed up the gold, distributed more glass beads, and in their boats returned to the ships and promptly set sail to distance themselves from the coastline.

After cruising around the base of the Yucatán peninsula, the Spaniards came to realize that the Yucatán was not an island, and Grijalva named the whole place New Spain. Later, at the suggestion of Cortés—who, like Julius Caesar and George Armstrong Custer, was a good writer—it was renamed New Spain of the Ocean Sea.

While passing a beach, the Spaniards saw Indians on shore waving white flags and landed to see what was happening. They were greeted by an elegantly dressed chief who spoke Nahuatl, the language of highland Indians; Julian and Melchior, speaking only Mayan, could not understand him. But by gesture the chief, who was the Aztec governor of the province, conveyed to the Spaniards that he was having gold brought to them by Indians from villages in the interior. And for several days the Spaniards encamped and, as Indian bearers came down from the hills, the Spaniards exchanged trade-goods for gold.

Happily back in their ships after another spurt of profitable and peaceful trading, the Spaniards proceeded westward off the Mexican coast, landing at one point on an island in Veracruz bay where in a prayer-house they found the bodies of two Indian boys who had just been sacrificed before a monster-faced idol. The bloody torsos of the boys lay on the ground with the chests slashed open; the arms and legs had been cut off; the stench of human blood was intense. Standing by were four black-cloaked, hooded Indian priests who were unperturbed, and the priests hastened to bring censers filled with burning copal. This was the Indian custom: Whenever Spaniards and Indians met, the Indians would perfume the Spaniards with these resin-filled censers, either as a gesture of courtesy or a kind of purification or because, in this case, the Indian priests who were used to the smell of human blood were not used to the smell of the Spaniards. Never before had the Spaniards objected to this fumigation. Now, though, they were outraged and drove the priests away. Most shocking to the

Spaniards was that the priests were surprised and seemed unable to understand the Spaniards' indignation.

By this time weevils infested the cassava bread the Spaniards had brought with them, and some decision had to be made on how to terminate the voyage. Either a settlement was to be founded, proper papers drawn up, a site selected, a fort built, and some of the men chosen to maintain the settlement while others in the ships returned to Cuba and more colonists could be sent out. Or else this trading voyage had to be wound up, and all the men in the ships would return to Cuba with the considerable amount of gold they had already collected.

The captains were at odds. Francisco de Montejo, who was an Estremaduran, favored the founding of a settlement; he was the one finally to conquer most of the Yucatán, and his family name is still incised over many doorways in the Yucatán city which he named Mérida. Pedro de Alvarado, who was infatuated with a girl in Cuba (perhaps one of the Suárez girls), claimed to be in pain from his longing for her and wanted to return to Cuba. What Alonso de Ávila thought was not recorded, except that he aggravated the situation. Grijalva himself equivocated. He thought there were not enough supplies to equip a settlement, nor enough men; thirteen had been killed or had died of wounds and four were crippled. Also, it was apparent now that this new land was enormous, with an incalculable population. He thought there should be more consideration before a settlement was made.

The upshot was that Alvarado was entrusted with most of the gold and in the smallest of the ships was sent back to Cuba to report to Velázquez and to turn over the gold to him. In the other three ships the remaining Spaniards continued to explore the coast all the way up to the mouth of the Pánuco River (where Tampico is now).

When Alvarado reached Cuba, Velázquez, having sighted the ship, promptly had himself rowed out in a boat. And when Velázquez saw the gold—and listened to Alvarado, who was renowned as a storyteller— Velázquez threw a party that lasted eight days. But he was furious with Grijalva for not founding a settlement. By not founding a settlement in accord with Velázquez's license, Grijalva had not legally established Velázquez's priority to develop this new, gold-laden land. Legalistically—and the Spaniards were forever absorbed with legal ramifications in the maze of their medieval law—what had taken place was simply a trading mission, which, though profitable, did not secure future rights for Velázquez.

Later, when Grijalva returned to Cuba with his fleet of three ships and still more gold, Velázquez was so mad at him that he refused to see him.

The Man for the Job

As soon as Velázquez became sober after the party celebrating Alvarado's return, Velázquez began to seek a captain-general for another expedition to go to the new land and establish his legal priority before news of this rich discovery spread. Velázquez turned from one to another of the leading men of Cuba. He was afraid of the noble or wellborn because they might be inclined to take over the project in their own names. His favorite lieutenant, Pánfilo de Narváez, was in Spain. Several of Velázquez's relatives were willing, but he did not want to repeat the disappointment he had just had with his nephew, Grijalva. Besides, Velázquez expected that now, since he had in hand proof of the potential in the gold Alvarado had brought back, whoever would lead the expedition should substantially contribute to its financing. After all, Velázquez not only held the license from Diego Colón and the Jeronymite fathers but knew to himself that his uncle was presenting his petition for confirmation to the king. Yet when Velázquez mentioned three thousand ducats as a suitable investment, several prominent citizens in Cuba backed off. Either they hadn't the money or hadn't the heart for the risk, and this reluctance became more pronounced after the return of Grijalva with the other ships. Both Montejo and Ávila took to grumbling in the streets and cafés that they had paid for equipment and supplies on Grijalva's voyage and they were not getting their fair share of the gold from the governor's treasury. Also, Grijalva was sulking about with his broken teeth and his arrow-wounds half-healed, and the effect he had on others was dispiriting. So Velázquez was in a quandary.

No one had suggested Hernán Cortés for the captaincy. Only recently Velázquez had been ready to hang him. But Cortés himself (this was the presumption of all the chroniclers) arranged a secret meeting at his house with Andrés de Duero, the trader with whom Cortés had two thousand castellanos on deposit and who also served as the governor's secretary, and Amador de Lares, who was the king's accountant responsible for calculating and certifying the royal fifth. With these two well-situated gentlemen, Cortés made a pact: that they should propose him for the captaincy and that the three of them would divide his share of the spoils.

The pact made, Duero and Lares at first startled the governor with the mention of Cortés's name, but then they argued eloquently in Cortés's favor. Cortés had money to invest; Duero attested to that. Cortés was not so wellborn that conceivably he could ever challenge Velázquez's authority. It may be that Cortés had the qualities desirable in a leader. Velázquez seemed momentarily to be well disposed toward the idea of appointing a friend like Cortés, instead of a relative like Grijalva. But the most curious argument advanced by the governor's secretary and the king's accountant was that, since Velázquez had stood up for Cortés at Cortés's coerced marriage to Catalina Suárez, Velázquez in some sense was obligated to Cortés as if he were Cortés's stepfather. It was known, of course, that Velázquez was carrying on with one of the younger Suárez sisters, but that would have made Velázquez and Cortés de facto brothers-in-law, not stepfather and stepson. In any case—the muddle of Spanish testamentary law being what it was—Duero and Lares convinced the governor to name Cortés captain-general of the new expedition.

As secretary, Duero prepared a contract that Velázquez and Cortés signed on October 23, 1518, officially confirming the appointment of Cortés and assuring him of his rights as captain-general. This contract in due course was approved by the Jeronymite fathers in Santo Domingo.

The people of Cuba, especially the men of means, were astounded by Velázquez's choice. Some were jealous of Cortés. Many were suspicious that a deal had been made behind the screen. But Cortés, after his appointment, calculatedly altered his demeanor. It was a thorough character transformation, and, in retrospect, less the intentional assumption of an idealized persona than the emergence in young maturity of his true self. Cortés was now serious and exuded an air of responsibility; *gravitas* was the Latin term Cortés had learned in school and now applied to himself; his resolution was evident and impressive. He changed the way he dressed, abandoning his casual, youthful style, and he had tailors make him a velvet cloak with tassels of gold, as befitted a prospective lord. In public he kept himself armed and had an escort. There was about him a sense of withheld power that made him, who was so recently carefree and gay, more than a little fearsome.

Cortés was thirty-three years old—too old for a coming of age to produce this change in him. The transformation of his character came about when his latent ambition was ignited by the happenstance of opportunity.

As soon as his appointment was confirmed, Cortés began to invest in the voyage without stint. He used all the money he had and pledged his *encomienda* to borrow more, with which he bought ships, arms and provisions. He paid in cash when he had to and bought on credit when he could, with repayment and a bonus to come from the spoils of the expedition. When Cortés approached Velázquez for ready money, the governor, pleading that he had none available at the moment, told him that he held a power of attorney for Pánfilo de Narvaéz, and from Narváez's estate Velázquez advanced a thousand castellanos.

Quickly Cortés enlisted three hundred men for the expedition. Some were able to equip themselves, and this was encouraged, but Cortés generously assisted those who did not have the means. Horses were most difficult to come by—so difficult and costly that Bernal Díaz, writing fifty years later, could recall each horse with its owner as well as the quality and characteristics of each horse. When one of Cortés's comrades from Medellín named Alonso Hernández Puertocarrero, who was a cousin of the Count of Medellín, wanted a gray mare he couldn't afford, and Cortés had used up all his own money, Cortés cut the tassels of gold from his cloak and with the gold bought the mare for his friend. Gestures such as this won for Cortés the loyalty of his assembling company.

Cortés had a fine banner made. On it in gilt thread was embroidered the Cross and the message: "Brothers and comrades, in true faith let us follow the Holy Cross and we shall conquer." This was his message, the message that had proved true in Spain's battle against the Moors, so why shouldn't it still be true? Cortés had this banner carried from town to town in Cuba, and he made his plea with such sincerity that Spanish men—the progeny of centuries of fighting—flocked to him. In concert with Velázquez, Cortés gave out that this expedition was sanctioned by the king, although royal approval had not yet come from Spain, as both Velázquez and Cortés knew.

After a few months, however, Velázquez began to worry that he might have made a mistake in his choice of captain-general. Cortés was spending money so fast and was building such a strong force that, when Velázquez's disgruntled relatives whispered to him that Cortés might be plotting to take over the project, the governor listened. But the stalwart men in Cuba liked Cortés; they liked the new Cortés, even though they had not served with him before and Cortés was not battle-seasoned. Even those Spaniards who had seen the horror of the mainland Indians volunteered to go once again—Montejo, Ávila, Pedro de Alvarado with his four brothers—and many new captains and knights joined them. The common soldiers as well signed on again, among them Bernal Díaz.

Cortés was gathering his fleet in the harbor of Santiago de Cuba on the south shore of the island when Andrés de Duero sent him a warning that Velázquez was about to revoke his appointment and advised that Cortés should sail without delay. The fleet wasn't ready yet. But, according to Las Casas, Cortés raided the local slaughterhouse and confiscated all the pork, which could then be salted aboard the ships. However, according to Bernal Díaz, Cortés bought the pigs and paid for them with his heavy gold chain that had a thistle medallion, the chain that Cortés in his new style had worn around his neck; the chain was the last item of value Cortés possessed that he could invest. (Bernal Díaz seems more credible: Cortés at this juncture would not have wanted to antagonize the people he was leaving and to whom he expected to return.) Likewise, according to Las Casas, Velázquez, who lived in Santiago, rode down to the shore but Cortés was already in a boat on the water and, refusing to return to land, with a wave bade a polite but ironic farewell to the governor and was rowed out to the ships. According to Bernal Díaz, Velázquez and Cortés met on shore; the governor took one look at the determined faces of the men who were escorting Cortés and decided that the course of wisdom was to accept the inevitable; then Velázquez and Cortés embraced and parted. (Again, Bernal Díaz's account seems more likely to be true.)

From the old town of Santiago, Cortés proceeded in his ships westward along the southern shore of Cuba, stopping at each port to enlist more men and to acquire more supplies when he could buy them on credit, and to be joined by *caballeros* (gentlemen cavalrymen) and soldiers who had crossed the island from towns on the northern shore. The horses for the expedition were kept ashore and were herded from port to port.

In a spasm of regret, Velázquez sent letters to the ports where the fleet would stop, desperate letters addressed to port officials and to many of the governor's friends and relatives who were with Cortés, instructing them that the fleet must not be allowed to depart, that Cortés's commission was being revoked, that Cortés should be arrested. But by this time all those with Cortés were exhilarated; they were pleased with Cortés as their leader; they knew how completely Cortés had pledged himself to this venture; and they scorned Velázquez's vacillation—first appointing Cortés, then wanting to retract the appointment, without having the nerve to oppose Cortés when the two of them had parted at Santiago, now wanting others to confront Cortés. Had Cortés without cause been relieved of his commission, there would have been a riot of resentment. So the port officials and Velázquez's relatives and friends chose to ignore the governor's entreaties.

It is difficult to understand the behavior of Diego Velázquez: He seems to have been a man who was tempted by adventure—but hadn't the courage for it.

In mid-February 1519, Cortés sailed for New Spain.

The Link of Language

It was not a neat fleet. Nor a well-organized sailing. Cortés had dispatched to the northern coast of Cuba two ships that were to pick up more men and supplies and were then to rendezvous with the rest of the fleet off Cape San Antonio at the western end of Cuba, and the fully assembled fleet would leave together for the island of Cozumel. But one of the ships sent to the north—captained by Pedro de Alvarado with a pilot named Camacho, who had been with Grijalva—returned ahead of schedule, did not wait for the rendezvous, and by itself sailed on to Cozumel.

When this ship reached Cozumel (Bernal Díaz was aboard), Alvarado led his Spaniards ashore only to find that, as when Grijalva had landed, the timid Indians had left their villages and fled to the low hills in the interior of the island, where they were hiding. In a prayer-house the Spaniards found some little gold offerings, which they took, and they caught about forty turkeys that were running about the thatched Indian huts.

On the following day Cortés arrived with the remainder of the fleet. Whereupon he began to impress upon the Spaniards his own code for the conduct of this expedition. He had the pilot Camacho put in irons for disobeying his orders. Cortés did not, however, publicly rebuke Alvarado. Cortés and Alvarado were both Estremadurans and they were the same age —thirty-three. Alvarado had more fighting experience, though both were expert at all the martial arts. Cortés from the moment he was appointed captain-general was acutely conscious of his prerogatives as commander, but Alvarado had four tough brothers, three of them reputedly legitimate, the fourth admittedly a bastard (no baptismal record exists for any of them, so they all might have been illegitimate). The Alvarados came from the tiny Estremaduran village of Lobán, though they boasted they were from the city of Badajoz. Pedro de Alvarado had a mane of long reddish-blond hair and a rakish, ready manner; he dressed as flamboyantly as he could for a man able to bring with him only a limited supply of clothing. The truth was that Alvarado resembled Cortés in many ways but had not undergone the character-change Cortés had imposed upon himself after his appointment as captain-general. In all probability, and according to their sensibilities, Pedro de Alvarado and Cortés liked each other very much. Cortés valued Alvarado and did not want to shame him.

But Cortés made Alvarado's men empty their pockets and their purses and give back the gold they had taken from the prayer-house; he was going to return it to the Indians. And Cortés lectured his men, all of them, and began to drum into them a message he was to repeat over and over and over: that this new land would be permanently pacified and truly conquered only if the Indians were induced to accept Spanish rule. The Indians could not be expected willingly to subordinate themselves if they were robbed or killed without cause. It was Cortés's firm policy—and his men should understand this and cooperate with him—that the Indians must be given the chance to welcome Christ and the king. It was too late to give back the turkeys, so Cortés proposed to pay the Indians for them with green-glass beads.

Sent out to search the countryside for Indians, the Spaniards found three, two old men and an old woman, and brought them to Cortés. Through Melchior (Julian had died in Cuba) Cortés told these Indians to go to their chiefs in the hills and tell them to bring back their people, that the Spaniards would not harm them but had come to do good. And he gave the three old Indians some beads and bells and put on each of them a Spanish shirt.

Then all the Indians came out of hiding—and Cortés gave them more presents. He also sternly told his men not to molest the Indian girls, an admonition that raised many eyebrows, coming from the man for whom one Suárez sister had not been enough. But the new Cortés did not invite backtalk. Soon the villages were teeming with easygoing island Indians who, happily trading with the Spaniards, brought them abundant supplies of fresh fish and fruit and especially the delicious island honey. Taken from the many small beehives the Indians maintained, Cozumel honey was a little tart for the Spanish taste, yet Cortés had several honeycombs packed in straw and stored aboard his flagship to send back as a sample to the king. Cortés ordered that the horses should be unloaded so they could be exercised and allowed to graze. And on the beach he held a muster of his force to see finally what he had with which to conquer a new world.

There were five hundred eight fighters in all. Most were swordsmen, pikemen and lancers. Sixteen were cavalrymen with mounts; in fact, there were now seventeen horses, since the mare belonging to Juan Sedeño had foaled en route. There were thirty-two crossbowmen and thirteen trained harquebusiers with shooting-pieces. Also in the company were several experienced artillerymen and they had ten small cannons, including four falconets (light brass cannons). Cortés had brought a couple of blacksmiths so the horses could be shod and the crossbows, shooting-pieces and cannons kept in repair. The crossbowmen had a good supply of cords and nuts and had tools for making arrows; the crossbows fired arrows at a low trajectory with great force and accuracy, and they compared in effectiveness with the firearms, though they were less shocking. Ample powder and shot were on hand, and the powder had been kept dry. A few of the *caballeros* had brought with them, as servants, Cuban Indians, including a few women, and there were a few Negroes.

The fleet at anchor consisted of eleven ships, the largest of which was Cortés's flagship, which displaced one hundred tons; there were three smaller ships of seventy or eighty tons; and the rest were either partially decked or open ships roofed with canvas. The larger ships carried boats that could be lowered for landing and could be rowed or sailed. In all, it was a motley armada. Several of the ships were owned by Cortés; several belonged to Velázquez (Cortés always maintained that Velázquez put up no more than one-third the cost of the fleet); Juan Sedeño owned the ship on which he sailed; the ownership of other vessels was shared by merchants in Cuba. Cortés had pledged the ships for supplies he had bought. These complications were typically Spanish; a Moor or Jew would never have allowed such a set-up. The ships were stuffed with supplies of salt pork, maize, yucca, cassava bread, chilis. And the ships were staffed by about one hundred pilots and sailors. The pilots were of particular importance; the chief pilot, Antón de Alaminos, had been on Columbus's fourth and last voyage and had been with both Hernández de Córdoba and Grijalva. These pilots recorded their sailing reports on rolls that passed among them.

After the muster Cortés had his banner with the Cross hung from the mast of his flagship and set his men to practicing—galloping the horses on the sand, firing the shooting-pieces and cannons, then cleaning the guns, and shooting the crossbows at targets. The watching Indians were most impressed by the horses.

During the next few days the Indians frequently came to the Spaniards and touched their beards and the fair skin of their arms when their sleeves were rolled up; the Spaniards' faces were tanned and weathered. Through Melchior it was learned that the Indians were not speculating about the return of Quetzalcoatl but talking instead about a recent memory: They had seen other white men years before Grijalva had come, bearded white men who, they said, were now held captive by Indians on the mainland— and they would wave toward the Yucatán, across the channel twelve miles away.

When this was reported to Cortés, he was aroused and asked the chiefs on Cozumel what they knew of white men in Yucatán. One old chief replied that he thought he knew where the captives were held, and he advised Cortés that, if he wanted to retrieve them, he should send envoys with a gift of green beads who could tell the Indian chief on the mainland of Cortés's wish that the white men should be freed and allowed to come to him. So Cortés prepared a letter addressed to whatever white men there might be. Then he tried to find island Indians who would serve as envoys and take the letter and a load of green beads to the mainland.

The Indians on Cozumel feared those on the mainland and were afraid, if they went there, they would be killed and eaten. But, finally, several island Indians were adequately bribed and agreed to undertake the mission. Cortés sent them on one of the smaller ships to the mainland, where the island Indians disembarked. On two accompanying ships Cortés sent an escort of fifty heavily armed men, with orders that the Spaniards on the three ships were to wait for six days to see if any white men would come to them.

While Cortés waited on Cozumel, a local temple caught his eye. It was a low pyramid made of limestone blocks with a thatched, open-sided pavilion at the top. In the pavilion were monstrous idols, including an idol made of baked clay with a hollow inside it where a priest could conceal himself; then, while the incense was wafting about, the priest would prophesy or respond to suppliants' questions (much like the oracle at Delphi in ancient Greece). The whole pavilion was spattered with blood, although these relatively gentle island Indians, according to Melchior, sacrificed partridges or their little castrated, barkless, fox-faced dogs more often than they sacrificed human beings.

Cortés decided to make a beginning. So he called together all the Indians who lived in the village where the temple was located and, through Melchior, he tried to explain the rudiments of Christianity. But Melchior could not understand what Cortés wanted to say and could not translate Cortés's thoughts into Mayan. This failure of communication was not due to Melchior's limitations—to his being, as Gómara reported, a fisherman who could not speak his own language properly or comprehend much Spanish. There were no words in Mayan to convey the concepts of Christianity. On divine matters the bridge between Spanish and Indian minds simply could not be made.

Aware that Melchior was bewildered and floundering, Cortés converted by demonstration. He led some of his men to the top of the pyramid and they smashed the Indian idols. Then Cortés had the interior of the pavilion swept out and whitewashed with fresh lime, including the floor and the bloody altar, and he had a Cross erected. On the altar, which had been used for sacrifices, the Spaniards fixed a painted, probably wooden figurine of Mary with Child and around the figurine set bowls of fresh flowers.

The island Indians had never seen anything like this before. A god that was not frightening? Passively they watched the Spaniards and tacitly accepted what was done. According to Bernal Díaz, they even promised to revere the Cross and the Lady, though translation in reverse on divine matters, from the Indians to the Spaniards, was probably no more dependable than had been the translation of Cortés's lecture on Christ.

The Spaniards wound up this exercise in conversion with a bit of practical and useful instruction: They showed the Indians how to make candles from the beeswax which was plentiful. The Indians had never before been able to make a long-lasting light. Cortés had Melchior tell the Indians that they should always keep candles burning before the statue of Mary.

After a week the three ships bearing the Indian envoys returned to Cozumel. The effort had been a failure. The island Indians who had gone ashore claimed to have delivered Cortés's letter and the beads to someone in a village in the interior. But no white men, nor any mainland Indians, had come to the shore.

Disappointed, and realizing that there was little gold to be obtained on Cozumel, Cortés reboarded his force and they set sail for Cape Catoche, only to have one of the ships spring a leak that could not be handled with the pumps, and the fleet had to return to Cozumel, where the damaged ship was careened for repair.

It was then—while work was being done on the leaky ship—that Cortés saw a canoe being paddled across the channel toward Cozumel from the mainland. The canoe was caught by the current, and Cortés sent some men down the beach after it. In the prow of the canoe was an Indian, naked except for a ragged breech-clout and with his hair braided and wound about his head like a woman. With him were six Indian oarsmen, all of whom were armed with bows and arrows, and they beached the canoe.

When Spanish soldiers with their swords unsheathed came near the Indians, the oarsmen moved to push off again. But the Indian at the prow spoke to them in the Indian tongue and apparently told them to wait.

Then to the soldiers he said in Spanish:

"*Señores,* are you Christians?"

The Spaniards embraced him and took him directly to Cortés.

The man was Gerónimo de Aguilar, from the town of Écija, which is between Seville and Córdoba in Spain. He was a priest. In 1511, while he was en route in a caravel from Panama to Hispaniola, his ship had grounded on a shoal off the island of Jamaica; he and fifteen other Spaniards, including two women, had escaped in a skiff that was blown in a storm all the way to the Yucatán, where, when they landed, starving and half-dead from thirst, they were captured by Indians. The Indian chief had promptly sacrificed eight of the Spanish men, and their bodies were eaten by the Indians in a riotous, barbaric ceremony. Aguilar and the others, kept in cages, were being fattened for another such feast when they had escaped into the jungle. But they had been captured again, this time by a chief who enslaved them. During the years that followed, one after another of the Spanish men had died from overwork, the two women had died from overwork and abuse, until now—after eight terrible years—only Aguilar and one other Spaniard were still alive.

(Writing more than seventy years later, Antonio de Herrera, Spain's official Historiographer of the Indies, revealed further details that he said were gleaned from contemporary reports of Spaniards in whom Aguilar, after his rescue, had confided. According to these reports, the Indians who held Aguilar captive came to realize that he was chaste, which was not a uniform condition among Spanish priests of this period. So they made sport of him and tried vainly to tempt him with women. Such reports about priests resisting temptation, however, were fairly common and may be doubted. The truth is more likely that Aguilar was sexually abused by the Indians, among whom sodomy was common, and finally the Indians, in scorn, made him serve their women as if he were a eunuch, which he was not. By the Indian women he was shown little mercy; he was, in fact, somewhat crippled from being forced to carry overly heavy loads. And he died at a fairly young age, a few years after his rescue.)

The island Indians sent by Cortés had found Aguilar, who was known as "the white slave," and they had given him Cortés's letter and the beads. With the beads Aguilar had, in effect, bought his freedom from the young chief who now owned him. Then with the letter Aguilar had gone to find the other Spaniard, Gonzalo Guerrero, who lived in a different village.

Guerrero was no longer a slave. Through feats of courage and strength (he was a sailor from Palos) he had established himself among the Indians and was war-leader in the retinue of the chief of his village; he had led his people to many victories over the Indians of other villages. He had been given one of the chief's daughters in marriage and had sons by her. His face and body were tattooed, his ears pierced, and he wore a gold bar through his nose and a jadestone in his lip. He read the letter from Cortés; he listened to Aguilar; but he refused to come. He would not cross back over to the Spaniards.

By the time Aguilar, having seen Guerrero, reached the coast, the ships Cortés had sent were gone. It was an Act of Providence, all agreed, that

Cortés had had to return to Cozumel to repair the leaking ship—or else Aguilar would have missed him completely.

In his eight years in the Yucatán, Aguilar had become fluent in Chontal Mayan. So Cortés had a link that he knew he needed: He could now speak freely in Spanish to Aguilar, who in turn could speak for him to the coastal Indians.

THE CONQUEST BEGINS

On March 4, 1519, the patched-up fleet of unmatched vessels left Cozumel and sailed for the mainland of Mexico. The weather was gusty and a storm blew up that dispersed the ships. When the storm abated, one of the ships was missing, and Cortés directed that a search along the Yucatán coast be made for it. When the missing ship was found safe at anchor in a cove, Cortés dispatched one of the smaller ships with a shallow draft to explore the large bay at the base of the peninsula. And the men who were sent out, when they went ashore, found the greyhound that had been left by Grijalva's expedition. The dog was running up and down the beach and leapt into the Spaniards' boat. Since the bitch was sleek and fat, the Spaniards concluded that this shore was rich with game.

Cortés did not want to bypass any Indians who had not been made to respect the Spaniards. So he intended to land at Champotón, where Hernández de Córdoba had been defeated by the Indians and Grijalva had been resisted. But the wind off Champotón was contrary, and Alaminos, the chief pilot, counseled against a landing. So they went on to the mouth of the Tabasco River, where Grijalva had been given the present of gold and had traded peacefully and profitably.

At Tabasco their trouble began.

When Cortés anchored his ships off the sandbar at the river's mouth and the Spaniards in boats went upriver, they were surprised when battle-ready Tabascans in a fleet of dugouts came out in force to confront them. The mangrove swamps along the riverbanks were teeming with armed warriors in battle paint—so many warriors that many of the Spaniards who had not been with Hernández de Córdoba or Grijalva and were seeing mainland Indians for the first time were astonished and shaken. But Cortés methodically disembarked his men on the headland below the town, which was on the right bank of the river going inland, and he had his cannons carefully unloaded, while his harquebusiers and crossbowmen stood at the ready.

Cortés had Aguilar shout to the Indians, massed in their dugouts on the river, that the Spaniards came in peace, to draw water because they had been at sea; the ships anchored offshore could not be seen by the Indians from this point upriver. And Cortés announced that they would like to trade the goods they had brought for fresh food—and perhaps receive another present of gold.

The Indians replied with threats and ominous gestures and told Aguilar that, following Grijalva's departure, they had been ridiculed by their neighbors because they had not attacked and repelled the intrusive strangers (further evidence that the Spaniards were not regarded as gods). All the towns of this region were allied in a kind of confederation, and their neighbors had heaped such abuse upon them that the Tabascans had vowed never again to have anything to do with white strangers and to kill all others who might come.

Cortés had Aguilar repeat his message, and the Indian repeated their message, because in these exchanges repetition was necessary before each side comprehended the other. Then, since the sun was setting, the Indians said they would return to their town; the chiefs would decide whether or not to trade; and they would reply in the morning. With a parting threat to kill all the Spaniards if they were to move from the headland, the Indians in their dugouts retired.

During the armistice of the night, both sides—both of these peoples who had evolved over untold millennia on utterly separate courses of human development—proceeded to cheat.

In the town the Indians hurriedly packed up all the things they regarded as precious and had their women and children with the bundles leave the houses and hide in the woods. Around the emptied town the warriors strengthened the barricades of tree-trunks and with other tree-trunks built obstructions to prevent a river-landing by the Spaniards.

Cortés, for his part, prepared a pincers movement. Men who had been here with Grijalva recalled an obscure path that led from the dune of the headland through the marsh that separated the headland from the mainland, and the path led around to the back of the town. So under cover of darkness Cortés sent a troop of one hundred men along this path to lie in wait behind the town and at the sound of gunfire to attack from the inland side while he and his men came in the boats to attack from the river.

In the morning, when the hostility of each side was obvious, Cortés and the men he retained—after hearing Mass from a priest named Bartolomé de Olmedo, who was an essential part of the Spanish company—reboarded their boats and proceeded upriver to the town.

Still, there was a nicety to be observed, the significance of which should

not be underestimated because it was understood by the Spaniards to be
a serious legal requirement and it was sincere. The policy of the Spanish
Crown was that the Indians had to be forewarned. Ferdinand and Isabella
had begun this practice, and Carlos had endorsed it. An official pronounce-
ment had to be conveyed to the Indians before there was any fighting. In
practice, what happened—when boatloads of tense, frightened Spaniards
were on the river, hugely outnumbered by fierce Indian warriors on the
riverbank who were eager to kill and eat them—was this:

Cortés had at his side in the prow of the first boat the king's notary,
Diego de Godoy, who served as a witness. So legalistic were the Spaniards
that the testimony of another soldier or a priest would not have been
acceptable; the witness had to be a notary. With Godoy witnessing, Cortés
had Aguilar deliver to the Indians in Mayan the required speech, the
requerimiento. The Indians were called upon to accept the primacy of
Christ and the king and to recognize the legitimacy of Spanish sovereignty
in America on the grounds of a papal donation; all Indians were urged to
accept their vassalage and consent to Christian preaching, thus assuring
themselves of peace and many other benefits; and the Indians were told that
horrors would befall them if they resisted, in which case whatever happened
would be the Indians' own fault.

Aguilar shouted this message at the Indians, but he could not possibly
have been heard over the noise; the Indians were shrieking, blowing
whistles and conches and beating on drums, vividly and vigorously miming
what they intended to do to the Spaniards. With the battle legitimized,
however, the Spaniards went at it. (Apparently no corresponding restraint
applied to the Indians.)

The beginning of the battle was a mess. With arrows, fire-hardened
darts, spears and slung stones pouring down on them, the Spaniards nearly
could not land. The Indians had a battle-cry that meant, "Kill their captain!" This cry was familiar to Spaniards who had fought with mainland
Indians before, when the Indians had shot ten arrows into Grijalva, and
Cortés knew what the cry meant. But he was so busy fighting that, when
he lost a shoe in the mud while forcing the landing, he rushed onto the
beach half-barefoot. Another Spaniard found the shoe in the water and gave
it to Cortés; he slipped it on and kept fighting, while the Spaniards tore
down the barricades.

With difficulty the Spaniards, firing and slashing, fighting in their organized, disciplined, integrated teams, which was second nature to them,
drove the Indians back toward the town—until the troop in hiding behind

the town attacked. The other Spaniards had had to cross a marsh and were late. Under pressure from two sides, the Indian warriors retreated and followed their women and children into the woods, while the Spaniards occupied the town.

When the panting Spaniards assembled in the central square, Cortés—with the notary Godoy attending—went to a giant silk-cotton tree that stood in front of the prayer-house, with his sword slashed the trunk three times, and proclaimed loudly that he had conquered this land in the name of "His Majesty the King." As the Spaniards sat down on the ground and stretched out to rest, it occurred to some of them—especially those related to Velázquez or who had been in the governor's employ—that Cortés in his proclamation had not mentioned Velázquez, even though it was to Velázquez that the license to conquer this place had been granted.

The next morning Cortés and his men were hungry. So Cortés sent out two troops of one hundred men each, one under Francisco de Lugo, the other under Pedro de Alvarado, to reconnoiter the countryside to see if some food could be found, and maybe to learn where the gold came from. Cortés told Alvarado to take Melchior as his interpreter. But Melchior was gone. His Spanish clothes were found, neatly hanging from a thorn-bush in a palm grove. The Tabascans fought naked, and Melchior had stripped, joined them and escaped. Cortés regarded Melchior's flight as treachery and disloyalty and he resented it—because Melchior had been baptized.

A couple of miles from the town Francisco de Lugo and his troop came upon fields of maize, nicely tended fields that were drained by well-planned ditches; the captain was inspecting the fields, appraising the corn as prospective food for the Spaniards, when he and his men were attacked by thousands of Indians who were coming from another town in the confederation to help the Tabascans. A desperate fight developed, and Lugo and his men were able to extricate themselves only because Alvarado and his troop heard firing and came up in support. The combined Spanish troops then were able to retreat in orderly fashion to the town. The Indians did not pursue them, because thousands of other Indians were coming over the hills and the attackers went to assemble with them. The Tabascan chiefs had informed both Grijalva and Cortés that they could field three *xiquipiles* (a total of twenty-four thousand men according to Bernal Díaz, forty thousand according to Gómara).

Three Indians had been taken prisoner by the Spaniards, and one of them, who seemed to be a captain, told Cortés through Aguilar that Melchior had told the chiefs how few Spaniards there were and had advised that the Indians would be victorious if they attacked without let-up. Cortés gave this captain and the other two Indians some green beads and released them to return to the chiefs to say that the Spaniards came in peace and wanted only to trade. These Indians with their presents left to relay Cortés's words.

That night Cortés had all the men who remained on the ships, except skeleton crews, come upriver as reinforcements, and he had them bring more artillery and the thirteen best horses. The horses were stiff after days aboard ship and, when they were released, they exploded with energy— bucking, rearing and running. By morning, though, after a cool night at pasture, they were ready.

Cortés led his force of, at most, five hundred men to the edge of the cornfields where tens of thousands of Indians awaited them, ready for battle. The Spaniards went through their usual ritual, hearing Mass before leaving camp, and again Cortés had Aguilar shout out in Mayan at the nearest Indians the assurances of the king.

Cortés liked pincers movements. So, mounting his own horse, which, according to Bernal Díaz, was a vicious dark chestnut stallion, he separated the cavalry from the rest of his little army. On the thirteen horses, which were hung with defensive plates of armor, were the men who were the best riders and best fighters from horseback; the cavalrymen preferred to use lances but used swords when they had to. Typically the horsemen were heavily muscled in the shoulders and arms, lithe and sinewy in body, with legs like spring-steel clamps and with lightning-quick reflexes. Cortés led the mounted unit on a route around the cornfields so they could attack the Indians from the rear.

Then the bulk of the army moved out from the woods into the open fields. The Spaniards were roughly in a rectangle, with cannons at the corners, the cannons protected by swordsmen and pikemen. The har-quebusiers and crossbowmen were interspersed along the sides and were similarly protected. The Spanish fighting team consisted of five men; and a team of harquebusiers, for example, would fire a volley in unison, then whirl to reload while protected by teams of swordsmen and pikemen, then would whirl again and fire a volley in another direction; then reload again; and they could do this with considerable rapidity. Likewise, the crossbow-men operated in teams and fired their arrows in volleys. The cannons as well were clustered. These were the tactics on which Spanish fighting men had been raised.

(Even in the early stages of warfare on the Eurasian side of the world, training was the determinant of victory. The Greek phalanx defeated the Persian horde. And the integrated cavalry and infantry maneuvers of Philip of Macedon and especially of his son, Alexander the Great—maneuvers which the Macedonians practiced again and again—brought victories over far larger forces. The Spanish tactics of the early sixteenth century, as devised by Gonzalo de Córdoba, made the Spaniards on land unbeatable for more than a century.)

The Indians, although brave, fought as a crowd. At first, keeping their distance, the Indians threw darts and slung stones, hurled javelins, and threw spears with the aid of spear-throwers that extended a man's arm and the arc of the throw and thus increased the distance a spear could be thrown. Mainly they shot arrows at the Spaniards, wounding many of them. But the Spaniards—even those with only Indian armor of quilted cotton—raised their shields and withstood the onslaught, until the excited Indians in a rush closed with the Spaniards. Then the practiced Spaniards in their interlinked teams at close quarters outfought the Indians, who had no strategy for bringing to bear their great superiority in numbers. Yet in this valley, called Cintla, the Indians continued to press the Spaniards. After being damaged by a series of Spanish volleys, the surviving Indians, still in great number, would withdraw a little and let loose more arrows, spears, darts and stones. It was nip-and-tuck, with the Indians closing, withdrawing, and closing again—until the Spanish cavalry came at the Indians from their rear.

This was marshy country, and Cortés and his horsemen had had to struggle through swamps, but they finally emerged on the cornfields. Then they operated like killing machines, not in unison, but like thirteen separate killing machines, each horseman spearing, slashing, breaking into an Indian crowd, racing about, charging another crowd, racing after the Indians who ran and spearing them one by one. The Indians, who prided themselves on being fast runners, were dismayed when their fastest runners were overtaken by the horses and speared. Shocked and deafened by the Spaniards' guns, the Indians were panicked by the strange animals. They had never before seen horses, with or without men upon them, and they thought that each horse and rider were one creature, a kind of centaur-dragon unloosed to destroy them. Routed, the Indians ran for the thick woods that lay beyond the fields. Cortés and his cavalrymen rejoined the weary foot-soldiers.

On the fields there were over eight hundred dead Indians—among whom Aguilar identified the tattooed corpse of Guerrero, the sailor from

Palos, who had been killed by a harquebus shot. Two Spaniards had been killed, and nearly all others were wounded, as were the horses. So the Spaniards cut up a dead Indian and removed the fat from his body; they heated and melted the fat; and with liquefied human fat they seared the wounds of both the men and the horses. Had the Indians been able to use the Spaniards' bodies, the Spanish fat would have served to tenderize the muscle-meat of the thighs, calves, forearms and biceps. Thus, had victory gone either way, the fat would have been put to use. Indians, incidentally, are smooth-muscled, like Asiatics, and their bodies contain an ample amount of fat.

The Spaniards held a few Indian prisoners. So, once more, Cortés talked to them and advanced his strategy; he had Aguilar translate for him in a gentle tone; and Cortés gave his usual reassurances that he and his men were peaceful and wanted to trade; he said that his men were hungry, and he freed the amazed Indians (who thought, if the Spaniards were hungry, then they as captives would surely be the food). Cortés told them to return to their chiefs. Then the Spaniards went back to their camp in the town.

The next morning Indian slaves came to the town bearing loads of tortillas and bringing many cooked fowl (usually translated as turkeys and often, incorrectly, as chickens; these birds are varieties of jungle fowl, similar to turkeys but quite different from chickens; most are small but some are as large as peacocks). The hungry Spaniards were about to snatch the food, but Aguilar, at the sight of the slaves' stained faces and ragged breech-clouts, angrily scolded these Indians; he had lived too long with his own face stained and a rag to wear, not to sense the impropriety of using slaves as envoys. He ordered these bearers to report to their chiefs that the chiefs must come themselves if they wanted or expected peace. The Spaniards, however, kept the food. And Cortés, advancing his diplomacy even when he was bloodied and tired, slipped each slave a few beads before the slaves left the camp.

And so the chiefs and priests in gorgeous feather-cloaks and embroidered tunics came. They knelt before Cortés and the Spaniards, touched the ground, then lifted their hands to the sky. They begged permission to be allowed to burn and bury their dead because pumas and rodents would feed on the corpses, and Cortés gave them permission. He asked them to bring Melchior to him. But it was too late. Melchior had already been sacrificed in atonement for the Indian defeat and as punishment for his bad advice.

Even when Cortés was under intense pressure, he liked to joke (it's a Spanish trait and talent). He caught on from talking to these Indians through Aguilar that they did not understand either the horses or the guns. So, after he had instructed the chiefs and priests to come back the next day and they had departed, he had the mare that had foaled led all around the shady grove where he had received the Indian delegation. He also had the biggest cannon loaded with a heavy ball and a great charge of powder and had it placed nearby. Then, when the Indian chiefs and priests returned the next day and were sitting with him in the shade, at his signal the cannon was fired and roared like thunder, the ball whizzing overhead toward the river. And the raunchiest stallion in the Spanish herd was brought up and, catching the scent of the mare, reared, pawed the ground, neighed, and tried to break away from his lead to get to the grove where the Indians and Cortés were sitting. The Indians were terrified, thinking the stallion wanted to attack them. But Cortés, like a good host, rose and went to the cannon and the stallion, whispered consolingly, and then returned to tell the Indians that they should calm themselves; the cannon and the horse were very cross with them; but he had explained that they were now sensible subjects of the king, so the cannon and the horse were pacified. (The Indians in the retinue attending the chiefs seemed to swallow this yarn, but the chiefs very soon afterward made obvious their comprehension that iron was inanimate and that horses, like dogs, were creatures of nature.)

While Indians were collecting and burning the corpses in the cornfields, the chiefs came again, and this time they brought a present of gold—all the gold, they said, that they had. Because they had been defeated, no wish was associated with the gold. The gold was their peace-offering to Cortés, or this king he talked about, or his God. It was a considerable amount of gold—masks, sculptures of dogs, lizards and ducks, diadems, even gold soles for sandals. When Cortés asked them where he might find more gold, they motioned northwestward and said, "Mexico" and "Culua," which was another name for Mexico. But this was meaningless to Cortés and to Aguilar, as it had been meaningless to Grijalva, Julian and Melchior.

The Indian chiefs presented to Cortés, along with the gold, twenty young women. This was a gift for which Cortés was most grateful, and said so, but he had reason to be even more grateful than he knew at the time because among these women was one whose name has come down to us with various connotations: In some circles her name is a spat-out invective that denotes a traitor to one's race; in other circles her name implies a true convert and a good servant of Christ; in still other circles, and only recently, her name forecasts the blending of the future; and to some who are romantically inclined her name suggests a rare kind of lover. The name by which she is generally called now is Malinche.

The Second Link of Language

The import of that name or word "Malinche" is obscure. The Indians called Cortés "Malinche." Later, the Indians addressed one of the Spaniards who had become fluent in Nahuatl as "Malinche." It has been suggested that this slave girl's name referred simply to her birthdate in the Nahuatl calendar—the day called Malin—and Nahuatl-speaking Indians called her Malinche (Malin-woman) and they called Cortés Malinche as a kind of joke because she eventually served Cortés with such constancy. But this explanation seems suspect because the Indians would not have been disrespectful of Cortés and because the explanation does not account for the name being applied to the other Spaniard who later learned Nahuatl. After she became a Christian, the Spaniards called her Doña Marina. Bernal Díaz suggested that Malinche was an Indian mispronunciation of Marina or Doña Marina or perhaps a Nahuatl reference to Malin-woman's captain. Both the Indians and the Spaniards garbled each other's language. The name of the Aztec war god was Huitzilopochtli, which the Spaniards simplified to "Witchy-lobos." But it is unreasonable to think that the name or word "Malinche" would have originated in Spanish; its root must be in Nahuatl because the Indians would not have applied to one of their own a Spanish appellation.

To the Spaniards, at first, she was simply one of the twenty slave girls given to them by the Tabascan chiefs. The giving of the women by the Tabascans, as an incidental phase of a general gift-giving, was casual and passive. Yet it pointed up an area of contrast between the Indians and the Spaniards that may suggest a fundamental emotional difference.

The Indians regarded all slaves—men like Aguilar and women like Malinche—as chattels to be owned and put to use and to work. The Indians did not denigrate women particularly; often in the upper circles of Indian society, as in Spanish society, women were prominent and powerful. Among all the Indian tribes slavery of both men and women was a deeply ingrained practice and an accepted social institution. Sometimes the slaves were people of another tribe that had been conquered. Sometimes the slaves were native to the tribe and were being punished for some offense; there was even an arrangement by which drunkards and wastrels could voluntarily sell themselves into bondage and make themselves the equivalent of indentured servants. Slavery was so universal among Indians that in the markets slaves were traded like cacao beans or any other commodity, as black slaves were traded in the southern United States before the Civil War, though in the Indian markets there was no racial distinction. In all of this there seems to have been a difference in moral and emotional sensitivity between the Indians and the Spaniards, and this difference is worth contemplating, for it sheds light on the behavior of both of these peoples.

In the contingent of nubile women delivered to the Spaniards were a number of very young girls, virgins and near-virgins, who were shy, scared and shivering. Malinche, who had been a slave since childhood, was not one of these, and her calm acceptance of her lot without embarrassment (some of the others, too, being calm and unembarrassed) relieved the Spaniards. The Tabascan chiefs, however, took no notice whatever of the emotions exhibited by the slave girls and women; these females were expected to do what they were going to do—and the most important use of the women, which the Tabascan chiefs clearly conveyed to the Spaniards, was that these women would make tortillas. The Tabascan chiefs deeply sympathized with the white strangers who seemed to have with them no women to make tortillas.

Obviously, sexuality for the Indians did not have the priority that it had for the Spaniards. Among the Indians no emphasis was placed on virginity; certainly no sanctity was associated with it. Girls began to be used sexually as soon as they were nubile. Nor did the bearing of babies spoil them for subsequent marriage. Among the Indians marriage was regarded as a serious matter because it was the basis for inheritance, though most Indian men of status had several wives. But the virginity of a prospective wife was never considered.

The emotional nature of the Indians apparently differed radically from the emotional nature of the Spaniards. The Indians frequently and regularly conducted ceremonies in which human victims were gutted and sometimes skinned while living, then dismembered, and the flesh of the sacrificial victims would be cooked and eaten. The Indian towns and cities were laid out with avenues along which the victims would be dragged and pulled to the top of a pyramid so the whole populace assembled on the rooftops could hear the screaming and watch the bloodletting. These were festivals all Indians were used to—orgies of shrieking—shrieking by the victims whose blood was about to spurt and the crowd's shrieking. The audiences for these ceremonies were treated to dramatic climaxes that within the whole range of human potentiality could not be surpassed or equaled. The climaxes of classical Greek drama were not as riveting as this because the audiences knew they were enactments. Nor were the public executions in

Europe or Asia so shocking and emotionally cathartic. The cruelties of Oriental despots, the atrocities committed by Europeans, the sometimes public torturing, the lashings and beheadings, none of these even began to match in orgasmic intensity the ceremonies familiar to these Indians.

To people used to such emotional intensity, what would the weeping of a virgin have meant?

Among the Spaniards, on the other hand, there was a respect for women which stemmed fundamentally from the concept of the Virgin Mary. The Spanish fighters, however they behaved, were imbued with the idea that virginity implied purity, that in God's eyes such innocence was good. All the Spanish men who were literate had read the popular romances, and all Spaniards had been thoroughly sermonized by the clergy. In practice, of course, in marrying and wenching, Spanish men did not conform to the teachings of the Church or to the ideals of chivalry. Nevertheless, respect for feminine purity was instilled in the Spaniards.

The Spanish mind was not imprinted with horror in the same way or to the same degree as the Indian mind—horror which for the Indians was ceremoniously presented, socially approved, and religiously exalted. So the Spaniards were more inclined to focus on the excitement of sexuality. They had more room in their souls, more emotional space, for sexual interest. When the slave girls were given them, they were titillated that such a delightful gift could be so casually made.

Spaniards simply could not be that casual about sex. They were passionate—their passion being concentrated on fighting and women. Cortés, for his part, accepted the twenty women in good grace and judiciously assigned one girl to each of his captains, and the remaining girls he assigned to tortilla-making for the army as a whole.

The young woman whom we call Malinche and who was christened Doña Marina was given by Cortés, a foresighted and calculating diplomat, to Puertocarrero, to whom he had already given a mare. As a cousin of the Count of Medellín, Puertocarrero had relatives he could contact at the Spanish Court; he was a fellow-Estremaduran; and Cortés foresaw the likelihood of important missions for him. (Regarding the few Cuban Indian women who accompanied the Spaniards, there is a record of only one dispute, of little significance.)

Since no more gold was to be obtained in Tabasco, Cortés organized his departure, which was on Palm Sunday, 1519. In the center of the town he had Spanish carpenters put up a large plain Cross and a pedestal on which they set a figurine of the Blessed Mary with Child. Cortés had brought, packed in straw, a large supply of these painted figurines. Cortés had Fray Olmedo, an exceptionally sweet singer, put on his vestments and conduct a solemn Mass, complete with palm fronds, while the Indians watched. Then Cortés paraded his troops before the rapt Tabascans. He had an intimation that these activities would be reported to Indians other than those present. Finally, in the ships' boats escorted and aided by Tabascans in a huge fleet of dugout canoes, Cortés and his men went downriver to the sea—where for the first time the Indians to their amazement saw the big ships.

Cortés wanted to go where the gold was. So Alaminos charted a course westward along the coast and a little northward to the place Grijalva had named San Juan de Ulúa, where the modern port of Veracruz is now. Cortés had his ships anchored in the lee of the island that partially created a natural shelter for the port. And within half an hour two large dugouts filled with Indian chiefs and priests came toward him. These Indians hesitated until they identified the largest ship—Cortés's flagship from the topmast of which his banner of the Cross was flying—and, at the Spaniards' invitation, they came aboard.

However, when the Indians were on deck and the chiefs were making obeisance in a tone pleasing to Cortés, it was clear that these Indians were speaking a different Indian language. Aguilar could not understand them. And Cortés was vexed; he was always acutely aware of the necessity of having a link of language so he could communicate; sign-language and mime frustrated him.

But one of the slave girls, the one he had given to Puertocarrero, was chatting easily with the newly arrived Indians. These Indians came from the highland, from the place called Mexico, and they were speaking the highland language, Nahuatl. They could not speak the coastal dialect of Mayan. *But Malinche could speak Nahuatl . . . and she could tell Aguilar in Mayan what had been said . . . and Aguilar in Spanish would tell Cortés.* This was the vital chain: from Spanish to Mayan to Nahuatl and back—from Cortés through Aguilar and Malinche to the Mexican king.

The Indian chiefs brought presents of fine cotton cloth and featherwork and some little gold objects, and in return they were given presents of glass beads, Spanish garments and iron tools. Both sides were pleased. Cortés sensed, and inferred from what the Indian chiefs said, that they had heard about the battle he had fought in Tabasco; in fact, they knew about all the previous Spanish landings. Among Mexican Indians there was a long-standing custom of receiving ambassadors and traders, and the envoys would be decently treated. Cortés was now being received in this spirit, as if he were an envoy from a distant land—and Cortés and all the Spaniards far preferred this kind of reception to the battlelines of warriors they had encountered so far. Cortés always asked to see the chief in charge, and these chiefs before they disembarked assured him that a greater chief would soon come.

During the next two days Cortés fortified his position on a large sand dune. He unloaded the horses and the artillery. With help from the local Indians his men built shacks to protect themselves from the sun, and the local people, knowing that palm fronds were insufficient roofing, brought enough thick cloths to make the roof coverings opaque. (Veracruz is a hellhole, flat and hot; the liveliest times there are the three or four hours after midnight, which are the least oppressive hours.)

When the greater chief came, Cortés received him on the fortified dune. The chief's name was Tendile. These Indian names are all phonetic renderings and reveal degrees of simplification: Bernal Díaz called him Tendile; Cortés called him Teudilli; Sahagún, who probably knew best, called him Teuhtlilli or Tentlil. He informed Cortés that he served a great monarch in the mountains whose name was, in Spanish usage, Montezuma. (If the deep-throated, guttural sound of Nahuatl is to be suggested, the name should more closely be pronounced "Mawk-tay-koo-soma.") And Tendile took from chests his bearers had brought many sculptures of gold, and gold jewels, and useful objects made of gold, as well as ten loads of the finest cloth and featherwork. So Cortés presented Tendile with a large quantity of fine glass beads, a Spanish cap on which was embroidered in gilt thread a medallion of St. George on horseback slaying the dragon (the Indians must have puzzled over this), and other items of Spanish clothing. To Tendile through Aguilar and Malinche, Cortés expressed his desire to meet Montezuma and, as a final present, he gave Tendile a beautifully made Spanish chair (the Indians had no chairs) in which Montezuma could sit when Cortés came to see him.

In his proposal to Tendile, Cortés happened upon a lucky ploy. Cortés told Tendile that he represented a great monarch who lived on the other side of the sea and that *his* monarch knew all about Montezuma and specifically wanted Cortés to present himself to the great king of Mexico. Cortés made this up, of course; no one in Spain had ever heard of Montezuma or Mexico; Cortés himself had just realized that Mexico was a place in the mountains and that there was a Mexican king called Montezuma. Tendile, however, was startled and somewhat dismayed when

Cortés, with exaggerated Spanish courtesy, said that *his* king knew of Montezuma, because this brought up the old Indian myth that one of the founders of the Indian race—king or god—had sailed away to the east and might return someday to resume his rule.

Tendile's attention was attracted by the helmet one of the Spanish soldiers wore, a gilded iron helmet. Tendile said this Spaniard's helmet resembled one that adorned an idol-image of Huitzilopochtli, the war god. (Gómara wisely suggested that the helmet on the idol had probably been found by coastal Indians in the wreckage from a Spanish ship, and had been regarded by myth-making Indian priests as evidence of the god who had sailed away, evidence which to rationalistic Indian war-leaders, on the other hand, may have indicated the possibility that enemies were coming.) Montezuma, Tendile was sure, would like very much to see the Spanish soldier's helmet. Cortés accommodated by having the soldier lend Tendile the helmet to take to Montezuma, with Cortés's suggestion that the helmet should be returned filled with grains of gold so that the Spaniards might verify that Indian gold was the same as their own gold. (Cortés could carry on this laconic joking while four thousand armed Indian warriors in attendance on Tendile were standing by.)

Although all the Spaniards' activities had been reported to Tendile and by him to Montezuma, now Tendile openly wanted to record these happenings by having artists in his retinue draw pictures of the Spaniards. The Indians had no phonetic writing, not even hieroglyphics or pictographs, but they had perfected a fast and simple kind of picture-making; their artists could quickly sketch whatever they saw, and the sketches, which lacked perspective or modulation, were drawn on stiffened, whitened pages made from hide or maguey, pages that were folded up in accordion fashion to make what passed for books. There were thousands of these "books." Most of them were burned in the years following the conquest by Catholic prelates who feared they might tend to perpetuate among the Indians the old heretical beliefs. The few "books" that remain in existence were mostly made after the conquest and are, for some esoteric reason, called codices; they are in museums chiefly in Europe and Mexico.

(Bernardino de Sahagún, a Franciscan monk who came from Spain to Mexico eight years after the conclusion of the conquest, was a philological genius. Sahagún learned Nahuatl and, with help from Aztec priests, he wrote explanations on the Indian drawings, which were mainly mnemonic devices. First writing the explanations in a phonetic Spanish transcription

eso parece ser cosa muy buena, y
sabrosa, ya me sano, y quito la en
fermedad, ya estoy sano: y mas
otra vez le dixo el viejo. Señor.
beued la otra vez, porque es muy
buena la medicina, y estareys
mas sano. Y el dicho quetsalcoatl,
beuio la otra vez, de que se embo
rracho, y començo allorar triste
mente: y se le movio, y ablan
do el coraçon, para yr se, y no se
le quito del pensamjento lo que
tenja, por el engaño, y burla,
que le hizo, el dicho njgromanti
co viejo. Y la medicina que be
uio, el dicho quetsalcoatl, era
vino blanco de la tierra: hecho
de magueyes, que se llaman teu
metl.

tlapia ieveuetlacatl, amo nono
tzazque. auh iniquac ticalmo
cuepaz, occeppa tipiltontli timu
chicaz. njman icmoioleuh in
Quetsalcoatl: auh inveuento ie
no ceppa qujlhuj, tlaoque xoco
miti, inpatli. njman qujto in
Quetsalcoatl reventzie caamo
niquiz. njmanqujlhuj inveue
to, macaxocon miti timotoli
miz, macannel noço mixquac
xocontlali motonal motolimiz.
macanachito xoconmopaloltiti.
auh in Quetsalcoatl: njman
conpalo achiton: auh catepa
vel conjc. njman qujto in Que
tsalcoatl: henj! cuccnca, qualli.
in cocolisitli caocenpolo. campa
noia cocolli caocmo mjnococoa,
njman qujlhuj inveuento, ca
occe xoconj caqualli inpatli ic
chicaoaz inmonacaio, auh ni
man ic icnoceppa ce conjc, mj
man icivintic, njman ieic
choca velitellelqujça, icvncan
moioleuh in Quetsalcoatl, vnca
tlapan injiollo. aocmoconmilca
cacaia, çaie inquimatinenca
inqujmatinemja velqujoima

A page from the Florentine Codex, which was prepared by Fray Bernardino de Sahagún on the basis of what old Aztecs, mostly former priests, told him fifteen to forty-five years after the conquest. The righthand column is Nahuatl phonetically rendered into the Spanish alphabet; the lefthand column is in sixteenth-century Spanish. The illustrations are typical Indian drawings.

of the Nahuatl, he then translated the Nahuatl into Spanish. Thus his annotated volumes are the best bridge we have to comprehend the significance of Aztec pictures.)

All the Spaniards were happy to pose for the Indian artists, and each captain had his portrait made. Bernal Díaz, in his old age recalling these days of his youth, wrote that, on the basis of the portrait of Cortés, Montezuma sent to the coast an Aztec chief who looked so much like Cortés that the Spaniards referred to them as "our Cortés" and "the other Cortés." This story, though, is likely a concocted Spanish joke because Indian drawings were simplistic; Cortés and all the Spaniards were heavily bearded and unshorn, wore helmets or cloth caps, and no smooth-faced Indian with cropped jet-black hair would resemble Cortés or any other Spaniard.

Cortés put on a good show for Tendile to report to Montezuma. Cortés had the cannons fired—and the artists did their best to depict the explosions. Cortés turned over all the horses to Pedro de Alvarado, who put bells on their harnesses and then led the jingling Spanish cavalry as they galloped over the wet sand at the water's edge and charged with their swords unsheathed, lances held high, past the watching Indians on the dune.

Tendile promised to convey Cortés's wishes to Montezuma—and the Indians departed.

MONTEZUMA'S GIFT-CUM-WISH

While Cortés and his men were awaiting Tendile's return, Cortés through Aguilar interrogated Malinche and learned her story. She told him, or so Cortés understood her, that she was wellborn, of parents who were of highland stock and who in Spanish society would be considered noble. She came from a village near the town of Coatzacoalcos, not far from Tabasco. (It's strange that these groups of Nahuatl-speaking and Mayan-speaking peoples should live in such close proximity and not meld. Yet this phenomenon exists today: At fairs in the city of Oaxaca, for example, people coming from different mountain valleys speak a number of different Indian dialects and languages, and the groups are unable to communicate freely with each other; they trade through sign-language or with the aid of clever interpreters like Malinche.) Her father had died when she was a child, and her mother had married a younger man, also considered noble among the Aztecs. Her mother had borne the new husband a son and, in order to make this son's inheritance unquestionable, her mother and stepfather had sold her into slavery and had given out the lie that she had died. She had been passed among slave-traders and had had several owners and she was in Tabasco and about to be traded again when, at the command of the Tabascan chiefs, she and the other slave girls had been given to the Spaniards.

This story evidently was accurate—because years later when Cortés was leading an expedition to Honduras and Bernal Díaz was with him, the army passed through Coatzacoalcos, and Bernal Díaz met Malinche's mother and her half-brother, her stepfather having died. The old woman, whom Bernal Díaz said Malinche resembled, and her grown son were terrified that Malinche, now with the Spaniards who were in control, would have them punished or killed. But Malinche took no vengeance at all. Instead, she told her mother and half-brother how thankful she was that, as a result of all that had happened to her, she had come to Christ and had become a woman of the Spaniards; this was her destiny, for which she was profoundly grateful and effervescent in her happiness. This account rings true.

The local Indians continued to keep the Spaniards comfortably supplied. There was some irritation on the part of Spaniards who were not captains, including Bernal Díaz, when the Indian chiefs who came to the camp would invite the Spanish captains to feast with them under a canopy of palm fronds and the common soldiers were not invited. But every Spaniard, even the lowliest, had brought his own little stock of trade-goods. So, while the chiefs and captains were feasting, the Spanish soldiers spread out their wares and traded with the common Indians for fish, fowl, fruit, and whatever else there was of value.

But the Spaniards' predicament was precarious. The sand dune on which they had established their camp was not suitable for long habitation; the mosquitoes were (and are) terrible. The anchorage for the ships was inadequately sheltered. The shoreline at Veracruz Bay is only slightly indented; the modern port has had to be protected with man-made breakwaters. Consequently the Spaniards were eager for Tendile's return. And after about ten days Tendile came back from the highland, leading a train of more than one hundred bearers. Seating himself with Cortés and a few of the Spanish captains, including the king's notary and the royal accountant (literally, *contador,* he who does the counting), Tendile had mats spread and displayed the gifts he had brought.

There was a calendar stone in gold, as big as the wheel of a cart, depicting the sun and its rays with many strange markings incised, and another wheel of highly polished silver depicting the moon. There were sculptures in gold of ducks, dogs, pumas, monkeys. There were ten magnificent and heavy gold collars, and gold necklaces inlaid with precious stones. The goldwork of the Aztecs was marvelous: They could make hollow sculptures of deer, and tubes or staffs of finely filigreed gold. A bow and arrows were made of gold with even the bowstring in gold. The Spanish soldier's gilt helmet, a little rustier than it used to be, was returned, filled with fine grains of gold. (The Indians both panned for gold in rivers and creeks and dug ore in the mountains. The frequent references to "mines" apparently meant simply places from which gold came. In the Indian culture, metalworking had begun in gold, silver and copper, though not in iron, which had not yet been discovered by them.) There were loads of dyed and embroidered cotton garments, as well as cloaks of featherwork so brilliant that, as Gómara recounted and Cortés recalled, had featherwork been durable, it would have been more precious than gold. Altogether, it was a dazzling, overwhelming, breathtaking presentation, an astonishing gift appropriate from a great king.

And along with this gift came Montezuma's wish. Tendile explained that Montezuma would not receive Cortés and his men; Montezuma would not allow them to come to the mountains to visit him nor would he come to the coast to see them. Montezuma was pleased to have them sojourn on the coast where they were, and he had instructed Tendile to say that the Spaniards, as envoys or ambassadors or traders, could stay until they were ready to go, that they should take with them as gifts everything he had sent them—but they should go.

This was not an attempt by Montezuma to bribe the Spaniards to go away; Montezuma had preponderant power, in spite of the Spaniards' horses and guns, and, as the ruler of millions, he would not deign to bribe a few hundred strangers. Nor did fear play any part in Montezuma's gesture; the Aztec empire was monolithic and considered itself invincible; the Spanish triumph over a coastal tribe was not cause for serious concern. And cowardice from the master of such a domain was inconceivable, especially considering that Aztec society was singularly dedicated to courage and the practice of war. Nor was there any substantial evidence that Montezuma thought that the coming of the Spaniards might be a fulfillment of the old prophecy about Quetzalcoatl; the contrary was implied, because Montezuma would never have chosen to deal in this mundane way with a deity.

The most reasonable interpretation of Montezuma's response is that, according to Indian practice, Montezuma was opting for peace: He was choosing the alternative to war, by giving a gift and expressing his wish, with the expectation that civilized people understood this practice and, by accepting the gift, the receiver was agreeing to accede to the giver's wish. But the Spaniards did not comprehend him. Nor would any Eurasians have understood this refined Indian gesture.

Cortés was beside himself with curiosity over the grains of gold in the helmet. Wherever these grains had come from, more could come. He wanted to know where the mines were. So Cortés implored Tendile to return once more to Montezuma, to say that Cortés's great king across the sea would not think well of Cortés if he were to go home without having presented himself to the monarch of this country. Although Cortés was running short of giftware, he gave Tendile for Montezuma some shirts of fine Dutch linen, a Florentine glass cup engraved with hunting scenes, and more beads.

Again Tendile went off—to return more promptly than before, with Montezuma's final word accompanied by another gift. Montezuma's gift this time consisted mainly of four green jadestones. But Tendile explained to the puzzled Spaniards that these jadestones, called *chalchihuites*, were to the Aztecs more valuable than gold. As for Montezuma's wish, it was the same: Montezuma would not come down from the mountains to meet Cortés, nor should Cortés think of coming to the mountains to see Montezuma because Cortés would have to travel through territories where Montezuma's enemies held out and these enemies, once they learned that the Spaniards were en route to Montezuma, would attack them.

At this point, had Cortés and the Spaniards understood the Indian procedure of peacemaking, the Spaniards might have retired, amply rewarded for their efforts. Had the treasure Montezuma gave them been taken to the king of Spain and displayed at the Spanish Court, Carlos undoubtedly would have sent further emissaries—to present more Spanish gifts to the Indians, to obtain additional gifts from the Indians, and to establish a line of communication. It may strain belief to think that peaceful communication could have been established between people with the customs of the Aztecs and people who were Christians. But if a moment passed when a bridge between these two peoples might have been made, it was this moment—when Montezuma presented to the Spaniards his generous gifts and, in doing so, expressed his wish for peace.

Uncomprehended by the Spaniards, the moment went by. Whereupon, both sides resorted to scheming and tried to outmaneuver each other.

Tendile went back to the mainland and—when the Spaniards did not comply with Montezuma's request, board their ships and depart—the local Indians ceased to bring them food. In accord with Montezuma's orders, the Spaniards were cut off and ostracized. There was no further trading or gift-giving. The huts the Indians had built for themselves on the sand dune were abandoned.

Cortés had sent two brigantines to search out a better harbor to the north, but the ships returned, having made their way, despite bad weather, nearly to the mouth of the Pánuco River without finding a satisfactory port. The cassava bread was giving out; what was left was moldy and infested. Thirty-seven Spaniards had been killed or had died of their wounds. Others were sick from the tropical heat.

Many men of prominence in the company wanted to return now to Cuba. These were Velázquez's relatives and friends. The expedition, they reasoned, had acquired a great load of gold. Why not return now, report to the governor, divide up the spoils, and, after rest and reassessment, assemble a larger fleet for another sally? This mainland was obviously enormous and heavily populated. There was no telling what would confront the Spaniards if they ventured into the highland. Now they were exhausted, their ranks depleted (even Cortés's horse had died), and supplies were running out.

In this souring atmosphere, amid rising dissension, Cortés appeared partially to agree with those who wanted to go back to Cuba, but he argued that, first, their immediate need was to remove themselves from San Juan de Ulúa before a northern gale, to which they were exposed, damaged or destroyed the fleet. In this he was supported by Alaminos. So a compromise was reached by which they would leave and try one more landing to the north, in a bay by a large rock which had been sighted from the brigantines. Atop the rock was a town of some sort. If this probe proved unpromising, then, Cortés conceded, the trading venture would be terminated and they would return to Cuba.

Consequently, they embarked, sailed to the north, and landed on a really sickening beach—a very shallow bay, only a dip on the coastline, less sheltered than the area around San Juan de Ulúa. At one end of the bay there was a rising rock face, and into the rock they drove wrought-iron pins that held rings to which the boats could be tied. At Cortés's direction, the Spaniards unloaded everything—the horses, artillery, stores. By this time the men were irritable and had formed factions. They were hungry, weak, and nearly out of food.

Cortés knew that, if he were to return to Cuba now, he would be ruined, financially and personally. Velázquez would seize the gold; Cortés would never get his fair share or even be repaid for his investment in the fleet. Other Spaniards, too, who were not relatives or friends of Velázquez, distrusted the governor's disposition of the gold. Cortés's *encomienda,* which he had pledged as collateral for loans that were outstanding, would be taken over by his creditors. Also, Cortés knew that his defiance of Velázquez at sailing-time, his refusal to relinquish his command of the fleet, would not be forgotten. Velázquez would bring charges against him and, with the slow working of Spanish justice, Cortés might expect, at the least, to spend years in prison; at the worst, he might be hanged. But, of greatest importance, Cortés knew that if he were to return to Cuba now, he would never again be given command of an expedition—and this was his chance, his only chance to work a miracle, to topple an empire, to achieve, as had the knight in *Amadís de Gaula*, fame, riches, a place among the nobility, lasting glory.

So—pressured by all the circumstances around him, with the partisans of Velázquez, many of whom were formidable men, set against him— Cortés worked quickly with legalistic finesse. Gathering together in his tent at night all those who were not allied to Velázquez and who wanted to be sure of their share of the gold, Cortés had them draw up a charter to establish a town and to found a colony on this forlorn beach; they called the town *la Villa Rica de la Vera Cruz,* the Rich Town of the True Cross. Formal papers were prepared in precise accord with the procedure prescribed in *Siete Partidas,* naming a council with a mayor, constable, quartermaster, all the required officials. Before the council of the new town Cortés resigned his commission as head of the trading venture. Then the council appointed Cortés captain-general and chief justice of Villa Rica de la Vera Cruz.

Through this legalism, Cortés totally obliterated Velázquez's authority—because a new town, a newly founded colony properly and duly established in a new land, was accountable directly and only to the king. The charter of Villa Rica was a preposterous document of questionable legality. It was such a brazen overreaching that even Cortés did not seriously consider the ramifications of all the provisions. He had himself put down for one-fifth of the spoils, the same as the king. In *Siete Partidas* it was stated that a conqueror, if he were a "natural" lord, would be entitled to one-seventh, if not a natural lord, to one-tenth, before the remaining spoils were distributed among the entire company. But since ultimate distribution seemed both unlikely and far-fetched, why argue over a specific provision?

In founding a new town, Cortés knew that he was taking an enormous risk. The jurisdiction of the Jeronymites in Hispaniola was vague, as was the authority of Diego Colón. But Cortés knew that Velázquez's uncle, Bishop Fonseca, was placing his nephew's petition before the king, to have Velázquez named as the king's appointee to lead in the exploration and settlement of the newly found mainland. If Fonseca, who was said to be very influential at Court, had obtained the king's endorsement of Velázquez, Cortés in setting up a town independent of Velázquez would be acting contrary to royal edict—and he would be on his way to the gallows. Knowingly, Cortés took this risk: He gambled that the king had not yet acted.

If the king had not yet acted, then the eventual judgment of this expedition in the king's eyes, Cortés calculated, would depend upon the degree of its success. Already packed aboard the anchored ships was a treasure such as no one in Europe had ever seen before. Cortés gambled that, if he could acquire enough treasure and could bring to the Spanish Crown extensive lands and multitudes of people to convert to Christ, the king would overrule whatever legal quibbling there might be and would favor Cortés.

When the supporters of Velázquez realized what Cortés had done, what had been done surreptitiously in his tent at night, they were furious. Several of Velázquez's men, led by Juan Velásquez de León (the León branch of the family spelled the name differently but was kin to the governor of Cuba), refused to take further orders from Cortés. So Cortés had the recalcitrants put in chains aboard a ship—while Cortés mingled with those who were uncertain and promised some gold here, some gold there, arguing openly that only through the establishment of the new town could each of them who had risked his neck and shed his blood avoid being cheated by Velázquez. Before long, the majority of the Spaniards supported Cortés. Then Cortés visited those who were in chains aboard the ship, talked to them in a friendly way, promised them a better share of the gold—and eventually even Velásquez de León came around. So Cortés had all those in chains released.

It had been touch-and-go, but Cortés by changing the purpose of the expedition from trading to settlement had made the expedition his own. And the Spanish force was still holding together, though bitter resentment continued.

After the Spaniards had come very close to fighting among themselves, unexpected dissension arose among the Indians.

While Cortés was leading some of his men inland to circle behind the high rock and from the inland side to approach the town that could be seen on the heights, he noticed some Indians who were watching from a nearby hill. So he sent a few horsemen to bring them in. These Indians appeared to the Spaniards to be revoltingly ugly because they had pierced their ears and the septum of their noses and split their lower lips, which many of the Indians did, but these Indians had enlarged all these openings and wore in them substantial chunks of colored stone, amber or gold. Their nose-rings pulled down their noses nearly to their mouths, and their lower lips were so split that their teeth and gums were exposed. Through their encumbered lips they spoke a language that was neither Nahuatl nor Mayan. But several of them could also speak Nahuatl. So the conversation went through the few who could speak Nahuatl to Malinche, then to Aguilar, then to Cortés.

These people were Totonacs. And they had been observing the Spaniards not so much in fear as in hesitation, in reluctance to ask a favor. Some of them had traveled down the coast to San Juan de Ulúa, having heard about the Spaniards. In fact, a number of the Spaniards had seen them and remembered them because the Totonacs were tall and had so much facial disfigurement, but the Totonacs had not come close and little attention had been paid to them. Now the Totonacs wanted Cortés to come to talk to the chief in their town, which they called Zempoala.

Cortés had with him horses and artillery, crossbowmen and harquebusiers, in case he was attacked or wanted to attack. So he was prepared for any eventuality. And he let the Totonacs guide him the few miles to their town.

Zempoala was a sizable town of about twenty thousand inhabitants with impressive stone buildings, the best buildings the Spaniards had yet seen. The walls were whitewashed with lime, the roofs well-thatched. Cortés and his men were led to a central square on one side of which was a pyramid with a temple on its top. A few Spanish soldiers reconnoitered the temple and reported that in it were the freshly killed corpses of several boys, but this was the case in practically every temple the Spaniards came upon, because the Indians, when the Spaniards were approaching, would make sacrifices to bring them safety or good luck. As if the Spaniards were expected guests, they were shown to spacious buildings that would serve as their accommodations. From the houses on the side streets Indian families came out and crowded about, to stare at the Spaniards and at the horses.

On his guard, Cortés placed his artillery at the corners of the square, kept his cavalry mounted, and aligned his soldiers around the square. Then he demanded to see the chief—who came promptly, carried in a kind of hammock that served as a litter. The chief was grossly fat, so fat he could hardly walk, and, after he left his traveling hammock, attendants at his sides held between them a stout stick on which the chief's belly rested.

In the shade of a tree in the courtyard of one of the buildings on the square Cortés and the Totonac chief held a parley. And Cortés was slowly informed—with the chief speaking the Totonac tongue, one of the other Totonacs who had brought Cortés to the town translating into Nahuatl, Malinche translating the Nahuatl into Mayan for Aguilar, and Aguilar telling Cortés—about an intriguing situation.

The Totonac chief was complaining that in a recent war he and his people had been defeated by the Aztecs; they were now subjects of the great monarch in the mountains. The Totonacs had fought fiercely to retain their independence, and now they had to pay tribute which was cruelly overtaxing them. Not only were they required to send goods to the monarch in the mountains but they had to turn over young men and young women to be sacrificed by the Aztecs, and the Aztec tax-collectors often took their wives as well.

Could Cortés have their taxes lowered?

Cortés had a ready answer: Of course he could.

THE DECLARATION OF WAR

Cortés's mind was set afire by his realization that there was dissension among the Indians. The partisans of Velázquez, dispirited and longing to return to Cuba, had been undermining the expedition by maintaining to every Spaniard who would listen that in this limitless land—in this nether world—they were facing a monolithic state peopled by numberless fierce dark warriors who had an unreachable king in the distant mountains, that this was why the Spaniards should retreat now, reequip themselves and reorganize. But after hearing the complaints of the Zempoalans, it became clear to Cortés that this nether world was no different from the world he and all the Spaniards knew: Far from being monolithic, this Indian world was as rife with discord as the Spains had been under the Moors. This was the truth of human existence as Cortés had known it—and he intended to spread the discord and crumble the mountains under Montezuma's feet.

Leaving Zempoala, Cortés led his force—greatly refreshed by the first ample gorging the Spaniards had had in weeks—to the town atop the rock, another Totonac town called Quiahuitzlan. The fat chief of Zempoala, who was carried after them in his litter, supplied several hundred porters for the army. So now the Spaniards who were not mounted could march with a swinging stride, while the porters pulled the cannons and shouldered the gear.

The Spaniards had to pick their way among boulders to reach Quiahuitzlan. The cavalrymen wanted to dismount for fear of having their
horses stumble and fall, but Cortés would not allow this: He wanted to
maintain the illusion that each horse-and-man were one. The Spaniards,
however, were unopposed at Quiahuitzlan; in fact, they were welcomed in
the central square by a delegation of chiefs and priests who hastened to
summon their people from hiding. And soon afterward the fat chief of
Zempoala arrived.

Again, the Spaniards were accommodated like guests and were bounte-
ously supplied with food and drink. The drink was Mexican chocolate,
made strong and frothed with little twirlers, wonderfully invigorating, even
served the Aztec way, which was thick and tepid; Bernal Díaz in his old age
recalled with delight the first times he had tasted it. The Indians also made
a raw-tasting liquor from maguey sap, *pulque,* which turns milky like
Pernod or absinthe when mixed with water. But as long as the Spaniards'
wine held out, they declined the *pulque.*

Then a coincidence presented Cortés with an opportunity. While the
Spaniards were resting after another feast, five Aztec tax-collectors with an
extensive retinue came to Quiahuitzlan. These were Aztec nobles sent by
Montezuma to collect tribute from the Totonacs and they were making
their way from town to town. Learning that strangers were present, the five
Aztecs came and haughtily stared at the Spaniards, refusing to address
Cortés or be drawn into discussion by him.

This lowland along the coast is scrub-jungle, and all sorts of smells were
strong in the air—human and animal feces and urine, the continuous decay
of the loam, the almost sickeningly sweet aroma of tropical blossoms, the
distinctive smell of near-naked Indian bodies and the odor of the sweating,
clothed Spaniards. The Indians' sense of smell is acute and accounted for
their frequent use of resin-filled braziers. In Quiahuitzlan the preferred
perfume came from bouquets of local roses, and both the local chiefs and
the Aztec collectors held these rose-bouquets close to their nostrils.

The Aztecs retired to quarters the Totonacs prepared for them, then
summoned the local chiefs and severely scolded them for daring to receive
these strangers without Montezuma's permission. The Aztec nobles told
the Totonacs that Montezuma had decided to capture and enslave these
bearded men and to crossbreed them. (This may have been true, because
Montezuma in his capital in the mountains maintained a zoo of animals
collected from all parts of Mexico and Central America; he was interested
in crossbreeding and raised many odd creatures.) The Aztecs said that the

Totonacs must be punished for their impudent and unauthorized behavior: They would have to deliver up, in addition to the regular tribute, twenty boys and girls for sacrifice by the Aztecs.

Parts of the Aztec diatribe were overheard, and the whole town of Quiahuitzlan was buzzing and frightened. A report was promptly passed through Malinche to Aguilar to Cortés. The Totonac chiefs were distraught at having to turn over even more victims for sacrifice—and they didn't know what to do. So Cortés told them: Tie up the Aztec nobles and imprison them. And tell them that, from now on, the Totonacs will pay no further tribute to Montezuma.

The Totonacs were nearly hysterical with fright and indecision. When they had been overrun by Aztec armies from the highland, they had suffered terribly. Now this fate would surely revisit them if they had the audacity to touch Montezuma's men. But Cortés was unrelenting. And he sent two of his hardest-faced captains to stiffen the Totonacs' spirit.

Reluctantly, but with increasing enthusiasm once they got going, the Totonacs told the shocked Aztecs that no further tribute would be paid— not the imposition of the extra twenty for sacrifice, *nothing* more—and that the Aztecs themselves were prisoners. The Totonac method for taking a prisoner was to bring a long pole and to tie to the upright pole the prisoner's neck, wrists and ankles. Then the pole and the prisoner would be laid on the ground, the pole lifted at each end by a couple of Totonacs, and the bound prisoner, pole and all, would be carried to a dark room somewhere and dumped on the floor. When one of the Aztecs refused to allow himself to be bound—while the Spanish captains were watching but, on strict orders from Cortés, not participating—the Totonacs brought out rush-whips and beat the Aztec until he complied.

The Totonacs wanted to sacrifice the Aztecs quickly, before word could be carried to Montezuma. But Cortés wanted these Aztecs held prisoner, and he sent some Spaniards to keep guard over them.

Then, in the middle of the night, Cortés—calculating far into the future—had two of these Aztecs released and brought to him (he had instructed his guards to bring him "the two who seemed brightest," for Cortés at this stage had not yet developed the profound empathy he would eventually develop with Indians). Blandly he asked the upset highland nobles what all this fuss had been about, as if he had played no part in it. He had the men fed and told them that he was going to release them to return as fast as they could to their king. Cortés assured them that he was Montezuma's friend, that he and Montezuma had often communicated before, that he looked forward to visiting Montezuma and exchanging more presents and discussing things that would be to the benefit of everyone. Above all, he desired the great king's friendship.

The two Aztecs were relieved and happy to be set free but were fearful that, if they had to make their way, especially at night, through this Totonac area, they would be captured again. So Cortés had several Spaniards escort them to the shore and in one of the ship's boats take them northward and land them in a Nahuatl area where they would be assisted on their trip into the mountains.

In the morning, when the Totonacs discovered that two of the Aztecs had escaped, they were frantic. The fat chief of Zempoala was stuttering and quivering. Cortés, however, pretended to be as surprised as they were by the escape and with a stern face he interrogated the Spanish guards. The Totonacs desperately wanted to sacrifice the three remaining Aztecs, the sooner the better. But Cortés prevailed and had the remaining three taken to the shore and put aboard one of his ships—on the premise that they would not be able to escape from a ship that was anchored far out in the water.

After this had been done, Cortés and his men left Quiahuitzlan and returned to their camp on the beach. Cortés visited the Aztecs on the improvised prison-ship, told them what he had told the others—how he wanted nothing more than Montezuma's friendship and wanted only to pay his respects to the great king—and promised them that they would soon be released to go home. This was the way Cortés declared war on the Aztec empire.

There were thirty towns in the Totonac confederation. Zempoala was the largest but they were all in the same region, either on the coastal lowland or in the hills, and the beach on which the Spaniards were encamped was central to all of them. Quickly the report spread among the Totonacs that these white strangers were allies who had abolished the Aztec tribute, had abolished all of it, not simply reduced it. Food in more than ample quantity was brought to the Spaniards daily, and the strength of the soldiers after weeks on cut-rations revived.

The food in itself was the most effective argument to counter the sentiments of Velázquez's party. And Cortés's men—the councilmen of Villa Rica de la Vera Cruz—proceeded to lay out the town: They paced off and marked plots where the fort was to be built, the church, arsenal, marketplace, storehouse. When the Totonac chiefs came to him, Cortés asked them how many warriors they could field, and they told him one hundred thousand. They also told him that there were other tribes who were as oppressed by the Aztecs as they were, tribes who would be willing and eager to fight. One tribe in a place called Tlascala was still holding out against the Aztecs and had never succumbed. If Cortés would lead a revolt against the Aztecs, there would be many hundreds of thousands of warriors who would rally to him.

Cortés found this most agreeable news.

THE TEN COMMANDMENTS REDUCED TO THREE

In the mountains Montezuma, of course, was also scheming—and he was trying within the scope of his own nature and experience to fathom these strangers. His priests, on the basis of their instincts and auguries, were recommending that the strangers be killed or driven out as quickly as possible. It was clear to Montezuma now that the strangers would not accommodate him but defy him, and he knew that his rule depended upon his inflexible requirement of obedience.

The Spaniards were continually preaching about Christianity to all the Indians they encountered, but only the simplest facts could get through the translation from one language to another to another and from the mind-set of the Spaniards to the mind-set of the Indians. It was impossible to transfer to the Indians the spiritual conceptions of Christianity. Yet, from the few facts that did get through, it was obvious to the Indians that the strangers wanted to substitute their gods for the Indian gods. To Montezuma, in the immediate sense, this meant a replacement of the Indian idols—the images of the Indian gods in stone and baked clay, graven images that were often stupendous—with the images the strangers preferred, the painted figurines of the Woman with Child and the Cross. (Actually the Indians had some appreciation of the figure of Mary, but the Cross perplexed them. In some Indian villages, by chance, the cruciform design was used as a decoration, but the design had no religious significance for the Indians.)

Montezuma, who had been a priest before he became king, realized that both the Indians' images and the Spaniards' images were suggestions of a spiritual nature. Montezuma's concept of spirituality was sophisticated, in some respects perhaps more sophisticated than that of the Christians. In the doctrine of Christianity there had been only one crossover from divinity to humanity—and this was Jesus Christ. In Montezuma's mind the idea of divinity was broader. For example, he knew that his stone and clay statues

were no more than symbols of spiritual forces—and he believed in these
forces. But he believed that divinity infiltrated humanity in more than one
case. Montezuma believed—or wanted to believe—that there was a degree of divinity in himself that accounted for his position, his power, his
success, and the success of his ancestors.

Montezuma was fifty-three years old (nineteen years older than Cortés)
and lately thoughts about his own mortality had been with him. He knew
that he was mortal, as mortal and as vulnerable and as bound to die as all
those around him. But he felt that, while he lived, there was within himself
some of the divine spirit. Otherwise, how could the great success of the
Aztecs be explained?

Now his priests were torn by conflicting emotions. On the one hand,
jealous of their privileges and prerogatives, they wanted these strangers
exterminated. On the other hand, fear had become rampant among the
priests that the prophecy about Quetzalcoatl might indeed be coming
true—that these strangers might be descendants of the bearded white god
who had once governed in Mexico, who had sailed away to the east, and
whose return had been foretold. This legend, Montezuma knew, was
especially popular among island Indians because it was a legend of the sea
and appealed to people for whom the sea was an everyday reality. But to
Montezuma, as a highlander who lived far from the sea—and most highlanders had never even seen the sea—this legend had much less significance
and appeal.

Even if the legend were true and these strangers were Quetzalcoatl's
descendants, Montezuma's interpretation was more subtle than that of the
Christians. In Montezuma's mind, his own family—the ruling family of
the Aztecs—must once have included Quetzalcoatl, a god-imbued man.
So, if Quetzalcoatl, as the legend recounted, had a long time ago and for
some unknown reason forsaken and abandoned his people and he had now
in the form of these strangers returned, why then these strangers were
probably blood-kin of Montezuma himself—and he and they shared a
degree of divinity.

To the Christians, had they understood, this would have been blas-
phemy. But Montezuma's mind was less restrictive. If, as he believed, he
possessed an essence of divinity, he found it reasonable to suspect that there
may be a bit of the essence in these strangers who, though so few, had
triumphed over many thousands of Indian warriors. These tolerant ideas in
the mind of the Aztec emperor slowed him, while in self-defense he plotted
and planned his next steps.

After the two released Aztec tax-collectors had reached Montezuma in the capital and had reported to him all they had seen and been told, Montezuma chose two of his nephews, appealing young men he thought might charm Cortés, and sent them with four old trusted chiefs on a mission to the coast. A train of many bearers went with them, carrying the usual gifts of gold, cotton and featherwork. In accord with long-held Indian custom, this embassy of Aztecs was allowed to pass peacefully even through Totonac territory, where the people were in open revolt.

Cortés received the Aztec delegates in Zempoala, and he thanked the young Aztec nobles for the gifts they brought him. Then the Aztecs diplomatically complained to Cortés: They said that he, probably unknowingly, had brought about the insurrection of the people in these parts. Such insurrection would cause Montezuma, whose friend Cortés claimed to be, to go to the trouble of putting down this rebellion, and there was bound to be much suffering.

Cortés heard them out and in turn complained to them: Had it been an act of friendship to order the Indians around San Juan de Ulúa to shun the Spaniards and leave them without food on an uncomfortable dune? Montezuma had not shown himself a true friend—if, in fact, he had ordered the Indians to ostracize the Spaniards. By dire necessity the Spaniards had been forced to get back onto their ships and to come northward to this spot on the coast in search of food.

Montezuma's nephews said to Cortés, as they had been instructed, that if—as legend had it—Cortés was a descendant of Quetzalcoatl, then Cortés would be kin to the ruler of Mexico because once, long ago, Quetzalcoatl himself had been a ruler of Mexico. (This was specifically said by the young Aztecs and with reasonable certainty was translated through Malinche and Aguilar to Cortés, because Bernal Díaz reported this verbatim in his chronicle; standing behind Cortés, he heard Aguilar's final version in Spanish.) But Cortés chose to ignore the implication that he and Montezuma might be distant cousins. The Spaniards regarded the Quetzalcoatl legend as a joke; had they taken it at all seriously, it would have offended them as Christians; and Cortés could not or would not see in this message from Montezuma the possibility that the Aztec emperor was extending to him a subtle peace-feeler.

Cortés gave the Aztecs green and blue beads and a few other items from his dwindling supply of trade-goods. And to them he turned over the three remaining tax-collectors who had been aboard his ship. The young Aztec nobles and the old chiefs were amazed that these three had not already been sacrificed and eaten, and they thanked Cortés profusely. Then with their bearers and the released tax-collectors the Aztecs returned to the highland.

The Totonacs were astonished. They had expected an onslaught. Instead, the Aztecs had sent to the Spaniards an embassy bearing gifts. The Totonacs saw in the Aztec gesture only a show of weakness, and this hardened the Totonacs' will.

Actually both Montezuma and Cortés were dissembling. The coming of Montezuma's nephews and their reception by Cortés was merely a reconnaissance on both sides.

The Spaniards proceeded to build a fort and a church as fast as they could. Cortés and all the captains helped with the labor. The Totonacs felled trees and trimmed the trunks; the Spanish blacksmiths made iron nails, while other Spaniards made bricks. Spaniards most familiar with fortifications constructed shooting holes in the log walls of the fort for the crossbowmen and harquebusiers and built platforms for the cannons at the corners. Cortés needed the fort because, when he would lead the army into the highland, he would have to leave some Spaniards on the coast to guard the ships. And the Spaniards wanted the church because they never for a moment doubted that from the church came their blessing.

The work went quickly; the church was completed and the fort enclosed. As the form of the fort became clear, all the Spaniards became more acutely aware of the significance of what they were doing: establishing in this savage land with its millions of dark warriors an independent colony for which they were accountable directly to the king of Spain. Most of the Spaniards were elated, but some of the Velázquez men remained disgruntled and dismayed.

While all the Spaniards and many Totonacs were at work on the fort, the chief of Zempoala with his leading men came to Cortés and begged for help in their campaign against another town, called Cingapacinga, twenty-five or thirty miles away. In Cingapacinga, they said, there were many Aztec warriors who were laying waste the town, capturing people for sacrifice, stealing whatever gold there was, even burning the maize in the fields.

Cortés did not like to be diverted from the construction of the fort, but he felt he had to show his strength, as requested, if he were to assure himself of Totonac support. So the next morning he had his men assemble, fully armed, with cavalry and cannons. The Zempoalans had two thousand of their warriors ready and waiting, and the joint expedition set out, with the chief of Zempoala in his litter at the rear.

As they approached Cingapacinga, however, toward dusk on the second day of their march, Cortés, leading the column, was met by the chiefs of Cingapacinga who asked Cortés why he had come with his army prepared for war. It was true, they said, that Aztecs had been in their town, but the Aztecs, when they learned of the Totonac revolt, had fled back to the highland and they had taken no victims for sacrifice nor any booty. They had been frightened and had left in a hurry. The chiefs of Cingapacinga told Cortés that they themselves were Totonacs; they spoke the Totonac language, with a few of them able to speak Nahuatl as well. They heartily subscribed to the revolt against Montezuma's rule and had pledged that their own warriors would support the Spaniards. When Cortés asked them why the Zempoalans would want to move against them, the Cingapacingans said that there were ancient land quarrels between the Zempoalans and themselves.

Quickly Cortés reconnoitered to see for himself (on his new horse, which he had induced two of his men, joint owners, to sell to him, a strong dark chestnut named Muledriver). He was amid little outlying settlements on the edge of the town of Cingapacinga—when he saw that the Zempoalans were gleefully looting the huts of the Cingapacingans, slaughtering and bundling the fowl, ransacking the huts for whatever they could find, tying up the young women and some of the men to take back to Zempoala.

Cortés was furious with this silly petty pillage. Since he had left Cuba, he had again and again repeated to his men his firm policy: that they would never cause this whole land to pledge its allegiance to the king of Spain and become a Spanish possession if they looted. Now his Indian allies were looting their own neighbors.

Cortés ordered the Spaniards to put a stop to this raiding, which the Spaniards quickly did. They forced the Zempoalans to release their captives and return the fowl and whatever else they had stolen. At a gallop Cortés rode back and found the Zempoalan chief in his litter; he called all the Zempoalan leaders together and castigated them for duping him into this stupid, self-defeating operation.

Cortés was under such intense pressure that emotionally it was sometimes difficult for him to control himself. When he saw one of his Spanish soldiers stealing from a hut, he reined Muledriver to a skidding halt. Damning the man for disobeying his standing order, Cortés had other Spaniards put a noose around the man's neck and had him half strung up—when Pedro de Alvarado rode over and with a slash of his sword cut the rope, dropping the throttled thief onto the ground. Alvarado said to let that be the end of it and rode off. Cortés could take such an admonition from Alvarado. Cortés may even have been grateful for his intercession.

In Cingapacinga Cortés reunited the Totonac leaders of both towns, forced them to clasp hands and embrace each other. Then he propounded to them the lecture he was subsequently to give at every stop he made— simple, clear points that could be translated quickly.

(1) All Indians—from Zempoala, Cingapacinga, or wherever—must stop human sacrifice and the eating of human flesh. They must give up their bloody practices and stop worshipping these idols they thought demanded blood from them. Instead, they must worship God with the Spaniards— and they would then see what blessings would come to them.

(2) They must give up sodomy. A caste of their priests openly practiced sodomy; these priests had pointed out to the Spaniards the conjoined Indian statuary that celebrated sodomy; in the streets giggling young men offered themselves for sodomy. This was a nefarious activity which Christians would not tolerate.

(3) They must stop stealing from one another—taking one another's goods and women and fowl and gold. This was what the Aztecs did to them, and they were doing it to each other.

Only if they agreed to (1), (2) and (3) would he, Cortés, win for them freedom from Aztec oppression. And they must abide by their agreement. Otherwise, he would abandon them and leave them to face the Aztecs by themselves. Cortés in his anger was not to be resisted.

It was a two-day walk for the Zempoalans and the unmounted Spaniards back to Zempoala. When they arrived, Cortés had the fat chief and all the leading men of the town with their two thousand warriors assemble in the central square before the pyramid atop which stood their temple. The streets around the square were crowded with goggling Zempoalans.

In wooden cages at the base of the pyramid there were four young men and women whom the Zempoalans had decided to sacrifice in rites of their own. The Spaniards had previously seen these unfortunates, dressed in feathers, dancing crazily in the streets and begging for tokens—bits of gold or curious stones—that would be offered to the gods at the ceremonies when they would be killed. (This kind of behavior, this dancing, was almost surely induced by feeding the victims hallucinogenic mushrooms, with which the Indians were familiar.) Now, in a later stage when sacrifice was imminent, the victims were being fattened. At a command from Cortés the Spanish soldiers broke open the cages and took control of the dazed victims.

Then Cortés told all the assembled Indians that they would never be able to become Christians until their idols were destroyed. The idols had to be smashed. The Totonacs were not passive, like the Indians in Cozumel and Cuba. They howled in rage and fear. They did not want their ceremonies interrupted or their idols destroyed. From their gods, they told him, came the rain, the sunlight, the thunder, and their own life-spirits.

Cortés told them his men were going up the steps of the pyramid to the temple—and down those steps would come the idols. Then they would see that nothing would happen. When Cortés ordered the Spaniards up the steps, the Totonacs put arrows to their bowstrings. Cortés had some of his men put swordpoints to the throats of the fat chief and the Totonac priests.

There was a momentary stand-off—and down the steps came the toppled idols, the stone images breaking into pieces, the clay images crumbling and raising a cloud of dust.

The shrieking of the Indian priests ceased. The Totonacs were dumb-founded. The dust was clearing—and nothing happened.

Cortés then set the Spaniards to work on the temple. Gradually Totonacs came to help them. The temple was freshly whitewashed and copal incense was used to fumigate the interior. The skulls from the skull-rack were taken down and were burned with the remnants of the idols. The dried blood on the interior walls and the thick clotting on the sacrifice-stone were first scrubbed with twig-brooms, then washed with water, then covered with several coats of lime. The sacrifice-stone was used as an altar, and on it a plain wooden Cross was erected. To a white pedestal was cemented the figure of Mary.

(It is hard to conceive how bloody the Indian religion truly was. The Indians not only made frequent sacrifices of human victims, offering up to their gods the gushing hearts, but would daily wound themselves and offer up a little blood; they would slash their forearms or thighs or would run thorned vines over their tenderest parts, along their tongues or penises, to draw blood for an offering; the priests cut their own ears until their ears were shredded. Blood was what the Indians believed their gods demanded. Blood was the ultimate proof of their faithfulness. Sometimes, before a feast, Indian priests would sprinkle human blood on the food to assure the gods' blessing—and this would test the appetite of the Spaniards.)

After his lesson had been made plain, Cortés and his men returned to their work on the fort.

EVERYTHING VENTURED, A NEW WORLD TO BE GAINED

Upon their return to Villa Rica, Cortés and his men found that a ship from Cuba had arrived. This was a ship that had been scheduled to sail with the original fleet but had required reconditioning to be seaworthy; the pilot had followed the coastline from the Yucatán until the other ships had been

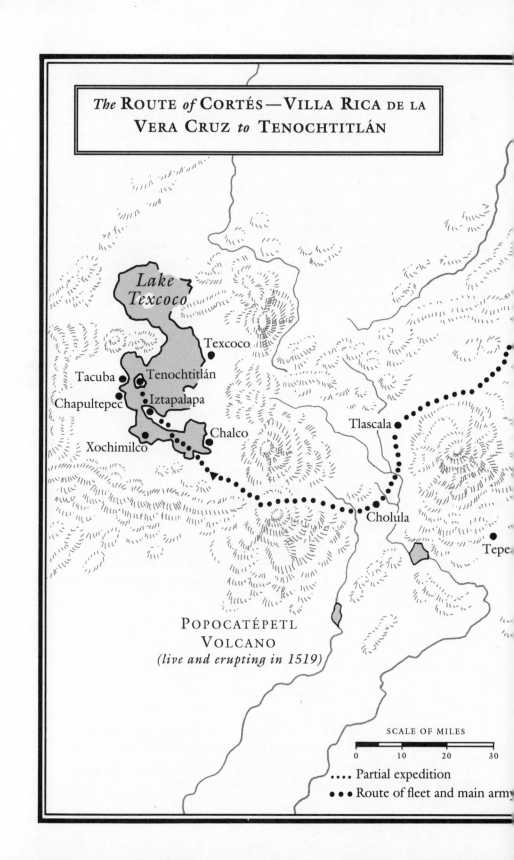

The ROUTE of CORTÉS—VILLA RICA DE LA VERA CRUZ to TENOCHTITLÁN

Lake Texcoco

Texcoco

Tacuba

Tenochtitlán

Chapultepec

Iztapalapa

Tlascala

Xochimilco

Chalco

Cholula

Tepe

POPOCATÉPETL
VOLCANO
(live and erupting in 1519)

SCALE OF MILES

0   10   20   30

.... Partial expedition

●●● Route of fleet and main army

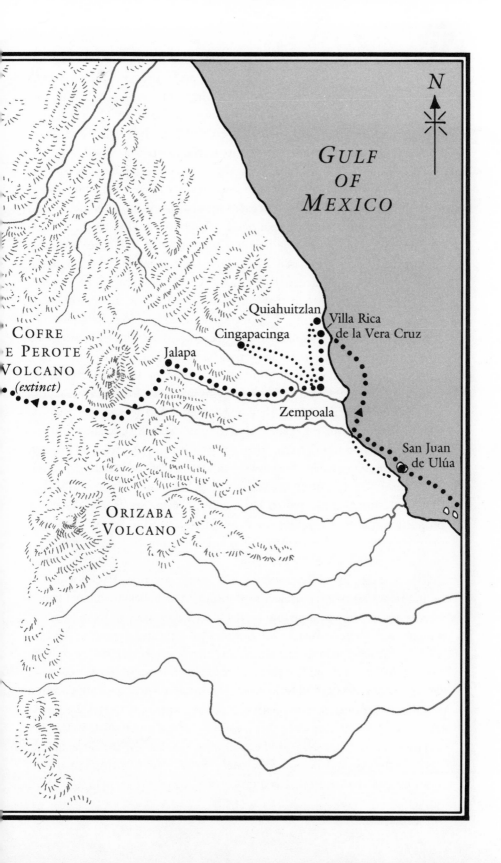

N

GULF
OF
MEXICO

Quiahuitzlan
Cingapacinga
Villa Rica
de la Vera Cruz

COFRE
E PEROTE
VOLCANO
(extinct)

Jalapa

Zempoala

San Juan
de Ulúa

ORIZABA
VOLCANO

sighted. The newly arrived ship was commanded by Francisco de Saucedo and had aboard sixty soldiers, nine horses and mares, as well as a fresh supply of trade goods. Cortés distributed a little gold to seal the enlistments of the fresh contingent and to whet their appetites. Saucedo, however, also brought the news that Velázquez had received from the king his authorization to trade and to found settlements in the newly discovered land.

This disquieting news caused Cortés to act promptly, and he and his supporters—knowing they would receive neither fair nor kindly treatment from the governor of Cuba—decided upon a daring stroke. They would immediately send a ship to Spain and submit to the king all the papers, prepared in accord with *Siete Partidas,* showing that Velázquez's trading venture had been terminated, that Cortés had resigned his commission from Velázquez, that a new town called Villa Rica de la Vera Cruz had already been founded, and that the council of the new town had made Cortés captain-general and chief justice. This was all dubious. What was not dubious was that they would send to the king, along with their notarized papers and long letters, *all* the gold they had thus far acquired—the whole treasure, not just the royal fifth but all of it, the wondrous jewelry, all the rarities (including the four Indians they had just saved from sacrifice), gold and silver in bulk, everything they had acquired in Tabasco, San Juan de Ulúa and here, from the Tabascan chiefs and from Montezuma and the Totonacs. By presenting to the king this great treasure Cortés and his men would be making evident their own confidence that they could get more.

At this juncture, Cortés wanted to delete from the charter of Villa Rica the provision which allotted to him one-fifth of the spoils. He knew this proportion was excessive. But the councilmen refused to rewrite the document, not because they wanted to give him so much, but because they lacked the patience for the rewriting.

The best ship in the fleet was selected for the journey. Alaminos was to be the pilot, because he knew a way through the Bahama Channel where he was not likely to be seen and reported to Velázquez, who would surely send ships in pursuit. To take the treasure to Spain and to present the case for Villa Rica to the king, Cortés chose Puertocarrero and Montejo. Both were of noble blood and had relatives at Court. Puertocarrero was Cortés's friend from Medellín. And by appointing Montejo—who was not Cortés's friend and who usually sided with the Velázquez men—Cortés was proving to his company that all of them, both those inclined toward Velázquez and those loyal to himself, could expect from him fair and equal treatment.

While the ship was being provisioned, the fat chief of Zempoala arrived in his litter at the head of a large group of Totonac nobles. The chief told

Cortés that in gratitude he wanted to give the Spaniards eight of his finest maidens, girls of noble blood who controlled many villages. The chief then had the eight girls brought forward. They were gorgeously dressed with jewels in their hair and wearing elaborate gold collars, and they had maids to attend them. The chief said that Cortés could give seven of them to the men of his choice, the eighth—who was the chief's niece—being for Cortés himself. This girl, even more richly dressed than the others, looked like her uncle. And the cranky Spaniards to a man respected Cortés when, with a flourish and aplomb, he accepted the fat and strikingly homely girl and thanked the chief with every show of sincerity. Cortés, as was his custom, distributed the other girls among his captains.

No time was allowed for dissension to arise among the Spaniards. The treasure ship departed on July 26, 1519.

It was far from certain that the ship would ever reach Spain, even if it were not intercepted, considering the storms that were likely to be encountered. Once in Spain, after it became known that a treasure was being brought from the New World to the king, Montejo and Puertocarrero could expect to attract the attention of Bishop Fonseca, Velázquez's powerful uncle, president of the Council of the Indies. Yet Cortés and his associates took the chance.

After Puertocarrero's departure, Cortés made Malinche his own mistress. Malinche passed to him easily; she was pleased and felt honored. Through all the months since she had been given as a slave to the Spaniards, she had been—as the Indians said—Cortés's "tongue." She was quick-minded and was rapidly becoming fluent in Spanish, which it has been said is best learned in bed. No one ever suggested—not even one of the captains allied to Velázquez—that Cortés sent Puertocarrero to Spain so that he could have Malinche. But this was the way it turned out.

Between Cortés and Malinche there undoubtedly existed a deep friendship and a profound affection. Later, Malinche became pregnant with Cortés's child and bore him a son that they named Martín after the baby's paternal grandfather. Cortés oversaw the boy's upbringing, as he oversaw the raising of all his children, illegitimate as well as legitimate. In his will he provided for the comfort of each of them.

The departure of the treasure ship upset and aroused the partisans of Velázquez. They hastily hatched a plot to provision another ship secretly, and several conspirators were to escape in it to Cuba, to alert Velázquez to intercept the treasure and destroy the town charter, and they would reveal to Velázquez the whereabouts of Cortés and his army so that Velázquez could send a stronger force to reimpose his authority. Many were involved in this plot, more than Cortés was able to act against; the degrees of implication were difficult to determine. So Cortés arrested five men who seemed to be the most obvious conspirators. The five were Juan Escudero, Diego Cermeño, Gonzalo de Umbría, a priest named Juan Díaz, and one of the sailors who were called "rockmen" (perhaps from Gibraltar or some other rock). Cortés's sentence upon them was severe: Escudero and Cermeño were to be hanged; Umbría's feet were to be cut off; the sailor was to be given two hundred lashes; and the priest (Cortés took this upon himself) was to be scared half to death. When Cortés signed the sentences, he said he wished he did not know how to write, so that he would not have to sign away men's lives. But he had to be harsh, as all those who had invested their fortunes and their lives with him knew.

This much was recorded: the harsh sentences passed upon the conspirators. The sentencing, however, apparently was an act calculated to frighten all the plotters, like the sentencing of Russians in the late nineteenth century to be shot when the firing squad, after the convicts had been blindfolded, would not pull the triggers. In this case, Cermeño obviously was not hanged because a year later he signed a petition along with many of his fellow-soldiers. Umbría could hardly have had his feet cut off when, later, he was put in charge of a troop that had to make a march of many days—and he most certainly was not carried. The sailor may have been lashed but he recovered. And the priest had a very unpleasant session with Cortés. As for Juan Escudero—who was the guard Velázquez had assigned to spy on Cortés when he had sought sanctuary in a church in Cuba and who had captured Cortés for Velázquez—there is no evidence that he was not, in fact, hanged.

This mutiny left Cortés and his cohorts with a lingering problem. These ships at anchor were a lure for all those who might falter from whatever was in store for them, who might want to retreat and seek reward from Velázquez. Besides, another Spanish ship was soon sighted; men in a boat from the ship were hailed and said their captain was Francisco de Garay, the governor of Jamaica; but the men refused to land and returned to their ship, which sailed on. So the governor of Jamaica, like the governor of Cuba, was coveting this newly discovered land. Which made it essential now for Cortés and his men to march into the mountains to find Montezuma—or they, who were the first to gain a foothold in this limitless place, would lose their advantage. There must be no retreat available for them. Everything must be bet on success.

Cortés's solution was to destroy the ships, to cut himself and all his men off from their means of retreat. If this were done, he would be able to add the ships' masters, pilots and sailors to his army. Everything then would be ventured.

At Cortés's command the ships were scuttled. They were stripped of all tackle and gear, anchors, sails and cables. This meant that the Spaniards could replace the ships by using the ironware and building new hulls with the wood that was abundant in the new land, but such rebuilding would take more time than a headlong escape would permit. Cortés gave out that the hulls were worm-eaten. This was a lame excuse but, before the Velázquez men could challenge him, Cortés had the masters drill holes in the hulls and sink the ships.

As one after another of the ships went down, Cortés's intention became obvious, and even the men loyal to him watched in grim silence. They were stranded now on the mainland of Mexico, on the side of the earth that until recently had been thought not to exist. In the fort they had built, their crippled and wounded would remain, to guard their few reserve supplies, and here perhaps—if they were victorious and returned from the mountains—they could build new ships and notify the rest of the world. Only dinghies and longboats were kept for the men who would stay at the fort, so the men might fish for their food if they had to.

THE EXHILARATION OF ALTITUDE

On August 16, 1519, the Spanish army of four to five hundred men with about fifteen horses and a few small cannons (the exact counts vary) left Zempoala for the highland of Mexico. The Spaniards were assisted by some two hundred bearers supplied by the Zempoalans; the bearers pulled the cannons and carried supplies; and the Spanish army was flanked by contingents of Totonac scouts.

Sometimes the chicanery of the Indians and the chicanery of the Spaniards—each stemming from a long, separate and radically different course of evolution—precisely coincided. Prior to departure from Zempoala, it occurred to Cortés that he was leaving over one hundred Spaniards— mainly his crippled, wounded and sick—in the unfinished fort at Villa Rica, and they might be overrun by the Totonacs if the Totonacs were to change their allegiance and revert to Montezuma. The same thought occurred to the Totonacs. So when Cortés suggested that a group of Totonac chiefs should accompany him as hostages to assure the welfare of the Spaniards left in the fort, the Totonacs agreed that his request was patently reasonable, and without argument they supplied the hostage chiefs. Cortés treated these chiefs as his advisors and kept them close to him while on the march.

By Indian standards this was a very small force. Cortés wanted it to appear small, because he wanted to be allowed to pass as a peaceful envoy en route to see his friend, the monarch in the mountains; Cortés did not want to appear to be going to war with the Aztec empire. Cortés did not, in fact, intend to go to war with the Aztec empire. He intended, rather, to steal it by guile, to convert Montezuma or to coerce Montezuma into willingly becoming a vassal of the king of Spain. Cortés knew that, by the Indians at large, his force was feared because the common Indians believed the Spaniards had magical power—in the cannons, in the horses.

Meanwhile in the highland Montezuma, to whom every move of the Spaniards was reported, was playing his own game of duplicity, calculatingly permitting these strangers, who thus far had only called at his distant shores, to advance toward his stronghold, where they would be hemmed in and enormously outnumbered and where they could easily be overwhelmed. (By whatever course of evolution—the American or the Eurasian—mankind seemed naturally to become adept at deception.)

With their Indian allies the Spaniards, after crossing the coastal lowland, began to ascend from the torpor of the tropics—and they were exhilarated. In the cool evenings when they camped, the air was bracing. During the days the Spaniards found the springiness returning to their legs while they walked upward—up the great mountain mass of Mexico, through the region they gratefully called the *tierra templada*, the temperate region in which they came first to the town of Jalapa. (It's life-saving to get out of the tropics; it's an illusion that the jungle, even a scrub-jungle, is delightful or enlivening; the tropics are draining and exhausting. But at an altitude of a few thousand feet above a tropical shore—Jalapa is over 4,000 feet— there is the pleasantest year-round climate in the world.) As the Spaniards continued to climb, their heads cleared and their spirits soared. Guided by the Totonac chiefs, the Spaniards were following a great natural throughway into the highland, along an unpaved and unmarked trail, just a path because there wasn't enough traffic between these places to keep the trail worn down, though the path had existed for many generations—upward between extinct volcanoes, past the towering, snow-capped peak of Orizaba (18,700 feet above sea level) and the massive Cofre de Perote.

Totonacs in the hilltowns were helpful to the Spaniards. But soon the Spaniards encountered Indians of other tribes who either fled from them or stared from a distance. Some of these tribes did not pay tribute to the Aztecs; they had not yet attracted the Aztecs' attention; but they knew of Aztec oppression and were pleased when the Zempoalans went to them, assured them they could safely approach and told them that Cortés had proclaimed that Montezuma was to receive no further tribute.

To all the Indians along the way Cortés propounded his message—(1), (2) and (3)—and the Indians seemed to respond favorably. Cortés's message could swiftly be put across because it was concise and translatable. Aguilar, Malinche and the Totonac interpreters, as they all became more practiced, translated with increasing gusto and emphasis. Moreover, to the Indians of other tribes the Zempoalans enhanced the effect of Cortés's set speech by describing how the cannons exploded like thunder and lightning combined, how a single Spaniard could defeat an entire Aztec army, how the horses could run faster than deer and bite worse than alligators.

In the prayer-house of each Indian village and town the Spaniards would come upon a few freshly slain, drawn, decapitated and dismembered corpses. It was an ineradicable habit for all the Indians—of all tribes—to perform sacrifices to their gods whenever something unusual was about to take place, even something no more unusual or threatening than the approach of a strange embassy. Cortés wanted to clean out each prayer-house, whitewash it, and erect a Cross and a figurine of Mary. But Father Olmedo discouraged him with the argument that these Indians needed thorough conversion, which took time; they would only destroy or defile the Cross and Mary after the Spaniards moved on. In spite of Olmedo, Cortés often could not restrain his impulse, had the prayer-houses cleaned, and put up Crosses and figures of Mary.

As they climbed and the weather became colder, a chill wind blew down from the mountains. The Spaniards and Cuban Indians were used to the Caribbean islands; the Zempoalans were used to the coast; none of them had prepared for cold. Spanish armor and Indian quilted cotton provided little warmth. At night, when the wind rose, they all shivered. Some of the Indians took sick and began to cough.

When they were deep in the mountains (and the mountains of Mexico cast a spell of their own; they are not like the smaller and greener Pyrenees, nor like the more extensive and open Rockies to the north; they are more enclosing, more striking and dramatic) the Spaniards and their allies came upon a large settlement of Nahuatl-speaking Indians, presumably Montezuma's own people, and then the atmosphere was forbidding and strained. These highland Indians with difficulty kept themselves from attacking the Totonacs, whom they regarded as traditional enemies and who were now rebels. The Nahuatl-speaking chief who met Cortés told him that Montezuma had ordered that the white strangers should not be opposed, but his instructions were so qualified that the chief and his people would render no assistance. Despite Cortés's request, they would not supply warm clothes or blankets, neither as gifts nor for barter. The highland chief allowed the Spaniards and the Totonacs to camp for the night in his town but he had only a little food brought to them. When Cortés tested him by telling him that Spaniards liked gold better than food, the Nahuatl chief— a huge man, as heavy as the chief of Zempoala but taller and more muscular—bluntly replied that he would give them no gold, tribute or help of any sort unless commanded by Montezuma to do so.

In the prayer-house of this Nahuatl-speaking group Cortés found fifty freshly slain corpses before an enormous, bloodied statue of Huitzilopochtli, the war god whom Montezuma had once served as priest. The extent of this sacrifice—the fleshy mass of fifty butchered bodies drenched in blood—baffled and dismayed the Spaniards. The Spaniards were used to war and blood; they were used to killing; they did not blanch at cruelty. But the killing they were familiar with had always been an act of passion— the slaying of an infidel, the repelling of an invader, the catching of a thief, or the taking of something they wanted: women or gold or land. What shocked them into silence in these Indian temples was the Indians' chilling indifference toward human life. These fifty bodies on the stone floor in front of the idol had not been killed in any passion that the Spaniards comprehended—neither in rage nor in the excitement of the attack nor in religious ecstasy. The fifty victims—fellow-Indians—had methodically been put to death in this awful way. Their screams had been ignored. Their struggling had been coped with. And their remains—their muscled limbs—had been put to practical use. It was the Indians' insensitivity toward human life, the Indians' seeming lack of feeling in making these routine sacrifices, that the Spaniards could not understand. And it sickened them.

The Spaniards now were a march of many days from the sea, and the sea was their connection to the world they knew. Amid these huge, sharp-ridged, rock-ledged mountains, deep within the highland, they had the sense of becoming lost in this strange other world. They were dizzy from the altitude; they did not understand the effects of altitude; they began to feel a queasy uneasiness—and their minds began to wander.

While standing guard during the cold nights, aware of the gigantic mountains there in the dark, the Spaniards were moved to speculate about who these Indians truly were—just as the Indians speculated about the true nature of the Spaniards. Some of the common Spanish soldiers (Bernal Díaz among them) advanced the suggestion that the Indians might be Jews. Among the Spaniards the Estremadurans in particular had been raised

In the Indian temples were various idols—the seemingly headless goddess who foretold the fate of the victims, the open-mouthed jaguar into which human hearts were put, huge serpents, monster-faces, all conceived to be horrific. But of the greatest gods—Huitzilopochtli and Tezcatlipoca—no representations endure.

on Roman history and they knew about the reigns of the Roman emperors Vespasian and his son, Titus. Both Vespasian and Titus had been governors of Judea and, after suppressing the Jewish rebellion around 70 A.D., they had sent whole tribes of Jews into exile. The Spaniards, trying not to freeze in the Mexican mountains at night, stomping and chafing their hands, wondered if perhaps these Indians were not descended from those ancient Jews who were exiled from Palestine more than fourteen hundred years before. But how, they asked themselves, would the Jews have got here? Well, the Jews knew how to build ships and it would have been possible to sail across the Mediterranean, through the Strait of Gibraltar, then across the ocean, wouldn't it? Furthermore, several of the Spaniards came up with an odd fact to support this theory: Indian priests in Zempoala had shown them how the obsidian knives—the sacrificial knives—were also used for circumcision, which was known to be a Jewish rite. Ergo, these Indians might be Jews.

This idea of the Indians being descendants of the ancient Hebrews may seem fantastic or absurd to us now—and revealing of the tumult in the heads of the Spaniards, which paralleled the tumult in the Indians' minds. In all the human minds dreams and realities mixed. Yet the idea of ancient Hebrews coming to America persisted into the nineteenth century, particularly on the vernacular level among street preachers and lay clergy who rode circuit. In the Book of Mormon it is revealed that the American Indians are descended from ancient Jews. The human mind is an amazing catchall.

Pressing on, the Spaniards were half-frozen by a hailstorm (hailstorms and rainstorms in the mountains of Mexico are sudden and blinding, and the temperature can drop forty degrees or more in a few minutes). In a high pass where for several days the army went without fresh food or water, several Indians died. Disoriented by their separation from the sea, the Spaniards were without bearings in this endless land and were giddy from the altitude.

At a place where the throughway forked to the north and south around a large mountain, Cortés paused, and an argument arose between the Zempoalans and some Nahuatl-speaking Indians who were accompanying the Spaniards. Cortés was aware that the Zempoalans were unsure of themselves and were beyond the territory where any of them had ever been before; they were proceeding on the basis of what they had heard from traders. But the Zempoalans vociferously argued that Cortés should take the route to the south which led to Tlascala and was shorter. The Nahuatl-speaking highlanders, with equal vehemence, wanted Cortés to take the route to the north which, they said, would keep the army on land under

Montezuma's control, would lead the Spaniards directly to the large town of Cholula, where the army would be comfortably accommodated, and from Cholula the trail was clear to the Aztec capital. This was a longer route, they admitted, but safer, and would be the route Montezuma would prefer for his guests.

The Zempoalans took Cortés aside. The Tlascalans, they explained, were age-old enemies of the Aztecs, and Montezuma had never been able to conquer them. The Tlascalans were among the most numerous and fiercest of all the Indian tribes; the Zempoalans were certain they would rally to Cortés if he were to have to fight Montezuma. In Cholula Montezuma was known to maintain a large garrison, and these Nahuatl-speaking highlanders were devious and cunning and would lead the Spaniards into a trap, into some canyon around Cholula where the Spaniards would have difficulty defending themselves and could be attacked and slaughtered.

Cortés decided to take the route to Tlascala. He sent ahead four Zempoalans to notify the Tlascalans that the Spaniards were coming in peace. And the army moved on—only soon to encounter a remarkable stone wall that stretched for five miles all across a mountain valley. The wall was built of uncemented stones; it was about ten feet high and twenty feet wide with a battlement built on both edges of the top behind which slingers, archers and spearmen could shelter themselves. There was only one passage through the wall, an avenue about ten paces wide, which was intentionally not direct but was overlapped by the walls on each side, so that warriors atop the walls could batter invaders as they wound their way through. This prodigious fortification, however, was unmanned. The whole place and the whole mountain valley were deserted, the only sound being the whistling of the wind.

This was the first castle-like construction the Spaniards had seen in the New World, and the horsemen reconnoitered it. They concluded that, even if the wall were adequately manned and stoutly defended, it could easily be flanked. So they were not overly impressed, though the construction was on a grand scale. Cortés asked the highlanders who had built this wall, and they told him their own ancestors had built it to protect themselves from the warlike Tlascalans. Then the highlanders left him and went back to their own town.

Cortés was watching for the return of the four Zempoalans he had sent to alert the Tlascalans but, as they had not returned and it was only midday, he had the army continue to advance, and with six horsemen rode forward as a van. In a great swale among these looming mountains Cortés and his horsemen sighted a small squad of about fifteen Indians, befeathered as if for war and with their shields and studded clubs gleaming in the sunshine. Riding toward them, Cortés through gestures tried to convey that he came in peace; he called out in a moderate voice and waved that they should approach him. Instead, the warriors turned and ran. So Cortés, who wanted to capture one of them to whom through an interpreter he could talk, galloped after them and with the other horsemen encircled them. But these Tlascalans, shrieking to others who were out of sight to come to their aid, made a stand against the Spaniards.

The Tlascalans had never seen horses before, but that did not deter them. Ignoring Cortés's repeated efforts to convey his peaceful intentions, the Tlascalans charged—and a terrible fight took place. The Tlascalans fought with a spirit the Spaniards had not yet seen. Dodging the cavalry-men's lances, they fearlessly rushed the horses and within a minute killed two of them. With smashing blows of their obsidian-studded bats they nearly cut off the horses' heads, slashing through the reins and protective plates. While the Tlascalans continued to call for help, Cortés himself hollered for his infantry to come running. By the time the infantry arrived, the Spanish cavalrymen had been forced to kill all fifteen Tlascalan scouts. From a distant canyon a few thousand more Tlascalans were coming to aid the scouts, but seeing that the Spanish army was deploying and that the scouts had been wiped out, they withdrew.

Cortés was deeply concerned—because now for the first time he was facing Indians who were not frightened by horses and who knew that horses were as killable as men.

WELCOME TO TLASCALA

The Tlascalans fought an all-out war, utilizing espionage, disinformation, tactics of feint and ambush, day and night maneuvering—and unrelenting fury. As far as the Tlascalans were concerned, the Zempoalans were still subjects of Montezuma. And the white strangers, en route to Montezuma, escorted by Totonacs, presumably were Montezuma's allies. All of which, to the Tlascalans, added up to another veiled invasion of their territory by the Aztecs—and the Tlascalans were determined to resist, indomitably, as they always had.

Actually the Tlascalans were Nahuatl-speaking Indians who centuries before had developed an extensive trading network, which eventually had brought them into conflict with the empire-building Aztecs, who had broken up the Tlascalan network and had isolated Tlascala, so that the

Tlascalans for many years had been denied cotton with which to make clothing. Their land was too high and cold for cotton plants to grow, and they were blocked from trading with the lowlands. Only rarely would traders dare to evade the Aztec prohibition and bring cotton, as contraband, to Tlascala. So prized had cotton become that some Tlascalans would be sold into slavery in order to make the trades. The Aztec blockade also kept out salt; for many decades the Tlascalans had been without salt for their food. In the coastal areas salt was made from the residue of receding seawater, and in the valley of Mexico from salt lakes, but for this part of the highland it came from mines in two remote areas under Aztec control and was made from natural deposits of saltpeter.

Like almost all the Indian groupings, Tlascala was a confederation, and the province comprised four cities with satellite towns and villages. In terms of social evolution, these Indian confederations were somewhat similar to allied city-states of ancient Greece. Within Tlascalan territory there were also Otomís, who were a more primitive people, and Pinomes, who were more primitive still, the oldest traceable civilization being Olmec, the extinct people who left huge stone carvings of their heads at La Venta and other archaeological sites, heads of remarkable roundness, like the heads of living Mayans but with distinctive features that had a semi-Negroid, though definitely Indian/Asiatic cast.

After the initial fight with the Tlascalan scouts and disengagement by the supporting force, the Spaniards encamped beside a stream and did what they could to bed down for another cold, threatening night. Cortés placed his cannons carefully, kept the horses saddled, and set out a strong ring of guards. But in the twilight two of the Zempoalans Cortés had sent to Tlascala returned and were brought to him in the camp. The Zempoalans said that the Tlascalans had told them that the scouts were really Otomís, who had not been ordered to fight; the Otomís came from outlying villages and had been surprised by the strangers. The Tlascalans themselves, having been informed by the Zempoalans of the strangers' peaceful intentions, would welcome the Spaniards the next day. Nevertheless, Cortés, as was his custom, visited his guards during the night, and all the Spaniards slept with their weapons in hand.

In the morning the Spaniards marched on and, when they were nearing a village, the other two Zempoalans who had been sent to the Tlascalans rushed to them, nearly hysterical. The report of these two directly contradicted the previous report: These Zempoalans said that they had been held captive and were to be sacrificed at dawn but in the excitement of the night, while the Tlascalans were in a frenzy preparing to attack the Spaniards, the

Zempoalans had been able to escape. All these two had heard from the
boasting Tlascalans was that the Tlascalans intended to sacrifice and eat
the Zempoalans and the strangers.

When the Spaniards began to move again in their roughly rectangular
formation, with bearers pulling the cannons and carrying baggage and
supplies in the center and Totonac scouts on the flanks, several thousand
Tlascalan warriors appeared on high ground. But a battle did not break out
immediately. The Tlascalans came within throwing distance to hurl a few
spears and sling some stones and to taunt the Spaniards and their allies.

Cortés through Malinche and some of the Zempoalans tried to tell the
Tlascalans that he and his men came in peace and wanted only to pass
through Tlascalan territory. With Godoy witnessing, he ordered that the
king's message should be read out as required. But the Indians were
gesticulating ferociously and soon a rain of stones began to fall on the
Spaniards. When the Tlascalans, having worked themselves up, attacked—
slinging, throwing spears with their spear-throwers, shooting arrows, and
trying to close to use their bats and knives—Cortés had the interpreters
give way, and the Spaniards defended themselves.

Above all else, the Spaniards did not want to break their formation
because, if they allowed themselves to be fragmented, the Indians could
surround and overwhelm each knot of Spaniards. So the Spaniards held
firm and fired their harquebuses and crossbows in volleys, brought up their
cannons, and, when the Indians would rush to close, the Spaniards would
meet them with their steel swords. Although the horsemen would charge
clusters of Indians, the Tlascalans were not frightened by the horses. Only
very slowly could the Spaniards, while keeping their formation and dragging their cannons, baggage and supplies along with them, move in pursuit
of the Tlascalans.

As this attack wave of Tlascalans fell back, however, and the Spaniards
followed them, the Spaniards were drawn onto rough ground cut by
ditches and ravines where the horses could not run freely. Then out from
hiding came about forty thousand Tlascalans who had been waiting in
ambush. Heavy fighting went on all day. The Spaniards could do no more
than hold their lines and endure the showering of stones, darts, spears and
arrows, while repelling the Tlascalans hand-to-hand whenever the Tlascalans closed.

The Tlascalans' technique to cope with the horses was the same as that
of the Otomí scouts the Spaniards had first encountered. Intentionally the
Tlascalans would cluster to attract a charge, then would isolate the horse
and horseman, seize the reins, grab the shaft of the horseman's lance, batter

the horse with their bats and try to pull off the rider. In this way they succeeded in killing a mare ridden by Pedro de Moron; with the razor-sharp obsidian blades on their bats they practically cut her head off. This was Juan Sedeño's mare that had foaled; Pedro de Moron was on her because Sedeño was too badly wounded to ride. The Spaniards, while holding their formation, moved en masse to aid the fallen rider, and though he was rescued from the Tlascalans who were dragging him away, he died of his wounds after a few days. The Tlascalans dragged off the dead mare. Later, the Spaniards heard that the mare had been cut up; pieces of her were exhibited in the cities and towns of the province; and her iron shoes were presented as offerings to the Indian gods.

At the end of the day the Tlascalans withdrew. It was not a victory for the Spaniards; their accomplishment was that they had survived. Miraculously, not a single Spaniard had been killed outright, though several were mortally wounded; all the remaining horses were hurt; almost all the men were cut and bruised and many had suffered arrow-wounds. The Spaniards were thankful that the Mexican Indians did not poison their arrows, as did the Caribs and other jungle tribes the Spaniards had encountered. (The poisons used by jungle Indians were made either from plants or from the sweat of little frogs native to the jungle. These frogs are not much bigger than silver dollars and are brightly colored with vivid designs. The Indians work the limbs of the frogs until there is an excrescence from the skin, and the excrescence, which is a thin liquid, is poisonous, but the poison may not retain its potency in the cold of the highland. On the other hand, curare, a resinous poison made from a variety of jungle plants, would have been transportable and could have been used by the Indians in trade. The most reasonable explanation for the fact that the Mexicans did not poison their arrows is probably that, since they intended to eat those whom they killed or captured in war, they did not want to contaminate the meat.)

After the battle, the Spaniards, holding a few prisoners, limped uphill to a village which had been abandoned by its inhabitants. In the center of the place was a pyramid, and the Spaniards used the village to set up a fortified camp. The Spaniards were hungry. The ready rations they carried had been eaten the previous night. But the little dogs the Mexicans raised for food slipped away from their owners who were in hiding and the dogs returned to the village. So the Spaniards and Zempoalans captured the dogs, cooked and ate them.

As his last act of an exhausting day, Cortés through Malinche interrogated the prisoners. They told him that the Tlascalan captain was Xicotenga the Younger (more correctly, Xicoténcatl, the "X" being a sound not used in English, like "cs"). His father, who was old and blind, was chief of the dominant city of Tlascala. Xicotenga could call upon more troops than he had used in this battle; troops were coming now from the other Tlascalan cities. The Tlascalans were accustomed to assembling quickly in response to Aztec attacks.

Cortés gave the prisoners some beads and released them, to go to Xicotenga and repeat Cortés's message: that he and his Spaniards came as brothers. But Cortés added that, if he were not allowed peaceful passage, he would destroy this land.

Within the Spanish camp everybody was sick or wounded. Cortés had tertian fever, which brought on bouts of chills and high fever every other day. As the wounded died, they were buried, and fortunately no digging of graves was required because few had enough strength to do it. In the village there were underground rooms that, when collapsed or sealed, served as tombs. For several days no one was capable of much action.

Some of the Velázquez men were grumbling again that Cortés was a Pedro Carbonero (according to a fifteenth-century ballad, Pedro Carbonero was a leader who in pursuit of his own vainglory in the fight against the Moors had caused both the deaths of the Spaniards who followed him and his own death). Scared, strained and nervous, these Spaniards who grumbled had comfortable establishments in Cuba and wanted to return. They said it was crazy for a force of four hundred to dare to invade this empire. They had nearly been overcome now by a tribe that was barely able to hold out against the Aztecs; God only knew what would happen when the Spaniards would face Montezuma's vast armies. Had Cortés not destroyed the ships, they could return to the coast and sail for Cuba, there to make adequate preparations for a venture of this magnitude. Even so, they might go to the coast now, with the saved fittings build a few ships—and escape.

In response to this talk, which was reported to Cortés, he called all his men together—and the theme of his argument was that, if they were to turn back now, the Indians would fall upon them from every direction. The Tlascalans would pursue them, Montezuma's people would attack them, the Totonacs would turn against them, and they would never reach the coast or, if they did, they would die there while they were building ships. Their only hope was the course of honor, which was to keep up their resolve to bring to the king infinite treasure, limitless land and innumerable subjects, and to bring to Christ invaluable souls.

Cortés prevailed, and temporarily the dissension quieted. In the style of the period, in dignified sixteenth-century Spanish prose, Cortés's speeches to his men and his pledges of loyalty were reported to the king in his own letter and were recorded by his biographer, Gómara, and by Bernal Díaz and others in the company. But the truth clearly alluded to behind the stately prose was that the Velázquez men cursed Cortés and cursed those who stood by him. Sword hilts were fingered, and tempers were barely under control.

What seems amazing, in retrospect, is that, while these Spaniards who were mercurial by nature fought with each other and formed rival factions, while the individual aims and commitments of the men varied and each man was ready to fight for his share of the treasure that had already been sent back to Spain, amid all this dissension and danger and difficulty which was to intensify and increase, still the proposal of a captain to replace Cortés never was put forth. There were many proud, admirable, capable and courageous gentlemen in that company, yet not one of them emerged as a rival for command. The Spaniards indulged themselves, immersed themselves in negative criticism—they blamed and damned Cortés—yet Cortés by force of character retained control. But the Velázquez men were not pacified, only put off.

On the other side, the Tlascalans were mourning and burning their dead. Many captains of noble blood had fallen. It was the Tlascalan custom to try to remove their dead from the field so that their enemies could not identify or desecrate the corpses and would not know how badly the Tlascalans had been hurt.

On the third day after the battle, which Cortés prayed would be for him a day without fever, he felt that he had to make a show of strength; otherwise, the Tlascalans would think the Spaniards were no longer to be feared. So he organized a force of a few cavalrymen, about two hundred soldiers who could walk and carry their arms, and some Zempoalans (all of whom, to a man, had remained resolute through the battle), and he led them out to explore the countryside. They were in a broad mountain valley, which was thickly populated and had many villages and well-tended farms. The weather was pleasant in early September, and the warm mountain sunshine was invigorating. Most of the people fled from the villages. Cortés did not want to raid; he wanted to demonstrate his peaceful intentions; but the practical Totonacs rounded up as many fowl and dogs as they could carry. Cortés captured a few old men and to them he emphasized that he came in peace. The old men told him that Xicotenga was assembling the full force of Tlascala, that troops were coming from all the cities and towns.

Cortés had the old men released. When Cortés was returning to camp, he looked back and saw that the Zempoalans had set fire to several of the villages. This did not displease him because he thought that his message of peace was more likely to be seriously considered if accompanied by a taste of terror.

By the fifth day Xicotenga was ready—and at dawn the Spaniards from their camp on the hilltop saw the valley swarming with warriors, more than a hundred thousand of them, their copper-colored faces and bodies aflame with bixa (a red dye made from the pulpy seeds of the annatto tree), which to the Spaniards gave the Tlascalans the appearance of devils. The bejeweled standards of each city were held high at the rear of each city's contingent. Xicotenga's emblem, pointed out to Cortés, was a huge white bird, probably a crane, with its wings extended as if for take-off. The air of the valley reverberated to the sounds of the conches and drums. And four hundred Spaniards took their places, wounded or not. Those unable to stand were propped up at critical spots around the perimeter of the village with guns or crossbows in hand. This time the Spaniards fought from a fixed defensive position. The high ground was theirs. The stone prayer-house afforded some shelter, and there were stone walls behind which they could crouch. From the top of the pyramid they had an overview of the enemy. Cortés had placed the cannons to protect the few narrow entrances to the camp.

After an overture of screamed threats and mimed feasting by the Tlascalans, the battle began. With their great superiority in numbers, the Tlascalans with a rush tried to overrun the Spanish camp, but they were repulsed by the disciplined volleying of the Spaniards and the thundering of the cannons and harquebuses. The Tlascalans were so close-packed that each Spanish shot—even the bolts from the crossbows—would pierce four or five men. The Tlascalans had never before encountered such efficient killing. They were not given time to carry off their wounded and dead. When an attack wave would falter, the Spanish horsemen, operating now in teams of three or four, never singly, would charge out but not venture too far—spearing and slashing—then wheel and return. Cortés ordered the horsemen to aim their lances at the Tlascalans' faces, the crossbowmen and harquebusiers to shoot at the bowels, the swordsmen to thrust low. For the Spaniards this was a battle of survival. Cortés's intention was to terrify the Indian mass.

The Tlascalans had so many men that, when contingents from different cities would converge to make a charge, the contingents would collide. Then the jostling crowd would be cut down by Spanish fire. In the midst of this savage struggle, Bernal Díaz noticed that Malinche remained stead-fast in the center of the Spanish camp. And the Zempoalans again fought with exemplary bravery.

The fight lasted four hours. By the end of it the Tlascalans were not defeated but were weakening, and the Spanish cavalry and infantry were leaving the camp to destroy or chase off any substantial contingent of Tlascalans that came close. When the Tlascalans finally retired, the Span-iards were too exhausted to pursue them.

The night passed tensely but quietly. In the morning, though, fifty Tlascalans approached the camp and said they were bringing food for the valiant strangers. These Tlascalans said that Xicotenga and his warriors did not want to vanquish men weakened from hunger (there was an implication that the Tlascalans did not want a victory over men who were emaciated), so Xicotenga was sending this food as a present. Cortés let them in, and with the fifty Tlascalans came a train of bearers carrying roast fowl, stacks of tortillas, and cherries that grow very well in the high valleys and are sweet and ripe in September.

While Cortés and Malinche were breakfasting on the cherries, some Zempoalans came to say that these Tlascalans who had been allowed to enter the camp were carefully inspecting the entrances, seeing where the cannons were placed and where the Spaniards' huts had been erected, and the Zempoalans had overheard them commenting to each other that the thick thatched roofs of the huts could easily be set afire. Promptly Cortés had one of the Tlascalans throttled and pulled behind the prayer-house. Under interrogation, which was not kindly, the Tlascalan confessed that Xicotenga had sent them to spy on the Spaniards, to find out where the camp would be most vulnerable to attack. Cortés had two more Tlascalans brought to him, and they made the same admission.

So Cortés assembled the fifty Tlascalans, denounced them as spies, and, according to many of the records including Cortés's own letter to the king, he had the spies' hands cut off. But this is a little hard to accept fully, not because Cortés would have been reluctant to do it, but because none of the chroniclers reported that any of the fifty Tlascalans died. Had their hands been slashed off with a sword, surely many of them would have bled to death, and they would hardly have been able to walk home. Bernal Díaz reported that Cortés had the Tlascalans' thumbs cut off, which is more credible. Earlier in history, of course, other peoples had engaged systemati-cally in mutilation, particularly the Scythians and the Persians. So this cutting off of hands or feet or even thumbs as a form of punishment was not uncommon and was regarded as proper, if deserved, by the Spaniards and their king. And when the mutilated Tlascalans went back to Xicotenga, Cortés's lesson was clear: that spies should not be sent to the camp of those who came in peace. The bloodiness of Cortés's rebuke would not have fazed the Tlascalans; on the contrary, they were impressed by his canniness.

The next day Cortés again led out a force of cavalry and infantry with Zempoalans in support—and this time they set fire to villages all over the valley. In some of these villages they captured Tlascalan warriors, including a few captains, and Cortés interrogated them. He learned that there was discord among the Tlascalans. Xicotenga had accused a leader from another city of not attacking with enough vigor, and the other leader had challenged Xicotenga to individual combat (this dispute being caused by the Tlascalans' inability to control the movement of their massed troops). The older chiefs of Tlascala, including Xicotenga's father, were meeting in Xicotenga's city and were discussing what to do. They had been told by the Zempoalans that the Spaniards were truly Montezuma's enemies and that Cortés had abolished tribute. At first, the Tlascalans had dismissed the Zempoalans' testimony as lies and had presumed that both the Zempoalans and the Spaniards were allied to Montezuma; all the Indians were used to hearing lies from each other. But now the Tlascalans were unsure.

When Cortés returned to camp, he was surprised to find an embassy from Montezuma. Six Aztec nobles with many bearers had followed him into Tlascalan territory. Probably these Aztecs, even had they been apprehended by the Tlascalans, would not have suffered because they were not a war party; they were obviously an embassy, which was acceptable among all Indians. The Tlascalans and the Aztecs were not unused to communicating with each other by means of embassies and messengers. These Aztecs had their bearers unpack and display another load of treasure: fine cotton garments, featherwork and gold.

Montezuma was beginning to realize that Cortés did not understand or did not want to understand the significance of a gift-cum-wish. So Montezuma, according to his emissaries, offered a definite deal. Cortés should accept this further load of treasure and should specify or find out from his king just how much the king wanted in yearly tribute—gold, pearls, jade, cotton, featherwork, slaves—and Montezuma would agree to pay it faithfully if the Spaniards would go away and not enter his homeland. Montezuma said that it wasn't that he would not be pleased to greet the Spaniards but that the trip through difficult terrain might be too much for them. So they should take the easy way out: name their price, to which he would agree—and go.

This kind of negotiating did not seem strange to the Indians. When a tribe, like the Aztecs, became dominant, the dominated tribes agreed to pay tribute. There was no assurance, of course, that Montezuma had any intention of standing by his bargain. If he felt stronger in the future—with Cortés gone—he might not pay the tribute, and the king of Spain or Cortés or Jesus Christ or whoever was intruding upon him could try to do whatever they thought it was in their power to do.

In reply Cortés said once again that his king would not think well of him if he did not meet Montezuma face-to-face, so the ambassadors should return to Montezuma to ask again for his approval of a meeting. But Cortés courteously invited the Aztec ambassadors to remain with him until they would be able to take back to Montezuma, along with Cortés's renewed request, news of his victory over Tlascala.

By now, the people in the valley were accommodating both sides and were bringing to Cortés information about the Tlascalan consultations. The older chiefs were said to be inclined to agree to peace with the Spaniards, but Xicotenga the Younger was defiant and wanted to continue to fight. The Indians, all the tribes, referred to the Spaniards as *teules*— which the Spaniards took to mean gods, but the precise meaning of *teule* is uncertain. It may have meant an inspired man or a demon; to Montezuma it is likely to have meant a man like himself with a bit of divine spirit that entitled him to his power; *teule* certainly did not imply superhuman invulnerability. Xicotenga boasted that he would kill all the *teules* and eat them, too, as he had already killed the mare. So the Tlascalan priests were asked to clarify the situation, and on the basis of their auguries they came to the conclusion that these strangers could be overcome only at night. *Teules* at night would have no strength.

It was a moonlit night when Xicotenga made his foray—and Cortés, forewarned, was ready. Cortés did not intend to allow the Tlascalans even to come close to the camp, where they might succeed in setting fire to the Spaniards' huts, a danger that Cortés took very seriously. So Cortés led out the cavalry, followed by troops of Spanish infantry and Zempoalans, and they intercepted the Tlascalans on a flat field where the horses could run and the Spanish infantry could maneuver to deliver their volleys.

The result was a rout. The Tlascalans were not used to night-fighting. That the Spaniards had anticipated them and attacked them while they were en route to the camp disconcerted them. The onrush of the horses and the flash of the cannons and harquebuses in the darkness terrified them. And after a groping, indeterminate fight the Tlascalans withdrew.

This struggle with Tlascala was a close call for the Spaniards—it was a desperate, dangerous, vexatious time when many Spaniards were killed and almost all were wounded—yet Cortés inserted a Chaucerian joke into the story as he told it to his secretary, Gómara, twenty-odd years later. Cortés remembered that, in an effort to cure his fever, he took some pills he had brought from Cuba, pills that were a very strong purge, probably cascara made from tree-bark. He took the pills at night, expecting them to take effect the next morning. But shortly after dawn and before the purge had worked, three large companies of battle-ready Tlascalans approached, and Cortés had to lead the cavalry from the camp to fight them. He had to fight all day. But the pills didn't work during the day, as might have been expected. At the end of the day he returned to camp—and only then did the laxative take effect.

Gómara, who was a lay priest, did not go so far as to state positively that this delay of the purge was a miracle. But he clearly suggested the possibility.

The first signs of peace were deliveries of food to the Spaniards without threats or nonsense. Then a messenger arrived to say that Xicotenga himself would come. And on the following morning Xicotenga came, escorted by many Tlascalan nobles, all in magnificent regalia but not armed for war.

Xicotenga was about the same age as Cortés, and built about the same way, strong in the arms and shoulders, lithe in body. His face was deeply pockmarked. After saluting Cortés and receiving Cortés's salute in return, Xicotenga said frankly that he was regretful that he had not been able to triumph over the strangers. But he had tried both by day and by night. Finally he and the older chiefs had decided that the Zempoalans were telling the truth and the strangers were enemies of Montezuma, in which case the Tlascalans would willingly become vassals of the strangers. The Tlascalans would be able to pay little tribute because they were poor, but they were and had always been men who would not yield and they would be staunch allies. If Cortés would come to their city (Xicotenga's father's city, which was a little under twenty miles away), they would consider themselves honored by his presence and would try to make his stay among them as pleasant and comfortable as they could.

Thus, in effect, Cortés had offers both from the Aztecs and from the Tlascalans to subordinate themselves to the king of Spain—and he trusted neither of them. The Aztec ambassadors had remained in the Spanish camp and, when they heard of Xicotenga's submission and his invitation to the Spaniards to come to his city, they derided all this as lies, obvious duplicity;

the Aztecs told Cortés the Tlascalans were so poor they would try to rob him of the cotton garments Montezuma had just sent; the Tlascalans could not be trusted and were trying to draw him into a trap.

The fact was that the Spaniards couldn't move. Cortés was still troubled by his fever; many of his men were barely able to hobble about. Several horses had sickened and were not reliably well yet. So Cortés stayed where he was.

The elders of Tlascala appeared at the camp and implored Cortés to come to their city. They offered to provide hostages if he distrusted them. The Aztec ambassadors, having reported to Montezuma the capitulation of Tlascala, received instructions from Montezuma (as well as another gift for Cortés) to redouble their efforts to convince Cortés that the Tlascalans were faithless.

When eventually the Spaniards were able to move, Cortés had a large Cross erected at the top of the pyramid. He had the local people assembled and told them to revere it. Then he opted for Tlascala—to the Aztecs' dismay. But the Spaniards moved out from their camp in formation, ready for war.

ON TO CHOLULA

After the fighting with the Tlascalans had subsided and peace between the Tlascalans and Spaniards seemed to be settling in, but before breaking camp in the village, Cortés sent a few horsemen back to Villa Rica. Cortés reasoned that, with the report of the Tlascalan capitulation spreading, whether or not this proved to hold true, the tribes along the route to the coast would be disinclined to interfere with the Spanish horsemen, which would not have been the case while the Spaniards were fighting for their lives. To the commander of the fort at Villa Rica (Juan de Escalante, who had been assigned to remain there with sixty ailing men) Cortés sent a letter instructing Escalante to dig at a certain corner of the dirt floor in Cortés's hut where there were buried two casks of sacramental wine and a box of wafers and to deliver the wine and wafers to the horsemen to bring back to the highland. As soon as Cortés realized that he and his men had survived, his impulse was to thank God—and the army in the highland for quite a while had lacked the accoutrements for a proper Mass. In his letter Cortés also told Escalante to be sure to maintain favorable relations with all the Totonac people, because the Totonacs with the army had fought like Christians.

In Tlascala Cortés and his men rested for twenty days. To the intense relief of the Spaniards the Tlascalans welcomed them wholeheartedly, with the exception perhaps of Xicotenga the Younger, whose pride as a warrior was hurt because he had not been able to overcome the strangers. By all the other Tlascalans who gathered from the surrounding cities and towns, the Spaniards were hailed as allies; for as long as anyone could remember, Tlascala had been standing alone against the Aztec empire. The fury of the recent fighting between the Tlascalans and the Spaniards seemed to have passed like the excitement of an athletic match that had been fought for the thrill of the game.

In the center of their main city the Tlascalans put up the Spaniards in commodious stone houses with shady courtyards and they helped the Spaniards to place cannons at the corners of the central square and establish guardposts. The Tlascalans brought delicious food in bounteous quantities (the province was fertile and intensively cultivated, and the fresh fish from the streams was and is especially good). With ceremony and sincerity the Tlascalan chiefs and captains presented their daughters to the Spaniards to culminate in sexual celebration the fusion of these two warrior-peoples who, the Tlascalans hoped, would proceed to victory over their age-old enemies, the Aztecs. The Tlascalans expected that war with the Aztecs would be fought for many generations, and they wanted conception of their next generation to take place as soon as possible. In the Aztec capital Montezuma with his zoo had an abstract interest in crossbreeding, but the Tlascalans put the idea into practice.

(In spite of the different styles of the chronicles of the conquest, the personalities of the various participants shine through. Cortés could not resist telling a joke. So he told Gómara, who recorded it in elegant Spanish prose, that a Tlascalan princess given to Pedro de Alvarado was so sexually fulfilled by Alvarado, so enamored of him, that she denounced her own brother, a Tlascalan captain, and confessed that her brother intended to betray the Spaniards to the Aztecs or Cholulans. Whereupon, Alvarado and Cortés quietly arranged to have the brother strangled, and his death or disappearance caused not a ripple in Tlascalan society. This whole story seems really to be Cortés's way of making fun of Alvarado's irrepressible sexual boasting and is not intended to be taken seriously. Cortés and all the Spaniards liked the Tlascalans, once peace was concluded and they lived among them, and Cortés respected the Tlascalans for their long stand against the Aztecs.)

Cortés was surprised when the Aztec nobles, who had come to him as an embassy, willingly entered Tlascala with him. The Aztecs as ambassadors appeared to be unafraid and confident of their safety, even though the Aztecs and the Tlascalans glared at one another and soon began to bicker vociferously. From this bickering, which was translated for Cortés by Malinche through Aguilar, Cortés learned a good deal about the Indian character.

There is a general assumption, which exists even now, that Indians are taciturn, but the contrary is the case. Indians—all Indians—love to talk. The Plains Indians of the western United States at powwows with U.S. Army officers and visiting U.S. Congressmen would talk until the Anglo-Americans were tugging at their britches, scratching or snoring, while for the Indians the powwow had hardly gotten started. Even the simplest and most hard-pressed of all the Indians, the Yahgans of Tierra del Fuego, had a vocabulary of over 30,000 words to describe the bleak circumstances of their lives.

The Tlascalans and the Aztecs—both groups obviously assuming beyond question that the sanctity of the embassy would be respected—railed at each other, accusing, recalling, threatening, and finding fun in the verbal fracas, as they found fun in fighting. Each group—after loudly making its point to the other group replete with grimaces and gestures—would turn to Cortés and make the point again, so that each point was made over and over, as Malinche's translations became fuller.

Cortés learned that for many years these two powerful tribes—poised against each other, with the Aztecs dominating but unable to prevail—had nevertheless maintained relations of a sort that Cortés at first found difficult to comprehend. These Tlascalans and Aztecs talked about "Flower Wars," which were battles that the nobles of both tribes agreed to conduct, the purpose being twofold: to give their young warriors experience in battle without having to send them to distant coasts, and to provide each side with victims for sacrifice. And the Tlascalan and Aztec nobles argued with each other over whose side had shown to best advantage in various of these staged battles. The Aztecs confidently asserted that they could easily over-whelm and finally conquer the Tlascalans and would do so if it were not that both sides wanted to continue the Flower Wars. A touch that im-pressed Cortés was that, after these staged battles, the Tlascalan nobles often were invited to the Aztec capital as "Enemies of the House" to witness the sacrifice of their own warriors whom the Aztecs had captured. The behavior of captured warriors during the ritual of sacrifice was regarded by both sides as a revelation of the mettle of the men, fully as significant an indication as had been the behavior of the warriors on the battlefield. The Aztecs particularly liked to have Otomís and Pinomes to sacrifice, because the behavior of these primitive Indians varied from that of the Tlascalans and Aztecs, who behaved in similar ways. (The testing of the ability of warriors to withstand pain and terror was a widespread practice among American Indians, and such testing was routinely conducted by many of the tribes who lived in the lands that became the United States and Canada.)

From his Christian and Spanish point of view, Cortés, in spite of his own training as a fighter and in spite of all the blood he had shed and seen shed, was frankly amazed by the cynicism and callousness of the Tlascalan and Aztec nobles. All the nobles admitted that these staged battles—"Flower Wars"—were regarded by the common people as real battles, real invasions, which the nobles knew they were not. As the arguing went on, Cortés came to appreciate the depth of Indian duplicity within a tribe. And he sensed, as he had sensed before but now more acutely, what seemed to him the Indians' indifference to human life. He noted that the Indians were capable of tremendous violence without the justification of any passion he could understand—save, perhaps, in battle, the simple thrill of fighting. He could not understand the religious ecstasy aroused by ceremonial human sacrifice. Eventually, and as a result of his listening to this self-revealing bickering between the Tlascalans and Aztecs, he gained an insight into the Indian character on which he would base his future strategy.

The Aztecs were importuning him to go on to Cholula; the city could be reached in less than two days. It was farther along on the natural throughway into the highland, and, as the Aztecs had assured him, from Cholula the route to their capital was open and easy.

The Tlascalans begged him not to go. Montezuma, they warned, kept a large garrison outside Cholula. The Cholulans, even by Aztec standards, were masters of deception and would lure him into a trap. The Cholulans were prepared to attack him. They had already dug pits in the road, set pointed sticks at the bottoms, and filled the pits with sand, so the horses would sink onto the sharpened sticks and be injured. On the flat roofs of the houses in Cholula there were piles of stones to throw down at the Spaniards in the streets.

The Tlascalans knew of these preparations because some of them had recently gone to Cholula. Cortés had reported to a Tlascalan chief that a certain Tlascalan had stolen some gold belonging to a Spaniard. The thief, it was learned, had fled with the gold to Cholula. So a squad of Tlascalans was sent to Cholula, where they found the thief and brought him and the gold back to Tlascala. Then the chief turned the culprit over to the Spaniards for punishment, but Cortés said that the Tlascalans should punish him according to the law of their land. So the squad of Tlascalans took the thief to the large public marketplace; a crier loudly announced his crime; and one of the men of the squad smashed the thief's skull with a club, shocking the onlooking Spaniards but causing hardly any interruption in the activity of the marketplace. According to Bernal Díaz, human flesh was bartered in the Indian markets like all other products and services, so probably the thief was soon offered for sale. (In all Indian societies, capital punishment was the only punishment for almost all crimes, enslavement being an alternative used in a few special cases.)

The Tlascalans pointed out to Cortés that, although the Aztec promises of how well the Spaniards would be treated in Cholula were florid and grand, no Cholulan chiefs had come to Tlascala to greet him and pledge their vassalage. Consequently Cortés sent a message to Cholula, summoning the chiefs. But the chiefs did not come. Instead, a few nondescript Cholulans showed up to say that the chiefs were sick. So Cortés sent another message: Either the chiefs came promptly or he would regard them as enemies and destroy them. Then the chiefs came. They excused their previous reluctance by saying that they feared to be among the Tlascalans, and they extended their greetings to Cortés, promised him hospitality, and pledged whatever he wanted them to pledge. It was not a reassuring performance.

Yet Cortés felt that he had to move. The Spaniards, amply fed, were healthy and hearty. His men were openly copulating with the Indian girls, and Cortés was fornicating with Malinche. (It's likely that Cortés disdained the Tlascalan daughters who had been given him. He was fond of Malinche, was grateful to her and dependent upon her; she was learning Spanish from him; and he impregnated her but none of the others.) Cortés did not want to allow himself or his men to become too comfortable. There was no gold in Tlascala, and the Tlascalans had been extravagant in their description of Montezuma's riches. The horses were adequately healed. So Cortés decided to go on to Cholula.

The Tlascalans turned out one hundred thousand warriors to go with him. The Tlascalan warriors were assembled in troops, armed, with food on their backs for the journey, on the morning when the Spaniards made ready to go. Cortés went to the top of the pyramid beside his quarters to have an overview of the Tlascalans—and this view made a deep impression upon him. He appreciated bravery and he appreciated loyalty, once it was honestly pledged. His Zempoalans, who had proved their trustworthiness, had predicted that the Tlascalans would be stout supporters of his cause, and he had wondered about the Zempoalans' judgment while he had been fighting Xicotenga and his men. Now the heartening sight of the Tlascalan army showed that the Zempoalans had been right.

Cortés had a final Mass held in the one Tlascalan temple that had been Christianized (the idols removed, blood scrubbed away, whitewash applied, a Cross and a figurine of Mary erected, flowers put out and candles lighted, all with Father Olmedo's blessing). During his stay in Tlascala Cortés had persistently lectured the Tlascalan chiefs on Christianity—as he always lectured Indians—telling them to worship the true God, destroy their idols, and cease human sacrifice and cannibalism. The Tlascalans had replied that, were they to do so, their people would stone them, and they would be turning from the habits of their ancestors, which would be disrespectful, but they would like time to study the Spaniards' practices, to become familiar with their ways, and perhaps in the future they would convert, which they were inclined to do since they had observed how well the Spaniards' gods supported the Spaniards in battle. In reply Cortés promised to send them teachers, brothers who would explain Christianity to them better than he could. And a reasonable compromise was worked out: The Tlascalans turned over to the Spaniards a single temple for Christianization. In this temple the Spaniards held their Masses and baptized the Tlascalan girls, which the Spaniards were scrupulously careful to do prior to copulating with them. Meanwhile, the Tlascalans studied the Spaniards—and pondered. This compromise was one of the very few bilateral acts of reason that marked the whole campaign.

After Mass, Cortés and his Spaniards, the Zempoalans, and the troops of Tlascalans left for Cholula. At the end of a day's march, however, Cortés sent back all except six thousand of the Tlascalans. He did not want to approach Cholula with an army such as the Aztecs had faced many times before. The Tlascalan chiefs had told him that, for every hundred thousand warriors they would field, Montezuma would field three hundred thousand or five hundred thousand. Cortés did not want to become involved in the kind of warfare that had existed in the past and at which the Aztecs excelled.

As Cortés approached Cholula, he had his strategy in mind. He was better informed about Cholula and the Cholulans than he had been about any place and tribe he had yet come upon, and he did not like the Cholulans he had seen. They made him uneasy. Cortés respected fighters, like the Tlascalans, and the Cholulans were mainly priests and traders. The Cholulans were Nahuatl-speakers who had not long been under the Aztec sway. In the city of Cholula, by all accounts, good pottery and cotton textiles were manufactured, and Cholulan traders distributed these goods all over Mexico, with the exception of Tlascala. Mixed in with the six thousand Tlascalan warriors who were accompanying Cortés were some Tlascalan traders who hoped to be allowed to exchange whatever they brought in their knapsacks for Cholulan blankets. Also, Cholula was famous as a religious center; the largest pyramid in Cholula had one hundred twenty steps and atop it was a temple that was a shrine of Quetzalcoatl.

Perhaps because Cholula was known to be dedicated to Quetzalcoatl, the Aztecs thought it an appropriate testing-place for Cortés. Many of the gifts Montezuma had sent to Cortés on the coast were supposed to be relics of Quetzalcoatl; Montezuma had intentionally sent them to see if Cortés would respond to things that might have belonged to his kinsman (a sculptured gold mask inlaid with jade that the god was believed to have worn, a gold crown with magnificent featherwork). Cortés, not understanding the significance of the things, had shipped them off to the king in Spain. But it is unlikely that Montezuma was doing more than toying with the idea, which was held by some of his priests, that these invaders were descendants of the legendary god who long ago had sailed away to the east. Montezuma's firmness of mind is more definitely evidenced by his repeated urging that the Spaniards go away, by his offer to pay tribute if they would go away, and by his continuous rearrangement of his forces so that he could overwhelm them if necessary.

Along the march to Cholula, Cortés at several places found that the main trail had been blocked by boulders and tree trunks and on the alternate trail he came upon some sand pits in which, as the Tlascalans had warned him, sharpened stakes had been set. To the Spaniards, on their guard, these obstacles were obvious and presented little danger. In the evening the Spaniards, Totonacs and Tlascalans camped beside a creek a few miles from Cholula.

At dusk several Cholulan chiefs came to greet Cortés. They were obsequious and were accompanied by bearers who brought food. The Cholulan chiefs were alarmed, however, when they saw the Tlascalans and they complained to Malinche that the Tlascalans were their traditional enemies and ought not to be brought into their city. (Actually the Tlascalans and Cholulans had once been allies; then, quarreling, they had fought with each other; the Cholulans had asked the Aztecs to help them against the Tlascalans and the Aztecs had done so, driving off the Tlascalans—but the Cholulans ever since had been forced to pay tribute to the Aztecs.) In the morning a great host of Cholulan chiefs and white-robed priests came to Cortés and welcomed him, the priests blowing trumpets and whistles, swinging braziers and beating drums. Like the chiefs who had come the previous evening, these chiefs angrily pointed to the Tlascalans and objected to having them enter their city. So Cortés accommodated the Cholulans, and he tactfully explained to the Tlascalans that they should remain outside Cholula because the Cholulans were afraid of them.

Cautiously entering the city with horsemen at the head of the column and the cannons pulled by a few exempted Tlascalans at the rear, the Spaniards were led to houses that had been prepared for them on the central square—spacious stone houses that faced a large courtyard around which were high stone walls. All the Spanish soldiers saw the piled rocks on the flat rooftops of the houses they passed and saw that breastworks of adobe brick had been built to protect the throwers. Once the Spaniards and the Zempoalans were settled, though, and the few Tlascalans at Cortés's direction had placed the cannons, the Cholulans brought ample food for all.

For two days Cortés held meetings with the Cholulan chiefs and delivered his usual lecture. But the Cholulans replied that they would not think of abandoning their gods or altering their practices; they upbraided Cortés for thinking he could enter their city and immediately make such suggestions to them. Cortés told them that he was on his way to confer with the great Montezuma, who was going to become a vassal of the king of Spain, and the Cholulans were somewhat interested in this proposal of vassalage, if Cortés was speaking the truth, thinking that whatever they might pay to the king of Spain they would no longer have to pay to Montezuma.

After three days the delivery of food to the Spaniards and their allies ceased. As did the visits from the Cholulan chiefs. Cortés summoned the Aztec ambassadors who were accompanying him and told them that he and his men required food. The Aztecs informed the Cholulans, who sent firewood and water but no food. And the Spaniards from their fortified stone houses, which were deep within the city, saw Cholulans laughing at them from nearby rooftops and from the tops of some pyramids.

What had happened was that a delegation of Aztec nobles had come to Cholula from the Aztec capital, which was said to be about sixty miles away. After these nobles had conferred with the Aztec ambassadors, one of the more prominent ambassadors promptly disappeared, presumably to report to Montezuma.

Then the leader of the newly arrived Aztec delegation came and told Cortés that Montezuma would not receive him in the capital because he could not provide him with food there. Nor could food be provided here. Nor could any arrangement be made for the Spaniards to visit the capital.

Cortés replied gently, saying that he most definitely intended to make the acquaintance of the great monarch about whom he had heard so many wonderful things, that his own king would never excuse him for failing to present himself courteously, and so on.

The Zempoalans reported to Cortés that the city was being evacuated, that women and children with bundles of valuables were leaving to hide in the countryside, that covered holes had been made in the streets with pointed stakes at the bottom as traps for the horses when they galloped, that many streets had been barricaded, and that Aztec warriors were installed in houses along the route the Spaniards would have to take to get out of the city. In addition to their arms, the Aztec warriors were equipped with long poles, leather collars and ropes with which to take the Spaniards prisoner.

As a final confirmation, a Cholulan lady of noble birth warned Malinche (who promptly reported to Cortés). According to this lady, Montezuma had sent thirty thousand warriors, who were waiting in ravines northwest of the city; some of these warriors were already inside the houses. Montezuma's order was that the Spaniards should be taken alive, if possible, and sent to him in the capital; the Cholulan priests were to be allowed to keep twenty Spaniards for sacrifice. The Cholulan lady offered to take Malinche with her into hiding—if Malinche would leave the Spaniards, as she must if she were to save her own life.

The Aztec and Cholulan strategy was clearly to starve the Spaniards and force them to leave and, as they wound their way out of the city through the narrow streets, to kill and capture them. The trouble with this plan was that the Cholulan chiefs did not want the Aztec army to enter Cholula. While the Spaniards were eating their last few stale tortillas, intense negotiations were being conducted by the Aztecs and Cholulans. Although the Cholulans were tribute-paying vassals of Montezuma, they still were allowed to manage their own affairs and to run their city with a degree of independence. If an Aztec army were to occupy the city, Cholula's days of even semi-independence would probably be over—because the Aztecs had occupied other cities on similar pretexts and Aztec governors had never left. Montezuma had sent bribes to the Cholulans (in particular, a drum made of gold, which was Montezuma's gift to the leading Cholulan captain, who happened to be the husband of Malinche's would-be protectress). In spite of the bribes, however, the Cholulans were stubbornly resisting Aztec occupation by maintaining that they had their own strategy and would capture the Spaniards without Aztec help.

Cortés had some of his men catch a couple of Cholulan priests and bring them to him. While he kept one of the priests, he had the other take a message to the Cholulan chiefs that he was about to leave Cholula and wanted first to speak to them. The chiefs came promptly, because they were eager to hear the Spaniards' plans. When Cortés berated them for sending him no food, they replied that Montezuma had ordered that no more food should be provided. When Cortés told them that he would need provisions and porters for his trip to the Aztec capital, the Cholulans were delighted— because they wanted to draw the Spaniards from their fortified stone houses and attack them in the streets.

That night it was reported to Cortés by the Tlascalans that the Cholulans were making their traditional sacrifices on the eve of war: According to one chronicler, they were sacrificing ten three-year-old children, five of whom were male and five female; according to another chronicler, there were seven victims, five of whom were children. Cortés sent a Tlascalan to alert those who were camped outside the city. The Spaniards had been expecting an attack and had been on alert each night. But this night they packed their belongings, and the horses were kept saddled. By dawn the Spaniards were ready.

In the morning, a good part of the populace of Cholula, having returned to the city in a jubilant mood, converged on the Spaniards' establishment. The Cholulan chiefs and captains directed troops of their warriors into the large courtyard before the Spaniards' houses and gaily announced that these troops, like honor guards, would escort the Spaniards from the city. Other troops of warriors would act as porters for the strangers; they had even brought hammocks slung as litters in which the strangers could be carried if they preferred not to walk (litters in which the Spaniards would be defenseless). All around the four entrances to the courtyard gathered the most prominent people of the city, women and children among them, to watch the Spaniards' departure. Cholulans were crowded on the roofs of the houses along the Spaniards' route (these roofs, *azoteas,* are customarily used as balconies or terraces).

Cortés had thirty of the Cholulan chiefs invited into his house to hear his farewell. They came in willingly, because their strategy seemed to be working so well. But when they were all inside, Spaniards closed and barred the door, and Cortés told them that he knew of their plot and that they had to be punished. A few Cholulans tried to fight and were killed by Spanish swordsmen. Most did not fight and were tied up.

Then Cortés and the men with him joined the rest of his army and the Zempoalans and few Tlascalans who were waiting outside, lined up with the baggage, as if ready to march. Cortés mounted his horse and had the signal given—a shot from a harquebus. Whereupon, all the Spaniards, Zempoalans and Tlascalans dropped the baggage and proceeded to massacre the Cholulans in the courtyard. The Cholulans were so close-packed that it was an easy slaughter; the harquebusiers and crossbowmen cut them down with devastating volleys. The Spanish horsemen burst out of the courtyard and attacked the horrified onlookers. Screaming, the women and children ran; Cortés had cautioned his men to try to avoid killing women and children; but many Cholulan men and the Aztec warriors in the houses fought back. From the wooden thatch-roofed temple of Quetzalcoatl atop the great stone pyramid, Cholulan priests were furiously rolling rocks down on the Spaniards. So the Spaniards deployed, rushed up the steps and burned the temple with the priests in it. The Cholulan warriors were not used to fighting, nor were the traders, priests and artisans. As the people

An Indian rendering of the massacre at Cholula, doubly prejudiced because this tapestry was made many years after the conquest by Christianized artists who were also Tlascalans. It shows Indian pitted against Indian, and Malinche standing behind Cortés.

fled from the city and tried to run off into hiding, the waiting Tlascalans fell upon them.

Contrary to the discipline Cortés had imposed ever since he had been on the mainland, he allowed this city to be sacked. The Spaniards took all the gold and jewels they could find. The Tlascalans stole all the salt and blankets they could carry. Temples atop pyramids all over the city were burning. The most credible estimates are that six to ten thousand people were killed.

With this lesson Cortés tried to pierce the veil of Montezuma's indifference toward human life—and he did pierce it, by his prescience and the suddenness of his attack. When Cortés recalled his troops, the nearby streets and the courtyard were carpeted with dead bodies. Returning to the room where the Cholulan chiefs were tied up, Cortés had them released and allowed them to go outside to see what, as he told them, they had caused.

The Cholulan chiefs returned to Cortés and blamed Montezuma. The Cholulans begged Cortés's forgiveness and asked to be permitted to go into the countryside to bring back the people, those who had escaped into hiding. Cortés agreed. And as the Spaniards and their Indian allies sat around and ate the food they had plundered from the houses and unpacked their baggage for the trip they were not ready to take, the city began to revive. Within a day or two Cholula was teeming again. The Cholulans, who had experienced Tlascalan and Aztec onslaughts and who in their own ceremonies exalted terror, did not seem to be scarred by the Spanish fury; the Cholulans did not even show resentment of the Spaniards but seemed simply to be chastised and grieved, and they accepted their lot with docile resignation.

Cortés had the Aztec nobles brought to him—the ambassadors who had come with him from Tlascala and the delegates who had been sent from the Aztec capital and had recently arrived in Cholula. He told them that the Cholulans had confessed to him that they had been ordered by Montezuma to attack the Spaniards. And they had been punished for their behavior. But, Cortés confided, he did not believe the Cholulans' lies. Not for a moment did he believe that Montezuma, such a great prince, would have given any such orders. Many times he and Montezuma had exchanged pledges of friendship. The Cholulans, Cortés had no doubt, were lying in a transparent effort to shift the blame from themselves and to avoid worse punishment.

The Spaniards stayed in Cholula for about two weeks after the massacre. Food was delivered to them daily. Cortés had the Tlascalans outside the city come into the center and, as he had with the chiefs of Zempoala and Cingapacinga, he forced the Tlascalans and Cholulans to embrace each other and promise to resume their amity. By reestablishing peace between Cholula and Tlascala, Cortés extended his safe route to the coast and his link to the Spaniards at Villa Rica.

Eventually word came from Montezuma in the capital that he would be happy to receive the Spaniards whenever they would come to him.

THE FANTASY FROM *AMADÍS DE GAULA*

Cortés and his men weren't self-possessed: They were transported. In the thin clear air of the highland they were physically elated, agitated, breathless and giddy, their blood vessels distended, throats burning as their lungs strained for oxygen. When in the midst of battle they would charge, their vision would be obscured by black specks (a symptom of anoxia). And they were amazed still to be alive—careening between, at one instant, disaster and death on the sacrifice-stone and, at the next instant, triumph that brought them not only gold but the promise of glory. They were rational men no longer. Their streak of luck was so incredible—how could they not believe they were blessed? When they would look up at the blazing mountain sun and see in the dazzle the figure of St. James on a rearing horse, they never doubted that it was St. James himself charging alongside them at the heathen hordes who fled like shades being driven back to hell.

Before Cortés left Cholula, the Zempoalans came and told him they wanted to go no farther. It was not that they were faint-hearted or did not want to support him or that they were relenting in their opposition to Montezuma; it was that they were too far from home, and this sense of being far away dispirited and disheartened them. None of them had ever been this far before. They were lost and felt poorly (lowlanders, they were suffering from the altitude). Cortés granted their request to leave. He was intensely grateful for the loyalty they had already shown him. In fact, he and his men shared their malaise, but inspiration made the Spaniards buoyant. Cortés divided up the feathercloaks and fine, embroidered cotton garments he had received and gave a generous portion to the Zempoalans, with loads segregated for the fat chief and his relatives. He also gave the Zempoalans an explanatory letter to deliver to their chief and another letter to deliver to Juan de Escalante in the fort at Villa Rica. Then he let the Zempoalans go. And most, though not all of them, left.

(It may seem absurd that the Spanish often sent letters to the Indians;

the Spaniards had sent letters to the Tlascalans before the battles and to the Cholulans and to Montezuma. Of course the Spaniards were fully aware that the Indians could not read the letters, neither translate from the Spanish nor comprehend writing. But the Spaniards had seen the Indian drawings on whitened sheets of pounded maguey, which looked like paper, and the Spaniards presumed that the Indians, when a message was verbally related to them, would be doubly impressed if the message were accompanied by a white sheet on which, instead of a drawing, there were curious and possibly magical markings. Also, the Spaniards kept copies of their letters to the Indians as evidence to present to the king's agents, were the propriety of the conquest ever to be questioned, as it certainly was.)

The Spaniards and the Tlascalans set out for the Aztec capital, Tlascalans pulling the cannons and carrying the baggage in the center, Tlascalan warriors and Spanish horsemen on the flanks of the formation. A few Zempoalans and a few Cholulans went with them. The Aztec ambassadors acted as guides. The whole assemblage traveled very slowly, warily, going only a few miles each day and camping at night in villages along the way, sometimes staying for two or three days before moving on. The villagers received them cautiously and a little fearfully, eyeing the unexpected mixture of Aztecs and Tlascalans in the Spanish train. The villagers would provide food and usually would present Cortés with modest gifts, including a little gold.

The first amazing sight the Spaniards saw en route to they-knew-not-where was a towering snow-capped mountain with a huge jet of white steam shooting from the summit, shooting straight up with such force that the smoke was not affected by the wind until it was high in the sky. This was the volcano of Popocatépetl at a point of near-eruption (Popocatépetl soon after erupted and remained active for ten years, then was dormant for one hundred thirty-five years, then became active again, and ever since has been dormant). Nearby was another great snowy mountain, called Iztaccíhuatl, but this mountain was quiet. The Aztecs and the Tlascalans said they had never before seen such smoke from Popocatépetl; obviously the mountain was upset in some way or perhaps was acclaiming the arrival of the Spaniards.

Cortés sent a few Spaniards to find out what was happening; he placed them under the command of Diego de Ordaz. The Indians were afraid to climb Popocatépetl; they said the spirits of bad rulers dwelt there. Cortés induced them to help find a path but they would go only part way up the slope of the mountain. After the Indians would go no farther, Ordaz and the Spaniards continued to climb. Near the summit they found that the earth underfoot was trembling, the air bitterly cold. The hard-crusted snow was being dirtied by a fall of fine ash. Large icicles, which were strange to the Spaniards, were hanging from the undersides of the rocks. The summit of Popocatépetl is 17,887 feet above sea level; it is a strain to move even slowly at this altitude; an effort must be made to breathe; all the symptoms of anoxia come on. But it is reasonably certain that Ordaz and the few men with him reached the rim of the crater because Ordaz's description, as expressed to Bernal Díaz, was so apt: that at the very top there was a mouth a mile and a half in circumference; this hole was filled with roaring but the hole was shallow and "looked very much like a glass oven when it is boiling its hardest." Which is just what an open volcano looks like. (The king later granted Ordaz the right to put a smoking volcano on his coat of arms.) When the Spaniards were on their way down, burning stones began to fall like rain, and the Spaniards had to take shelter under some rocks. But they got down safely and showed to Cortés and the others a few volcanic cinders, icicles and snow. Some of the Indians kissed the hems of the mountain-climbers' scorched clothes.

While high on the slope of Popocatépetl, Ordaz and those with him saw that the trail Cortés and the army were following came to a fork and at the fork one branch of the road was clear and the other branch had been blocked at the junction and in several other places with huge felled trees. Beyond the felled trees, however, the road that was blocked seemed to be the better route. So when the army reached the fork, Cortés called a halt and summoned Indians from a nearby village. Out of the hearing of the Aztec ambassadors who were serving as guides, Cortés interrogated the village chiefs and they told him that the cleared road led to a narrow place where Aztec troops had prepared a trap by cutting out the side of a hill, digging ditches and erecting barricades, and they were waiting there. These were probably troops that had withdrawn from the vicinity of Cholula after the massacre; it is doubtful that they had orders to attack the Spaniards, but they had positioned themselves to be able to do so if Montezuma were to issue the command.

Cortés summoned the Aztec ambassadors and asked them why one branch of the road had been blocked. The Aztecs replied that the blocked road led to a town allied to Tlascala and this was a very poor town, while the cleared road led to a large prosperous town loyal to Montezuma where the Spaniards could be accommodated in the manner that Montezuma desired for them.

Cortés took the road that had been blocked. The Tlascalans cleared away the trees, and the army passed through to the town which was not under

Aztec control. In that town the chiefs warned Cortés not to go on to the capital, where there were countless Aztec warriors and where the Spaniards were sure to be killed in battle or, if they were captured, sacrificed and eaten. These chiefs had heard rumors that the priests of Huitzilopochtli, the war god, had busily been making auguries, that they had been sacrificing daily; as was well known, Montezuma himself had been a priest of Huitzilopochtli, not of Quetzalcoatl; and the auguries varied, indicating sometimes that the strangers should be prevented from approaching the capital and sometimes that they should be induced to come because, when surrounded by all the warriors in the capital, they could easily be defeated and taken.

For Cortés this information from the allies of Tlascala coincided with the protestations he had been receiving both in Cholula and on the road from Aztec messengers who every few days had come to him from Montezuma, each message being accompanied by a courtesy gift of gold. These Aztec messengers had continued to argue that there was no food available in the capital, that the terrain was dangerous and difficult, that tribes along the way would resist the Spaniards, and (a really imaginative excuse) that the ferocious wild animals in Montezuma's zoo in the capital would be let loose and would tear the Spaniards apart. Finally Cortés had told the messengers to stop their nonsense: He was coming to the capital, confident that the great Montezuma would receive him in friendship, as Montezuma had many times promised. Cortés's own great king expected nothing less. When Cortés threatened to come in war if he could not come in peace, the messengers relented and assuaged him.

The Tlascalan allies provided the Spaniards with ample food, though unsalted, and a small gift (a little gold and a few female slaves) because they were truly poor. In mid-morning, after eating and repacking, the Spaniards went on and climbed a few miles to a high pass between the mountains. The weather was frigid, and snow was being driven at a slant by the wind in the pass. The Spaniards could hardly see through the snow, and they worried because, had Aztec troops attacked in this pass, the blinded Spaniards might have been in difficulty. But the Aztecs had laid their trap on the other road that the Spaniards had not taken.

Once through the pass, the snow ceased, the wind fell, and the Spaniards looked out over the grand valley of Mexico, gleaming in sunshine because clouds tend to gather over the mountain rim and the sky above the valley is clear. You cannot see the whole valley from any spot on the ridge, but you can see all the close-in places. And this was enough to quiet, even to gentle the Spaniards by its astounding beauty. On the valley floor there were many lakes, mirroring the blue sky above, and in the lakes were villages and towns on islands connected by causeways to the shore. All the villages and towns were of whitewashed stone, with many pyramids towering above the houses, the surfaces of white lime made vivid by paintings in red, yellow and black, and on the water of the lakes were thousands of canoes in which people were paddling about, crossing between the islands and the mainland and in canals making their way through the villages and towns. The fields after the harvest were trimmed and well-tended, and there seemed to be verdant fields afloat even on the surfaces of the lakes.

To the Spaniards, it was a view of a sort never seen before or even dreamed of. It was a fantasy from a romance. Such fantasies had been in the minds of all the Spaniards since they were children, half-believed, hardly hoped for. Yet there it lay in golden glory, a heavenly vision glimmering like a mirage on the floor of this extensive valley among these great mountains on the other side of the earth.

The Spaniards were so overcome by this, their first panoramic view of the valley of Mexico, that some of the Velázquez men wanted to turn around. They said it was ungodly for them to delve into such a scene from heaven, and, punished, they would not survive. While the Spaniards stood and stared from the mountain ridge, mutiny once more became imminent. But again Cortés, who was as awed as any of them by the spectacle, through the force of his character and by his example prevailed. Then they started their descent.

As they came into the valley they began to appreciate the infinite richness and luxury of the Aztec empire. Guided by the Aztec ambassadors, in mid-afternoon they came upon an enormous country villa that had been vacated for them; it was large enough to accommodate all the Spaniards and the thousands of Indians with them. The villa was made of matched kinds of stonework, some of it limed and adorned with brilliant paintings, decorated here and there with inlaid cedar. There were interior courts filled with aromatic plants, in the rooms rich hangings on the walls, and also in the rooms were mounds of logs ready to be lighted, with more logs stacked alongside, so the Spaniards would not have to endure another cold night (and nights in the valley of Mexico at the foot of the mountains are chilly). All around the villa were gardens with flowers cascading over walks shaded by cotton awnings, and there was a pool of fresh water.

The Tlascalans were suspicious that they would be attacked and they warned Cortés. They had seen warriors spying from the woods. So Cortés set out a formidable guard, with the cannons and harquebusiers at high-points where they could be seen, while the horses were kept saddled.

Then to the Spaniards in the evening came another Aztec delegation, led by a richly dressed Aztec noble who said that he was Montezuma's brother, or so Cortés came to understand after translations (this was not likely to have been Montezuma's brother but a more distant relative). After the customary presentation of some gold, this noble, in effect, laid out Montezuma's ultimate offer. Montezuma, having realized that gift-cum-wish meant nothing to the Spaniards, thought that perhaps Cortés had not clearly understood his previous proposals. So this noble recited all the difficulties that the Spaniards' advance on the capital posed—the shortage of food in the capital, the uprising of the people, and so forth, adding the danger of drowning since the Spaniards would have to enter the capital by canoe—and he laid out explicitly the promised reward if Cortés would turn back: Cortés could have whatever treasure he wanted for himself, which he could take with him, plus whatever yearly tribute his king wanted, which would be delivered to a designated port on the coast for the Spaniards' convenience.

Cortés replied that, if he were able to accept Montezuma's generous offer, he surely would, but his king had commanded him to present himself in person to the Aztec monarch, about whom the king had known for many years. Again, this assertion of foreknowledge by Cortés, groundless though it was, disturbed the Aztecs.

Then Cortés took the Aztecs on a tour of the villa and its grounds before they departed, and he showed them the cannons and guards. Cortés told them that, were any curious Indian strangers to enter this place at night, they would be killed without question. So there was no attack that night and no spying, and the Spaniards and their Indian allies slept well. (They were all feeling better as they came down from the heights.)

In the morning the Spanish train moved on a few miles to a substantial town of about twenty thousand people. There the Aztec chiefs welcomed the Spaniards and gave them forty slave girls and gold worth three thousand castellanos. The Spaniards were fed well and stayed a few days, after which they proceeded to the next town, which was partly on land and partly on water. They were intrigued by the canoes gliding by and even passing among them on canals. But these waterborne Indians were bold, and at night, while the Spaniards were settled in the town, they tried to infiltrate the Spanish camp—and the Spaniards and Tlascalans on guard killed fifteen or twenty spies, if they were spies—without creating a disturbance.

On the morning of the next day a great Aztec lord arrived, one of Montezuma's nephews named Cacama (the Aztec honorific suffix "tzin" was usually added, to make Cacamatzin, phonetically rendered). With his arrival the Spaniards were treated to an exhibition of grandiosity they had not yet seen. First, a dozen chiefs in magnificent regalia with many attendants came to announce Cacama's approach. When the prince came, he was carried in a litter by eight great chiefs, themselves the lords of towns, and his litter was resplendent with green feathers set in holders of silver and gold. Cacama was about twenty-five years old and was lord of Texcoco. The Spaniards did not yet understand that the major towns and cities of the valley, including Texcoco, were allied in a confederation, the dominant city being the capital. When Cacama stepped down from his litter, the attendant nobles swept the path he would tread and picked pebbles from it.

These dignified Aztecs with their rigid decorum were startled when Cortés greeted them with a warm *abrazo,* the Spanish bear-hug. Cacama, once he had recovered his composure, explained that Montezuma was sick and consequently could not come to greet the Spaniards, and Cacama had been sent to escort them. Then the whole combined group moved onward—the Aztec nobles with their large retinues, the Spaniards, the Tlascalans and a few other Indian allies—and people from all the nearby villages converged upon the road to gape, so that it became difficult to make progress through the crowds.

The Spaniards were led to a straight causeway built of stone, no wider than a lance-length and extending nearly two miles into a fresh-water lake. (These lakes in the valley of Mexico, some fresh and some salt, were shallow; most of them have been drained.) The Spaniards were reluctant to advance along this causeway because they were vulnerable in such a confined narrow space. But Cortés never wanted to show fear, so on they went. In the town at the end of the causeway they were received by local notables who presented the usual gifts of gold and girls; Cortés always responded by giving a few Spanish trinkets. From this place, the Spaniards, directed by Cacama, went to a larger town, which was built on the shore of a salt lake.

The lord of this place was Cuitlahuac, who was Montezuma's brother and Cacama's uncle. He was ruler of this town, Iztapalapa, and the adjoining town of Coyoacán. Cortés was approaching the center of the valley of Mexico (Coyoacán is now a suburb of Mexico City and is the place where the Mexican government housed Leon Trotsky and where Trotsky was killed by an ax-blow from a Spanish assassin sent by Stalin). Cuitlahuac was more reserved, more measuring than the other Aztec lords who had come to Cortés, and Cortés might have done well to remember his dark somber face. But Cortés and all the Spaniards with riotous colors about them, iridescent feathers, gleaming gold, shining silver, sparkling jewels, were trying hard not to let themselves yield to one of the crescendos of a culture utterly alien to their own.

In Cuitlahuac's city they were shown the grandest villas they had yet seen and a number of unfinished villas the Aztec rulers were building, because this was a new neighborhood favored by the nobles. The rooms of the villas were gracefully linked by interior courts, corridors opening upon gardens, and in the garden of Cuitlahuac's villa there was a square, stone-lined pool with fish swimming in it and, on the surface, water fowl paddling about. Cortés himself measured the pool and found it to be four hundred paces per side, sixteen hundred paces all around.

The next day the Spanish party continued to move along, escorted by Aztec nobles, enveloped by crowds, until they were brought to the foot of a causeway that stretched for six miles into the lake. This causeway was two lance-lengths in width, space enough for eight horsemen to ride abreast. There were two towns along the causeway: one probably was Coyoacán; the other was where Churubusco, the movie-making center of Mexico, is now. And beyond the towns was the capital of the fantasy, the largest city the Spaniards had ever seen, floating on water, elegantly white, surrounded by fleets of canoes, with pyramids so high they seemed skybound.

The Aztec capital was called Tenochtitlán (which is the Hispanicized spelling, the Nahuatl "ch" tending to be a back-of-the-throat sound similar to the "loch" in Loch Lomond, and the accent being on the penultimate, "Teh-noach-*tee*-tlan"). It was the capital of this side of the world.

"MAWK-TAY-KOO-SOMA"

On the bank of the lake Cortés halted the army and paused, while from horseback he appraised the situation. It was intensely dangerous. On the water all around the narrow causeway were hundreds of canoes filled with Indians who at the moment seemed peaceful. At several places the causeway had gaps of about twenty-five feet through which the water flowed, and canoes full of Indians were passing through these sluices which at road level were bridged by long straight timbers. The timbers could easily and quickly be removed to prevent the Spaniards from leaving Tenochtitlán, or the timbers of two bridges could be removed to trap the Christians on a segment of the causeway. Jammed together in the narrow confine, strung out over a long distance, the Spaniards and their Indian allies would be unable to maneuver, and they would be easy targets for warriors attacking from canoes. Furthermore, Cortés saw that at a point partway out to Tenochtitlán another causeway from the left joined the main causeway, and at this juncture there was a substantial stone battlement, resembling the gateway of a castle. The Spaniards would have to march to, through and under this battlement. Another great general, the Carthaginian, Hannibal, who was always reluctant to attack fortified places, would have stayed ashore where he could maneuver and circle around the city. But not Cortés. Acutely aware that the eyes of all the Indians in the massing crowds of onlookers were upon him, Cortés shook the reins, pressed with his heels and urged his horse forward onto the narrow causeway.

It was a parade of scared men—led by Spanish horsemen with lances up, harquebusiers next, crossbowmen, pikemen and swordsmen following, about four hundred Spaniards in all, then Tlascalans pulling the cannons and more Tlascalans carrying supplies of powder and shot and the baggage, with six thousand Tlascalan warriors, a few Zempoalans and even a few straggling Cholulans at the rear. The army, which was probably regarded as no more than an embassy by the Aztecs, had to abandon its usual, defensive rectangular formation to converge into an elongated, fragile, exposed column on the causeway. Filling the causeway in the wake of the army and blocking any possibility of retreat came the crowds from the Aztec villages around the lake.

At the battlement a thousand Aztec nobles, dressed in gaudy splendor, awaited Cortés. There the army stopped, and for one hour Cortés had to sit astride his horse while each Aztec noble took his turn to touch the ground and kiss his own hand—in token of what? Subservience? Hardly. Most likely, this elaborate greeting was simply the performance of the elegant, formalistic courtesy practiced by these Indians, a degree of slow-paced courtesy uncomprehended by the Spaniards. (It is amazing, yet true, that, on the one hand, the Aztecs in their ceremonies sacrificed screaming human victims and worked up to a pitch of terror that was an emotional catharsis, followed by greedy cannibalism, while, on the other hand, the Aztecs in their treatment of embassies, in their custom of gift-cum-wish, and in many of their social procedures were exquisitely and patiently fastidious.) On his horse Cortés no doubt wondered what the Aztec warriors in the city were doing during this enforced delay. But he had no choice except to wait and see, since the causeway both in front of him and behind him was packed.

After all the nobles had made their gesture of welcome, Cortés continued to lead the army through the battlement and onto the segment of the causeway that connected this junction point with Tenochtitlán. On this

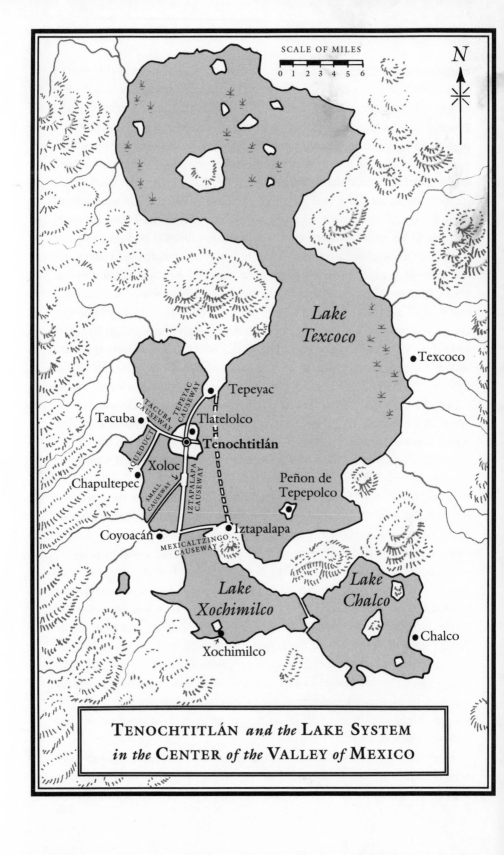

SCALE OF MILES

0 1 2 3 4 5 6

N

Lake Texcoco

• Texcoco

Tepeyac

TACUBA CAUSEWAY

TEPEYAC CAUSEWAY

Tacuba •

Tlatelolco

Tenochtitlán

AQUEDUCT

Xoloc

Chapultepec •

SMALL CAUSEWAY

IZTAPALAPA CAUSEWAY

Peñon de Tepepolco

Coyoacán •

MEXICALTZINGO CAUSEWAY

Iztapalapa

Lake Xochimilco

Lake Chalco

• Chalco

Xochimilco

TENOCHTITLÁN *and the* **LAKE SYSTEM**
in the **CENTER** *of the* **VALLEY** *of* **MEXICO**

segment there was another bridged gap, and Cortés glanced at the removable, unnailed timbers, but he did not slow his horse's gait.

Ashore on the island of Tenochtitlán, Cortés came upon a wide straight avenue lined on both sides with handsome, flat-roofed stone houses whited with lime and decorated with inlaid wood, interspersed with towering pyramids topped with temples. In this avenue, coming to greet him, were more Aztec nobles, about two hundred of them, even more elaborately dressed than those who had met him at the battlement, wearing feathered headdresses and embroidered dyed cotton garments glittering with gold, silver and precious stones, and the nobles were attended by a multitude of servants who followed them, filling the street. The nobles were in two lines, one line on each side of the street close to the front walls of the houses. The side streets and *azoteas* were crowded with onlookers.

Walking slowly toward Cortés in the center of the avenue came the monarch. On his left hand was his nephew, Cacama, on his right hand his brother (or half-brother), Cuitlahuac. Montezuma was touching the forearm of each of his relatives, not to support himself but in token of the vassalage of these kinsmen. The nobles aligned along the sides of the avenue all averted their eyes toward the houses so as not to look directly at the emperor, in order to avoid the slightest hint of impertinence. All the nobles, including Cacama and Cuitlahuac, were barefoot, while Montezuma wore sandals that had gold soles and precious stones sewn onto the leather thongs.

Cortés dismounted, and promptly Malinche and Aguilar came to him. Cortés presented himself—and the monarch confirmed that he was indeed Montezuma. Whereupon, Cortés flung wide his arms and tried to give Montezuma a heartfelt *abrazo,* having come so far and gone through so much to meet him. But Cacama and Cuitlahuac interceded to stop him, while from the nobles in the avenue rose a high-pitched wail in objection to this unheard-of behavior. So Cortés took from his own neck a chain of pearls and cut-glass beads, and Montezuma allowed the necklace to be placed around his neck.

They had a good look at each other, close up. Even a good smell. To Montezuma, Cortés's paleness and dark full beard must have seemed strange. But the emperor, who was used to appraising men, saw in Cortés the vigor of a man in the prime of life, strained and toughened by months of fighting and constant danger—and perhaps he could see the determination and daring in Cortés's eyes. To Cortés, Montezuma appeared as an older man who, although he may have been a fighter in his youth, was now pampered and long retired from fighting. Within the flamboyant Indian regalia, Montezuma was dark and thin, had his black hair cropped around his ears and cut straight across his forehead, and Cortés judged him to be more inclined to contemplation than action.

Montezuma hesitated, uncertain how to communicate. So he instructed Cuitlahuac to accompany Cortés, while Montezuma turned and, with Cacama attending him, went to some of the other nobles. Then, again, each noble in Montezuma's retinue approached and greeted Cortés, touching the ground, kissing his own hand. Before the whole assemblage moved up the avenue, servants brought to Montezuma two necklaces of red snail shells with eight exquisitely carved gold prawns attached to each necklace, and Montezuma placed these chains around Cortés's neck.

The Spaniards were led to a very large and beautiful palace, an extensive compound of low buildings with a large walled courtyard; it had been the home of Montezuma's dead father, Axayacatl; and gradually they were all installed, not only the Spaniards but their Indian allies who, as part of the embassy, were tolerated by the Aztecs. The Tlascalans, by now practiced, quickly set up the cannons in the courtyard with supplies of powder and shot at hand, but the Aztecs paid no attention to the defensive measures of so small a contingent deep within the stronghold of their empire. As Bernal Díaz wrote of the Tlascalans, "they were so numerous they could have blinded us with handfuls of earth," and this threat was obviously more enforceable by the Aztecs.

Since it was early afternoon, Montezuma left the Spaniards so that they could eat and rest, and he retired to do the same. (At the high altitude— Mexico City is 7,347 feet above sea level—the main meal is best eaten at midday and given ample time for digestion. Fortunately, since the Spaniards did not understand that the low oxygen content of rarefied air slows digestion, a large midday meal followed by a siesta happened to be the Spanish habit.) The Aztecs had provided everything for the Spanish army—a swarm of women to cook, servants to bring the many dishes, huge supplies of food, even fodder for the horses because the Indians had carefully observed the habits of the horses. So a banquet was served up, after which all the Spaniards except those on guard took a nap. Cortés liked with his meal a half-pint of wine cut with a half-pint of water. Whether or not it was sacramental wine that he drank is not known.

In the late afternoon (one of the pleasantest times of day in Mexico City, and this was at one of the pleasantest times of year; the day was the eighth of November, 1519) Montezuma with many nobles in attendance returned, and Cortés met him in the great hall of the palace. Montezuma had bearers unload his presents: many objects made of gold, jewels, silver, feather mantles, and fine, dyed, embroidered cotton tunics. Cortés thanked him and gave Spanish things in return.

Then Montezuma, with Malinche and Aguilar translating, delivered a speech of some length, a speech he had considered and prepared, which explained his thinking and feeling. This speech, however, invites interpretation and raises many questions. Surely Malinche was under stress simply to be in these circumstances. A slave girl, here she was being talked to by the great king who all through her life had been revered and feared as the most powerful force in existence; she could not have been free of fright. Her translation from Nahuatl into Mayan for Aguilar must have been stuttery and uncertain; even to be in Montezuma's presence must have astonished her. In turn, Aguilar's Mayan, although serviceable for all practical purposes, was in all likelihood inadequate to convey the nuances intended by the Aztec emperor. And Cortés, the ultimate recipient of this chain of communication, had his own fixed mind-set into which Montezuma's thoughts, stemming from an entirely different background and context, had to fit.

There are various accounts to go by: Cortés's letter to the king, which was the account closest in time to the incident; Gómara's account, given him by Cortés twenty-odd years later; Bernal Díaz's memoir, written about fifteen years after that; the recorded comments of several of the Spanish captains; and the works of the Franciscan fathers, Diego Durán and Bernardino de Sahagún, which were written years after the conquest and were based on the testimony of Aztec priests. So all that is possible now is to try to apply to this speech the calipers of reasonableness, in an effort to fathom its meaning. And this is worth doing because in the speech may lie an explanation for the subsequent conduct of Montezuma.

Cortés's interpretation is preposterous. What Cortés comprehended, what he heard or thought he heard or wanted to hear or, at least, what he related in his letter to the king, was a self-serving conglomeration of ideas and phrases from *Siete Partidas,* from the Bible, and even from traditional Spanish sayings. According to Cortés, Montezuma told the Spaniards that they should treat his father's house as their own. To Cortés this meant *"Aquí es su casa,"* which is a traditional Spanish expression to a guest, a typically Spanish exaggeration, "Here is your house." Whatever Montezuma had in mind, he could hardly have intended to express himself like a Spanish gentleman. And Cortés was pleased to take this courtesy literally, as if Montezuma were legally turning over the premises to him.

In Montezuma's formal speech—and the sequence of topics varies between Cortés's close-in-time letter to the king and Cortés's recollection to Gómara a quarter-century later—he explained that he had discouraged the Spaniards from coming to Tenochtitlán because his people were frightened by stories about the Spaniards and about their horses that ate people and their guns that cast killing bolts of lightning and belched thunder. But he assured the Spaniards that he himself was under no such delusions. He knew they were mortal men like himself, that the horses were animals like deer, and that the cannons and firearms were like blowguns.

This was a little deflating to the Spaniards, because they liked to believe that all Indians regarded them as gods; this was the way the Spaniards chose to understand the term *teules*. The Spaniards, having first heard this notion expressed by the island Indians, found it amusing; and among the common run of Indians this belief in the Spaniards' divinity occasionally seemed to be held.

Montezuma, according to all accounts, lifted his garments to show his naked body and declared that obviously he was mortal, like them. Something of the sort undoubtedly happened, but there is a striking similarity between this gesture by Montezuma and statements in the Bible (Jesus to his disciples, "A spirit hath not flesh and bones as ye see me have," as well as statements by Paul and Barnabas). So whatever Montezuma intended by his gesture was made to conform to the precepts from the Bible that the Spaniards had in their minds.

Montezuma went on to tell them that he knew what nonsense about him they must have heard from his enemies, the Tlascalans, and from the Zempoalans, who had rebelled against him. "But I shall clip their wings," Montezuma stated flatly. He said the Spaniards must have been told that, in addition to Montezuma himself being a god, in Tenochtitlán the buildings were made of gold and the accumulated treasure was infinite. All this was silly. The pyramids, he told them, were made of mud and had stone facing. The houses were made of mud and wood and sometimes stone. The treasure in gold and jewels, which was the accumulation of all the Aztec kings, was limited.

Montezuma told the Spaniards, or so they understood him, that the Aztec people were not native to this land, that in misty past time they had come here, led by a great chieftain who for some reason left his people to go back where he had come from, then returned and wanted again to lead the people and to take them elsewhere, but the Aztecs had interbred here with the local Indians and were prospering and they would not obey their "natural lord." So the natural lord had gone to the coast and had sailed away to the east with the promise that one day he would return again and resume his rule.

Obviously Montezuma was recounting the story of Quetzalcoatl. But there were two versions of the Quetzalcoatl legend. In one version, Quetzalcoatl was purely a god, companion of the other creator-gods of Aztec mythology; all were represented by fantastic-faced idols throughout Mexico. Chief among these gods was the ferocious Huitzilopochtli, whose eagle had descended on a fruited cactus to indicate where Tenochtitlán should be founded and who demanded sacrifices in human blood. Quetzalcoatl, the Feathered Serpent who was satisfied with sacrifices of doves and partridges, was god of the air, wind and light. In the other version, Quetzalcoatl, a man who may have been named for the god, was the semi-legendary, quasi-historical chief of the Toltecs, an ancient people (long gone) who had built the city of Tula north of Mexico City and probably the great ceremonial center of Teotihuacán outside Mexico City. The lofty pyramids of Teotihuacán were already covered by windblown dirt and were grassy mounds in the time of Cortés. Finally the Toltecs had trekked to the Yucatán, where they had built the Toltec/Mayan city of Chichén Itzá—and it was from there that Quetzalcoatl had departed. Quetzalcoatl, the Toltec chieftain, was said to have been pale and bearded. So the story of Quetzalcoatl that Montezuma told the Spaniards was the semi-historical version about a god-imbued man (god-imbued or else he would not have been chief and had the successes that he had) who may possibly have been the progenitor of Montezuma's line.

Montezuma was happy to regard Cortés and the Spaniards, who came from the east, as descendants of Quetzalcoatl. The previous visits of white men (the expeditions of Hernández de Córdoba and Grijalva) had been reported to Montezuma and he had wanted to meet them. Now he was pleased to have the white men come as guests to his capital and, from what had been told him about Cortés's lectures, he thought it was likely that the great king of whom Cortés spoke was, in fact, the direct descendant of Quetzalcoatl, Montezuma's forebear, especially since Cortés said that the great king knew of Montezuma and the Aztec people. Montezuma was careful to add, "if you are not deceiving or tricking us."

This rationalistic view of Montezuma's speech to the Spaniards is in contradiction to the testimony of the Aztec priests that Sahagún and Durán collected years after the conquest. The Aztec priests told them that Montezuma was terrified by a prophecy that Aztec rule was coming to an end and that all would be lost. There had been a portent—a comet in the sky that in the first flush of dawn seemed to hang over Tenochtitlán. Montezuma had bemoaned this awful omen, which had been interpreted for him by the king of Texcoco, another city in the Aztec confederation.

Montezuma's reception of the Spaniards, according to the Aztec priests, was in acquiescence to this awful prophecy. These Aztec priests, however, were testifying in Nahuatl to Franciscans who had made themselves bilingual. And the Aztec priests were already, in the aftermath of the conquest, accommodating and encompassing the fact of the conquest. What seems faulty in their presentation is that the omen they described—the comet in the sky—had occurred ten years before the coming of the Spaniards, during the reign of that particular king of Texcoco. And it is unreasonable to think that whatever effect the omen had upon Montezuma would have lasted for ten years and would not have been obliterated by the unbroken string of Aztec triumphs during that decade.

(It may be pointed out that religious mythologies—whether they result from the course of human evolution in Eurasia or in the Americas or elsewhere—have in common a tendency to rely upon metaphors and allegories. The Aztec priests after the conquest were retelling their stories, adapting their metaphors, allegories and allusions, reweaving the tapestry of their tales to absorb and include the conquest.)

Cortés especially approved of Montezuma's description of Quetzalcoatl as the "natural lord" of the Aztecs (if such a concept as "natural lord" could have come from Montezuma). "Natural lord" was a term familiar to and used by the Spaniards. And Cortés confirmed to Montezuma that the king of Spain was indeed the natural lord. Furthermore, if the mantle could be spread a bit, Cortés himself, if he could be labeled a "natural lord" as defined in *Siete Partidas,* would be entitled to a larger share of the profit from this conquest.

It also pleased Cortés's legalistic mind that Montezuma, by saying that his people were not native to this land, was confessing to being an usurper. So Montezuma could not claim legitimacy if he chose not to yield his authority to the king of Spain. On the contrary, according to the Quetzalcoatl legend, the king of Spain would be the legitimate ruler.

Reasonably, Montezuma may be viewed as saying whatever seemed advantageous to himself from his own point of view, while Cortés derived from Montezuma's speech whatever seemed advantageous for the Spanish undertaking. Obviously Montezuma was suspicious and skeptical, as he made clear when he qualified all he said by adding, "if you are not deceiving or tricking us." But even so, he would still deal with the Spaniards because they had shown themselves to be such good fighters, with such effective support from their gods. Earlier he had offered to reward Cortés and to promise to pay tribute to the king of Spain, so he was not making a further concession. And one payment or two from Montezuma's huge treasury would mean little. If Cortés could be induced to go away, Montezuma would have a breathing spell to think over what to do next and to consult his own gods and auguries.

It is scarcely credible that Montezuma was afraid of the Spaniards. Montezuma had drawn them all the way onto this island from which they could not escape. He knew about their horses and guns and was confident that he could overwhelm them whenever he chose. But he was intensely curious about them. The amount of treasure at stake seemed insignificant to him. Cagily, he was negotiating with these ambassadors, and from his point of view it was the Spaniards who had come from the nether side of the earth. He was even offering them a peaceful resolution to their invasion of his land, a resolution that would be temporary if he changed his mind, or that might involve a permanent arrangement whereby he would continue to pay tribute to a formidable white-skinned tribe. To pay tribute was an arrangement the Indians were familiar with and with which they were comfortable.

Cagily, Cortés—with expansive Spanish courtesy, and from his own point of view—accepted with thanks the kind hospitality of this blood-besotted, heathen, cannibal king.

THE STRATEGIES OF MONTEZUMA AND CORTÉS

For five nights Montezuma prayed. He was devout by nature. He had always sensed a divine presence. Without acknowledgment of that presence, he could not explain the achievement and glory of his people. He prayed to Huitzilopochtli, the god of the Aztecs, founder-god of Tenochtitlán. Huitzilopochtli was Montezuma's god, the god Montezuma had served when a young man. Huitzilopochtli was the divine drum-beater, the god of war, the god who had given Aztecs their strength. And their luck. Montezuma would not pray to Quetzalcoatl, the windy god; Montezuma disdained praying to the god of the Cholulans. Quetzalcoatl was the god of the unremembered Toltecs, the god of craftsmen. To Huitzilopochtli Montezuma fervently prayed—prayed that Huitzilopochtli would send him a sign to indicate what he should do. These strangers who had come to Mexico were different from all the human beings Montezuma had ever known or seen. If Montezuma were to command their annihilation, would Huitzilopochtli continue to bless and favor the Aztecs? Or would Huitzilopochtli prefer that Montezuma deal with the strangers and learn the secrets of their flashing blow-tubes that made so much noise? Montezuma was certain that he could trade with these strangers; perhaps he could obtain from them some of these animals that carried them and could breed the horses in his zoo. These strangers were avid for gold. Why, Montezuma did not know. The Aztecs valued gold because it was ornamental and beautiful, and it was malleable and could easily be sculpted. But jadestones were rarer and more precious. Montezuma tried to grasp the meaning that gold had for the Spaniards, but the concept of money eluded him, even though quills filled with grains of gold were sometimes used to balance barter deals in the Aztec markets. That these strangers were god-imbued seemed likely, even obvious, to Montezuma. The strangers prayed to their gods—they knelt before the Cross (a symbol Montezuma found meaningless) and the figure of the Woman with Child (which he found puzzling). Both symbols were pallid and passive in Montezuma's eyes. Yet the strangers' gods had given them victories against enormous odds at Tabasco and Tlascala. Could the blessing of the strangers' meek gods be more potent than the blessing of Huitzilopochtli, the blessing that had inspired the Aztec empire? Montezuma didn't know—and he prayed for his god to guide him.

How Montezuma prayed—in the opinion of the Spaniards, when they learned of it—was hideous. The temple of Huitzilopochtli topped the highest pyramid in Tenochtitlán. In that temple each night, by torchlight, Montezuma would kneel before a horrific stone idol with an inhuman face, a nightmare figure. And Montezuma would pray only after his priests had sacrificed half a dozen young people, both male and female—slaves or prisoners of war or Indians of other tribes who had been delivered to the Aztecs as tribute with the expectation that they would be sacrificed. To the Spaniards (to whom all Indians looked alike) Montezuma seemed to be killing his own kind. But this was not the way it seemed to Montezuma, for whom the distinctions among Indians, the tribal differences, were the only means he had for distinguishing among the human beings he had known, the Aztecs and all others. Huitzilopochtli, according to tradition and according to the experience of the Aztecs as proved by their success, required human blood as the price for his attention: He demanded sacrifice in the most emotionally explosive way that could be devised. It was after the god's attention had been gained that Montezuma would pray. Meanwhile, Montezuma's priests would try to foretell the future by studying the entrails of doves and partridges. After Montezuma prayed, while the smell of fresh human blood remained heavy in the air and smoke rose from the torn-out human hearts on the braziers, while Huitzilopochtli was surely attentive, Montezuma, still kneeling, would think—because he knew that the god frequently sent his sign in the form of a thought.

In a room within the palace complex where the Spaniards were lodged, Cortés had a makeshift chapel set up, where Father Olmedo said Mass.

Montezuma, through Malinche and Aguilar, inquired who among the Spaniards were the brothers of Cortés, who were his captains, who were of noble birth, respectable or low-born. Then Montezuma sent appropriate gifts—for the *hidalgos* handsome gold sculptures and jewels, which were delivered by Aztec nobles; lesser gifts for the soldiers, delivered by Montezuma's attendants; trifles for the Spanish sailors and the few servants, delivered by Indian lackeys. Both the Aztecs and the Spaniards assumed that social stratification existed. Neither side of the world was egalitarian.

At first, Cortés cautioned his men not to leave the palace complex until they learned more about the way they would be treated. Promptly he put the whole army to work, fortifying the complex, closing off entrances, limiting access, building platforms for the cannons, trying to protect the flammable thatch that roofed the servants' areas, assigning vantage-points to the harquebusiers and crossbowmen. The Aztecs, however, continued to ignore the Spaniards' activities, as if they were insignificant.

During the days Aztec nobles followed by large retinues would call upon the Spaniards, and the nobles escorted groups of Spanish captains and soldiers about the great city, which was estimated to have three hundred thousand to five hundred thousand inhabitants. Cortés always insisted that a strong guard should remain at the complex that served as their quarters. Proudly, gravely, proceeding at a stately pace through the streets, the Aztec nobles showed off the handsome palaces where the lords lived. Montezuma insisted that subject lords should maintain residences in the capital and, when the lords were not present, that their wives and children should remain, which was an effective hostage arrangement utilized by many monarchs on both sides of the world.

The palace in which Montezuma was living (he had many residences throughout the city and country) was not far from the Spaniards' quarters. In Montezuma's palace the Spaniards were shown the state in which Montezuma lived—the guard of three thousand warriors that was always on hand, the cordons through which a visitor had to pass even to approach the emperor's residence, the great hall where Montezuma heard petitions and resolved disputes. Thousands of servants waited upon the king. Hundreds of dishes would be prepared for each meal, from which Montezuma would choose—upon the chefs' recommendations—the few he would deign to taste. His women would serve him his drinks. At mealtimes a few elder chiefs would sit with Montezuma but the chiefs seldom spoke. Occasionally, as an act of favor, Montezuma would allow them to taste the food from one of his dishes. And while Montezuma ate, he was amused by foot-jugglers who kept large logs spinning in the air and by jesters who were dwarfs or deformed cripples. But there was no overt levity in the monarch's court. Rigid decorum was enforced, because the Aztecs felt that dignity demanded gravity, which was the acceptable evidence of fear.

The Spaniards were shown the zoo where wild animals were kept, animals that were said to feed on the torsos of humans who had been sacrificed. These animals included roaring, snarling and screaming pumas and jaguars, as well as deadly rattling snakes which the Spaniards had never seen before. The Spaniards were taken to visit an aviary where fierce birds of prey were kept and another aviary where birds of gorgeous plumage were raised and plucked. The Spaniards were shown (and made special note of) the treasuries where the tribute was stored—gold, silver and jewels—and the armories adjoining the temple-topped pyramids. The Spaniards noticed that the people of Tenochtitlán did not go about armed; the Aztec nobles said that only when the gods were threatened or when Montezuma issued a call to go to war were arms issued to the populace at large.

The Spaniards were especially impressed by the huge and orderly market-place, which was strictly policed, regulated and taxed (a flat 20 percent sales tax went to the Aztec lords) and where sixty thousand people gathered daily and the exchange of an enormous amount of merchandise took place. Trains of bearers from distant provinces brought in food and wares, while people came by canoe from all the surrounding cities and villages. Food of all kinds was abundant, although it seemed to Bernal Díaz that the lowliest people got very little; yet fear kept them obedient. Slaves were traded in the market. Tobacco, which the Spaniards had never seen, was sold in paper tubes, to be lighted and the smoke inhaled after eating. All kinds of medicinal herbs were offered. In one section of the market, people from a nearby town prepared featherwork cloaks and curtains, setting each feather precisely in place, and the Spaniards thought the pictures these craftsmen made with the brilliant feathers were wonderfully realistic. In another section of the market, goldsmiths and jewelers worked on their sculptures until the reproductions, to the Spaniards' eyes, seemed flawless. Of these Indian artisans, Cortés observed and later said to Gómara, "Few nations have such patience, especially short-tempered ones, like ourselves."

The hoop on the side of what the Spaniards called a *pelota* court, an Indian ball court. Around the rim of the stone hoop are commemorative inscriptions.

The Aztec nobles without explanation showed the Spaniards their ossuary, a kind of theatre of the dead, in which, set on tiers and pegged to poles, were exhibited over 136,000 skulls of warriors whom the Aztecs had captured and sacrificed. Andrés de Tápia with a couple of other Spaniards later went back and counted the skulls, not including those that had been conglomerated with mortar and used to make two towers.

What attracted an instant, sympathetic response from the Spaniards were the ball games. In neighborhoods throughout Tenochtitlán—and in cities throughout Mexico—there were ball courts as carefully constructed as ancient Greek theatres; these rectangular ball courts had banked, elegantly made stone stands for spectators and end-walls with niches for idols and carved symbol-stones. The game was played with a rubber ball that seemed wonderfully bouncy to the Spaniards, and the players would knock the ball about with their hips, knees, feet and heads (not the hands), the aim being to send the ball through a vertical stone hoop; stone hoops were mounted at midcourt on both sides. It was a very difficult, low-scoring game because the hoops were high and the holes in them were small. The players, who were indefatigable even at the high altitude, wore pads for protection against the solid ball and each other, and people who filled the stands gaily cheered. The Spaniards quickly caught on to the game; they understood less the rituals that went with it; but in sports Aztecs and Spaniards found pleasurable common ground.

In all, the Spaniards were treated as if they were a visiting embassy temporarily staying in the city: At Montezuma's direction, his nobles were showing them the sights. To Montezuma and the Aztec lords, this seemed to be the courteous and sensible thing to do, to provide these ambassadors with pleasure and at the same time to impress them. That this embassy of weirdly bearded, white-skinned men was being accommodated within the capital, that the strangers had had the temerity to come to the very heart of the empire, was to the Aztecs obvious evidence that a course of peace had been decided upon by both peoples—themselves and these strangers. Still, the vivaciousness and jocularity of the Spaniards somewhat disconcerted the Aztec nobles. As the Spaniards became more used to the atmosphere of Tenochtitlán, they joked and swaggered and flung themselves about in a way that conflicted with the Indians' notion of propriety.

At night, while Montezuma was praying, Cortés was scheming. What was he to do with his few hundred men in the midst of this metropolis? They were utterly dependent upon Montezuma's goodwill, which might be withdrawn at any moment. If the bridges were lifted, the Spaniards would be isolated. If food were not delivered to them, they would starve. And they were so outnumbered that if every inhabitant of this place were to throw a single stone, they could be wiped out. Cortés knew what he wanted— but he groped for the means by which to advance his cause.

The emotional make-up of the two peoples was markedly different. Despite the periodic outbursts of the Aztecs, despite their ferocity in war and the violence of their sacrificial rites, and despite the whimsical delight the Indians took in featherwork and flowerwork and in their many games and dances (delight which remains so charming in Mexicans today), the Indians in general and the Aztecs in particular were deliberate and very slow to change. In contrast, the Spaniards were impulsive and quick, eager to improvise and invent, and practical rather than whimsical.

One night when Cortés was pacing about his quarters, he happened to notice a wall that had been freshly limed and that seemed newly built. So, by torchlight, he had some of his men bring iron crowbars and break through this wall—and they came upon a series of windowless, closed-off chambers in which the treasure of Axayacatl, Montezuma's father, was stored. In the rooms were stacks of chests filled with jewels, all kinds of goldwork, heaps of feathercloaks. Cortés and his captains were amazed by the limitlessness of the wealth. But, for the present, they were overburdened with the gifts they had already been given. So Cortés ordered that the treasure-rooms should not be disturbed and that the wall should be put back together and fresh lime applied.

On the morning of the Spaniards'. fourth day in Tenochtitlán, Cortés asked to be received by Montezuma. His request granted, Cortés with several of his captains and several soldiers went to Montezuma's palace. Cortés had a way of joking with Montezuma which Montezuma seemed not to resent; in fact, the emperor seemed to like the Spaniards' informality. Montezuma was perhaps the only one in the empire who felt that he could afford to tolerate any deviation from strict observance of protocol: downcast eyes, respectful silence, a show of obedience and fear. Such behavior did not suit Spaniards—not any of them, not even the lowliest. So, after some banter, Cortés told Montezuma that he and his captains would like to visit the great temple of Huitzilopochtli atop the highest pyramid in the capital. Montezuma hesitated; this was his sanctum. But he agreed and said that in the afternoon he himself would escort the Spaniards on their visit.

This was more cumbersome than had been the previous outings with the Aztec nobles and their retinues. Montezuma traveled in a litter. The Spaniards—Cortés and some of his captains and about a hundred harquebusiers and crossbowmen—were enveloped by the regal entourage. In the temple courtyard at the foot of the huge pyramid Montezuma got down from his litter and asked the Spaniards to wait while he first ascended and spoke to his priests. The pyramid had one hundred fourteen steps, a few less than the great pyramid at Cholula, but these difficult steps were not uniform. Montezuma was helped by many of his attendants. And after a short wait the Spaniards were invited to ascend.

Then down the temple steps came running a swarm of Aztec priests.

Instantly sharp words passed—Cortés's tone made clear his meaning. He would not allow the priests to touch or even to come close to the Spaniards. The captains had their hands on the hilts of their swords; the harquebusiers and crossbowmen deployed and were ready. The Spaniards knew how the priests would hold down a victim for sacrifice with a priest clutching each arm and leg. But these priests had been instructed by Montezuma to assist his visitors on the arduous climb, and the priests in confusion backed away. When the Spaniards reached the top, which wasn't easy for them because many were chafed on the insides of their thighs from marching and others had blisters, boils and abscesses on their legs and feet, Montezuma said that he hoped the climb had not tired the Spaniards. To which Cortés replied that Spaniards never tired.

Montezuma pointed out the view—the glorious panorama of Tenochtitlán, the city with its hundreds of lesser towers, the roof gardens, the network of canals and the lakes. It was the finest view of the city the Spaniards had had. Some of the interlinked lakes surrounding the capital being fresh water and some salt, it was a feat attempted by Aztec engineering to separate the lakes with causeways in which there were adjustable sluices and with segmented dikes to achieve a degree of flood control. On the glittering surface of the lakes was a great array of canoes. None of the lake water was drinkable; even the fresh-water lakes were too brackish. A stone aqueduct containing two huge pottery pipes brought spring water to the capital from the hill of Chapultepec on the farther shore, the potable water running in crystalline channels all through the capital and crossing the canals in smaller pottery pipes. From the banks of the salt lakes the Aztecs collected the salt and prepared bricks of it that were traded throughout Mexico, except with the Tlascalans. On the fresher water floated the artificial gardens the Aztecs knew how to make, with crops planted in soil deposited on interwoven thickets. The Spaniards were profoundly admiring, as Montezuma expected them to be. (Aztec priests after the conquest maintained that Tenochtitlán was founded in 1325 with the landing of Huitzilopochtli in the guise of an eagle, and this date is generally accepted as the time of the founding, yet such a date seems unreasonable because two centuries would not be enough for people without iron tools to build a city of such size, complexity and cultural refinement; this island in the valley of Mexico must have been inhabited for a far longer period of time.)

Then Montezuma showed them the interior chambers of the temple. He showed them the fearsome bejeweled monolith of Huitzilopochtli, black with dried human blood, with awesome eyes glowing though obscured by clots, and the statue of Tezcatlipoca, Huitzilopochtli's brother, and another idol made of seeds and dough from which all life was said to spring. A small army of priests stood by. (It is interesting to realize that no statues at all of Huitzilopochtli or Tezcatlipoca have endured, and of course none of the dough-god. Images of other gods, like Tlaloc, the rain god, have endured, particularly in the lowland, but none of the two chief Aztec deities. This may be coincidental, or evidence of thorough Christian eradication, but the thoroughness of the eradication was likely assured by some of the highland Indians themselves who were acutely disappointed in the failure of their own gods to support them.)

Cortés, as always, was sickened by the sight of the idols and began to explain to Montezuma that he should worship the true God and that even better fortune would come to him, but Father Olmedo tugged at Cortés's sleeve to dissuade him. So Cortés asked Montezuma if a small area within the temple might be cleared where the Spaniards could set up their Cross and the figurine of Mary; he even implied that, were the Spaniards allowed to do this, there would be a tacit competition between Montezuma's idols and the true God—and Montezuma could then see which force would prevail. But Montezuma became indignant and said no, he would not allow the Spaniards to intrude upon the sanctuary of his gods. And they must leave now. Nor would he accompany them, as in courtesy he should, because he had to stay and propitiate his gods for the indignity to which he had exposed them.

So down the steps the Spaniards went—and Cortés had the unhappy awareness that several more victims were about to be sacrificed to atone for his brashness.

On their fifth day in Tenochtitlán Cortés thought of the means by which he might advance his cause. And on the sixth day he acted.

Cortés had in his possession a letter that had been brought to him in Cholula; it was from Pedro de Ircio, who had succeeded Juan de Escalante as commander of the fort at Villa Rica on the coast. A few Spaniards had been killed (seven or nine; the accounts vary). Apparently the Zempoalans had induced fifty Spaniards from Villa Rica to go with them to another town where there were Nahuatl-speaking Indians who were historic enemies of the Zempoalans and were willing vassals of Montezuma, the purpose being to force the Nahuatl-speaking Indians to renounce their allegiance to Montezuma and to pay some tribute in gold to the king of Spain, with a percentage going to the Zempoalans. In the fight that ensued, Juan de Escalante and several other Spaniards had been killed; the Spaniards had been defeated; and the chief of the Nahuatl-speaking Indians, named Qualpopoca, remained defiant and, according to Pedro de Ircio, had announced to the countryside that he had been ordered by Montezuma himself to kill the strangers. The defeat of the Spaniards had upset the whole region, because now all the Totonac people, including the Zempoalans, were doubting the Spaniards' invincibility and were wondering which way they should turn. Deliveries of food to the fort were uncertain—and the Spaniards were fishing from their dinghies.

Sending word to Montezuma that he had to see him on a matter of great importance, Cortés left half his force to guard their quarters, and he led out the other half, heavily armed. He posted groups of harquebusiers and crossbowmen at critical street corners on the way to Montezuma's palace; other groups he placed in Montezuma's courtyards. Although the Spaniards always went about armed, now they hid their arms under their cloaks and tried to dissemble so as not to alert the Aztec guard. With thirty captains and soldiers Cortés entered Montezuma's reception hall.

Even then, with the letter from Pedro de Ircio in his pocket and his strategy determined, Cortés joked with Montezuma. They joked about women. Montezuma's palace, Tecpan, was maintained by a thousand (or three thousand) women, including his high-born wives and all the daughters of subject lords who had been given him. Cortés asked him how many women he kept pregnant at one time, and Montezuma replied about a hundred fifty. Montezuma summoned a young girl he said was one of his own daughters and gave her to Cortés, but Cortés declined with the excuse that he was married and God allowed him only one wife (though he may already have impregnated Malinche) and Cortés turned the girl over to Pedro de Alvarado, who was a bachelor and ever-willing. This was the kind of badinage Montezuma liked and was used to from the sassy white men.

Then Cortés took out the letter from Pedro de Ircio and read it very slowly to Montezuma, allowing Aguilar and Malinche ample time for full translation. Cortés emphasized Qualpopoca's assertion that he had killed the Spaniards on orders from Montezuma. But, Cortés confided to Montezuma, he was sure that Qualpopoca was a liar. Montezuma would never have given such orders. Montezuma was host to this embassy from the king of Spain, and tribute-sharing was being discussed. Cortés could not believe that Montezuma would be so perfidious.

Vehemently Montezuma denied ever having given orders that the Spaniards should be opposed. He called for some of his nobles and, taking from his wrist a sealstone of Huitzilopochtli, he gave them the seal and told them to send to the coast for Qualpopoca, to have him brought to the capital, and, if he resisted, to call up Aztec armies from towns Montezuma specified to overwhelm Qualpopoca and force him to obey.

All of which was fine, Cortés said, but, until this matter was resolved, Montezuma would have to come with the Spaniards and stay in the palace where they were living. He would be treated with the utmost courtesy and with the love that all the Spaniards, who were grateful for his generosity, felt for him. But he had to come with them because, otherwise, the king of Spain would not excuse Cortés for failing to take action in response to the murder of the Spaniards. From Axayacatl's house Montezuma could and should continue to rule his domain, hear disputes, render his judgments, in short, conduct all his customary business.

This was a stroke so daring that Cortés had a hard time getting out his words. He sometimes paused and for a minute or two said nothing—then went on.

And Montezuma understood that he would not be at liberty. The holding of a great lord for ransom or advantage was a familiar tactic in medieval Europe. It was a familiar tactic in ancient Greece and Persia. It was not a familiar tactic in Mexico, where defeat and the sacrifice-stone were nearly simultaneous. Montezuma—shocked, puzzled and hurt—replied that he could not be taken prisoner.

But Cortés pulled closer his bench, and for four hours he and Montezuma—with Aguilar and Malinche standing by and translating—discussed this novel prospect. Cortés assured Montezuma that he would not be a prisoner but an honored guest. Would a prisoner be allowed to administer his empire? Cortés wanted, insisted, that Montezuma should maintain the continuity of his reign. Over and over and round about they went. It would not be strange for Montezuma to stay for a while in the house of his dead father, would it? If every day his nobles would come to receive his instructions?

The fact was that Montezuma had not yet had a sign from Huitzilopochtli. So after four hours of cajoling, bargaining and wheedling, Cortés prevailed, and Montezuma consented to become the ward of the Spaniards.

CONQUEST BY GUILE

For five months Cortés got by with it: conquest of the Aztec empire through cleverness, through adroit diplomacy, through pressure and manipulation, by the use of wit and guile—without having to fight and with minimal bloodshed.

The transfer of Montezuma to the Spaniards' stronghold was quickly accomplished. Montezuma, after consenting to come, gave instructions that a suitable chamber in the house of his dead father should be prepared for him, which was done within an hour by scores of scurrying servants. Then Montezuma, escorted by Cortés and the Spanish captains, was carried in his litter from his own palace to the Spaniards' quarters. Word was passed that on the next day Montezuma would hold court in the place from which his father had ruled. This was not unseemly; it could even be viewed as respectful.

Yet the Aztec nobles who attended Montezuma—and there were hundreds of them—were shaken. Warriors were seen racing around the city. In a distant neighborhood a drum began to beat. Worried people crowded the streets—because there had been a deviation from the deliberate routine of Aztec life. Something untoward had happened, which could be an ill omen.

Montezuma himself took steps to quiet the distress. To his nobles he affirmed that he made this move of his own volition. And Cortés continued to emphasize that Montezuma would continue to rule, that this arrangement was only temporary until the Qualpopoca matter was cleared up, that Cortés and the king of Spain wanted Montezuma to rule, that it would be Montezuma's destiny to rule not only over his own empire but over all the lands that Cortés and other agents of the king of Spain would conquer and add to the Aztec domain. Cortés never slackened with these reassurances.

Promptly Cortés sought to divert attention from what the Spaniards regarded as Montezuma's arrest, what Montezuma himself probably regarded as his concession to these strangers. Ever since Cortés had seen all the canoes on the Mexican lakes, he had been acutely aware of danger from the water: If the bridges were taken away, the Spaniards would be surrounded and cut off on the island, and they could be attacked by Indian warriors coming in canoes from the lakeside cities and towns and infiltrating the capital on the network of canals. So Cortés explained to Montezuma that he intended to build four brigantines—the kind of ships, though smaller, in which he and his soldiers had crossed the ocean. Montezuma was intrigued and placed battalions of Indian laborers at the Spaniards' disposal. Cortés put in charge Spaniards who were experienced shipbuilders. While the Indians were felling trees and trimming planks, the Spaniards began to steambend the timbers to form the hulls. Cortés sent to Villa Rica for some fittings and tackle that had been stripped from the ships he had destroyed.

Also, Cortés told Montezuma that the Spaniards wanted to see where the gold came from. Montezuma replied that most of the gold came from three different locations; if the Spaniards were curious about the sources of the gold (which they were), he would have his chiefs guide them to the mines, for the mines were distant. Cortés was reluctant to disperse his small force, but for such a worthwhile project he would do so and he chose Spaniards who were familiar with mining and assigned them in groups of three or four to go and see the gold *in situ*. These small groups of Spaniards then went off to unknown destinations with Aztec chiefs as guides and with trains of warrior-bearers, without interpreters, on trips that were expected to take more than a month. Very soon these little knots of Spaniards were trekking through mountains and jungles among dangerous, alien people. These venturesome Spaniards were stiff with fear—yet they went without balking. All the Spaniards, all of them, were borne along on the crest of their daring.

Cortés asked Montezuma where on the east coast there was a good harbor where ships crossing the ocean could anchor and be safe from storms. Montezuma did not know since he had never had any need for harbors, but he understood Cortés's interest and readily cooperated. Montezuma dispatched his best artists to map the coast and to draw pictures of all the inlets and river mouths where the great ships might rest. Montezuma thought that perhaps the king of Spain, if there were such a person, would come—and Montezuma could negotiate with him. At the least, trade would be developed for all the odd and often useful commodities of these strangers. And if more white-skinned warriors—nobles, captains and soldiers—were to come, if the human nature of these strangers was similar to the nature of the Indians with which Montezuma was familiar, who knows what dissension and strife among the white men might erupt? This kind of thinking had to be in the mind of a seasoned Aztec king. Montezuma knew that, twice before Cortés, other Spaniards had come; inevitably more would come; and rivalries were almost sure to develop.

Of course Montezuma was aware—every moment he was aware—and Cortés was aware—that with a whispered word he could bring about the Spaniards' end and the end of this whole unprecedented encounter. But Montezuma chose not to give this word. In the audiences that he held in the great hall of his father's house where the Spaniards were lodged, Montezuma was meticulous and careful, as he always had been; he showed no evidence whatever of being fearful or coerced; he continued to reign customarily, habitually, firmly and with dignity, as he always had. Montezuma never hesitated to impose his will on his subjects. So, despite the stricken looks that sometimes came over the faces of his nobles, and despite the buzzing in the marketplace and the whispering on the rooftops in the rose-glow of Mexican evenings, life in the Aztec capital went on without disruption.

Twenty-odd years later, when Cortés reflected and passed on his reflections to Gómara, his conclusion was that Montezuma was a man of little courage, fearful for his own life, and this was why Montezuma did not call up his forces for a battle in which he himself, as well as all the Spaniards, might have perished. But at the time of Montezuma's detention Cortés did not feel this way. Nor did he so describe Montezuma when he wrote his second letter to the king. And the facts suggest that there could be an interpretation of the behavior of the Aztec emperor quite different from Cortés's eventual recollection.

In his youth Montezuma had served for a few years as a priest, which was the tradition for young Aztec nobles; then he had been a vigorous war-leader; and later, as emperor, he had aggressively extended his domain. Montezuma was not afraid of risking his own life; he had done so many times in battle. It is an unsympathetic Spanish view—a view that is self-serving in that it indirectly compliments the courage of the Spaniards—to think that the purpose of Montezuma's inaction was to preserve his own life. It is more reasonable to believe that Montezuma decided to play out and to further his association with these remarkable strangers who intrigued and amused him. In Montezuma's eyes, and according to Cortés's own words in his letter to the king, what was actually taking place was essentially what Montezuma had proposed—a trial partnership, an agreed-upon peace between the Aztecs and the Spaniards. Montezuma had already offered to reward Cortés and to pay tribute to the king of Spain: in effect, to share the tribute which Montezuma received from his empire. In return, Montezuma expected to learn the secrets of these strangers and to benefit from his association with them.

Twenty days after Montezuma moved to the Spaniards' quarters, Qualpopoca arrived in Tenochtitlán. He was, it appeared, a great lord, for he came in a litter, accompanied by his sons and some of his nobles. There had been no trouble in having him come. Montezuma's messengers had simply shown him the sealstone and told him that Montezuma wanted him—and Qualpopoca, as Montezuma's vassal, had complied. In an audience with Montezuma, Qualpopoca admitted that he had killed the Spaniards. When Montezuma turned him over to Cortés, Qualpopoca made the same admission. In private, Cortés asked him if he had acted on orders from Montezuma—and Qualpopoca said no, although he was rather indefinite because Montezuma's orders had been vague. When Cortés asked Qualpopoca conclusively if he were indeed a vassal of Montezuma, Qualpopoca replied by asking who else's vassal could he be when there was no lord as great as Montezuma.

Cortés sentenced Qualpopoca and his sons and nobles to be burned at the stake. The sentence was carried out in the public marketplace. There are two accounts of the execution. According to one account, when Qualpopoca and his followers were burned, the crowds in the market were distracted from their haggling and dealing, not because a killing was going on, but because burning was to the Aztecs a novel way of killing. According to another account later rendered by a *conquistador,* after Qualpopoca and his followers were tied to the stakes, the Tlascalans killed them with a fusillade of arrows; then the bodies were burned, arrows and all. The first account seems more credible because it includes a description of the onlookers. Also, Aztecs probably would not have countenanced violence by their despised enemies, the Tlascalans.

Before the execution of Qualpopoca and his followers, they had all confessed—under torture applied during interrogation—that Montezuma had ordered them to resist and to kill the Spaniards, which was what Cortés reported to the king.

With careful calculation Cortés varied his approaches to Montezuma in an effort to unhinge or undermine or further to subvert the Aztec monarch. After Qualpopoca confessed, Cortés went to Montezuma, denounced him for his treachery and had chains put on him. Montezuma was furious. At that moment, the partnership of the Aztecs and the Spaniards nearly ended. Montezuma in his mind must have been considering how best to pass word to his people to rise up. But immediately after Qualpopoca's execution, which brought no reaction from the Aztecs, Cortés went back to Montezuma, removed the chains with his own hands, and begged the monarch's forgiveness—because, Cortés said, he had always trusted Montezuma and had never believed the lies of Qualpopoca that obviously were told only in a vain attempt to avoid just punishment.

On the coast the Totonacs and the other Indians quickly calmed down, once they heard that Qualpopoca and his followers had been killed. Deliveries of food to the Spaniards in the fort at Villa Rica resumed.

Within the context of the strange relationship between Montezuma and Cortés, occasionally Montezuma prevailed. When Cortés and some of his captains went again with Montezuma to the temple of Huitzilopochtli, Cortés in a burst of overconfidence announced that he wanted to knock down all the idols, whitewash the whole temple and set up the Christian symbols. He even tried to hustle Montezuma into compliance by ordering his men to begin to smash the idols. But Montezuma forbade it. And he would not yield. Montezuma told Cortés that these gods of old would remain in place, or else he and all his people would fight to the death to defend them. So Cortés backed down.

Montezuma devoutly believed that a contest between his gods and the Spaniards' gods was taking place. And he was not ready to concede that the Spaniards' gods had triumphed. Montezuma's strategy was that this whole accommodation might be temporary; he could change his mind at any time; and he had armies waiting to enforce his will. The steps to which he had so far consented meant little to him—to move into his father's house, to dispense some gold, to make gifts as was his custom, to indulge in prolonged talk which he enjoyed, even to agree to share some tribute. But he was not ready to destroy his gods.

Cortés in disgruntlement carried on against human sacrifice, and Montezuma, to pacify him, agreed to have the practice curtailed. But the truth the Spaniards learned was that, during the whole five months of Cortés's attempt to conquer by guile, the Aztec priests continued to conduct nightly sacrifices because never before had Montezuma so needed the gods' attention. And every night Montezuma—with Cortés's knowledge and permission—went to the temple of Huitzilopochtli and prayed.

With help from the Indian laborers, the brigantines were quickly finished (Cortés said there were four ships; Bernal Díaz said there were two). They were sloops, single-masted, and Cortés had the sails that were brought from the coast recut and the ships decorated with pennants and with awnings in the sterns. Each sloop could transport seventy-five men and a few horses. Cortés had cannons mounted in the bows. The Spanish sailors tested the ships, which proved to be fast and maneuverable. Then Cortés invited Montezuma to come for a ride, in fact to sail down the lake to an island that was reserved for the monarch's hunting. So in a cannon-nosed brigantine with harquebusiers and crossbowmen at the gunwales, propelled by a stiff breeze, Montezuma, lounging in the shade of the awning, sped down the lake, outdistancing by far his attendants who were being paddled in canoes. After the monarch debarked, Cortés had the cannons fired in salute, serving notice on the Aztec nation that the Spaniards were masters of the water.

The Spaniards tried to amuse Montezuma while they strengthened their grip on the country. When men of different cultures meet, they tend to behave toward each other as they would toward children—playing, mimicking, intentionally being silly. The Spaniards counted the hairs on Montezuma's chin; there were six to ten black bristles about an inch long. And Montezuma taught the Spaniards how to play *totoloque,* an Aztec game of pitch-and-toss that the Spaniards especially liked because Montezuma's *totoloque* set was made of pure gold. When Montezuma would play Cortés, however, while one of Montezuma's young nephews kept score for the monarch, Alvarado would keep score for Cortés—and Alvarado consistently cheated, making an extra mark whenever Cortés gained a point. This was obvious to Montezuma, who said so (the Aztecs had a word for cheating, *yxoxol*), but it was a laughing matter because, when Cortés won, he would give his winnings to Montezuma's attendants and, when Montezuma won, he would give his winnings to the Spanish soldiers. All the Aztecs admired and liked Alvarado, whom they called *tonatiuh,* "the Sun."

Montezuma also liked a Spanish boy named Orteguilla, who served as Cortés's page and who had come from Cuba with his father. Orteguilla was young enough to pick up Nahuatl the way children learn to speak, without having to translate, and, although not as dependable as Malinche and Aguilar, Orteguilla soon came to be an effective go-between.

Often Montezuma expressed a wish to visit one of his other houses in Tenochtitlán or on the far side of the lake. Cortés always obliged him, sending along an escort of Spanish captains and soldiers. Cortés even took to taunting the monarch by suggesting that he no longer need stay in the Spaniards' quarters since Qualpopoca had been punished. But this was a transparent mockery, as Montezuma knew, and Montezuma responded by saying that he preferred to stay with the Spaniards because, were he to return to his people, they would rally to him and he would be obliged to lead them against the Spaniards. So he chose not yet to move back to his palace. Whenever Cortés perceived a threat, he would remind Montezuma that the Spanish captains would kill him instantly if they were attacked.

When Orteguilla reported to Cortés that the collection of tribute from all the provinces was imminent, Cortés told Montezuma that he would like gold to be collected for the king of Spain, either as a share of the tribute or as a kind of surtax. This was agreeable to Montezuma; actually it was part of his plan. So a great deal of gold was brought to the capital and was duly turned over to the Spaniards.

Cortés wanted to keep this load of treasure intact; the Spaniards already had more than they could carry (and there was the treasure of Axayacatl on their premises, besides). But most of the soldiers were restless after months of inactivity; they worried that stored gold would disappear into the pockets of the captains and priests; and they wanted to divide it. So they did. They melted down the gold bars and grains and cast new bars, which were stamped. The gold, after being weighed, was estimated to be worth 600,-000 pesos or more. The silver likewise was melted down and recast. The jewels were set aside as priceless. But the actual division (without a Moor or Jew to act as purser or paymaster) resulted in a terrible squabble.

First, the royal fifth was deducted and set aside. Then Cortés's fifth was withdrawn. Then a schedule was followed by which the captains and priests got more than the horsemen, who got more than the harquebusiers and crossbowmen, who got more than the soldiers, who got more than the sailors. Besides, some gold had to be apportioned to repay mainly Velázquez and Cortés for the sums they had advanced for the fleet in the first place. Some gold had to be put aside for the men at Villa Rica, as well as gold for the men who had been sent to Spain, and some for those who had lost horses. So little was left for the common soldiers that many of them refused to take their shares, whereupon Cortés said that, as far as he was concerned, he would give any loyal comrade whatever the comrade felt he ought to have because, Cortés told them, this was only the beginning.

When the gambling began—not *totoloque* but Spanish gambling with a deck of handpainted cards a sailor from Valencia had made by cutting up drumskins—fights broke out among the Spaniards, and Cortés had to chain up a few, including Velásquez de León, until their tempers cooled. Thus the Aztecs were able to see how discipline among the Spaniards could disappear when the spoils were at issue.

As the days, weeks and months passed, the strains inevitable in the situation became more apparent. The Spaniards Cortés had sent to see the gold sites returned safely and reported that much more gold could be obtained if the Aztecs used better methods to obtain it; the Indians just scooped up the silt in gourds and, flushing the silt with water, picked out the grains of gold. In one place in Oaxaca a local chief had refused to allow the Aztecs to enter his territory; this local chief, who was not a vassal of Montezuma, traded with the Aztecs but distrusted and hated them. The local chief had invited only the Spaniards to enter, and the Spaniards, showing real pluck, had gone with him to his village, where they had been well treated, given some gold, and also given to understand that, if the Spaniards were to fight the Aztecs, these people would side with the Spaniards. Which pleased Cortés when he heard it, because it meant that opposition to the Aztecs was even more general than he had thought.

On the other hand, in the empire-wide tax collection that was going on, several Aztec chiefs, knowing that some of the gold to be collected was to go to the Spaniards, refused to pay tribute. One of these chiefs, who happened to be in the capital, left at night and returned to his home province. Throughout the empire Aztec chiefs were grumbling over Montezuma's toleration of the Spaniards, over his delivery of tribute to them, over his failure to serve the old gods in the old ways—and Montezuma could no longer rely on the Aztec habit of obedience.

The rebelliousness of the Aztec chiefs came to a head when Cacama, Montezuma's nephew, the lord of Texcoco, a city on the farther shore of the lake, openly defied Montezuma and declared war on the Spaniards. This was a hurtful blow to Montezuma. Often Cacama had come to him in Tenochtitlán and begged him to escape from the Spaniards and to join his own people in a battle to kill the strangers or to drive them from the land. Though Montezuma had been king for eighteen years, he seemed to have no legitimate son to succeed him, and Cacama regarded himself as the next in line to reign.

The matter of Montezuma's children is a little mysterious. In the chronicles, mention was made occasionally of Montezuma's sons, but either such sons seemed to be illegitimate and unable to succeed to the kingship or they were not Montezuma's offspring, because there was no clear heir apparent. Sahagún was later told by Aztec priests that succession was by consensus of the nobles rather than by primogeniture; still, direct descendancy seemed to be the preferred course, and the Aztec priests with whom Sahagún spoke had come to know that the Spaniards were devoted to bloodlines. Cortés in his second letter to the king mentioned that Montezuma had three sons, of whom one subsequently died, one was mad, and one was palsied, but this is difficult to reconcile with Montezuma's supposedly numerous progeny. Often Montezuma would refer to girls he gave to the Spaniards as his daughters, which they may or may not have been, and sometimes he would call them his nieces. But it remains difficult to believe that Montezuma, had he been able to sire an heir, would not have had a son who was recognized as ready for succession, or sons who were being considered for the succession, or bastard sons with aspirations.

Cortés wanted to respond to Cacama's rebellion by promptly marching on Texcoco with his army and the Tlascalans and whatever troops Montezuma would furnish. But Montezuma was more experienced than Cortés in the problems presented by fighting in this mountain valley and in the means available to solve these problems. Montezuma cautioned Cortés and explained that Texcoco was strongly situated at the lakeside and would be very difficult to attack. Approaches by land were narrow and few, and an approach by water would be fiercely resisted. In a frontal attack Cacama's people, Montezuma's people, the Spaniards and their allies, all would suffer greatly. Also, other nobles and other tribes might support Cacama, so general had the dissension become, and the rebellion might spread. But, Montezuma confided, there were several nobles close to Cacama who were loyal to Montezuma (actually they were Cacama's brothers). For many years Montezuma had regularly been sending them gifts. It was only natural for a ruler, any ruler, to be wary of a spirited nephew who held considerable power. Montezuma had maintained his arrangements with Cacama's brothers so that he might have recourse to them were Cacama's ambition ever to become excessive. Now what Montezuma proposed was to plot with these brothers to lure Cacama to a meeting in Texcoco at which Cacama would be seized, forced into a canoe, and brought to Tenochtitlán to account for his impudence.

Montezuma prevailed. Cortés held his own simpler impulses in abeyance. Montezuma sent a few trusted messengers across the lake to Texcoco. At the meeting set up by Cacama's brothers, Cacama was waylaid and brought back to Tenochtitlán—where Cortés had him put in irons. Then Montezuma and Cortés made one of Cacama's brothers the lord of Texcoco. In the following week Montezuma identified several other chiefs who were talking rebellion—and Cortés had them arrested and manacled, and all of them were attached to the same heavy chain to which Cacama was bound.

Proceeding in his customary style, Cortés went at night and talked to Cacama, recalling how they had pledged to be friends when they had first met, assuring Cacama that he was liked by all the Spaniards and that he would be well treated if he would only calm down. But Cacama railed against Cortés and all he stood for—his gods and the king of Spain—and Cacama in rage swore to take revenge.

As the sixth month of this strange, static period began—when the Spaniards were unopposed, even abetted, and violence was withheld—both Cortés and Montezuma realized that circumstances were reaching a breaking point.

Cortés wondered how he could get out. And get the gold out. How could he reestablish communication with the Caribbean islands and with Spain? How could he contact the world that he knew? He had not so lost his bearings that he envisioned himself living permanently in isolation in this barbaric place. But he did not know even if the treasure he had sent to the king had reached Spain. He did not know if the king had expressed any opinion on this independent venture he had fashioned. He did not know what was going on elsewhere in the Spanish world. But from the Aztecs Cortés felt the growing hatred of himself and his men—among the Aztec priests whose gods were being disserved, among the Aztec chiefs whose tribute was being diverted, among the Aztec people who were bewildered by the prolonged presence of strangers in their midst. Cortés knew that within Tenochtitlán, as well as in the lakeside cities and in the country towns, warriors were standing by, tens of thousands of them, probably more than a hundred thousand, tense with anticipation.

Montezuma knew better than Cortés how rampant was the desire of the Aztecs to attack the Spaniards. The Aztecs were the most violent people ever to achieve ascendancy in the valley of Mexico, and after six months of restraint they were desperately eager to break loose. The chaining of Cacama and the other chiefs who dissented from Montezuma's policy had only caused the flames of Aztec fury to spread. Repeatedly, Montezuma told Cortés that, were he (Montezuma) to leave the stronghold of the Spaniards, he would be forced by his own nobles to lead them against the Spaniards in a war to the death—the death of all the Spaniards and of many of his own people. If Montezuma would not lead them, he would be replaced. So Montezuma stayed where he was, within the Spanish camp, and he continued to tell his nobles that Huitzilopochtli was counseling him and was assuring him that the course he was following was the best course for his people.

Montezuma's motives will always remain mysterious. Perhaps he was sincerely convinced that he was obeying the will of his god. Perhaps Montezuma, like the experienced king he was, stubbornly was pursuing his own policy and continued to believe that he and his people would benefit by accommodating the Spaniards. Maybe Montezuma feared for his own life. Or perhaps he—a king without a male heir and possibly a childless man, possibly a sexually impotent man—had come to love the Spaniards and wanted a fusion between the Spaniards and the Aztecs to take place.

There is only indirect evidence to suggest that Montezuma may have been impotent. Malinche told Cortés, and Cortés later told Gómara, that the wellborn women in Montezuma's houses, when they became pregnant, would try to abort themselves by doing contortions and by taking herbal potions. Historically, this has not been the behavior of women impregnated by kings.

As Montezuma aged and his own life dwindled, he may have had a premonition that the Aztec empire would change and meld and become something different from what it had been. Montezuma believed in pre-destination.

Yet finally Montezuma went to Cortés and begged him to go, to leave Mexico. Montezuma told Cortés that his people could be restrained no longer. The ultimate indignity was that the Spaniards in a corner of the great temple of Huitzilopochtli had set up a Cross and the figure of Mary with Child—and the Aztec priests had rushed to Montezuma to say that Huitzilopochtli was being disgraced and to demand that Montezuma should drive out the Spaniards or kill them. Montezuma had not been able to appease the priests with his own interpretation of Huitzilopochtli's intent. All the priests had heard the command of their god—that the Spaniards must go.

Cortés played for time. Later, he wrote to the king that he had three options in mind: (1) to have ships built at Villa Rica with which to reestablish his connection to Santo Domingo, so that he could arrange for reinforcements of men, horses and fresh supplies; (2) to link up with the tribes that wanted him to defeat the Aztecs and to wrest from the Aztecs control of the whole empire, which was wishful thinking because the Spaniards were scattered and few and their supplies of powder and shot were low; and (3) to achieve a mass conversion of all the Aztec people, to smash all their idols, scrub the blood from their temples, ban human sacrifice and cannibalism throughout the empire, and institute Christian worship, all of which Cortés thought the king would be pleased to hear, though Cortés was afraid to begin a thorough cleansing even in the temple next door to his quarters.

What Cortés said in reply to Montezuma was that, as soon as a few ships could be built, he would comply with the monarch's request, grateful as he and all the Spaniards were to Montezuma for all the gifts they had been given and for the favors they had received and for the gold that had been given them for the king of Spain. Cortés ordered two Spanish shipbuilders to set out for the coast to begin the construction of the ships at Villa Rica. Montezuma assigned a battalion of Indian laborers to help out. Before the departure of the shipbuilders, however, Cortés took them aside and told them to go slow—because he was not about to abandon this rich country.

What brought to an end this period of artifice, this peculiar balance of peace, was the intrusion of a factor that neither Cortés nor Montezuma had anticipated. A fleet of eighteen ships was sighted off the east coast and came to anchor at San Juan de Ulúa. Drawings of the fleet were brought to the highland by runners who went straight to Montezuma, and Montezuma received the news with good grace. Maybe this was the timely intervention of Huitzilopochtli. At the least, Montezuma's understanding of human nature was being sustained. Montezuma sent the runners back to the coast with gifts of jewels for the newly arrived strangers and with instructions to his subject tribes in the area that the new arrivals should be welcomed and amply provided with food.

For three days Montezuma kept this news to himself and did not tell Cortés, although they saw each other daily. Not until the fourth day did Cortés become suspicious because Montezuma, who had lately been glum, had a beatific smile on his face. So Cortés came back a second time in the day to see him. Then Montezuma told Cortés of the arrival of the new fleet, adding that he knew how happy Cortés must be, because now Cortés would not have to build ships in which he and his men could leave Mexico; they would be able to leave in these ships that had arrived—just as soon as Montezuma had exchanged courtesies with the new arrivals.

Montezuma showed Cortés the pictures of the fleet and relayed the details he had been given: eighteen ships, fourteen hundred soldiers, seventy with firearms, ninety crossbowmen, eighty horsemen, twenty cannons, and mountainous heaps of supplies.

Cortés did not need to have a picture drawn for him: He knew the fleet had been sent after him by Velázquez.

THE WRONG MAN FOR THE JOB

The commander of the fleet, Pánfilo de Narváez, was the trusty lieutenant of Diego Velázquez and had long known Hernán Cortés. It was under the command of Narváez that Cortés years earlier had gone from Hispaniola to Cuba. Velázquez owed his long-lasting designation as *conquistador de Cuba* to Narváez. Undoubtedly, Narváez, as Velázquez's favorite, had carefully eyed Cortés while Cortés rivaled him for Velázquez's favor. Unlike Cortés, who to the governor of Cuba had seemed an engaging young heller, Narváez was in many respects a mirror-image of his patron: blustery, hefty, testy—but, in contrast to Velázquez, brave and tough.

Three of Cortés's men, looking for gold sites, were in the vicinity of San Juan de Ulúa when the fleet anchored and the army debarked. These three ran to the newly arrived Spaniards and, relieved of fear for the first time in so many months, feeling fear drain from them, they prostrated themselves before Narváez and thanked God for the coming of what seemed to them a relief force. Narváez plied them with wine and Spanish food, and in the warming company of Spaniards who were not stiff with fear these three—

who until now had been courageously exploring on their own—poured out a torrent of complaints: how Cortés had tyrannized all his men, including them; how Cortés had coerced them into foolhardy adventures; how all those with Cortés despaired of ever seeing home again.

Meanwhile, Indian runners were on their way to Montezuma, and within a few days, in compliance with Montezuma's instructions, Indians came to Narváez making signs of welcome, bearing gifts and bringing food. The three Spaniards who had been with Cortés and who had switched to Narváez could make themselves understood to these Indians in pidgin Nahuatl, and they conveyed to the Indians the message Narváez told them to convey: that Cortés was a renegade and a criminal; that he was wanted by the governor of Cuba and the king of Spain; that Narváez and his great army had been sent to bring back Cortés, dead or alive; and that Narváez, once he had captured or killed Cortés and all the men loyal to him, would restore to the Indians everything Cortés had taken from them and would leave them in peace. The three turncoats also told Narváez how few men Cortés had, how low were his supplies of powder and shot, how his men were dispersed all over Mexico, and the exact disposition of Cortés's forces in the capital where Cortés held Montezuma prisoner. They told Narváez that on a bay twenty-five or thirty miles up the coast was the town Cortés had founded, Villa Rica de la Vera Cruz, where there was a fort with sixty or seventy or, some said, a hundred Spaniards in it. So Narváez sent overland to Villa Rica a delegation— consisting of a priest, a notary, and a wellborn relative of Velázquez—to demand the surrender of the fort.

In command of Villa Rica at this time was a young captain who had rapidly risen in the esteem of Cortés and all his company. When the expedition had first set out, Gonzalo de Sandoval, then in his early twenties, had been too young to receive any assignment of importance. Like Cortés, Sandoval came from Medellín, although Cortés, who was thirteen years older than Sandoval, did not know or could not remember the boy from home. Now, after nine months in Mexico, Sandoval was respected for his fighting ability, his courage and his character.

Before the delegation from Narváez reached Villa Rica, Sandoval was informed they were coming, and he had the oldest and most crippled men go to a friendly Indian village in the hills, keeping with him only those who were fairly battle-ready. When the delegation came before him and the priest began to denounce Cortés as a traitor to Velázquez and the king, Sandoval curtly shut him up. When the priest told the notary to read aloud the letters from Velázquez ordering Cortés to surrender himself, Sandoval had the three delegates netted; the nets were slung on long poles; Indian bearers hoisted the poles at each end; and Sandoval sent off Narváez's delegates in this awkward position to Cortés in the highland. Villages along the way provided changes of bearers, so the same bearers did not have to carry the bagged delegates all the way to Tenochtitlán.

When bearers with the three delegates neared the capital, Cortés, having been alerted, ordered the delegates released and sent horses for them. Then he welcomed them to Tenochtitlán. The three were amazed by the capital and, as Cortés took them about, they saw that he was in control of it. And Cortés, while he told them how he had conquered the country and how rich it was and how he was Christianizing the Indians, filled the delegates' purses with gold and jewels. In the Spaniards' quarters, the delegates were further impressed, in fact were dazzled, by the sight of the card game in which a heap of gold was staked on each hand.

Quickly won over to Cortés's side, the delegates told Cortés that Narváez had lost a ship in a storm at sea; nineteen ships had started out, and all hands aboard the ship that foundered had drowned. In order to raise this army, Velázquez had traveled all over Cuba seeking enlistments, and whenever a man hesitated, Velázquez threatened to take away his Indians; so among the forced enlistees there were many who were resentful. Also, Velázquez had provided Narváez with numerous letters of authorization, several of which the notary had with him. Sandoval had not been willing to listen to these letters, but Cortés read them carefully. In Cortés's opinion the letters were not conclusive. Furthermore, the delegates told Cortés that Velázquez and Narváez had been opposed by the Jeronymite fathers in Santo Domingo, who were now a royal tribunal and represented the Council of the Indies. The Jeronymites had sent to Cuba a judge named Lucas Vásquez de Ayllon, who had tried to block the departure of Narváez and the army because the Jeronymites foresaw that a clash between two Spanish forces would be disadvantageous to the cause of the king and might ruin the Spanish effort to Christianize and colonize the new land. But Velázquez and Narváez had ignored the judge's pleas and threats, which had caused the judge to accompany Narváez on his flagship in order to be able to make a final attempt to avoid bloodshed when the two armies should meet.

Cortés found all this information very interesting, and he promptly packed up more gold for the delegates to take to the judge. Then he packed up yet an additional load of gold for them to take back to Narváez's camp, not to give to Narváez but to the soldiers in Narváez's company, especially the captains who most disliked their commander and resented the way they had been forced into his service. Another passenger who at the last minute had joined Narváez on his flagship, according to the delegates, was Andrés de Duero, Cortés's partner, who, having heard about a treasure, had come to see after his share.

The delegates were able to describe for Cortés Velázquez's frame of mind, and for the first time Cortés learned a little about the fate of Puertocarrero and Montejo and the treasure and the charter of Villa Rica that he had sent to the king in Spain. Contrary to Cortés's orders, the treasure-ship had stopped in Cuba, where Montejo had visited his house in the country. But the ship had slipped away again, though not before word had leaked out about the treasure that was being taken to the king and about the charter for a newly founded town. So Velázquez was aware of Cortés's scheme to freeze him out of this venture; he was also aware that it was a proven bonanza; and he was aware that the founding of Villa Rica was Cortés's tactic to seize control of the conquest and win the approval of the king.

Velázquez had sent fast schooners in pursuit of the treasure-ship, but it had safely reached Spain, where both the ship and its cargo were promptly impounded. The delegates had heard that letters had passed back and forth between Velásquez and his uncle, Bishop Fonseca, and Bishop Fonseca had advised Velázquez to send this fleet to capture or kill Cortés.

Immediately upon learning of the arrival of the fleet from Cuba, Cortés had called in his men—the gold-seekers and the surveyors—from all over the country. Juan Velásquez de León with a hundred fifty men was in Cholula because the Cholulans were disinclined to render their tribute in gold. Cortés had this force remain in place because they were situated on the route to the coast.

Each side—Narváez's and Cortés's—busily tried to subvert the other, and disaffections spread. When Narváez's delegates returned from Tenochtitlán and praised Cortés as a valiant Spaniard and a good Christian, Narváez shouted them down. So the delegates went among their friends, passing around the gold Cortés had given them. The judge, Vásquez de Ayllon, after he received his gold, again went to Narváez and argued that peace should be made between the Spanish factions. So Narváez had the judge put forcibly aboard a ship and sent back to Cuba. Had the ship gone to Cuba, Velázquez would surely have treated this judge harshly. But at sea the judge threatened to sentence the captain of the ship and all his sailors to be hanged if they took him to Cuba. So they took him instead to Santo

Domingo on Hispaniola, where he reported to the Jeronymite fathers in Cortés's favor.

Narváez sent a letter to Velásquez de León in Cholula. Velásquez de León was not only a kinsman of Governor Velázquez but Narváez's brother-in-law. Narváez told Velásquez de León that it was his duty as a kinsman to bring all his men to the coast and join the newly arrived army. But Velásquez de León, a big, strong and stormy man, would not switch sides. When after the gambling binge Cortés had punished Velásquez de León for being obstreperous and had him manacled to a heavy chain, Velásquez de León had dragged the heavy chain through the halls all night, making so much noise that Montezuma had been awakened. Having been through so much with Cortés, however, Velásquez de León trusted and liked him. Besides, he had fought alongside Cortés for all the gold they had won together, and he was not about to turn it over to his brother-in-law or his cousin in Cuba.

Trying another tack, Narváez paraded his army before the Indians on the coast; all the cannons were fired; the cavalry charged; and the Indians changed sides. Narváez through the coastal Indians sent messages to Montezuma, denouncing Cortés and promising justice and restitution, as well as eventual independence for all Indians. In the highland Montezuma didn't know what to do. The newcomers greatly outnumbered Cortés and his men; they had many more horses and cannons; and they apparently worshipped the same God. But, as long as Cortés remained in the capital, Montezuma was unable to do very much.

Cortés wrote a long letter to Narváez, recalling their old friendship and repeating again his, Cortés's, list of accomplishments, boasting of the gold he and his men had acquired in the name of the king, and asking what to Cortés's legalistic mind was the crucial question: Did Narváez have a letter from the king which denied the founding of Villa Rica and authorized Velázquez to conquer and colonize this land? If Narváez had such a letter, Cortés would have to obey it and would subordinate himself and his men to Narváez's command. But if Velázquez and Narváez did not have specific authorization from the king, then Cortés, as duly and properly appointed captain-general and chief justice of the recently founded town of Villa Rica de la Vera Cruz, was ordering Narváez to pack up his army and get out. Cortés generously offered to assist him in his departure, should Narváez be in need of anything that Cortés happened to have on hand.

Cortés assigned Father Olmedo to carry his letter to Narváez. As soon as Olmedo reached the coast and delivered the letter, Narváez detained him. Then Narváez moved his headquarters to Zempoala. Cortés's men left the fort at Villa Rica and retired to the Totonac town in the hills. In Zempoala Narváez established himself atop the central pyramid (it's a modest pyramid really, but it dominates the small city). He placed his cannons on the steps of the pyramid and quartered his men in the best houses. Whereas Cortés had never accepted gold from the Indians except as gifts encouraged by a little coercion, Narváez confiscated from the fat chief all the gold that he had, including the load of treasure Cortés had sent him. When Cortés and his army had departed for the highland, the well-born girls the chief had given to Cortés had been left with their mothers in their own homes. These girls were taken by Narváez and given to his men. Narváez, who had been calling himself captain-general of the army acting in the name of the governor of Cuba, declared that he was founding his own town and he named a council, mayor and sheriff. But Narváez did this in a slipshod way, not in precise accord with *Siete Partidas*. Narváez was not as good a lawyer as Cortés.

When Cortés learned that the fort at Villa Rica had been abandoned and that the Indians on the coast had switched to Narváez or had fled, Cortés prepared to march. He had very few men and few resources with which to contend with Narváez's army. To maintain his position in Tenochtitlán, to guard the accumulated treasure and to continue to hold Montezuma, he left about eighty soldiers under the command of Pedro de Alvarado. They were well-fortified, with all the cannons, and they had five horses. With the remaining men—and there could not have been more than one hundred fifty to two hundred, plus Malinche—Cortés set out. Before he left the capital, Montezuma offered to send with him five thousand warriors, but Cortés could not trust Montezuma's warriors so he declined the offer. When Cortés had a messenger go to Tlascala to ask for the support of more Tlascalan warriors, Xicotenga replied that the Tlascalans would support him against the Aztecs but not against other *teules*. In Cholula Velásquez de León and his hundred fifty men joined Cortés, but the force was still at the most only a few over three hundred, without cannons and with about eight horses.

On the trail they were met by a party sent by Narváez, who had empowered a notary to serve papers upon Cortés requiring him to surrender. When Cortés demanded that the notary produce his notary's license, however, the notary could not do so, and Cortés would not allow him to read his proclamation and serve the papers. But Cortés dismounted, put his arm around the neck of the notary (a timid soul named Alonzo de Mata) and had him mingle with his soldiers, all of whom were wearing heavy gold chains that the Aztec goldsmiths had made for them and had gold bangles on their arms and wrists. Cortés of course gave the notary some gold for himself.

With the notary was Andrés de Duero. His message to Cortés, which he delivered in private, was that Narváez could not be swayed, that Velázquez had sent an army so powerful that Cortés would not stand a chance against it, and that Cortés ought to give up and plead for leniency. But Duero recognized that the Cortés who politely listened to him was not the ambitious, green adventurer with whom he had made a pact in Cuba. Cortés now was tempered to a steely hardness by the ordeals he had been through, by the unending tension he had endured. Cortés heard him out, gave him a clap of affection on the shoulder, and remounted. Cortés sent the notary and Duero ahead of the army back to Narváez.

Other messengers from Narváez came to Cortés along the way. A parley was proposed whereby under mutual safe-conducts Narváez and Cortés would meet face to face and each would bring with him ten soldiers. But Cortés learned from these messengers, after he had given them a little gold, that Narváez planned to seize him at the parley, as Cacama had been seized. So nothing came of the proposed parley. Cortés sent a messenger to Sandoval, who with his men was hiding in the Totonac hill town, and Sandoval brought his men and joined Cortés. With them came five Spaniards who had deserted Narváez and had sought out Sandoval; they were friends and relatives of the judge Narváez had packed off, and they, too, joined Cortés.

It is likely that Cortés planned to use gold as the lure to induce Narváez's men to side with him. Cortés and his men were all loaded with gold. If Cortés could find enough ways of contacting Narváez's men, of having his own men mix with the newcomers and spread around some gifts, the sense in combining forces rather than fighting would become obvious. Also, Cortés hoped that, when the coastal Indians saw him again, they might rally to him. But nature intervened to present a different kind of opportunity— and Cortés took instant advantage of it.

When Cortés and his men were about three miles from Zempoala and had paused for the night, rain began to fall—the tropical rainfall of the coast (purple on the weather maps), a torrential downpour which makes so much noise that commands cannot be heard, and under the cloud cover the darkness is absolute. It was this weather that gave Cortés his chance—and he unhesitatingly adjusted his strategy. Instead of taking refuge from the storm and settling under wraps for the night, Cortés ordered the march to continue. (When men who have been active in the highland descend to the lowland, there is a physical reaction in reverse of that which takes place when the men ascend: They abound with energy and are capable of action they would not have been able to manage in the oxygen-thin air of the highland. Cortés's men had marched all day, but they were not tired.)

Warned of the approach of "Cortés and his three cats," as Narváez and his troopers scornfully referred to Cortés's little army, Narváez had all his horsemen mount and led them out to block the road. But when the road appeared to be empty, and in their armor and leather clothes Narváez and his cavalrymen were sopping, Narváez ordered the cavalry to return to Zempoala, while he left two men as lookouts on the road.

Advancing in the darkness and noise of the rainstorm the men in Cortés's vanguard captured one of these guards, though the other escaped and carried the alarm to Zempoala. Quickly Cortés extracted from the captured guard the disposition of Narváez's forces, where the cannons were placed, how the cavalry and infantry were deployed. Cortés and his men were thoroughly familiar with all the streets, alleyways and plazas of Zempoala. Cortés assigned Sandoval with sixty men to take the temple at the top of the pyramid and to capture Narváez, who had his quarters there. With the rest of the army Cortés would cover the base of the pyramid and the surrounding palaces and compounds and would neutralize Narváez's artillery, cavalry and infantry.

It was in the pitch black of the night and in the awful downpour that Cortés and his men sprinted into Zempoala, raced through the streets they knew—and they were already among Narváez's men when the alarm was sounded. Even then, Narváez's men could see nothing, and they weren't used to fighting in darkness or to fighting at all. Sandoval and those with

The remains of the Totonac pyramid in Zempoala on the hot flat coast.

him swarmed up the steps of the pyramid, engaged Narváez's guards hand-to-hand and quickly subdued them. Cortés and the others reached Narváez's horses before the cavalrymen could mount (and the cavalrymen were hesitant to mount because in the darkness they didn't know where to go and their horses could slip and fall) and Cortés and his men cut the girths and unsaddled the horses. Then Cortés turned to the artillery, but the gunners had filled the touchholes with wax to keep out the rain so the cannons couldn't quickly be fired—and Velásquez de León, Lugo, Ordaz and Cortés's other captains with their men disarmed the confused and terrified artillerymen, while Cortés and those with him captured the infantry. One team of gunners, frantically digging out the wax, got off a single shot from a cannon, and with this shot two of Cortés's men were killed. When Narváez came roaring from his bedchamber, sword in hand and ready to fight, a pikeman named Pedro Sánchez Farfán called on him to give up and, when he wouldn't, lunged and knocked out one of Narváez's eyes.

The rain had ceased by the time dawn came—a dim gray dawn under still-threatening clouds. The jungle air was heavy. And Narváez's defeated men, disarmed and standing about, were appalled and dismayed to see how Cortés with so few had overcome them. Cortés showed little pity for Narváez, who was moaning loudly and trying to stanch the blood from his ruined eye socket. But Cortés, instructing that food should be prepared for all, went from one of Narváez's captains to the next; he knew almost all of them; and he mingled with the defeated soldiers, liberally giving away gold and describing the riches still to come. By noon Cortés was enlisting the newcomers, who were standing in a long line, with a notary and four witnesses attesting.

GÖTTERDÄMMERUNG

Pedro de Alvarado was desperate. Of the eighty men Cortés had left with him in Tenochtitlán many were gimpy, old, or sick with dysentery. Two of the five horses could not gallop. The fortification of the compound had been well planned, but many men were required for the guard, and Alvarado often had difficulty rousing enough men when the guard had to be changed. When the cannons were staffed, there were too few men at the gates.

The attitude of the Aztecs perceptibly altered as soon as Cortés and the others were gone. Montezuma kept to his chamber, and a steady stream of Aztec nobles with calculatedly blank expressions came to confer with him. When Alvarado would call on Montezuma, the emperor no longer joked with him as he used to, and when Alvarado would propose a game of *totoloque,* Montezuma was not interested. The Spaniards guarding Cacama and the other chiefs in chains had to chase away Aztec nobles who were trying to talk to the prisoners.

Obviously the presumption of the Aztecs was that Cortés and his men would be annihilated by the larger army on the coast. Narváez had given the Aztecs notice of his intention. Nor could Alvarado refute the prevailing presumption. Alvarado and the men with him had every reason to fear for their own safety and to doubt the likelihood of Cortés's return. They were threatened by both the Aztecs and Narváez, but the Aztecs were the ones who surrounded them.

What could eighty men or one hundred twenty (as usual, the figures vary) do to protect themselves in a city of hundreds of thousands of ferocious Indians bent on war? It was a miracle that for the past half-year four hundred Spaniards had been able to maintain themselves in Tenochtitlán and even exert some control, as a result of Cortés's amazing combination of intimidation and diplomacy. Now the Aztecs were hoping that Narváez, after he had killed or captured Cortés, would make good on his promise to return the empire to Aztec control and would leave. But Alvarado knew that the Aztecs were bursting with pent-up hatred of Cortés and all his men and were eager to seize the remaining Spaniards in the capital and sacrifice them in atonement for the indignities the Aztecs and their gods had suffered. By killing Alvarado and his contingent the Aztecs would only be anticipating Narváez.

The Tlascalans who were with Alvarado brought to him confirmations of the Aztec plans—and there was no reason to doubt the honesty of the Tlascalans' reports. The Tlascalans were just as fearful for their lives as were the Spaniards. In the temple of Huitzilopochtli, the Tlascalans reported, sharpened staves were being collected on which to impale the stripped Spaniards, once they were taken. And the Tlascalans told Alvarado that the Aztec attack was to come at the climax of the forthcoming ceremony of Toxcatl. This was a particularly dreadful Aztec ceremony that went on for days of crazed dancing and that traditionally culminated with the sacrifice and eating of the warriors, usually Tlascalans, who had been captured in Flower Wars, only this time the white men, too, would be sacrificed and eaten. Montezuma notified Alvarado that the Toxcatl would be held in the expansive courtyard at the foot of the pyramid atop which was the temple of Huitzilopochtli and that the Spaniards, if they so desired, might attend. Alvarado needed no further confirmation of what was in the wind.

Alvarado had always been a self-directed man. When he had captained a ship in Grijalva's fleet, he had once cut out from the fleet to explore a river, for which Grijalva had reprimanded him since the other ships in the fleet would not have been able to come to his defense had he been attacked. Now, under intense pressure, Alvarado, more than ever, was impelled to strike out on his own. The example that occurred to him was the action Cortés had taken at Cholula. There, similarly, the Spaniards had been heavily outnumbered by Indian warriors planning to attack, and the Spaniards had been enveloped within a populous city. Cortés had struck with such suddenness and fury that the Indians had been quelled and had not risen again.

The Toxcatl was an awesome festival. The largest drums of the Aztecs, made from huge hollowed tree trunks elaborately carved and painted, were set in rows around the courtyard, and the drummers—ranks of them— kept up a rhythmic beat that never stopped, a thunderous, intoxicating thrumming. Only the Aztec nobles were allowed in the courtyard but there were thousands of them, and the rhythm of the drums kept them dancing and dancing, immune to exhaustion. Outside the courtyard and throughout the city the people heard the drumming and in their neighborhoods echoed the rhythm with their own drums, and the people probably accentuated their fervor with pulque and mushrooms.

Alvarado had his men organized like a mailed fist when he burst into the courtyard. Teams of Spaniards blocked the exits while the others fell upon the unarmed Aztecs. Volleys from the harquebusiers and crossbowmen systematically felled the crowded Indians, but most of the work was done with swords and pikes. The Indian drummers, themselves entranced by their drumming, did not leave their drums, and the Spaniards, running down the rows, hacked their hands off as they drummed. The Spaniards slashed and thrust—and the shrieking Aztecs could not flee or fight back; they were still in the mood of their dancing. The slaughter went on until the floor of the courtyard was carpeted with bloody corpses. Then the Spaniards, climbing over the heaped bodies, retired from the courtyard and retreated to their quarters.

Most of the top echelon of Aztec nobility was wiped out at the festival of Toxcatl. But cessation of the drumming was the signal that alerted all of Tenochtitlán. The Aztec people came thronging through the streets. In every neighborhood people screamed out that there had been a massacre.

From every direction furious crowds converged upon the Spaniards huddled behind the walls of their fortress.

The cannons boomed, the harquebusiers and crossbowmen fired volleys from their ramparts, and Spaniards held the entrances to their compound. But from rooftops all around them and from nearby towers and pyramids, stones, arrows and spears rained down. The Aztecs set fire to the sheds where the Spaniards stored provisions and supplies. At night the Aztecs tried to dig under the walls and, wherever they could break through, they battled the Spaniards—obsidian-studded clubs against steel swords, copper lances against iron pikes. The Spaniards were unable to leave their fortress to protect the brigantines they had built, and the Aztecs burned the ships which were at anchor in the canals.

During a lull in the fighting on the third night following the massacre, a Spaniard from the coast was able to slip into the Spanish stronghold; he brought news of Cortés's victory over Narváez. But Alvarado quickly sent him back to Cortés with the dismal news from Tenochtitlán.

On the coast Cortés—now with eighteen ships at his disposal, and with more men, horses, arms and gunpowder—was methodically planning to continue what had been his almost bloodless conquest by guile. He had enlisted nearly all of Narváez's men, excepting Narváez himself and a few of his more insulting captains who remained prisoners. Cortés had compelled his own men, not without difficulty, to give back to Narváez's former soldiers the horses and saddles that the soldiers personally owned, as well as their personal armor and weapons. Cortés would not condone what he regarded as stealing; his belief in individually held, private property was unshakable; tribute and gifts extorted from the Indians under pressure were another matter. Cortés was assigning a troop to go to the Pánuco River to prepare a harbor, another troop to go to Coatzacoalcos to build a fort that would be a gathering-point for gold; he was sending to Jamaica for more horses and equipment; now, when he had gold to buy with, he did not feel in need of anyone's permission. But these pleasant plans had to be set aside when he was informed that the Spaniards in Tenochtitlán were under siege, starving, likely to be overrun and killed, and the treasure that had been accumulated would be taken from them.

Quickly assembling about thirteen hundred Spaniards and with plenty of horses and cannons and lots of Indian bearers supplied by the Totonacs, who were loyal once more, Cortés set off at a fast pace for the highland.

In his force there were many of Narváez's former soldiers, who volunteered for the chance to win favor with Cortés and to establish their right to a share of the treasure. But en route to the highland no Nahuatl-speaking Indians approached them; the towns and fields along the throughway were deserted. Cortés suspected that his bastion in Tenochtitlán had fallen. So he sent scouts far ahead and far out on the flanks to avoid an ambush. And he didn't pause until he reached Texcoco on the shore of the lake in the valley of Mexico.

There were no chiefs in Texcoco whom Cortés recognized; the nobles known to him had gone to the festival of Toxcatl in Tenochtitlán and had been killed by Alvarado. But the Indians who came to him said that the Spaniards in the capital were still alive. Since learning of Cortés's victory on the coast and that he was returning, the Aztecs in Tenochtitlán had ceased to attack, and a tense stand-off was in effect.

Cortés camped in Texcoco, and to him in a canoe crossing the lake came a Spaniard escorted and protected by several Aztec nobles who were attendants of Montezuma. To Cortés the Spaniard confirmed that Alvarado and his men were still holding out, though they were short of food and water. And the Aztec nobles relayed a message from Montezuma: that the emperor was deeply sorry for all the fighting that had taken place, that he knew Cortés would blame him for it, but that he welcomed Cortés's return and would command his people to cooperate again as they had before Cortés's departure for the coast.

Cortés wasn't so sure. The next day in close formation he approached the capital, paused again on the lakeshore for the night, then at midday, after hearing Mass, crossed a causeway and entered the city. The streets were nearly deserted; he saw only a few people at a distance, scurrying about. He noticed that several of the bridges had been removed and that there were barricades in a few of the side streets.

When he and his men reached and entered the Spaniards' compound, Alvarado and his survivors fell upon them with joy and thanksgiving, though Cortés, when he was told the detailed story of the massacre, could scarcely control his temper. Also, in the courtyard Montezuma with his retinue was waiting to welcome Cortés. But Cortés, sensing the danger of the impending situation and aware of the advances Montezuma had made to Narváez, could not keep himself from spewing out a stream of curses when Montezuma's attendants came to him (the attendants did not understand his curses but fully comprehended his tone). Cortés would neither greet nor receive the emperor, so Montezuma sadly returned to his chamber. To Cortés it appeared that Montezuma and the people in this city were fearful that he would punish them—and he did not want to diminish their fear.

In the morning shortly after dawn Cortés sent a horseman to the coast with a letter stating that he had reached the capital and that all was safe and secure. In half an hour, however, the horseman galloped back, bleeding and beaten. He had been ambushed by Aztecs before he had reached the causeway but had broken away. Everywhere, he reported, the Aztecs were lifting the bridges. The streets were filled with warriors who had been hiding in the houses. It was Cuitlahuac's name they were shouting— Montezuma's brother, Cuitlahuac, was their leader. While the horseman was still reporting, there was a rumbling noise as the whole massed population of Tenochtitlán bore down on the Spanish stronghold—Aztec warriors filling all the streets, lining the steps of the pyramids, crowding onto the rooftops, finally bringing to bear the crushing burden of their numerical superiority, screeching, slinging stones, with their spear-throwers hurling high-arching spears, troops of warriors under the banners of their chiefs knotting up to try to force the entrances while others raced around with pitch-pine torches, trying to set fires wherever they could.

Cortés knew he had been duped. He recognized that the Aztecs had let him come into the center of their city only to trap him—so now they would have, to sacrifice to their gods, not only Alvarado and his men but Cortés and his army as well. The newcomers who had come with Narváez were horrified and nearly hysterical, never having seen attacking hordes of Indians before.

But Cortés reacted decisively, without hesitation, sending cadres of his veterans to block each Aztec incursion. The outbuildings of the palace compound were burning again, and the Spaniards had to collapse a section of the outer wall to block the spread of a fire, then stand in the gap and hand-to-hand beat back the Aztecs who tried to enter the compound. All day long the fighting went on until the stones, darts, arrows and spears so littered the flagstone floor of the courtyard that the Spaniards slipped and slid as they scrambled about.

At night Cortés had the broken wall repaired, and his men caught their breath. But at dawn the Aztecs attacked more fiercely than ever. To break the pressure of the Aztecs all around Axayacatl's palace Cortés organized a squadron of cavalry and led them in a charge out from the fortress. So many Aztecs were crowded together that they could not break and run before the charging horses and their slashing riders. So the riders were enmeshed in the crowd. Behind brick parapets on the rooftops other Aztec warriors stoned the Spaniards, while the Aztecs in the crush around the horses tore at the reins and stabbed at the armored horses and riders. In this fight Cortés was dealt a bat-blow that smashed and disabled his left hand. All his men were wounded and they had to retreat to their fort.

The cannons continued to blast away, but the Aztecs had called up their whole nation and, though the gunners did not even have to aim for each shot to fell a dozen Indians, the press of Aztecs seemed not to be lessened at all. Volleys from the harquebusiers and crossbowmen did not thin the Indian ranks. Cortés sent out a captain with two hundred infantrymen to try with their swords and pikes to cut a path through the Aztec mass, and these men, like the cavalry, were driven back, wounded and mauled. As Bernal Díaz wrote, revealing the classicism in the minds of these sixteenth-century Spaniards, "even if ten thousand Trojan Hectors and as many more Rolands had been there, we could not have broken through."

During the night Cortés ordered carpenters to rig up some wheeled carts with sides and roofs of strong planks. His plan was to place in each cart about twenty men who would be safe from the stones, arrows, darts and spears from the rooftops. These men would be equipped with iron crowbars. And when the carts, escorted by cavalry, cannons and infantry, were pushed up to the barricades the Indians had erected in the streets, the men with the crowbars could get out, demolish the barricades, and break into the houses from the roofs of which the Aztecs were doing the most damage. All through the next day the carpenters worked on the carts, while the soldiers held their positions on the walls and at the entrances. On the following morning the carts, under strong escort, went out. But the Aztecs on the roofs had boulders ready, and they pushed off or threw down these boulders and smashed the carts. The Spaniards fought until they were exhausted, and they broke through a few barricades and set fire to some houses, but they could not lessen the Aztec pressure and were driven back to the fort, dragging the wrecked carts. Each time the Spaniards would attempt to counter the Aztec offensive, some of them were killed, most were wounded, and some were captured alive by the Aztecs.

After days of fierce fighting, Cortés sent for Montezuma and demanded that he call off this attack. The role Montezuma had played in causing the attack was uncertain. He had stayed in his chamber since Cortés's arrival, and his chamber was on the second story in the center of the compound, so he had not been threatened by the fires and the battling on the perimeter. It was Montezuma's brother, Cuitlahuac, who was said now to be the war-leader. But Montezuma—to himself and to Cortés—was the emperor. He was the one the people must obey, or the whole scheme of Aztec society would lose its tension, its discipline, its order, and its luck.

So Montezuma—who for more than six months had contrived with Cortés to reach an accommodation and who had probably pursued his own strategy to counter the strategy of the Spaniards—went out into the courtyard and ascended a stairway to a flat roof along the outer wall from which he would be seen by his people and from which he could call to them. The Spaniards protected him with their shields while he made his way to the edge of the roof, then withdrew their shields to reveal him.

And Montezuma was stoned by his own people. Later, Aztec apologists said the people did not recognize him. Or the people threw by mistake. But this is not reasonable. The wildly agitated Aztec warriors on the roofs opposite, on the pyramids and in the streets, could not be calmed or stayed—they were fighting for their identity and their freedom, as well as for possession of their own wealth. Later, Aztec priests, trying to create a new mythology, said that a young Aztec noble, Guatémoc, who would eventually assume the throne, in disgust with the old monarch threw the stone that struck Montezuma on the temple. Other priests said to Sahagún and Durán that the people denounced Montezuma for betraying them. But it is not reasonable to believe that anybody heard anything in the din of battle. The Aztecs saw that it was Montezuma there on the roof of the Spaniards' fortress; Montezuma chose a spot where he could be seen and recognized; he always dressed identifiably as the emperor. Yet the Aztecs continued their slinging and throwing. Montezuma was hit at least three times and he fell. Raising their shields over him, the Spaniards carried Montezuma from the roof.

The battling went on and on—while word spread among the Aztecs that Montezuma had appeared on the roof and had been stoned. But the Aztecs redoubled the intensity of their attack, and the Spaniards kept fighting to save their own lives. Montezuma lived for a couple of days, but he would not allow his wounds to be tended nor would he eat or drink. He was mortally injured in spirit. Rejected by his own people, he may have viewed his fate as a reprimand by Huitzilopochtli, or as the working out of the ancient omen, or as the triumph of the Christian God (according to one story, highly doubtful, he had once asked to be baptized). Or perhaps he viewed his fate simply as the failure of his own strategy to achieve an enlightening of the lives of the Aztecs through a peaceful fusion with these new people.

The Spaniards mourned him, to the extent that they had time to mourn. Montezuma with personal warmth had been very generous to them. When

Bernal Díaz had asked Montezuma to give him a pretty girl, Montezuma had done so and said that the girl was noble, which to Bernal Díaz meant a great deal since his own claim to being noble was treated with laughing suspicion by his fellow-soldiers. Cortés, though he was scheming all the time, knew that it was only through Montezuma's goodwill that he had been able to advance by guile toward an end that both he and Montezuma thought might be good. The chroniclers recorded that the Spaniards mourned for Montezuma, and it is easy for modern cynics to doubt this, yet I think it is reasonable to believe it.

When Montezuma was dead, Cortés had some Aztecs the Spaniards had captured lift his body and carry it back to his people. The Spaniards opened the gates to let the corpse-bearers leave and watched them disappear into the streets of Tenochtitlán. Neither Cortés nor any of the Spaniards ever learned what happened to Montezuma's body.

The Spaniards were nearly dying from thirst and hunger. In the courtyard they had removed some flagstones and dug a well from which they obtained a little water that was not too brackish. They still had some stiff and stale tortillas. But the pressure of the Aztecs was visibly and actually increasing as more troops, summoned from nearby cities and provinces, entered the capital. The Aztecs were not only lifting the bridges and blocking the streets but were dismantling the causeways so that the Spaniards, with their brigantines burned, would have no way of escaping, while the Aztecs, who had stores in reserve, could resupply themselves with their fleets of canoes.

From the top of a pyramid adjoining the Spaniards' stronghold, Aztec chiefs had an overview of the Spaniards' compound and were directing the fighting. While the Spaniards weakened, the Indians fought in shifts, with troops relieving each other, attacking on one side, then on another, wherever the Spaniards were fewest. Atop this pyramid was the temple of Xipe Totec, "the Skinned God," and in it the Spaniards had placed a Cross and figure of Mary. So Cortés strapped a shield onto his left arm, since his left hand was limp and useless, and led his men up the steps of the pyramid, while the Aztecs rolled down boulders and tree trunks. But many of the boulders and tree trunks stuck on the terraces of the pyramid—and the Spaniards took the temple at the top (the Aztecs had thrown out the Christian symbols). Setting fire to the temple, the Spaniards killed or drove off the Aztec chiefs and their warriors.

At night Cortés left the compound and burned more nearby houses where warriors could hide or use the roofs. But he saw that the whole city was occupied by fighting men. The bridges were gone, and the only causeway remaining was the link to Tacuba, a city on the mainland shore. So for several days Cortés and his Spaniards tried to open a path for themselves to this causeway. They would fight their way to a gap where a bridge had been removed, then would knock down a wall or a house and fill the gap with rubble. But at night the Aztecs would remove the rubble and reopen the gap.

Cortés had to face the fact that their position in Tenochtitlán was hopeless. So he prepared to flee while the causeway to Tacuba remained open. He had all the treasure the Spaniards had acquired brought to the hall of the palace. It was impossible to get it all out. So he had what he approximated to be the king's fifth loaded onto a mare and a few lame horses. And he let his men fill their pockets and purses, though he warned them they would do better taking what food there was. Bernal Díaz, knowing that Indians most highly prized jadestones, slipped a few *chalchihuites* under his breastplate and took a few gold boxes. Narváez's men so loaded themselves with gold that many of them could not carry their weapons.

The plan was for the Tlascalans at night to lead the Spaniards from the city and to guide them to Tlascala, where they might revive themselves and reestablish contact with the coast. The carpenters had built a portable bridge, a movable section that could be carried and placed across the gap wherever a bridge had been removed; then the portable section would be lifted again and carried to the next gap. Forty Tlascalans were needed to carry this portable bridge, so two hundred were assigned to work in shifts, with one hundred fifty Spaniards to guard them.

In a heavy fog on the night which was probably the tenth of July, 1520, the remaining Spaniards, all of them battered and wounded and many limping, weighed down with gold, opened the doors of their fortress and followed their Tlascalan allies. But the fog did not hide them for long. At the first gap when the bridge was set in place, the noise roused the Aztecs, and promptly there was a call to arms. The Tlascalans and Spaniards made it across their bridge at the first gap, but then the Aztecs were on them — and there were eight gaps along the route to Tacuba.

The Spaniards ran through the streets, the Aztecs pelting them with stones slung from behind parapets on the rooftops and behind barricades in the side streets. The Spaniards could not counterattack. They ran — and when a Spaniard slipped or was felled by a stone or staggered under the weight of the gold he was carrying, the Aztecs swarmed over him and carried him off. At the gaps the frantic Spaniards slid down into the water and tried to wade or swim to the other side. The horses slipped and fell on the underwater rocks. The Aztecs in the capital had summoned those on the mainland to come in their canoes, and Aztecs in the capital came in canoes, to throttle and drown the Spaniards who floundered in the water. Riderless horses were swimming alongside the causeway in the shallow lake.

After each gap on the causeway to Tacuba there were fewer Spaniards. Cortés, Velásquez de León, Sandoval and the other captains tried to rally the Spaniards and fight off the Indians, but it wasn't a battle, it was a rout. Alvarado tried to maintain a rear guard. When finally the last stretch of the causeway to Tacuba was reached, Cortés led a charge and broke through a cordon of Aztecs. Then the surviving Spaniards got through to the shore. But Cortés was called back to save many who were trapped.

Charging back, Cortés and Sandoval met Alvarado, who was on the other side of the last intervening gap. Alvarado was on foot, bleeding and exhausted, without a horse, and had his sword in one hand and an Aztec spear in the other. And the story is that Alvarado used the spear to vault across this last gap and that he was the last Spaniard to leave Tenochtitlán. Bernal Díaz, however, candidly reported that he never heard of "Alvarado's Leap" until years later when a Spanish minstrel made up a song about it, and that even if Alvarado did leap, no one would have been looking at him anyhow because each of them was concerned solely with saving his own life.

In Tacuba, as day dawned, the Spaniards staggered into the central square of the town and dropped to the ground in exhaustion or milled about, dazed. The Aztecs had prepared to kill or capture all the Spaniards before they were able to escape from Tenochtitlán—and had nearly done it. Only about four hundred Spaniards survived; eight or nine hundred had been lost. Only twenty-four horses remained; not one of them could gallop. All the people and all the horses were wounded. His left hand crippled, Cortés had been struck on his knee, and he was afraid to dismount for fear he could not mount again. All the cannons had been lost, all the powder. Most of the gold was gone. The Spaniards retained only the gold and jewels they carried; the Tlascalan bearers had some gold bars; most of the gold had been taken by Narváez's former soldiers, and they had paid for their greediness and inexperience, for very few of them escaped. The survivors preferred not to think of the sacrifice-stone that awaited those who had been captured, on whose flesh the Aztecs would feast. Velásquez de León was dead. Malinche survived, as did two daughters of Montezuma and a few other noble Indian girls and one or two Spanish women who had accompanied Narváez's men. It is interesting to note that both the Spaniards and the Indians profoundly respected social distinctions; these so-called daughters of Montezuma were later married by Spanish *hidalgos* and were granted extensive domains as their just inheritances; one of these girls was given Tacuba.

In their writings Cortés, Gómara and Bernal Díaz agree that in the flight from Tenochtitlán the Spaniards had taken with them Cacama and the other chiefs they held prisoner and that these captive Aztec nobles were killed in the melee. Years later, however, many Aztec priests reported to Nahuatl-speaking chroniclers that Cacama and the other chiefs were executed by the Spaniards in their compound before the Spaniards departed from Tenochtitlán. There were even reports that Montezuma had not died from the stoning but had likewise been executed by the Spaniards. Bernal Díaz, who wrote his memoirs when he was in his late seventies, had Gómara's work to go by, and Gómara knew only what Cortés told him. So Cortés himself in his second letter to the king is the chief source for the idea that Cacama and the other captive chiefs were killed by their own people in the course of the night's fighting. Yet it seems reasonable to believe that the Spaniards with sword thrusts would execute Cacama and the other lords, all of whom were vociferous in expressing their hatred of the Spaniards, rather than take the chance that these Aztec leaders might escape in the night to rejoin and further inspirit their people. But it is not reasonable to believe—and it is in conflict with many eyewitness ac-counts—that Montezuma was only slightly injured by the stones and was killed by the Spaniards. It would not have been in the Spaniards' interest to kill Montezuma, because he always seemed to them a valuable hostage for whom they might ultimately bargain with the Aztecs.

Cortés feared they would be trapped in Tacuba. There were Aztec warriors in the town, though not in massed force; three Spaniards on the edge of the crowd of refugees were picked off and killed by them. The Aztecs had not yet manned the rooftops. So Cortés got his people up and they straggled from the town in what they thought was the direction of Tlascala. But the Tlascalans, who had known the way out from the capital, wanted now to avoid the main road and go by a little-traveled route to avoid an Aztec ambush, which seemed sensible. The result, though, was that the surviving Spaniards and Tlascalans often got lost and meandered around before they found their direction again.

They were starving, and during the day, with the Aztecs pursuing them, they were able to move only a few miles. In the evening they all bedded down in and around some stone houses and a little temple in the country and set up a perimeter defense. Whistling and screaming, the Aztecs surrounded them but did not attack in the night. While it was still dark,

Cortés roused his people and, leaving bonfires burning, they set out again. But the Aztecs saw them and came in pursuit, alerting towns along the way to rally warriors to exterminate the last of the *teules*. So the Spaniards had to fight as they tried to move along. The Spanish horsemen and soldiers were so tired they could hardly hold up their heads or lift their arms, yet they sallied out again and again to keep the hostile Indians at bay. In the evening they took refuge in some stone houses and maintained a guard.

After fighting all through the next day as they tried to march, the Spaniards reached a town from which all the people fled at the sight of them. So the Spaniards occupied the town and found a supply of maize; they boiled and ate some of it and roasted the rest to carry along with them.

On the following day the Spaniards passed a hill from which local Indians were threatening them, and the horsemen rode after these Indians only to find that there was a large town on the far side of the hill, and a fierce fight ensued on bouldery land where the horses could not run freely. Cortés's helmet was knocked off and he was hit in the head by two slung stones, so hard that he suffered a concussion and lost consciousness. But, slumped, he did not fall from his horse, and other horsemen brought him back to the remnant of his army, where he recovered himself. The Indians had killed one of the horses, and the Spaniards succeeded in dragging the animal's carcass from the fighting. The Spaniards left the vicinity of the town, though the inhabitants pursued them, and finally bedded down again in stone houses around a small pyramid; it was the kind of stopover place that served them well. They promptly butchered the dead horse, cooked it and ate it—in the Spaniards' words—down to the hair and the bones.

Cortés had crutches fashioned for those who could hobble. The most seriously wounded were laid over the rumps of the horses that were too lame to be used for fighting. Other people held onto the horses' tails or the stirrups of the horsemen to keep awake and to keep going.

And so they went on until, after setting out one morning, they came to the valley of Otumba, which was thick with warriors waiting to attack them. This was the final trap the Aztecs had arranged. Reflexively, the Spaniards formed to do battle again. Most of those left alive were veterans of many past fights. They had no cannons; there were no ranks of harquebusiers; few of the crossbows worked. They had their swords, daggers, pikes, and a few lances. In the center of their defensive rectangle were the wounded, both Spaniards and Tlascalans, and the few women. As usual, the horsemen were in the van, and they rode out to force their way through the Indian mass.

What resulted was more a confused riot than an organized fight. For this final onslaught the Aztecs had called up the Otomís who inhabited the region. The Otomís were not used to discipline in warfare and, promised rich spoils, too many Otomís had shown up. Contingents of warriors from different Otomí towns got in one another's way; arguments and scuffles broke out. The valley was so packed that effective attacks could not be mounted. Some of the Otomís were trampled, others panicked, though fighting went on for most of the day.

When the Spanish horsemen saw an Otomí chief with an enormous plumed headdress carrying a banner, they charged at him—and Cortés knocked the banner from the chief's hands while another Spaniard, Juan de Salamanca, tore the plumed headdress from the chief's head. Cortés speared the chief, and the Otomís broke and ran, leaving the field to the Spaniards. Separating into village groups, the Otomís departed for their homes. (After this battle Juan de Salamanca gave the chief's plumed head-dress to Cortés, who later sent it to the king in Spain with a true account of what happened, and several years later the king awarded to Juan de Salamanca the right to use the headdress on his family coat of arms.)

When the Spaniards and the Indians who remained their allies made camp that night, they could see the mountains of Tlascala. But Cortés was not sure of his welcome there. In defeat, in retreat, he no longer would represent to the Tlascalans the hope for relief from Aztec tyranny that once he had represented. Yet he and his people hadn't the strength to march any farther.

In the morning they staggered into a Tlascalan village on the border. The Aztecs and tribes allied to the Aztecs no longer pursued them, and the Tlascalan villagers came out to stare. Cortés had the wounded put in the shade to rest. The Tlascalan warriors and bearers who were with Cortés demanded food from the villagers—and the people brought food, though reluctantly, and they insisted on being paid for it in gold. So the Spaniards had to dig into their pockets and purses for bits of gold and negotiate for each meal.

Soon the Tlascalan chiefs arrived, led by Xicotenga the Younger's father, blind Xicotenga the Elder, for whom the plight of the Spaniards had to be described. There was another dominant chief named Mase Escasi. And the ranking Tlascalan chiefs commiserated with the Spaniards. They had heard, they said, of the fighting in Tenochtitlán and were raising an army to support the Spaniards in the valley of Otumba where they knew the Aztecs had prepared an ambush, but obviously they were too late. They invited

Cortés to come to their city, where the Spaniards would be p
and where they could rest and revive themselves.

The Spaniards stayed three days in the Tlascalan village or
before they were able to get themselves up to travel the ten or
to the city. During these three days Xicotenga the Younger, in counc..
the city with the other Tlascalan chiefs, was said to have urged that the
Spaniards should all be killed and that the Tlascalans should seek a rap-
prochement with the Aztecs. But the elder chiefs spurned his argument,
maintaining that, once the Spaniards were eliminated, the Aztecs surely
would turn again on Tlascala, more ferociously than before since Tlascalans
had fought as allies of the Spaniards. True, the Spaniards had lost a battle,
but there remained on the coast many more Spaniards with guns, horses
and ships. It was beginning to dawn on the Tlascalan leaders that the sea,
which had hitherto marked the boundary and end of the Indian world, was
for the white men not only their means of access but their channel for
reinforcement. From the Aztecs the Tlascalans knew what they could
expect (merciless fury) but with these Spaniards, while the Spaniards survived and had a chance, an attractive accommodation might be worked
out—and now was the time to dicker for it. Thanks to the Spaniards, the
Tlascalans were eating salt on their food and were weaving cotton to make
new clothes. So the elders decided not to dishonor their alliance with the
Spaniards. The Spaniards heard that in a heated argument Xicotenga the
Younger was thrown down the steps of his father's palace by other Tlascalan chiefs. It is more likely, however, that the Tlascalan chiefs in council
through hard reasoning reached the canny conclusion that it was in their
best interest for the while to stand by the Spaniards.

When the bedraggled Spaniards limped into the city, Mase Escasi took
Cortés into his home. The other Spanish captains were similarly received
by other Tlascalan nobles. The Spanish soldiers were taken into the homes
of the people. For the first time in weeks Cortés had his armor removed
and was able to lie down on a bed. His skull was cracked on the left side.

(As the result of a series of amazing twists of history, the details of
Cortés's skull fractures are reliably known. In his will, Cortés specified that
his remains should be kept in the Hospital de Jesús in Mexico City, and
there they were kept in an ornate casket for more than two and a half
centuries. Then, during the Mexican war of independence from Spain in
the early nineteenth century, Cortés's bones were hidden by priests for fear
that the nationalists would regard Cortés as a symbol of Spain and would
desecrate his remains. A century after that, during the Mexican revolution,

there was yet another threat of desecration, so the secret of the location of Cortés's remains was kept—until in 1946 a young Spaniard, following clues from a paper trail of ancient documents, traced the bones to their hiding place within a thick old wall of the hospital. Carefully chiseling out the stones of the wall, a team of archaeologists discovered a crypt, and in it was the casket with Cortés's bones. In the casket along with the bones was a notarized statement attesting to their authenticity, which was an elegant touch of legalistic Spanish precision. The extant skull shows how severely Cortés had been injured.)

While Cortés was inert and semiconscious, one of the Spaniards deft at surgery amputated two fingers from his crippled left hand, cauterized the stumps of the two fingers with boiling oil, and removed splinters of bone or stone from Cortés's head. Cortés's knee was purple and swollen to double its size. His whole body was covered with bruises, arrow-wounds and cuts. Almost dead on an Indian pallet, prostrate and in a coma, lay the conqueror of Mexico.

III

The Distorting Mirror of the Black Legend

THE NAY-SAYERS

It was Bartolomé de las Casas—the implacable denouncer of Spaniards in the New World—who initiated the Black Legend during the course of his long lifetime of persistent, inspired, flamboyant and furious propagandizing. Las Casas was born in 1474, eleven years before Cortés, and lived until he was ninety-two, dying in 1566, nearly nineteen years after Cortés. For more than fifty years Las Casas spoke out vehemently and wrote voluminously, longevity—as well as moral certainty—giving him a considerable advantage. Yet in the estimation of most contemporaries while Las Casas and Cortés were both alive, Cortés was little affected by Las Casas. Only in the longer run—over the span of centuries—may the influence of Las Casas be seen as prevailing, in that Las Casas put an imprint upon Cortés, upon Spaniards and upon Spain that has been impossible to erase and difficult even to mitigate by shedding light from different angles.

To refer to him as *Fray* Bartolomé de las Casas, which is common usage, serves to emphasize his role as a Dominican monk, but he was not accepted into that order until he was forty-nine years old. Actually, Las Casas's youth had many points of parallel with that of Cortés: Las Casas attended the university at Salamanca (unlike Cortés, however, Las Casas graduated with degrees in law and divinity); Las Casas came to the New World in the fleet of Nicolás de Ovando (whose departure Cortés missed because he fell from the garden wall following an assignation); Las Casas received an *encomienda* of land and Indians on Hispaniola and worked his Indians in both mines and fields more mildly perhaps but in the same manner as other acquisitive Spaniards; and, crossing to Cuba when that island was occupied, he ingratiated himself with Velázquez and received a better *encomienda* than he had on Hispaniola. Grateful to Velázquez, Las Casas afterward tended to favor Velázquez contra Cortés, though Las Casas also fell out with Velázquez over the issue of *encomiendas*.

Not until Las Casas was forty—four years before Cortés set out for Mexico—was he inspired by the idea that not only were the Indians being cruelly overworked but the Indians were God's innocents on earth and ought not to work at all; that black African slaves or white Andalusian serfs ought to be imported to do the labor the Indians were doing; and that it was the holy duty of Spain and Spaniards to Christianize these Indian innocents solely by education, by persuasion without resort to force, and, most of all, by example. The Indians Las Casas knew at that time were the island Indians, who were remarkably passive and to the virile Spaniards seemed to be effeminate; he did not know the cannibal Caribs from the Outer Antilles or, of course, the Indians on the yet-to-be-discovered mainland. Responding to his inspiration, Las Casas freed his own Indians and for the rest of his life eloquently expounded the Indian cause with sincerity and exuberant fervor.

This concept of conversion solely through education, through persuasion without ever using force, and by setting an example of Christian goodness had its history in the Spanish Church from the time of the Moors; then it had been argued that the Muslims should be converted only in this pacifistic way. But the religious reeducation of the Moors by such means was rejected for many reasons: There were not nearly enough Christian priests who could speak Arabic; also, among those being proselytized, there was bound to be frequent backsliding; thorough conversion could never be proved; and conversion could not be dated and made definite. So harder courses were followed: The Moors were subjugated by force, given the choice of conversion or exile, and Catholic ritual, once instituted, was trusted to be the effective device to maintain the forms of Christian worship while over the years Christian teaching would sink into the converts.

The situation in the New World was similar. There were hardly any priests fluent in the Indian tongues, and the few who eventually came along were obsessed with linguistics; also, the horrific nature of the Indian religion on the mainland made the threat of backsliding more to be dreaded; and there were many millions of Indians in countless tribes spread all over this vastness. Conversion through education and persuasion and by the setting of a Christian example seemed too uncertain and slow. So most priests, in fact nearly all of them, accepted the soldiers' decision to command conversion and institute ritual. Whereupon, the priests—especially Franciscans and Dominicans—heroically devoted themselves to instilling the spirit of Christianity in the Indian nature and to deepening and extending the habits of Christianity in Indian society.

Another consideration that the *conquistadores* and the priests with them had to face was that somebody in the New World had to do the tilling, the digging and the carrying. Only the Indians were numerous enough for the tasks at hand. So the *encomienda* was invented, by which Indians were entrusted to Spaniards who were duty-bound to provide priests who would catechize the Indians—and, incidentally, the Spaniards would make the Indians work. In tropical and subtropical climates the native Indians were used to doing very little work.

Of course excesses resulted. There were Spaniards who, in their greed for gold, worked their Indians to death, and Spaniards sometimes committed inexcusable atrocities. There were provocations by the Indians, who did tend to slide back toward their old religion, which involved idolatry, human sacrifice and cannibalism, and whose notion of working was not at all in accord with the Spaniards' schedules.

Las Casas chose to attack this situation in a typically Spanish way: through unrelenting negative self-criticism (it's a form of self-flagellation, a strong impulse among Spaniards). He repeated and magnified every story that he heard about Spanish cruelty. He deplored and damned every Spanish punishment of the Indians. He wildly exaggerated the number of Indians oppressed (up to forty million) and the geography involved (making Hispaniola larger than Spain). And Las Casas initially focused his vituperation upon Hernán Cortés. Las Casas condemned Cortés for being unfaithful to Velázquez. Las Casas depicted Cortés as engaging in a pirate-raid on the slaughterhouse in Cuba prior to sailing for Mexico, although Bernal Díaz's more credible depiction was that Cortés used his own gold chain with the thistle medallion to make a fair purchase. Las Casas accused Cortés of massacring the Cholulans absolutely without cause, even though Las Casas knew nothing of the circumstances, and Las Casas made no allowance whatever for the fear and jeopardy of Cortés and his men.

During the course of his long life Las Casas returned to Spain many times to vilify the Spaniards in America and to plead for mercy and beneficence on the Indians' behalf. Las Casas appealed directly to the king/ emperor. Carlos Quinto, always interested in issues of conscience, had debates held between Las Casas and eminent Christian philosophers in an attempt to define what the proper moral relationship between the races should be. And it is significant that Las Casas was heard sympathetically.

The essential problem confronting the government in Spain was to enunciate principles of administration that could be applied on the other side of the world, not to primitive savages, but to people who over many millennia had evolved a high civilization which was radically different from European civilization. This problem was unique. And the legal positions that Spain took—despite deviations in execution—should be made clear.

The Catholic Church in Spain always valued and regarded with respect the souls of subjugated peoples, and the Church influenced the Spanish government either to disfavor slavery or at least to question the legitimacy, propriety and morality of slavery. When Columbus brought back a few Indians from the New World and recommended that these timid island Indians would make ideal slaves and that more should be imported and sold because humankind was one of the New World's most readily usable and plentiful commodities, Isabella in a generous gesture freed the captive Indians. In fact, Las Casas's father, who had accompanied Columbus on the second voyage, had brought back an Indian boy who, when the Queen's edict was announced, was a servant to Las Casas at the university in Salamanca—and Las Casas duly lost his slave. But in the New World the practical demands of the work to be done severely restricted magnanimity. The *encomienda* was invented as a compromise, to avoid outright enslavement, to Christianize, and yet to get the work done, not only the mining of gold but the raising of food for a growing population, the building of a network of roads connecting inland cities with never-before-used harbors, the construction of ports and the building of port cities.

The *requerimiento* (the required reading of a message to the Indians prior to battle), however impractical and absurd, was a considered attempt by the Spaniards to make themselves understood by Indians whose society was so different from Christian society that understanding was impossible. But the Spaniards *tried*—and even risked their lives in the effort.

It was after one of Las Casas's impassioned pleas that Cardinal Jiménez, the co-regent in Spain who preceded the rule of Carlos Quinto, sent the first Jeronymite fathers to Hispaniola and empowered them to investigate the excesses of Spaniards in the New World. But when the Jeronymites established standards and set limits for the *encomienda*, rather than following Las Casas's advice and abolishing the *encomienda*, Las Casas furiously denounced his fellow clerics. Las Casas in turn was furiously denounced by one of the most selfless Franciscans, Toribio de Benavente, who was called by the Indians in Nahuatl something which was phonetically rendered as "Motolinía" (the "poor one" because he was always barefoot and his cassock was in tatters). Motolinía was one of a team of twelve monks, priests and lay priests sent to the New World by the king—at Cortés's request—to work with the Indians. Motolinía did teach and preach and set a Christian example, and he baptized over four hundred thousand Indians under the mantle of Spanish control. Motolinía, though he, like Las Casas, deplored the cruel practices of the Spanish settlers, bitterly resented Las Casas's insistence on a period of probation for the Indians that Motolinía felt would postpone adult baptism indefinitely; when Indian people or any people appealed for Christ, Motolinía wanted to satisfy them; and this argument pitted Franciscans against Dominicans, passionate Spaniard against passionate Spaniard. Nevertheless, Las Casas kept on.

At one point the king granted to Las Casas the right to set up a utopia in Venezuela (as Plato once tried to set up an ideal republic). But the ideal state that Las Casas set up failed amid intense dissension, disgusting both the Spaniards and the Indians and disappointing even the priests who in company with Las Casas undertook to convert solely through education, persuasion and example.

As Las Casas lived on and on and on, debating publicly both in the New World and in Spain and writing histories that were selective and slanted compilations of everything he had ever seen or heard, his horror stories of Spanish cruelties were eagerly taken up in Europe, where Spain was being opposed by England, France, Holland, and the cities of Italy. All across Europe the enemies of Spain made spectacular use of Las Casas's outpouring, which portrayed Spain and Spaniards as exquisitely cruel and fanatical in their treatment of meek and mild Indians. A century and more after the conquest of Mexico, European engravers were making drawings of Spaniards butchering peaceable, pitiable Indians. Many of these engravers didn't know what Indians looked like, so they drew bald-headed creatures that had no likeness to any human beings anywhere. Yet these drawings were widely distributed and continue to be shown today.

This calculated and self-serving defamation of Spain and Spaniards by Spain's enemies reached a crescendo around the time of the Spanish armada (1588) when Spain in the extension of its empire clashed with England, which was extending its empire. English privateers had been out raiding the whole world—stealing, burning, raping. The French were the chief rivals of the English. But it served the purpose of the English and the French to identify the Spaniards as the most glaring offenders against everything European civilization was supposed to stand for, thus neatly diverting attention from themselves.

This propaganda campaign, which came to be called the Black Legend, stereotyped Spain and Spaniards as unbridled agents of evil. In truth, during the seventeenth and eighteenth centuries, while England and France were ruthlessly and vigorously extending their empires in North America and Africa and the East and were contesting with each other, Spain was peacefully maintaining its dominion in Latin America. Never mentioned by the purveyors of the Black Legend was the extraordinary fact that Spain as a government and Spaniards as a people from the beginning of European incursion into the New World sought to redeem the souls of the Indians.

This exhibition of Christian conscience was not emulated by the English, French, Dutch, Danes, or those who became Americans. Yet—in all our minds—the Black Legend lingers today. The clichés are reiterated, the images are traced and retraced, in historical novels, costume dramas and movies of derring-do.

There is no denying the facts of the past. But the worthwhile challenge is to abjure the distortion which has been foisted upon us and to see— amid all the foibles of two distinct branches of humanity that had followed separate courses of evolution for thousands of years—the shining qualities that humanity holds in common.

IV
THE REGRETTABLE TRIUMPH

BARELY HANGING ON

One Spaniard after another died on his pallet in Tlascala—following into death the many hundreds of Spaniards who had been killed on the night of the retreat from Tenochtitlán, or who had been captured alive by the Aztecs and by now had certainly been sacrificed and eaten, and those who had fallen along the reeling route of the retreat, in skirmishes or by blood-loss from their wounds. Within the past short span of frenzied days and nights, there had been a great scything of people on both sides. Solemnly the Tlascalans watched Cortés as he lay immobile. The Tlascalans were not unused to grief or to the stoicism that was called for after a battle had gone poorly. Patiently they tended the Spaniards, brought water and food, did what they could to aid in the healing of the wounds, burned the corpses and buried the charred remains. Many Tlascalan warriors fighting or carrying for the Spaniards had been lost and some wounded, though most of the Tlascalan bearers loaded with gold had survived, which was a tribute to their toughness and caginess.

Among the Tlascalan chiefs, Mase Escasi, who had given his daughter to Velásquez de León, mourned with particular intensity, because both the girl and Velásquez de León were gone. No tears were shed for Cacama and the Aztec chiefs; in the atmosphere of warfare, which was the familiar environment of both Indians and Spaniards, tears were not shed for enemies. The Spaniards, however, regretfully noted that two of Montezuma's children who were with them had been killed, a son (it was Cortés's impression that this was Montezuma's only son who was not mad or palsied) and a daughter who was pregnant. Never able to forgo black humor even in this ambience of defeat and death, the Spanish soldiers lying exhausted on their pallets passed along the rumor that, since St. James had been too busy fighting on the Spanish side, it must have been Cortés who had quickened her—which added another little touch to Cortés's growing reputation. Malinche, who either was carrying or would soon be carrying Cortés's child, had not been seriously wounded in the flight, and she nursed Cortés, urging upon him a little water and a little food, taking care of his defecation, washing him.

After a week, when Cortés was able to sit up, his head ached and his skull along the lines of the fractures itched unbearably. When helped to his feet, he was dizzy, and every muscle hurt where he had been bruised by stones and clubs or pierced by arrowheads, lance-points or chips of obsidian. In the yards and houses all over Tlascala, Spaniards, leaning on their hosts, were limping about, trying to regain their vigor. Many never regained their health and remained as cripples in Tlascala. Fortunately for those who survived, the climate in Tlascala was salubrious; in the dry clear mountain air, scabs formed cleanly and scar tissue developed quickly; in the jungle, infection would have been much more prevalent.

The twenty-four horses that were left restored themselves. In the cool pastures their wounds and sprains healed. Horses have an instinct to exercise stiffened limbs, and this was beneficial and curative.

The Tlascalan chiefs called on Cortés and laid out to him the terms they expected in return for the assistance they were rendering. The Tlascalans were not grandiose; they had no imperial ambitions; they did not aspire to be the successors of the Aztecs. If the Spaniards, reinforced by their brothers on the coast, were able eventually to prevail, the Tlascalan chiefs wanted for themselves and their people perpetual exemption from tribute of any sort, a share of the spoils, and control of two provinces that bordered their land. Cortés agreed. And—although the terms of Cortés's agreement were later adjudicated and could never be precisely defined because Cortés himself was hazy, as were most of the Spanish captains who witnessed the agreement—Spain substantially kept its promise to the Tlascalans and exempted them from tribute for the entire period of Spanish rule in Mexico, nearly three hundred years. History is not studded with many such instances of good faith by Europeans in respect to their agreements with Indians.

When the Spanish captains met in council with Cortés and took stock of their situation, the indications were forbidding. Cortés, while on his way to the coast to confront Narváez, had with him more gold than he was able to carry (gold with which to bribe Narváez's soldiers) and he had left some of it in Tlascala in the care of a few ailing Spaniards; he had also left the reserve supply of Spanish clothing. After Cortés, having defeated Narváez, had raced back to Tenochtitlán to rescue the garrison there, the Tlascalans reported that a Spanish captain with five horsemen and forty foot-soldiers had come from the coast with additional provisions for Cortés; this captain had proceeded on the road to the capital and had taken with him the Spaniards Cortés had left, along with the chests filled with gold and the reserve supply of clothing. The entire company had been massacred either by Aztec troops sent from the capital or by tribes along the way who were subject to the Aztecs, and all the Spaniards and the gold had been lost. The Tlascalans had heard that many Spanish horsemen from the coast, thinking the routes to Tenochtitlán were safe, had followed roads which did not pass through Tlascala and had been ambushed and killed. All the tribes who had ever been subject to the Aztecs were up in arms against the Spaniards. It was not known if the Spanish settlement on the coast still endured.

So Cortés picked a few of his healthiest men and sent them to the coast on the healthiest horses. He arranged for Tlascalans to guide them on obscure trails where the Aztec tribes could be avoided. He wanted word brought back to him immediately on the condition of Villa Rica. And soon word came back: Villa Rica endured; the Totonacs had not turned against the Spaniards there.

Then many Spanish captains—including many of those Cortés regarded as most valorous and trustworthy, and including Cortés's old partner, Andrés de Duero—strongly urged Cortés to break for the coast as soon as they were able, to unite with the Spaniards in the fort at Villa Rica and be ready to defend themselves, while ships would go to the islands for help. The logic behind this course was irrefutable. The Spaniards in the mountains had almost nothing left to fight with—no cannons, no harquebuses, no powder, no fittings for the few crossbows. This was the time, the opportune moment, perhaps their only moment, for a strategic withdrawal.

About two weeks had passed since the Spaniards had taken refuge in Tlascala. Cortés was able to walk again, although his head still hurt. But his thinking had not changed. If they were to try to flee to the coast, he replied, they would most likely never make it. A couple of messengers with guides on the back trails could get through and return, but the whole army— what remained of it—was sure to be sighted and attacked all along the way. They would not be able to travel rapidly; even troops sent from Tenochtitlán could overtake them. That is, *if* they were allowed to leave Tlascala— because it would be clear to these brave and loyal Tlascalans that Spaniards lacked courage and were running from the Aztecs. Most likely, the Tlascalans would fall upon them, kill them, take whatever they had. All the Spaniards knew that Xicotenga the Younger had his men on alert, even now, while he abided by the will of the older chiefs.

As Cortés later wrote to the king, he quoted to his captains the Spanish saying—"Fortune always favors the bold" (he did not add Ricardo Palma's disclaimer that Fortune is blind)—and he affirmed his faith in their ultimate victory. Why was he so sure? Because they were Christians and God would not forsake them. And because they were Spaniards and owed this service and their lives to the king, who, if they succeeded, would reward them with both glory and riches. Cortés never said to his men that, if he were to seek help from Cuba, his own vulnerability would be revealed to Velázquez, who had just sent Narváez and a whole army to kill him. Possibly, Cortés never had any thoughts other than the positive propositions he laid out to his captains.

Cortés made no effort to discredit those who argued with him. Nor did he openly question their motives. Some of the captains now proposing a dash for the coast were and always had been partisans of Velázquez. But the fates of all the Spanish leaders had been fused in battle with the fate of Cortés. Many of them owned commodious estates in Cuba or Hispaniola and sensibly longed to return to comfort and safety. But with Cortés they had all faced and withstood the heathen horde. Now their only option— the only option Cortés left them—was to refuse to obey him, which was the military crime of insubordination.

So, at the end of a long afternoon of debate, often desperate and sometimes angry, the captains agreed to hang on—not because the soundness of Cortés's reasoning caused them to change their minds, not because they succumbed to the eloquence of his exhortations, and not because they were afraid to be insubordinate. They agreed because they and Cortés were comrades—and, as often happens in war, comradeship won out.

While the Spaniards rested and recuperated in Tlascala, it occurred to Cortés and his men to wonder why the great armies from Tenochtitlán were not pursuing them, why Tlascala was not under attack or intensive siege, why they were being allowed time to recover. They presumed they were being shielded by the Tlascalans. What they did not know, however, and did not learn until later, was that an epidemic of smallpox was devastating much of Mexico. Smallpox had been brought to America by a stricken crewman in Narváez's fleet, a Negro sailor, and the disease had spread with amazing rapidity through the coastal tribes and up into the highland. Because Tlascala was always in a state of semi-siege, the sickness had not yet affected Tlascala. But American Indians had never before been exposed to smallpox (in spite of the complexion of Xicotenga the Younger) and they had no resistance or immunity to it.

What made the disease spread so quickly was that the Indians were in the habit of bathing to alleviate almost any ailment that afflicted them. These baths were either communal or the same bathing water was used consecutively by many. But after someone with an open smallpox sore entered the bath, the disease was transmitted to everyone who followed. The Spaniards, fortunately for themselves under the circumstances, never bathed; they would wash off the dirt and the blood when they could, but they believed that bathing *per se* was weakening.

In Tenochtitlán Cuitlahuac was dying of the new sickness. While Montezuma was held prisoner, Cuitlahuac had been battle-commander of the Aztecs, and after Montezuma's death he had succeeded Montezuma. In all likelihood, it was at Cuitlahuac's coronation ceremonies that the captured Spaniards were sacrificed. Now the doubly decimated Aztec nobility was in confusion, trying to settle upon another successor.

After twenty days in Tlascala, Cortés felt that he could ride again. As his wounds healed, the pain shrank to the areas around the wounds and no longer debilitated his whole body. He felt that his first move must be to restore the respect the Indians had once held for the Spaniards—to reinstill fear. So he decided to make an example of Tepeaca, an extensive province about thirty miles from Tlascala along an alternate southern route to Tenochtitlán. The Tepeacans were part of the Aztec confederation and part of the Aztec bulwark against Tlascala; while Cortés had been victorious, the Tepeacans had pledged allegiance to the king of Spain; after the Spaniards were driven from Tenochtitlán, the Tepeacans reverted to the Aztecs— and, it was confirmed, had then killed twelve Spaniards who were en route from the coast to Tenochtitlán. Now warriors from Tenochtitlán were known to have joined and reinforced the Tepeacans.

Cortés had the Tlascalans send an embassy for him to Tepeaca: He commanded the Tepeacans to resume their allegiance to the king of Spain, in which case he would forgive them for their recent treachery; otherwise, he would punish them as they deserved. The reply from the Tepeacans was contemptuous: They needed more victims for sacrifice to their gods; their supply from the Flower Wars had been used up; they dared the Spaniards to come on.

So Cortés assembled all the Spaniards who could walk, a total of about four hundred men. Seventeen horses were usable, and Cortés assigned them to his best riders and led the cavalry himself. The Spaniards had no powder at all, so they could not use their few cannons and harquebuses even if the weapons would function. There were only a few crossbows with strings. But the men still had their swords, pikes, lances, daggers, and body armor. This time they would not have to leave a perimeter defense around their camp; Tlascala habitually defended itself. As usual, a Mass was said prior to their departure.

Xicotenga the Younger decided to support them—with forty thousand Tlascalan warriors. He had been provoked by the insolence of the Tepeacan reply, and he sought battle to assuage his pride.

While the Spaniards and Tlascalans were marching on Tepeaca, they were joined by substantial contingents of warriors from Cholula and a town near Cholula. The Cholulans told Cortés that Cuitlahuac was determined to reverse Montezuma's policy of accommodation with the Spaniards, and he had sent Aztec governors and troops into all the provinces surrounding Tenochtitlán. Prior to the coming of the Spaniards, the Aztec tax-collectors had been oppressive enough, but these new Aztec governors and their men were ransacking the cities and towns, stealing everything the people had. In their arrogance the Aztecs violated the Cholulan women—wives, sisters, daughters—forcing the Cholulan men to stand by and watch. And the Aztecs enslaved the young women and children. The Cholulans preferred the orderly administration of the Spaniards to this despoliation by the Aztecs. So the Cholulans and their neighbors rallied to the Spaniards.

This was the first good news Cortés had heard since the defeat in Tenochtitlán. And he welcomed the Cholulans with a hearty *abrazo*.

Confident of another victory, the Tepeacans and Aztecs had not established their defense in a cranny or atop a cliff but, screaming their taunts and waving their weapons, had formed their battlelines in front of their city on flat fields of maize and maguey—ideal terrain for the Spanish cavalry. The warhorses had lost some of their cunning and at first were confused by the tall stalks and sharp spikes, but Cortés and his clever riders soon had the horses charging, wheeling, pursuing. The cavalry performed in sets of three for better safety and aimed their lances at face-level for maximum frightfulness and to avoid embedding a lance in a body and perhaps losing it. The Spanish infantry fought with grit and efficiency. On the flanks the howling Tlascalans and Cholulans came on like a whistling wind and operated in harmony with the Spaniards, responding promptly to commands from Cortés. Again and again the Tepeacan and Aztec lines were broken, their warriors speared, hacked down or sent running from the fields.

Forcing their way into the main city of Tepeaca, the Spaniards and their allies burned the temples atop the pyramids, toppled the idols, cracked the sacrifice-stones, and swept on to the other cities and towns of the province. In a relentless campaign that took nearly three weeks, the Spaniards and the Indians with them smashed all opposition. The troops from Tenochtitlán deserted the Tepeacans and fled back toward the Mexican capital. In the entire campaign the Spaniards did not lose a man and lost only one horse, though a number of Spaniards were wounded. The Tlascalans and Cholulans, less disciplined and overeager in the fight, suffered heavier losses.

All eyes then were on Cortés—at the center of the smoking desolation of Tepeaca. Into the central square of the main city he had his men herd all the people from those towns where Spaniards were known to have been killed, and there were several such towns in the province; in one of the towns fifteen Spaniards had been invited to rest and had been killed as they slept. Now Cortés's own men watched him with curiosity to see what in Christian conscience he would do. The Tlascalans and Cholulans keenly anticipated vengeance. The assembled Tepeacans trembled as they awaited his judgment.

Cortés had promised punishment. But what outrage of the flesh could impress these people? Indians were used to the vicissitudes of battle and in their ceremonies exalted a degree of barbarism which exceeded anything Spaniards had ever dreamed of. Yet Cortés needed to teach these Indians a lesson.

The crime at issue was unique. It was not that the Tepeacans had bravely defended their homes against strangers who demanded their subservience. Spaniards respected brave fighters. But these Tepeacans had pledged allegiance to the king of Spain, then had reneged on their allegiance. Their crime was that they had turned against the king. Cortés had his strategy ready.

He enslaved the Tepeacans. Slavery was a degradation with which all the Indians were familiar; it was a condition, an ancient custom, recognized by all the tribes and accepted by them without question. He had a brand made to mark the slaves, with the letter *"g"* for *"guerra"* (war) crossed by a bar and decorated with two dots, and he branded all the Tepeacans—women, children, and surviving men from those towns where Spaniards had been killed. Though the women and children screamed, the punishment administered was less severe in terms of immediate harm and torture than the Tepeacans expected. It was the permanence of slavery—not as the Spaniards perceived slavery but as the Indians understood slavery—that appalled the Tepeacans.

This was all a show. Cortés knew that the Spanish Crown viewed slavery with disfavor (this imposition of slavery was later undone by the Crown). He was too familiar with Spanish law to think that his use of this form of chastisement would last. But there was no other way he could think of, or did think of, to accomplish his short-term aim. And his purpose was served. All the Indians—on his side the Tlascalans, Cholulans and the Cholulan neighbors, on the other side the Tepeacans and the Aztecs who were watching from a distance—accepted his justice.

Carrying out his show with Spanish legal precision, Cortés allotted a fifth of the slaves to the king and turned them over to Spaniards who had been appointed royal agents; he took a fifth of the slaves for himself, and apportioned fixed percentages to his captains and to the Tlascalans and his Cholulan allies. The judiciousness of Spanish procedure always won the admiration of the Indians. The Spaniards themselves, however, became entangled with their own routine.

They seemed to get drunk at the end of each episode of fighting. In Tepeaca they had no wine, nor is there any record that they drank *pulque*. Perhaps it was just the relief from tension that made them bicker and bluster as if they were carousing. In Tepeaca they argued over the disposition of the branded slaves.

Certain Spaniards maintained that the slaves (women) they had turned in for branding weren't the same slaves who were given back to them. One of the Spaniards who had formerly been with Narváez swore that he had wrapped around the hips of an Indian woman he favored a shawl that had belonged to his mother, he had turned in the woman for branding, and another woman without a shawl had been returned to him; so where was his mother's shawl? Bernal Díaz himself was one of a group who argued that, in a situation like this, the women should be auctioned off to the highest bidder, and the royal fifth should be taken from the gold thus collected. Narváez's men, for their part, maintained that a fifth should not go to Cortés because there couldn't or shouldn't be two kings to skim off the cream. Besides, the Narváez men wanted to know, where was this gold to come from? Cortés's men confessed that each of them might have a bar or two hidden away in a pocket or purse. And on and on the bickering went.

There were many more Indian women, enslaved or available, than the exhausted Spaniards needed or could use. And Cortés diplomatically agreed that, if they were ever to do this again, an auction would be the right way to do it. As for the gold, Cortés said, everyone should turn in all that he had for a redistribution. And nobody turned in anything.

There must have been an aspect of conscious buffoonery in this very characteristic Spanish fractiousness (as, among Spanish people now, there is often an aspect of humor underlying what by Anglo-Saxon standards seems histrionic behavior). Exaggerated accusations were made against Cortés by his own captains, and the common soldiers made accusations not only against Cortés but against all the captains and a few of the priests. Without taking offense, Cortés defended himself, parried, proposed alternatives. Yet never—in any of these melodramatic blow-offs—was it suggested that Cortés should be replaced as captain-general. Cortés was the natural as well as the designated leader of his men—whether leading them into battle, plotting strategy, or later letting down.

After the Tepeaca campaign Cortés felt that he had to hold this place which was a way-station on a route to Tenochtitlán. So, even as new bone was forming in his skull and his many wounds were healing, while his dizziness and aches diminished, he founded another new town, precisely in accord with *Siete Partidas*. He named a council, had a charter written, appointed the required officials, ordered the construction of a fort, church, storehouse, just as had been done for Villa Rica. He called the new town *la Villa de Segura de la Frontera*, the Town of Safety for the Frontier.

SECOND WIND

The Tepeaca campaign promptly had two effects. One, the route from Segura de la Frontera in the highland to Villa Rica on the coast became open and safe. The tribes along the way—both Nahuatl-speakers and others—quieted, and they treated Spaniards passing through with respect. Two, Cuitlahuac and, after he died of smallpox, his successor, Guatémoc (phonetically, Cua-uh-tay-mawk), dispatched from Tenochtitlán substantial Aztec armies to hold the mountain passes around the valley of Mexico and to strengthen garrisons in the nearby provinces. Cuitlahuac, while he lived, was especially aggressive and invented new weapons. He took Spanish swords that had been captured on the night of the Spaniards' defeat and had them bound to long poles for attacking the horses, and he had very long copper lances made and distributed (but the Indians had not discovered the effective tactic to fight cavalry, which is to butt the lance in the earth and have a gutsy man hold it firm and steady so that a charging horse impales itself). The improvement in Aztec weaponry, however, was offset by the depredations of the Aztec troops, whose excesses roused the hatred of the adjoining tribes.

From the Spaniards at Villa Rica to Cortés in Segura de la Frontera came a number of reports which revealed that a trend of significance in history was taking place. Irresistibly—sometimes by chance, sometimes by design, sometimes in strength or in the aftermath of a disaster, often as the result simply of a mix-up—Europeans were landing on the mainland of the New World. Cortés was in the vanguard but, even had he not persevered, it is reasonably certain that invasion of the New World by Europeans would have continued. As it was, Cortés knew that Francisco de Garay, the governor of Jamaica, was trying to establish a settlement at the mouth of the Pánuco River to the north of Villa Rica. Now a report reached Cortés that two of Garay's ships had sought shelter at Villa Rica. There had been three ships; one had sunk. The ships had entered the Pánuco River, been attacked by the Indians and driven off. Cortés ordered that Garay's men who survived should be provided with supplies and assisted to depart, if they chose to depart, or they should be offered some gold as an inducement to enlist under Cortés's banner. To no one's surprise they enlisted and soon joined Cortés in Tepeaca.

Also, there arrived at Villa Rica a supply ship from Cuba. Apparently Velázquez presumed that Narváez had succeeded in overcoming Cortés, and he was sending to Narváez additional men and equipment. The commander of the ship was a gentleman named Pedro Barba. The Spaniards at Villa Rica warmly greeted the newly arrived crew and welcomed the new men ashore. Then Cortés's men uncovered their weapons and announced that they were loyal to Cortés. They explained the situation to the newcomers, gave them a little gold—and the officers and crew of the supply ship were enlisted in the ongoing crusade.

Eight days later, another supply ship from Cuba arrived under the command of Rodrigo Morejón de Lobera. Velázquez obviously had set up a rotation of supply ships to support his hitherto-reliable lieutenant, whom Cortés had jailed. So the officers and crew of this second ship were enlisted in the same manner as those of the first ship, and the cargo was brought ashore.

Then another supply ship arrived, a large ship from Spain very heavily loaded. This ship was owned by a merchant who was aboard and who, having heard of the gold discovery in the newly found land, had brought merchandise to sell, especially powder, cannons and shooting-pieces. The men in Mexico had received no recent reports from Spain; they did not know what had eventually become of Puertocarrero, Montejo, and the treasure that had been sent to the king. But from the men on this supply ship they learned that the Council of the Indies, under the direction of Velázquez's uncle, Bishop Fonseca, had placed an embargo on all goods destined for the New World. In order to evade the embargo, the merchant-owner of this ship had sailed it empty to the Canary Islands and there had loaded the goods which he had previously dispatched from Spain. The Spaniards at Villa Rica—upon instructions from Cortés—paid for the whole lot in gold.

Thus, up from the coast to the highland began to flow an intermittent line of supply, which included items desperately needed, like twine to string the crossbows and load after load of powder, all sorts of ordnance, and men, horses, even broodmares. Pedro Barba, it turned out, was an old friend of Cortés and they had a back-slapping reunion in Segura de la Frontera. Cortés placed Barba in command of the crossbowmen. Cortés rewarded and gave important assignments to all the incoming gentlemen who joined him.

Reassured now of his ability to continue with the conquest and less chary of his relationship with Velázquez, Cortés composed another letter to the king, confessing to his defeat and attesting to his survival and resolve. He sent this letter to Spain in the care of a couple of his captains, using one of the many ships now available. He also entrusted gold to these captains with which to buy more supplies. Though Cortés on the night of the retreat from Tenochtitlán had lost most of the enormous treasure he had accumulated, he retained the gold bars the Tlascalan bearers were able to bring out, and this was the financial capital with which he worked. Cortés wrote letters to men he knew in Jamaica and to the Jeronymite council on Hispaniola and sent the letters with other captains, along with gold to buy horses and mares. Cortés dared to send his old partner, Andrés de Duero, to Cuba with some gold to buy more supplies. Duero had no appetite for further daredeviltry, and Cortés felt that Duero, who had been Velázquez's secretary and knew a great deal about Velázquez's affairs, would be able to withstand or evade the governor's disapprobation. In Duero's care Cortés even sent a letter to his wife, La Marcaida, a letter undoubtedly replete with formalities, courtesies and niceties, but it is unknown what Cortés essentially said to her.

Some chiefs from a town beyond Cholula, farther up the throughway toward Tenochtitlán, came to Cortés in Segura de la Frontera to beg for his help against an Aztec army of occupation. They said that thirty thousand Aztec warriors were encamped in the countryside around their town, while Aztec captains had ensconced themselves in the best houses within the town. If Cortés would aid them, they promised to seize the Aztec scouts on watch along the road, to guide the Spaniards into their town (a walled town with well-built battlements) and to besiege the Aztec captains so that the captains could be killed before the Aztec army could come to their support.

Cortés assigned for the task three hundred foot-soldiers and cavalrymen under the command of Cristóbal de Olid, a hard-bitten captain who had served as quartermaster in Villa Rica. Olid in turn chose officers to go with him—and the officers he chose happened to be mostly men who had formerly served Narváez. The Spanish force set out, with the best horses

and with many Tlascalan auxiliaries, and in a day reached Cholula, which
was about twenty-five miles away. The town occupied by the Aztecs was
ten or fifteen miles farther up the valley. In Cholula, however, Indians came
to Olid and his officers and warned them that they were being drawn into
a trap, that the Aztecs planned to block their retreat route after they had
entered the town and to massacre them while they were in the narrow
zigzags of the town walls. Narváez's men had little heart for another fierce
battle and they influenced Olid so that he hesitated and sent back to Cortés
in Segura de la Frontera both the chiefs from the occupied town and the
Indians who had warned him of the trap.

In Segura Cortés interrogated these Indians. He was becoming expert
at this kind of examination, as he developed—instinctively, intuitively—
an empathy with Indians. He had outgrown his earlier disdain of the
Indians; their courage had knocked this out of him; and his tendency now
was to assume that they thought as he did, boldly and cleverly, in what they
perceived to be their own self-interest. For questioning, he would put each
Indian in a separate room under guard, then with Malinche and Aguilar
would go from room to room, chatting easily, proffering friendship, cajoling, sometimes threatening torture, comparing details, catching contradictions. And Cortés concluded that all these Indians had been telling the
truth; Olid had misunderstood those who seemed to warn him of a trap.
The trap they were describing was the trap proposed by the town's inhabitants to capture or kill the Aztec captains.

So Cortés with a cadre of veterans went to Cholula and took over the
command from Olid. In accord with the original plan, the Spaniards
proceeded against the Aztecs; the local Indians performed precisely as
promised; and there was another significant Spanish victory. Evidently there
had been prominent Aztec nobles in charge of this army because the armor,
feathered headdresses and weapons taken from the dead were heavily laden
with gold and precious stones.

Returning to Segura de la Frontera, Cortés posted a captain and sixty
men to oversee the continued construction of the fort and to hold the new
town. Then he went back to Tlascala, where he put into effect the preparation for the next stage of his strategy. Cortés ordered that thirteen brigantines should be built from the abundant wood on the hillsides, and they
should be made in unassembled pieces—keels, crossbeams, planks—so
the pieces could be transported over the mountains and down to the lakes
in the valley of Mexico. He ordered that all the remaining sails and fittings
from the ships he had scuttled at Villa Rica should be brought from the

coast. Pitch could be made from local trees. In addition, all kinds of ships' equipment could be taken from the many vessels now in harbor and at his disposal. Cortés had excellent shipbuilders who supervised the thousands of Indians who turned out for this work. And Cortés sent word to the coast that all blacksmiths should come to the highland and their forges should be brought with them.

Cortés did not intend again to flaunt his daring by crossing the spider's thread of a causeway into Tenochtitlán, only to be besieged and starved there. Next time he intended to be the besieger, to hold the land all around the island, and to let that heavenly capital, that dream city, starve itself while he waited in force ashore and with his brigantines kept all commerce from the water.

ENCIRCLEMENT

From Tenochtitlán, at the center of their web of empire, the ranking Aztec nobles, led by their new young emperor, Guatémoc, were ready and eager to match wits with Cortés and the Spanish captains. Slowed in their response though the Aztecs were by the smallpox epidemic and the consequent problem of the royal succession (smallpox had now spread to Cholula, even to Tlascala, where Mase Escasi died of the disease), Guatémoc and his commanders vigorously countered the moves of the Spaniards.

The Aztec generals ordered that in all the cities and towns in the valley of Mexico new ramparts should be built, ditches dug and sharp pointed stakes set at the bottom, hillsides cut out and ambushes prepared along the paths down into the valley from the mountain rim. After Cortés's victory in Tepeaca, the Aztecs knew he was coming. So Guatémoc sent word to all provinces in the empire that Spaniards were to be attacked and killed wherever they were. He sent gifts of gold and jewels to the chiefs of subject tribes and promised them exemption from tribute for years to come. More Aztec armies were on the march.

Both the Spaniards and the Aztecs were trying to restore the respect in which they had formerly been held, and both the Spaniards and the Aztecs were trying to do so by reinstilling fear. But for the Aztecs this reassertion of their exalted status was more difficult because they carried with them a greater burden from the past. When Aztec warriors now fanning out from the capital abused subject tribes as they had abused them while first achieving supremacy, many of these tribes, instead of being terrorized into submission, informed the Spaniards, conspired against the Aztecs and supported the Spanish cause, especially after the Spaniards humbled the Aztecs at Tepeaca.

There was no sense of community among the Indians, no feeling of racial cohesion, no comprehension that a vital racial clash was taking place. Prior to the coming of the Spaniards, the Indians had never known there were any human beings except Indians, and tribal distinctions—which were obvious to all Indians in appearance, accent, manner, locale—to the Indians meant everything. And, tribe to tribe, the Indians were infinitely cruel to one another in ways that had no counterpart in anything the Spaniards had done or ever did. For example, the tribute, from which Guatémoc promised subject tribes temporary exemption, included as part payment young males and females for sacrifice. The Aztecs never sacrificed their own; from the subject tribes they collected victims as tribute and, because the Aztec need for sacrificial victims was so enormous, the Aztecs had to amplify the collected tribute with captives from Flower Wars and wars of exploration and conquest. During the early years of Montezuma's reign Aztec military expeditions to gather victims had gone as far as Nicaragua. This awful underpinning of the interrelationship among the Indians had no reflection in the relationship that Indians of any tribe had with the Spaniards. So Guatémoc's temporary exemption from tribute was received by those who had been paying the tribute with less than gratitude. Contrarily, the religion of these Spaniards—focusing strangely on the figure of a woman with child, the cruciform design, flowers, lighted candles—had a gentleness about it that the Indians, all of them, even the Aztecs, found curious and appealing.

Only two tribes along the route from Segura de la Frontera to Villa Rica obeyed Guatémoc's command and waylaid passing Spaniards. Promptly Cortés, while he was still in Tepeaca, sent Gonzalo de Sandoval with twenty horsemen, two hundred foot-soldiers and a substantial contingent of ever-ready Tlascalans to restore the safety of the road.

It was mid-December, 1520. In the highland the days were clear and crisp. It never rained. The nights were cold but endurable under a good cloak. The ground underfoot was firm for marching; the horses never became mired. The weather was ideal for war.

More and more tribes were resorting to Cortés for confirmation of their successions, especially in cases where the chiefs had abandoned their people to flee with the retreating Aztecs. The passing of governmental control from one chief to the next had always been troublesome for the Indians, and disposition by Cortés was welcomed. He made many Solomonic judgments. To settle a dispute between a bastard and a legitimate heir, Cortés had the legitimate heir, who was ten years old, anointed as chief, but he made the bastard regent until the boy's maturity. In Tlascala after the death of Mase Escasi, Cortés approved transfer of the control of his land to his son, who was twelve or thirteen years old. But Xicotenga the Younger was discomfited because he would have liked to annex Mase Escasi's land.

Two days before Christmas, Sandoval returned, his mission accomplished, and brought with him as captives the chiefs who had followed Guatémoc's orders. But Cortés pardoned them, after they promised once more to be faithful to the Spanish cause, and he freed them to return to their people. Not that Cortés believed them, but his fundamental policy was to accept and accept again the Indians' promises of allegiance in the hope that finally faithfulness, supported by practical self-interest, would prevail. Also, he did not have enough men to enforce compliance throughout the land.

Two days after Christmas, Cortés held a review and took stock. He had forty horsemen, five hundred fifty foot-soldiers (eighty of them crossbowmen and harquebusiers), with eight or nine cannons and a reserve of powder so small as to be worrisome. This force was actually only a little larger and in some respects weaker than the force with which he had first accosted Mexico—and it was much smaller and weaker than the force with which he had returned to Tenochtitlán after defeating Narváez.

Nevertheless, to these men Cortés laid down the ordinances he expected them to abide by when again they returned to the valley of Mexico in pursuit of their prize, which was the magical city of Tenochtitlán. He told his men that they would be victorious because they were Christians contending with barbarian heathen; that the Aztecs, having sworn fealty to the king of Spain, had turned treasonous and killed many Spaniards; that the Aztecs, having resolved to kill all Spaniards, were their mortal enemies; and that the Aztecs were opposed by those Indians who to the Spanish had been saviors and were loyal friends. These premises were all valid justifications for warfare, as defined in *Siete Partidas* and as required by the Spanish Crown. To these justifications, Cortés added a number of prohibitions, most of which were the same prohibitions he had first set forth when he had landed with his men on the island of Cozumel: No Spaniard was ever to blaspheme the Holy Name of God; or quarrel with another Spaniard; or wager either his arms or his horse (both too valuable to be used in gambling); or force a woman; or rob or harm any Indian other than in battle, unless the council of the army, for good reason, condoned a sacking;

or insult friendly Indians in any way; or, specifically, use an Indian who was acknowledged to be a bearer *(tameme)* as a gift. The aim of the Spaniards must be to compel and induce these unenlightened people willingly to accept Christ and the king and to do nothing which might impede their voluntary submission.

The Tlascalans heard Cortés's speech to his army. It was translated for them by Malinche and by a few Spaniards, particularly the young pages, who were picking up Nahuatl. And the Tlascalans were amazed by some of Cortés's provisions. They passed on their amazement to the Cholulans, the Tepeacans, and the news spread from tribe to tribe, even eventually reaching those in Tenochtitlán.

For conquerors not to force women? Unrestrained and unaffected by the concept of purity and innocence personified by Mary, all Indians, when conquering, would use force with women of another tribe in order intentionally to shame and disgrace the men of the tribe that had been conquered. But Spaniards took only the women who were given them as gifts, women who passively came to them, and the women of tribes they were punishing, and even with these women the Spaniards exhibited little savagery. Furthermore, the Spaniards, as conquerors, accepted only the tribute—in gold, jewels, clothing, food, never victims for sacrifice—which was with some degree of volition delivered to them. This tribute, though often elicited with some pressure, nevertheless was accepted in a manner that did not infringe upon the dignity of the givers. Now, even the Spaniards who were common soldiers were being told not to steal, not to rob houses, not to abandon themselves in the frenzy of pillage with which all the Indians were quite familiar. These white-skinned strangers would not even regard as a slave one whom the Indians themselves regarded as good for nothing other than bearing burdens. Cortés probably proclaimed this ordinance regarding the *tamemes* because he was grateful to the Tlascalan bearers who had carried gold from Tenochtitlán, and his feeling was seconded, if not prompted, by Aguilar, who had labored for years as an Indian bearer.

The whole Indian world was befuddled by the inkling of morality which was perceived from these Spanish military ordinances—imperfect in execution though these ordinances inevitably would be.

On December 28, 1520, Cortés and his army with twenty thousand Tlascalan warriors (not counting *tamemes*) departed from Tlascala and began their climb to the mountain rim. There were three passes available to them—one pass that was easy and most often used, another pass that was more difficult and occasionally used, and a third pass that was extremely difficult and very seldom used. Cortés guessed that the most difficult pass would be the one in which the Aztecs would be least prepared to oppose him—and he was right. His troops suffered from the cold during the night, but the pass itself proved to be unmanned by the enemy.

Descending from the rim in the chill of early morning, the eight horsemen and foot-soldiers who comprised the point of the army found the road blocked by recently felled trees. With difficulty making their way past the roadblock, the point men found another roadblock a little farther on, and past that, another. So they sent back for Cortés who quickly joined them. On this unmanned route, roadblocks had been set up at intervals for a considerable distance. Cortés, however, decided to persist on his course. He called up the Tlascalans, who dismantled the roadblocks as the army came to them—until eventually they all emerged upon a clear path and came to a ridge from which they had a view of the valley of Mexico.

There in the center of the valley were the interlinked lakes, drawn into focus by the surrounding orchards and fields, which were more brown than green in winter, and by the ring of mountains interspersed with snowy volcanoes and peaks. The lakes, like mirrors, reflected the clear sky. On and around these lakes were the true jewels of Mexico—the lakeside cities and, in the middle of the largest lake, the glittering island capital of Tenochtitlán. The Aztec cities were different from any cities the Spaniards or any Eurasians had ever seen. The Aztec cities were not jumbled, like European cities, energized, tossed-up, overcrowded, nor were they soaring like some modern cities, New York or Hong Kong. Instead, the Aztec cities seemed geometric, planned, and in a spiritual way strangely calm; they were so horizontal, with many flat rooflines, tier upon tier, composed largely of extensive compounds of low-lying buildings, one or two stories high; the Aztecs took their leisure on the *azoteas,* the roof-gardens of their homes; and in this horizontalness there was an expansiveness and air of repose. The horizontalness was varied by the upthrusting, aspiring pyramids, like token mountains with precise triangular sides that modulated the light, all the whited, stuccoed limestone together producing a kind of glow. The straight boulevards and rectangular plazas were paved with flagstones, and the lines of the boulevards, like trunks of trees, drew together the narrow curving lanes. Actually, the geometry of Tenochtitlán was deceptive because it implied a mathematical perfection the Aztecs had not achieved. The Aztecs had corbel arches but no true arches and consequently favored horizontal lintels. And the pyramids were basically mounded rubble faced with receding layers of stone, not true pyramidal arrangements of stone blocks. Thus the Aztec cities were illusions of geometric perfection—

probably unintentional, perhaps unperceived by their makers—with the assertion of the stone moderated here and there by expanses of thatch, where the huts of the poor were roofed or the market stalls covered. But, altogether, the Aztec beauty charmed the Europeans. Because so many of the Spaniards knew Tenochtitlán, for better and worse, their overview now recalled for them in detail the carved images, friezes, inlays of rare wood, the brilliant painting in black, red, blue and yellow on white, even the smells of the marketplace, of strange fruits and foods and exotic brown women. Multi-faceted Tenochtitlán was the most glorious jewel of the Aztec empire. And every Spaniard in his romantic imagination was inspired to take it—Cortés most of all. Having once possessed the treasure lode of this valley, he was determined never to leave it again until he had triumphed.

The Spaniards and Tlascalans had been sighted by the Aztecs. The Aztec armies that had been guarding the easier passes where the Spaniards were expected to cross were now falling back to positions on lower land. Signal fires burned in towns on the slopes, and columns of smoke were rising in the windless air. More smoke signals were being lighted all over the valley, warning of the invasion. The smoke signals were ominous—yet the Spaniards, elated by the gorgeous vista and relishing the prize in their minds, bravely swung along on the downward slope, a few hundred Europeans with Indians flanking their column, tackling once again a valley in which dwelt well over a million Indians renowned for their ferocity.

Cortés had selected Texcoco—Cacama's city—for his initial base. Texcoco was nearly as large as Tenochtitlán and was situated on the eastern shore of the lake system. Texcoco was not connected by a causeway to the capital; it was set off amid rich farmlands, and the Texcocan part of the lake was separated from Tenochtitlán and the cities on the southern and western shores by a very large, segmented dike. The lakes of Mexico, linked by straits, were only partially understood by the Spaniards and, for that matter, by the Mexicans. The fresh-water lakes were runoff from the mountains; the salt lakes were residual. In winter the level of the salt water was considerably higher than the fresh-water level.

Having taken the unexpected route into the valley, the Spaniards were not immediately opposed; the Aztecs were not as quick as the Spaniards in responding to surprise or adversity; so the Spaniards and their allies were able to proceed toward Texcoco in an uneasy quiet, bothered only by people who hollered at them from distant hilltops. The Spaniards and Tlascalans stopped for the night at a town from which all the people had fled. Cortés always countenanced the taking of maize, fowl and dogs for food. In the morning the march continued.

Cortés did not know what reception he would get from the Texco-cans—whether they would yield in fear, or would stand and fight, or would try to ambush him. But a few miles outside Texcoco he was met on the road by four Texcocan chiefs who brought with them on a pole a heavy banner made of gold, a showy offering of the commodity the Aztecs knew the Spaniards liked best. These chiefs—one of whom Cortés recognized and knew—made polite obeisance to him and asked him to accept the gold banner as a sign of their renewed allegiance to him and to the king of Spain; they blamed all the trouble he had had on the people of Tenochtitlán; and they begged him not to harm their people or their homes. Cortés replied through Malinche that in this province many Spaniards had been killed and much treasure taken, treasure which had been given the Spaniards by the great Montezuma, and, though he could not expect them to restore life to the dead, he did want his treasure back. If they would return the treasure, he would forgive them for their previous crimes. The Texcocans said the people of Tenochtitlán had taken all the treasure, but if Cortés and his men would rest in the pleasant garden-palaces prepared for them on the out-skirts of Texcoco, these four Texcocan nobles would speak to their reigning chief and see what could be done toward restoration of the treasure.

The then reigning chief of Texcoco was not Cacama's brother whom Cortés, on Montezuma's recommendation, had left in control. The reign-ing chief was Cacama's other brother, Cacama's two brothers together having connived to turn over Cacama to the Spaniards. This brother, incited by Cuitlahuac or Guatémoc, had murdered the brother who had been appointed by Cortés and Montezuma and had seized control for himself—a sequence which came as no surprise to sixteenth-century Spaniards.

Cortés declined the offer of the garden-palaces, declaring that it was his intention to occupy the center of Texcoco. Compliantly the Texcocan chiefs said they would hasten to their city and prepare his reception.

Warily, Cortés moved his army into Texcoco, where he found quarters prepared for him in an extensive compound beside the highest pyramid. But there were very few people in the streets and the people he saw seemed fearful. Without delay he disposed his forces to defend their position and he sternly forbade his men to venture from the compound and ordered the Tlascalans to stay close by, while he sent Alvarado and Olid to the top of the pyramid to look over the city.

What the Spanish captains saw from the top of the pyramid was that Texcoco was being abandoned. On the lake were thousands of canoes carrying people and their goods to the safety of Tenochtitlán. Roads into

the country and surrounding woods were crowded with people bearing
burdens. People were fleeing into thickets along the shore. The streets of
Texcoco were deserted. Obviously the Aztec ploy, once again, was to starve
out the Spaniards, to leave to the Spaniards and their allies a swept-out city
with no one to supply or sustain them.

When this was reported to Cortés, he dispatched a squad of horsemen
to bring to him the reigning chief and the Texcocan nobles who had met
him on the road. But the chief and those nobles had already left in canoes
for Tenochtitlán. The greeting Cortés had received on the road with the
gift of the gold banner had been simply a ruse to delay the Spaniards'
occupation of the city. Now only a few minor officials could be found.

What Cortés needed was not the nobles, unless the nobles would
command the people to come back to their homes: He needed the people
themselves—the women to make the tortillas and to cook the fowl and the
fish, the farmers to bring maize and fruit from the fields. But Cortés had
in his entourage a noble Texcocan boy the Spaniards had taken with them
in their flight; the boy was said to be the grandson of a great Texcocan king
who had preceded Cacama and his brothers. This boy was remarkable
because in the company of the Spaniards he had become bilingual and had
been baptized: Since Cortés was his godfather, the Spaniards jubilantly had
named the boy Don Fernando Cortés. (The Spaniards are broad-minded
about names. Cortés himself was called Hernán and Hernando and Fernán
and Ferdinando.) Now Cortés produced this boy and proclaimed him the
new and rightful ruler of Texcoco.

As word of the new boy-king spread, the common people of Texcoco,
who had not fled to Tenochtitlán but were hiding in the woods and in
thickets on the lake, returned to the city to look at the boy. And they liked
him and respected his descendancy. Probably they had been mistreated by
Cacama's generation. Then within a few days Texcoco was repeopled,
tortillas were fluffing on the griddle-stones, sacks of corn were being lugged
through the streets, and food was being brought regularly to the Spaniards
and their friends.

Cortés's policy, especially in view of Aztec oppression, was to encourage
the subject tribes willingly to come to his side. So he stayed in place in
Texcoco, and within three days chiefs from two large towns nearby came
to him to make excuses for their past conduct and to repledge their
allegiance. Cortés welcomed them, and on the following day these chiefs
brought to him, tied up and slung from poles, messengers from Tenochtitlán who had been sent to threaten them with all kinds of punishment for
consorting with the Spaniards. Various lies were told by all sides, though

almost all were seen through. The Aztec messengers denied making threats and claimed only to have asked the local chiefs to mediate between the Aztecs and the Spaniards. Cortés hopefully was angling to renew his conquest by guile. So he had the Aztec messengers freed and put into a canoe to return to Tenochtitlán to tell Guatémoc that he (Cortés) was aware that the war against the Spaniards had been instigated by Cuitlahuac, now dead, and Cortés wanted only to restore the harmony that had existed during the reign of Montezuma.

None of these schemes worked. No reply came from Tenochtitlán. Consequently, after about a week, and after the Spaniards had dug in at Texcoco, Cortés organized a raiding party of two hundred foot-soldiers with cavalrymen, crossbowmen and harquebusiers and with four or five thousand Tlascalans in support, and he set out for Iztapalapa—one of Cuitlahuac's two cities—which was about a two days' march around the lake.

Before departing from Texcoco, however, Cortés had to cope with another spasm of fear and resentment among his own men, especially those who had come with Narváez and who were terrified by the audacity of what they were doing. Cortés was informed of a plan to mutiny and to send to Velázquez for help. Cortés identified the plotters, who really had no leader, and had confessions taken from a few of them, but he chose to play down the whole confused affair and, as a lesson to firm up discipline, he ordered and saw carried out the execution of a single plotter, a common soldier named Antonio de Villafaña who came from Zamora. In executing Villafaña, Cortés was not individualistically demonstrating his iron will; on the contrary, the execution was the act of the army as a whole. All the men with Cortés knew that their lives were at desperate risk, and almost all of them knew that, if they allowed their chronic bickering and bitter joshing to turn to mutiny and weakness, they would be undone. After the execution, which was probably by hanging in the courtyard of the compound, Cortés led the raiding party for Iztapalapa. His godson, Don Fernando, sent several Texcocan chiefs to act as guides.

The city of Iztapalapa seemed exceptionally beautiful to the Spaniards because about half the houses were built on the land of the lakeshore and half were built on stilts in the water where canals served as streets, so the city blended into the lake. After camping overnight in the hills, the Spanish force approached Iztapalapa shortly after dawn, and they were opposed by Iztapalapans reinforced by troops from Tenochtitlán. Only after a grueling daylong battle did the Aztecs fall back past their houses on the land to their houses and canoes on the water. The Spaniards and Tlascalans, weary and flushed with victory, occupied the houses on the land and, while the Tlascalans ransacked the houses, the Spaniards caught their breath.

But then there was a rush of rising water as the houses on the land were flooded. The Aztecs had opened a dike that separated the nearby salt lake from this fresh-water lake, and now a torrent of water descended on Iztapalapa. Only the Texcocan chiefs who were with the Spaniards comprehended what was happening and they screamed and gestured for the Spaniards to leave the city and run for high ground. In the dimness of oncoming night the Tlascalans dropped much of their booty and the Spaniards tried to lace up their armor as they all waded through the water coursing in the streets and stumbled into or leaped over ditches, now water-filled, that the Aztecs had dug to impede them.

Several Tlascalans drowned (the Tlascalans could not swim) and in darkness the soaked army in wretched shape staggered uphill. Cortés was ashamed of himself for falling into this trap. At dawn, while he was regrouping his force, the Aztecs, inspired by the success of their tactic, landed from their canoes—and the Spaniards and Tlascalans in ragged formation had to fight their way back nearly to Texcoco (the Spaniards' powder was wet and useless) while they listened to jeers from the Aztecs.

In Tenochtitlán there was no inclination toward peace. Guatémoc's silence in response to Cortés's overture, followed by the trap of the flood, made this clear. And Cortés longed for the loquaciousness of Montezuma, for the connection through language and reasoning that held out the only possibility for linking these two peoples without the destruction of one or the other—in spite of the bluffing, innuendo, evasiveness and duplicity.

The Spaniards' setback at Iztapalapa, however, did not prevent chiefs from continuing to come to Cortés in Texcoco, begging his pardon and pledging their allegiance. They continued to report that troops from Tenochtitlán had taken up positions in their towns or near them and were oppressing them, and they asked Cortés for Spaniards to drive away the Aztecs. Cortés fully understood that these people in outlying areas could and would go with whichever side appeared likely to win, but he hadn't enough men to relieve them. So he assured them as best he could, and significantly he tried to make peace between some of these subject tribes that had been at odds with each other, uniting them in opposition to the Aztecs. When the Aztecs landed at shore towns near Texcoco, the Spaniards were able to drive them out, but the Aztecs would fight and then withdraw, little harmed, in their canoes.

Cortés, short of powder, was wondering what to do next when a Spaniard slipped through from Tlascala with two messages of importance: (1) another ship had arrived at Villa Rica with a large supply of powder as well as more men, horses and arms; and (2) the brigantines that were being built in Tlascala were nearly finished. Promptly Cortés ordered Sandoval with a substantial complement of cavalry and infantry to return with the messenger to Tlascala. Cortés wrote a letter to his commander at Villa Rica to have the supply of powder brought to Tlascala and also to send all the newly arrived Spaniards who wanted to come. While holding out the bait of gold, Cortés always tried to maintain this volunteer aspect among his men, although, as Bernal Díaz commented, those who volunteered would never have done so if they had known what was in store for them. In fact, Cortés from Tepeaca had allowed a few men who wanted to withdraw from the expedition to do so, telling the men who remained (and telling himself) that they were better off without those who lacked heart for this adventure. With Sandoval, Cortés allowed a proportion of the Tlascalans to go home because it was becoming difficult even from the rich farmland around Texcoco to provide food for Cortés's whole army. Sandoval was again to make sure the way was safe, and he was to bring back from Tlascala the brigantines, the powder, and whatever new men there were with their arms and horses.

En route to Tlascala, Sandoval left the trodden roadway and went to a town that had been complaining of oppression from an Aztec garrison. There he found the Aztecs awaiting him ready for battle, and the Spaniards and Tlascalans defeated and dispersed them. After the battle, though, Sandoval and his men discovered in a village near the town the grisly remains of some Spaniards who had been killed. The local people—with little affect—described what had happened. These were Spaniards who had come with Narváez, about fifty of them led by a *caballero* named Juan Juste, and the local Indians, pretending to be helpful, had led them into a narrow rocky defile where the horsemen had to dismount and lead their horses. Indians in hiding behind boulders on both sides of the defile had attacked and killed most of the Spaniards, taking some alive to the village. On the wall of a house in the village Sandoval and his men found a message Juan Juste had scrawled in charcoal on the wall: "Here the luckless Juan Juste was held prisoner." In the village temple the Indians pointed to the Spanish blood that had been sprinkled by the Indian priests around the idols. And immediately before the idols were hung the tanned hides of five horses with the hair and even the horseshoes preserved and the faceskins of two Spaniards with the beards still on. (Such flaying of human beings, which was not uncommon among the Indians, would be done just after the victims had been sacrificed, and Indian priests would wear the faceskins while the skins were slippery with blood and body fluids. At such moments—like the moments of human sacrifice—the mental, emotional and spiritual state of the Indians was beyond the comprehension of Europeans.)

Often, when Indian chiefs came before Cortés, confessed their crimes and begged forgiveness, Cortés would have difficulty keeping his temper, not showing his revulsion and unloosing his anger; he had to impose steely self-control in order to stick to his considered policy, which was to accept all offers of peaceful submission. Now Sandoval and the Spaniards with him smashed the idols and punished some of the villagers, but they did not punish the chiefs of the province, though these chiefs seemed responsible. In accord with Cortés's policy, Sandoval accepted the chiefs' profuse promises of renewed allegiance.

Inevitably, as the crimes against humanity mounted on both sides, all toleration was being squeezed from this conflict—a conflict more fundamental than any of the participants grasped. And the raw fury of both Aztecs and Spaniards was intensifying, emerging.

In Tlascala Sandoval found the brigantines ready. The master Spanish shipbuilder was Martín López from Seville. Being the third son of an *hidalgo*, López had little inheritance to look forward to, so he had to go adventuring, and with him from Spain he had brought his own team of ship's carpenters. Like most of the captains and men of any background, he had made a financial investment in the expedition. López had assembled the brigantines and tested them on a river near Tlascala that had been dammed for the purpose; then he had disassembled the ships—and the Tlascalans turned out eight thousand bearers to carry the pieces to Texcoco, plus eight thousand warriors to serve as a guard, plus two thousand *tamemes* to bring along food, with one of the senior chiefs of Tlascala, Chichimecatecle, in command. Sandoval was delighted. He sent the horseman with Cortés's letter on to Villa Rica, and he turned his own force around to escort the Tlascalans.

The column—Cortés reported with pride to the king—was more than five miles long, and the pieces of the thirteen ships were transported over rough ground for about fifty miles. It took six hours for the column to pass a given point. Strict order was maintained so there was no gap in the column and the column was not unnecessarily extended. Spaniards were at the front and rear, Tlascalan warriors on the sides. The Aztecs did not attack—though more smoke signals than had ever been seen before were rising all over the valley of Mexico, while the dismantled ships were brought down from the mountain rim. Cortés was elated when the column reached Texcoco, and he ordered that the ships should be assembled as quickly as possible and a canal should be dug to facilitate launching.

Chichimecatecle and the warriors with him were excited and eager for battle; also, the Tlascalan multitude was difficult to feed; so Cortés organized a formidable force of Spaniards that he led himself (twenty-five cavalrymen, including Alvarado and Olid as captains, three hundred swordsmen and pikemen, fifty crossbowmen and harquebusiers, with six field guns) and thirty thousand Tlascalans in support. Leaving Sandoval in charge of the base camp, Cortés set out on a mission he did not disclose to anyone, for fear those in Tenochtitlán would be forewarned.

Cortés's destination was Tacuba, which had been the Spaniards' first stopping point when they fled from Tenochtitlán. It was on the western shore of the lake and was the base for the shortest and most important causeway connecting Tenochtitlán and the mainland. A large city, Tacuba was one of the three original cities of the Aztec alliance, along with Tenochtitlán and Texcoco, Tenochtitlán having become the dominant capital and the Aztec alliance having become the focus of the empire. After the Spaniards and Tlascalans overran the first lakeside town they came to (the inhabitants escaping in their canoes), the Spaniards found the other towns on their way to Tacuba deserted.

But in Tacuba the Aztecs stood and fought. Since it was such a large city, the Spaniards could not occupy or control all of it, and Cortés let the Tlascalans proceed with looting and burning, which they did with a vengeance because they, too, had suffered in Tacuba on the night of the retreat. Now they took their revenge with an efficiency that impressed even Cortés. His aim was to test this place through which flowed most of the supply to Tenochtitlán and to try once again to work his way by guile.

Cortés led his horsemen with the infantry behind them onto the causeway to Tenochtitlán, as far as the first bridge, which had been lifted. Then, with the burning city of Tacuba as background, he called out to the Aztecs who were on the other side of the narrow strip of water. When the Aztecs calmed and stopped hooting and jeering, shooting arrows and throwing their darts and stones, Cortés had Malinche translate his words.

He asked if a lord were present with whom he could speak.

The Aztec warriors retorted that they were all lords (an assertion of their tribal pride, since actually Aztec society was fully as hierarchical as Spanish society).

Cortés told them he wanted only to resume the harmony in which he and they had lived in the past.

Sneeringly they asked if he expected another Montezuma who would obey him.

Cortés was frustrated by the Aztec refusal to talk—a refusal even to try to throw a lifeline of reasoning across the gulf that separated them. One of Cortés's men shouted to the Aztecs that they would face starvation and death, that all food would be kept from them on their island. Though Cortés himself would not have chosen to reveal his strategy, he allowed Malinche to translate.

The Aztecs replied with scorn that they had plenty to eat. They tossed a few tortillas on the water in case the Spaniards were hungry. And they said that, if ever Aztecs were hungry, they would eat both the Spaniards and the Tlascalans.

Cortés knew that he was a good talker; he relied on his ability and used it to maintain control of his rambunctious army; Spaniards generally had faith in their talent for dickering, bickering, cajoling, threatening, exaggerating. With Malinche serving him well and adding little fillips of her own, Cortés tried repeatedly to talk the Aztecs into moderating their belligerence.

He got nowhere. And turned back. The Spaniards and Tlascalans held Tacuba for six days, destroying part of it and fighting off Aztec attacks almost constantly. Then Cortés led the booty-burdened Tlascalans and his own men, who were not empty-handed, back toward Texcoco. Thinking the Spaniards and Tlascalans were retreating in defeat, the Aztecs rushed after them. So Cortés invented a new tactic: the rear-guard cavalry ambush. He and his horsemen hid off the road while his army passed by; then when the Aztecs came hurrying along in pursuit of the army, the cavalry charged out, panicking the Aztecs, and there was a spearing binge. This ended the nuisance, and Cortés returned to Texcoco. From Texcoco, a large number of Tlascalans, including Chichimecatecle, left for their home.

Cortés had to balance his various objectives while he attempted to surround Tenochtitlán—with a few hundred Spaniards and ever-increasing popular support from Indians rebelling against Aztec rule. Cortés had to protect the brigantines which were nearly assembled in Texcoco; three times Aztec warriors came at night by canoe from Tenochtitlán and tried to burn the ships as they had burned the four brigantines that had been left in the capital, but the Aztecs were detected and repulsed. At the same time, Cortés had to keep open his supply route from Tlascala and the coast; again and again he sent Sandoval and his men to eliminate threats to the roadway, particularly in the large province of Chalco, which lay to the east of the lake system. Eventually the Chalcans, cooperating with neighbors who had previously been their enemies, were able to defeat a fresh Aztec army without Sandoval's help, so the anti-Aztec alliance Cortés had been urging upon the mountain tribes was beginning to take hold. Whenever Sandoval would bring in captured Aztec captains, Cortés would free the captains to return to Tenochtitlán to repeat once again his plea to Guatémoc that peace and harmony should be restored—but silence was always the answer from Tenochtitlán.

Heartening news, though, was reaching Texcoco from the Spaniards at Villa Rica on the coast. At least three more ships had arrived, with more powder, arms, men, horses. Trains of Spaniards and Totonac bearers were working their way up the mountain trails.

Among the newcomers who reached Texcoco was a wellborn Spaniard named Julián de Alderete. His ship had sailed from Spain to Hispaniola, where the Jeronymites had appointed him a royal treasurer (to keep track of the royal fifth); in Hispaniola he had been told where to look for Villa Rica. Alderete boasted that he was an expert crossbowman, and Cortés welcomed him warmly. It was Alderete who brought the news from Spain that Puertocarrero and Montejo had been received by the king, who was now informed about what Cortés was doing; consequently, there was an awareness in Spain of the potential richness of Mexico, which was why Alderete had come. Perhaps most important, Velázquez's uncle, Bishop Fonseca, had lost some of his power to the king's Flemish advisors.

Leaving Sandoval in charge of the camp, Cortés departed from Texcoco and led a fresh force of Spaniards and tens of thousands of Indian allies on what he intended to be a thorough reconnaissance of the whole lake system in the broad valley of Mexico. It was timely and sensible to make this reconnaissance, because Cortés had been proceeding haphazardly, intuitively, exploring as well as conquering (like Alexander the Great when he invaded India, and Genghis Khan when he crisscrossed Asia and southern Russia). Cortés had only a dim notion of the geography to the south and west of the lake system. Panoramic views from the eastern rim of the mountains were indefinite. And Cortés could not tell, when he came upon Indians he did not know, whether they were true Aztecs, or were subject tribes willing to go with whichever side seemed the stronger, or were tribes resentful of Aztec rule and thus eager and willing to support the Spaniards in throwing off the hated Aztec yoke.

While Cortés was marching along the slopes of the mountains through the borderland between the province of Chalco and Aztec territory, he passed a series of isolated plateaus (created by differential erosion). On the tops of these sheer-sided hills whole villages of Indians had gathered—

men, women and children, all hooting loudly, the men brandishing weapons. Cortés was not much interested in further local encounters, yet he was disinclined ever to turn his back on Indians who had not been chastised. So he reluctantly ordered an attack on the hills, but the attack went poorly. These Indians rolled down boulders that splintered like fragmenting cannonballs; the Spanish cavalry was neutralized; the battle went on all day and the Spaniards could not take the heights. There was no water in this area and the Spaniards suffered from thirst during the night. The next morning, while the horses were taken for water to a spring a few miles away, the Spaniards again attacked; newcomers like Pedro Barba and Julián de Alderete were receiving their indoctrination; and the Spaniards succeeded in establishing themselves atop a plateau that commanded other plateaus and from which they could shoot their crossbows and harquebuses.

At which point, the Indians appeared to give up. The men calmed and stopped shrieking, slinging, shooting arrows and hurling spears—while their women came forward and made a perplexing sign: The Indian women held their hands in front of them parallel to the ground, one hand on top of the other, and they patted their palms together; then they reversed hands and patted their palms again. The Spaniards, covered with stone dust, were parched, winded and exhausted, having suffered at least eight killed and twenty or thirty seriously wounded, and, staring, they found this sign to be inexplicable. Foot-soldiers around Bernal Díaz mumbled that this was a sign of the Devil. Others took it to be a gesture suggesting copulation perhaps in a position with which the Spaniards were unfamiliar. But what the sign turned out to be was simply the Indian sign of surrender: The women were miming the making of tortillas, patting the pancakes to make them flat, to indicate that they wanted peace and feasting should begin. The fact was that the Indians on these plateaus had failed to supply themselves with any water at all and were dying of thirst.

In accord with his policy, Cortés accepted their pledges of allegiance, however dubious. As was his custom, he gave the defeated Indians a stern lecture to the effect that they had brought this calamity on themselves. And he forbade his men to take as plunder so much as a kernel of corn. Bernal Díaz unsuccessfully tried to evade this prohibition on the grounds that Cortés had winked, but Cortés made him disgorge his plunder. Then Cortés sent back his wounded to Texcoco and moved on.

Why Cortés led this force down through a break in the mountains to the plain of Morelos and the city of Cuernavaca is not clear. There is a fairly precipitous and distinctly noticeable drop of more than two thousand feet, so he could not possibly have thought that the lake system in the valley of

Mexico would be affected by this lower land. Probably, with about fifty thousand men (he had been joined by more Indian allies as he went along) sweeping over the countryside, all sorts of reports were being brought to Cortés. And most likely it was reported to him that in Cuernavaca there was a substantial army loyal to Guatémoc. When Cortés would lay siege to the Aztec capital, he did not want this army to come up and attack him from the rear.

On this expedition, as on most expeditions, the Spaniards were not continuously fighting. The Spaniards always hoped they would not be opposed; Cortés always tried to succeed by guile; and often they were accommodated. In the pleasant little town of Oaxtepec, Cortés and his Spaniards were welcomed by a chief who wisely chose not to fight and they were housed in the chief's own palace, which was exceptionally enchanting. On the long horizontal lintels of aromatic hardwoods were carved friezes; the walls were alternately of different kinds of stone; gauzy hangings covered the doorways; and flowering plants overhanging from the *azoteas* littered the air with blossoms.

The extensive compound of the palace was set amid a garden and orchard that covered several square miles. After lookouts had been posted and a perimeter defense established, the Spaniards were able to take off their armor and let their bodies cool while they sauntered along shaded walks past flower beds of varying hues and subtle shades. Remembering Talavera pottery and the patios of home, the Spaniards admired the Indian talent for inventing odd color combinations, juxtaposing textures and designs. Summer houses or gazebos were interspersed at intervals that the Spaniards calculated as being about two crossbow shots; at these resting places on whitewashed walls and pillars were painted fantastical, stylized versions of birds, insects, blossoms, antelope.

This region around Cuernavaca is one of the loveliest in the world, with one of the most agreeable year-round climates. April—this was April 1521—would be the warmest month of the year, yet at an altitude of five thousand feet there is always a freshness in the air. Savoring the perfume of the flowers, the Spaniards cleared from their lungs the dust of the trail and the battle smells of urine, sweat and blood.

During these rare moments of repose the Spaniards were able to perceive that there was a great calm middle span in the emotional nature of the Indians, an unaffected calmness that had little counterpart in the Spanish make-up. Spaniards were not good farmers (the Moors had been much

This painting on bark is an example of the kind of charming fantasies that were painted on the walls and pillars of the gazebos in the extensive garden at Oaxtepec.

better); the Spaniards in Spain preferred to be herders. Spaniards by nature were explorers, fighters, born for a crusade like the one they were on. To make palaces and gardens, to cut stone and carve hardwood and gems, called for patience and a passivity inherent in the Indians. It was this calmness and patience that a few years later appealed to Motolinía and caused the devout, selfless monk to feel profound affection for the Indians, whom he found to be, as a people, fun-loving, artistic and imaginative, and in their everyday lives easygoing and much less individually acquisitive than Spaniards.

The Spaniards realized, of course, that this Eden they were in had been built for and was used by the Indian nobility. But both Indian and Spanish societies were rigidly hierarchical, so it did not surprise the Spaniards that only Indian lords lived in this refined luxury. The artfulness and joy of creation obviously came from the people, and there wasn't a cranky drive of individual self-assertion among the Indians, as there was among Spaniards. In this long emotional middle span of human nature—where imagination and patience produced such beauty—the Spaniards felt a deep liking for the Indians, sensed the promise in ultimate fusion, and appreciated a common ground that both peoples loved.

Yet the Spaniards had to wonder: How could the same human beings who created this beguiling, lassitudinous bliss be the ones who in the frenzy

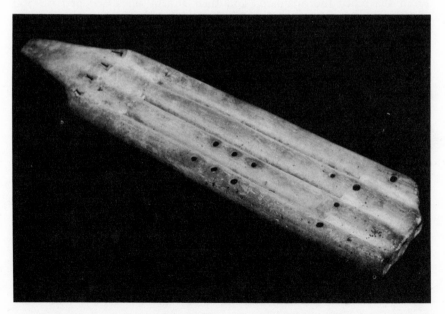

On this four-tube Aztec pipe, sweet-sounding chords can be played, and this may be one of the earliest chordal instruments.

of their ceremonies tore the hearts from living victims and frolicked in
human skins? Untold millennia of evolution had produced these two strains
of human beings on different sides of the world unknown to each other,
and in their frenetic extremes they were radically different. The Indians—
though patient, artful and playful when producing handicrafts or making
gardens and palaces—in ecstatic moments were able to cast off restraint
and abandon themselves in ways and to degrees that for the Christians were
so forbidden as to be unthinkable.

The Spaniards were also aware of a dim, dull end in the emotional span
of the Indians, an absence of resentment alien to the Spaniards and
amounting almost to apathy. Among the Indians the slaves and the poor
of all tribes had so little—they went naked or wore rags and ate anything,
mice, moles, worms, snakes, lice—and these slaves and poor were the ones
who made up the majority of the victims for sacrifice.

Although puzzled, the Spaniards, as Christians, sensed that the structure
of Indian society with its almost incomprehensible extremes was held
together and maintained by the devilish spell cast by the priests—a hypno-
sis of horror. Yet in the Indians' very long, emotional middle span of
patience and grace there was hope for the future.

From Oaxtepec the Spaniards and their Indian allies marched on and
burned other towns, perhaps as pretty as Oaxtepec, because the local chiefs
would not submit, and the Spaniards and allies forced their way across the
ravines east of Cuernavaca and overran and destroyed the Aztec bastion
there. (The Spaniards habitually Hispanicized Nahuatl names, producing all
sorts of corruptions. The Nahuatl name of Cuernavaca, phonetically rendered, was Cuauhnahuac. Cortés, who had very little patience with Indian
tongues, in his letter to the king spelled it Coadnabacad. He never referred
to any Indian god as other than "Witchy-lobos.")

Then Cortés in his quickness and determination, acknowledging that he
was in a region too low to be of importance to the lake system around
Tenochtitlán, turned abruptly northward to return to the valley of Mexico
by the most direct route—and nearly had a disaster. The Spaniards' return
route took them and their Indian allies to a mountain pass that was over
10,000 feet high. The way was arid and desolate and was wholly unknown
to the Spaniards and the Indians with them. Cortés would not turn back,
so they continued climbing, though some died of thirst and cold every
freezing night. When food ran out, the Spaniards ate artichokes, which

were unfamiliar to them, and the sharp points of the leaves cut their tongues and throats.

Stumbling down from the mountain rim, the Spaniards and allied Indians found themselves at Xochimilco, at the southern end of the valley of Mexico. This large handsome city was mostly built on a fresh-water lake that was connected by a strait to the larger lake where Tenochtitlán was situated. Thus it was close to the Aztec center; the cities and towns on the southern and western shores of the lakes were adjuncts of Tenochtitlán; and Guatémoc decided that it was time to retaliate. Smoke signals were rising, and calls to arms were being shouted from farm to farm, house to house, warning of the Spaniards' approach. Causeways linked the various neighborhoods of Xochimilco, which was subdivided by many broad and deep canals. New ditches had been dug and staked, ramparts erected. Famished and parched, the Spaniards, Tlascalans and other Indians with them raided the outlying farms for food and water.

On a campaign Cortés tried always to begin a march before dawn, and they reached Xochimilco around eight in the morning. Aztecs in great numbers were deployed at the very first canal. In the battle that followed, the Spaniards could not force their way across the canal, though volley after volley from the harquebusiers and crossbowmen cut into the Aztec mass. Battalions of Aztecs—ten thousand warriors to a battalion—were coming up on the Spaniards' flanks, and Cortés ordered the horsemen to form two squadrons, each squadron to fight on a flank.

According to Bernal Díaz, who mixed praise and complaint in commenting on Cortés, wherever Cortés was the fighting was hottest. Like the Spaniards, the Aztecs always sought to capture the leader. When Cortés's horse collapsed under him from exhaustion (Bernal Díaz blamed this on the horse for being too fat and pampered), the Aztecs swarmed around Cortés and he fought them off with his sword and lance. A Tlascalan warrior and a young Spaniard named Cristóbal de Olea ran to help him, but Olea's head was smashed by a bladed Aztec bat. Then other soldiers, including Bernal Díaz, and other horsemen forced their way through. Cortés's dazed horse was urged up, and Cortés, who had again been wounded in the head, was rescued. The Spaniards tried to retire behind a stone wall to treat their wounds but the Aztecs rushed upon them—until the squadron of horsemen from the other flank charged back and momentarily relieved the pressure.

Sheltered within a stone-walled courtyard, the Spaniards seared their wounds with hot oil. Olid, who commanded the horsemen from the other flank, could hardly see through the blood pouring from cuts on his scalp. Olea was critically hurt. All the men and horses were wounded. Then a fresh Aztec battalion burst into the courtyard, and the Spaniards had to respond frantically. Scrambling onto their mounts, the horsemen began fighting where they were, the infantry formed ranks and pressed forward, and the Aztecs were pushed out.

The Spaniards fought their way down a street until they came to a larger courtyard before a temple-topped pyramid. Since it was late afternoon, Cortés was looking for a place to set up his defense for the night. He sent men to the top of the pyramid—and they saw a flotilla of two thousand canoes on the water, bringing more Aztec warriors to the battle.

All through the night the Spaniards and their allies worked feverishly. Wherever bridges over the canals had been removed, Cortés had the Tlascalans fill the gaps with stones and rubble so the horses would be able to cross. Along the banks of the central canal he stationed guards to prevent landings by the Aztecs from their canoes. Cortés and his captains made continual rounds of the guardposts—and Cortés had two Narváez men flogged for sleeping. The warhorses were kept bridled. The harquebusiers had used up all their powder, the crossbowmen all their arrows. So the Spaniards on guard at the central canal, including Bernal Díaz, gathered stones to throw, as their only resort before, at close quarters, they would have to use their swords. All night long, the crossbowmen were making new arrows, using the spare shafts, copper arrowheads and feathers they carried with them. Twice during the night Aztecs in canoes, using muffled paddles, approached the central canal but were reluctant to land, not knowing in what strength (or weakness) the Spaniards held the banks. So the warriors in the canoes rejoined the flotilla, and the whole flotilla landed elsewhere, the men from it combining with a fresh Aztec army that was advancing overland.

At dawn the battle resumed, and in the fighting the Tlascalans took prisoner five Aztec captains who revealed that Guatémoc was sending more battalions by land around the lake so that, had the warriors in the flotilla of canoes attacked from the water, the Spaniards would have been caught in a pincers, as the Spaniards had so often caught the Indians. When the fresh Aztec troops came on, the land battalions and those who had come by canoe, they were in gorgeous array, and the captains leading them held aloft captured Spanish swords tied to long poles and boasted loudly that they were about to kill the Spaniards with the Spaniards' own weapons. In a furious fight the Spaniards broke the ranks of the new army but succeeded only in dispersing the Aztec warriors throughout the city. From other captured Aztec captains it was learned that Guatémoc was sending another flotilla and more battalions by land, to keep up this assault until the Spaniards were overcome.

Late in the afternoon, the battle died down—from exhaustion on both sides—and Cortés, in council with his captains, decided to withdraw from Xochimilco the next day, before pressure from the Aztecs increased. Cortés reasoned that, if he had the whole Spanish army together, he might withstand greater pressure, but with only part of the army his limited purpose was to make a reconnaissance in force. The Spaniards had won back from the Aztecs a few of the captured Spanish swords tied to long poles, but the battle had been a stand-off.

That night several Spaniards and Tlascalans ransacked palaces in Xochimilco and returned to camp with gold, silver and bales of cloth. But when other Spaniards and Tlascalans went to do the same, they were ambushed by Aztecs from canoes. Four Spaniards were taken alive by the Aztecs and were carried across the lake and brought before Guatémoc. They revealed how few Spaniards there were and that all the Spaniards and their horses were wounded. Then Guatémoc had the four Spaniards sacrificed, their hearts and blood offered to the gods, and he sent a butchered piece—a white-skinned arm, a white-skinned leg, or a bearded, white-skinned head—to each of the tribes that had turned against him.

Before dawn the Spaniards, Tlascalans and other allies assembled, formed a defensive column and fought their way out of Xochimilco. The Aztecs tried to fall on the rear of the column, but Cortés again and again used his rear-guard cavalry ambush and discouraged them. Yet it was all the Spaniards could do to disengage and flee.

The Spaniards and their allies were sporadically attacked as they made their way to Coyoacán, which was deserted, and on to Tacuba. In one of the skirmishes two more Spaniards, young pages, were captured alive by the Aztecs and were taken to Tenochtitlán for sacrifice. What had happened was that Cortés and his cavalrymen, while attempting a rear-guard ambush, had in turn been ambushed by Aztecs—and three pages had dashed to the column for help. Only the fleetest made it. But before the column could be turned around, Cortés and his horsemen returned at a funereal pace. Cortés was used to men falling in battle; this was the fate expected by fighters; but he was sickened by the loss of the boys, knowing what would be done to them, so heartsickened that he could not talk.

The rainy season was beginning. When the Spaniards reached Tacuba, there was a downpour, and, bedraggled, they took refuge once again in the plaza where they had assembled on the night of their defeat. With an eye to the future, the Spanish captains looked through the rain and appraised the Tacuba causeway, the shortest, broadest and most heavily trafficked link with the island of Tenochtitlán. The Spaniards marched on, through towns from which the people fled at their approach, and after several days of trudging through deep mud they arrived back at Texcoco. Sandoval rode out with a strong force to meet them.

Cortés had made his reconnaissance of the lakes. It had been costly in terms of men, energy, powder. But Sandoval related the good news that more men, powder and equipment had arrived from Villa Rica. And— of utmost importance—the brigantines were completed and ready for launching.

DEVASTATION

Cortés's most effective stroke of tactical genius stemmed from his realization that waterborne military power was vital for victory over the Aztecs. Apparently he alone had this realization; it was not an idea generally held among his men. Cortés was the one who sensed that only if the Spaniards were able to dominate the lakes in the valley of Mexico would they be able to succeed in their conquest. Spaniards were not by nature seafaring people; they were not like the ancient Cretans and Phoenicians or the later Vikings, English and Portuguese, whose explorations and aggressions were always by sea. Spanish power had been and was to be exercised chiefly on land. Yet Cortés had recognized the importance of the lakes while he consorted with Montezuma; this was why he had built the first four brigantines, which the Aztecs had burned when the Spaniards were driven from the capital. And his first move—after the defeat—had been to order the building of thirteen more.

The Spaniards were dependent on sea power, an idea that did not initially occur to the Indians. The Indians never went to sea, other than offshore to fish, and it took them quite a while to appreciate the fact that these few invading Spaniards could be and would be continuously reinforced from the sea. But this use of the sea was for transport. Cortés foresaw the need to be able to fight on the Mexican lakes. He knew that if he could not prevent the Aztecs from attacking in their canoes while the Spaniards were strung out along the causeways, if the Aztecs could withdraw in their canoes whenever they chose, if the Aztecs were allowed to resupply Tenochtitlán by canoe and quickly to send reinforcements to their armies on the mainland while the Spaniards were trudging overland, this war could turn toward slow attrition, in which case the indigenous people would have the advantage.

The so-called brigantines that Cortés had built were not what would be called brigantines today. A brigantine, in modern usage, is a small sailing ship that has some of its sails fore-and-aft rigged and some of its sails square-rigged. A ship so rigged is very adaptable to conditions in which the winds are variable, puffy and uncertain. What Cortés called a brigantine was a heavily built ship of shallow draft about forty-five feet long (twelve of the ships were forty-two or forty-three feet long, one was forty-eight feet) with a beam (width) of about nine feet. From drawings based on the recollections of participants, the ships seem to have been single-masted and lateen-rigged, though conjectures have been made that they had two masts and were square-rigged (with lateen-rigging they would be more maneuverable). If there were no wind, the ships could be rowed like galleons, with six oars on each side. Again, it has been conjectured that a beam of nine feet would be insufficient to accommodate rowers so the ships had to be paddled by men standing along the rail, but this does not seem reasonable. With about four feet of freeboard from rail to waterline, the paddles would have to be very long, allowing little leverage for paddling, and paddling would be less effective than rowing. Besides, a nine-foot beam would be adequate to accommodate rowers. Also, the Spaniards would have been inclined to replicate their own galleons, which were rowed, rather than Indian canoes, which were paddled. Actually, few specific details about these brigantines were given by any of the Spanish chroniclers—further evidence of Spanish disinterest in maritime matters.

The ships were assembled in Texcoco on the bank of a creek more than half a mile from the lake. Why the ships were not assembled on the lakeshore, where they could be launched easily, is another mystery that has attracted some attention. There are many credible explanations. The Tlascalans' advice undoubtedly was to select an assembly site away from the lakeshore since the lakeshore would be vulnerable to attack by Aztecs coming in canoes from Tenochtitlán. Also, López and his shipbuilders had to fashion some new timbers for the ships, and the forest did not extend to the lakeshore. To bend new timbers, or rebend transported timbers that had lost shape, the shipwrights had first to float the wood in water to soften it (several pieces were reported floating in the creek); then they needed well-set posts to use as fixed points against which to bend the timbers. The site on the bank of the creek suited these purposes.

When López and his men had tested the brigantines on the dammed river in Tlascala, they had assembled the ships without caulking. Now, when reassembling the pieces, they carefully filled the interstices between the planks with caulking of flax, hemp and cotton. To be less degradable in water, the caulking had to be treated with fat—and the fat, according to Gómara, was taken by the Tlascalans from the corpses of Indians who had recently been killed in the fighting. Though the Spaniards had used human fat before to sear wounds, they were slightly nauseated by this degree of improvisation to caulk ships. Nevertheless, the improvisation worked. After the treated caulking was carefully tapped in, the crevices were covered with pitch.

These particulars about the brigantines are known because, in the aftermath of the conquest, Martín López and several Spanish carpenters who worked on the ships sued Cortés, and the court records are extant. In his court complaint López claimed that he had to spend his own money to equip the ships, sending for fittings to friends in Villa Rica who charged him high prices. With all the Spaniards there was perpetual confusion over whose money went to pay for what—the acquired gold that Cortés used for the sake of the conquest, Cortés's and the captains' personal money, investments by minor entrepreneurs like López, gold borrowed from the royal fifth, Velázquez's underlying interest, et cetera. Cortés won, or at least succeeded in evading, all the lawsuits brought by the shipbuilders.

A very difficult job, foreseen from the beginning of the assembly project, was to dig a canal from the site where the ships were assembled to the lake, a distance that was approximated at a quarter-league (a Spanish league was 2.63 miles). The canal had to be twelve feet wide and at least that deep. The creek, which flowed over boulders, was unsuitable for the passage of the ships. Boards were needed to reinforce the sides of the canal so there would be no crumbling when the lake water rushed in. The digging of this canal, following the track of an old irrigation ditch, was started when the assembly of the ships was begun, and it was accomplished by forty thousand Indians working in shifts of eight thousand at a time, mainly Texcocans sent by their chief, Don Fernando.

A remarkable characteristic of all the Indians was that they were able to turn out huge numbers of workers for a project, and these workers were cooperative and productive. For battle the Indians turned out huge numbers of warriors, though the warriors lacked the tactics to take advantage of their numerical superiority. Undoubtedly, huge numbers of Indian workers had built the causeways and dikes, the pyramids, the city on the island in the lake, and the cities along the lakeshore. These were phenome-

nal accomplishments by people without iron tools, and such mass cooperation had no reflection whatever among the individualistic Spaniards. As the
result of this social phenomenon, the canal for the brigantines was dug and
was ready when Cortés returned to Texcoco.

Manning the ships, however, was a problem for Cortés because Spaniards didn't like to row, they didn't like the water, they all preferred to be
on land. For each ship about twenty-five men were required: twelve to row
if necessary, to set the sails, and to fight at the gunwales; ten or twelve
crossbowmen and harquebusiers to shoot at approaching canoes; an artil-
leryman or two, a captain and a lookout. No Spaniards volunteered. So
Cortés himself went down the roll and assigned to the brigantines all the
men who had ever served as sailors on ships. When this proved insufficient,
he assigned all those who were known to have gone fishing. Still short a
few, he assigned those who came from port towns in Spain. For captains,
he selected gentlemen who sought his favor, like Pedro Barba, others who
were ambitious and of an amenable nature, like Juan Jaramillo, and a few
who confessed to having some sailing experience. The truth was that many
Spaniards could sail.

Bernal Díaz commented that one of the men chosen to captain a ship
had a handsome wife, thus pointing up the fact that by this time in the
conquest there were a few Spanish women accompanying the army. These
women probably had first come with the Narváez men; more had come
with later arrivals; and there may have been a very few before Narváez. How
these women were treated, how they got along on a march, bedding down
with the men, washing, defecating, mixing with the Indian women, has not
been detailed in the chronicles. Surely, during battles the Spanish women
were kept in the center, along with Malinche, other Indian women, and the
tamemes with supplies. The tone of Bernal Díaz's comment implied that
the Spanish women were treated respectfully, in accord with sixteenth-
century proprieties, as they would have been in their hometowns in Spain,
despite the primal and turbulent circumstances of the New World. Presumably, if and when fighting developed, these Spanish women would pound
on the attacking Indians just as Spanish women had pounded on the Moors
and, before the Moors, on the Visigoths.

As evidence of the importance Cortés placed on the brigantines, he took
command of the fleet himself, overruling the cavalrymen and foot-soldiers,
who wanted him to lead them on land.

During Cortés's absence on the reconnaissance around the lakes a letter
had reached Texcoco that, when Cortés read it, pleased him very much.
While Montezuma had been held hostage and Cortés was hoping to

acquire this land peacefully for Spain, Cortés had sent Spaniards in small parties all over Mexico—to seek out harbors, mines, potential bases for settlement. After the Aztecs drove the Spaniards from Tenochtitlán, Cortés assumed that the Spaniards he had sent out had all been killed, as most of them were. But this letter, brought by Indians first to Tepeaca, was from two young Spaniards Cortés had sent to the province of Oaxaca, which was not under Aztec control. The letter recounted that, after the Spanish defeat, these two Spaniards had made themselves war-leaders of local tribes (Zapotec or Mixtec, both good fighters and admirably independent in spirit to this day) and they were contending fiercely with Nahuatl-speaking people all around them. Cortés was reminded of the sailor from Palos who had been shipwrecked along with Aguilar and had made himself a prince among the Indians, though that sailor from Palos had abandoned Christianity. These Spaniards, it was clear from the letter, retained their allegiance to Christ and the king and asked for at least thirty Spanish soldiers so they could break the ring of their Nahuatl-speaking enemies. Cortés in reply told them to hold out a little longer.

At the end of April 1521 the canal to the lake was opened, the brigantines were launched, and Cortés held a review of the force he now had. Passing on parade were more than nine hundred Spaniards, eighty-six of them on horseback, one hundred eighteen with crossbows or harquebuses, the remainder with lances, pikes, shields, swords and daggers. There were three heavy cast-iron cannons and fifteen small, mostly bronze field guns and falconets, a thousand pounds of powder, and plenty of shot. Not as large a force, in all, nor as well-equipped, as the force Cortés had led into Tenochtitlán after the defeat of Narváez—but Cortés had improved his strategy.

He dispatched to the brigantines the crews he had coerced into serving, and he had a field gun set in the prow of each ship. The largest brigantine, called *La Capitana*, served as flagship with Cortés's tattered banner hung from the masthead, and he had the three heavy cannons placed in its hold, since the iron cannons were cumbersome to take overland. Then Cortés divided his remaining men into three troops of roughly two hundred each, with a mixture of cavalry, crossbowmen, harquebusiers and foot-soldiers in each of the three troops. Alvarado was named captain in command of one troop, Olid of another, Sandoval of the third. Serving as auxiliaries were seventy-five thousand Indians who were willing to fight on the Spanish side against the Aztecs. Then Cortés issued a call to all tribes that had ever pledged allegiance to him that they should come with all the warriors they could muster to lay siege to Tenochtitlán. And more Indians poured in—

Tlascalans came, led by Chichimecatecle and Xicotenga the Younger, and more Texcocans responded; warriors came from Cholula and Chalco, all excited by the prospect of battle, liking to fight, greedy for booty, and especially eager to settle scores with the domineering Aztecs. Cortés apportioned these Indian allies to his three troop-leaders. It took about ten days for the three troops to be organized, stores distributed and the brigantines equipped, while the crews practiced sailing the vessels near the shore.

During this waiting-time Xicotenga the Younger deserted. He did not lead away the men who were under his personal banner of the white bird with outstretched wings; his men would not have followed him; they were caught up in the spirit of the impending battle. Instead, Xicotenga departed at night, secretly, with only a few attendants. Not until morning, when Chichimecatecle looked for him, was his absence noticed, and it was said that he was returning to Tlascala. Various reasons for his defection have been offered: that there was a fight between a Tlascalan and a Spaniard in which the Tlascalan suffered, and that this Tlascalan was a relative of Xicotenga (the matter was never taken to Cortés, who would have severely punished the Spaniard); or that Xicotenga was resentful because the older chief, Chichimecatecle, was in over-all command of the Tlascalans (this explanation is credible). But the most reasonable explanation, considering all of Xicotenga's vacillating behavior, may be that he alone among the Tlascalans—and perhaps alone among all the Indians, for even those in Tenochtitlán regarded this war narrowly as a conflict over the right to exact tribute—sensed the fundamental racial subordination that was being imposed. And, in spite of his occasional spirited responses in conjunction with the Spaniards, Xicotenga ultimately rebelled against this subordination, which he foresaw would become universal. Whatever his reason, which never became clear even to the Tlascalans, Cortés denounced Xicotenga as a deserter, as did Chichimecatecle. Cortés had never liked Xicotenga. Many times their eyes had met, and Cortés had never felt that he could rely on Xicotenga; he always suspected Xicotenga of plotting. Chichimecatecle sent a delegation of Tlascalan nobles to pursue Xicotenga and persuade him to come back. When this delegation failed to achieve its purpose, Cortés, knowing the trouble Xicotenga could stir up in Tlascala while most of the Tlascalan nobles and Spaniards were gone, dispatched a squad of horsemen who overtook Xicotenga on the road before he reached Tlascala—and they hanged him. Then the horsemen returned and rejoined Cortés.

To each of his three troop-leaders, Cortés assigned a mission, and the combination of these missions was critical. Alvarado and Olid were to proceed from Texcoco around the lake counterclockwise to Tacuba, at the base of the most important causeway to Tenochtitlán, and Alvarado was to block and hold the causeway. Olid was to continue past Tacuba to Coyoacán and hold that place, from which there was a link to the causeway from Iztapalapa to Tenochtitlán. Sandoval was to wait until the others were in place, by which time Cortés would be able to calculate the pattern of Aztec resistance. Then Sandoval was to go from Texcoco around the lake clockwise to take Iztapalapa and to block the causeway there. When these three coordinated missions were accomplished, most of the flow of supply to the capital by causeway would be shut off, because the only remaining causeway that would be open connected Tenochtitlán with Tepeyac on the north shore, and this causeway was not much used.

In designing this strategy, Cortés and his captains in council were relying on their experience over the half-year they had spent in Tenochtitlán. They had then been free to roam the city and they had assiduously observed the pattern of supply. In addition to traffic on the causeways, there was a constant coming and going of thousands of canoes. But, to counter the canoes, Cortés would wait with the brigantines in Texcoco until his three troops were in place at the bases of the causeways.

Having barely escaped from Xochimilco while on his reconnaissance, Cortés was acutely aware of the pressure Guatémoc could exert by applying the full force of Aztec might against any segment of the Spanish army. So it was Cortés's order to his three troop-leaders that in this early stage of the siege, while the army would be divided, they must move fast because each separate troop would be vulnerable. If Guatémoc were to direct a full-fledged onslaught against any one of the troops, that troop would be in serious jeopardy—and the whole Spanish strategy would be endangered.

But, though the island of Tenochtitlán was packed to bursting with Aztec warriors, Guatémoc did not seize the initiative and concentrate an attack on one of the Spanish troops. Perhaps the Aztecs were mystified or surprised by the maneuvers of the Spaniards, who had ships on the water and troops in movement on the shore. The ranking nobles who comprised the Aztec command, under the aegis of their unseasoned young emperor, were hesitant and indecisive, and undoubtedly among the Aztecs there were spats and mix-ups, as there were among the Spaniards, but the Aztecs did not chronicle their indiscretions. Guatémoc, for his part, assured both his generals and his warriors that they would win because their war god, Huitzilopochtli, had so decreed. To symbolize his faith in ultimate Aztec victory, Guatémoc ordered the sacrifice to the god of the several Spaniards he had been keeping in cages and saving for the occasion, including Cortés's two young pages. With homage thus paid to Huitzilopochtli,

Guatémoc and the Aztecs concluded that they could wait in confidence until a weak spot on the Spanish side became apparent to them. Cortés, from experience, had come to bank on a slow reaction from the Indian opposition.

Not that the Spaniards' plans went smoothly, nor could the Spaniards avoid petty flare-ups. On the very first night out from Texcoco Alvarado and Olid—tensed, energized, resolved, and scared—quarreled bitterly over which of them would occupy the best house in the deserted town where they stopped, and their dispute became so intense that they were ready to draw swords on each other. A horseman was sent racing back to Texcoco to inform Cortés, who immediately dispatched a mediator. The mediator Cortés sent was a monk named Pedro Melgarejo, who was an excellent choice. Melgarejo was a Franciscan who had arrived in Villa Rica in February, bringing with him a large supply of indulgences, specifically papal bulls *(Bulas de Cruzada)* stamped with the official seal; any Spaniard who bought one of these embossed sheets was guaranteed absolution from any sin whatever that he may have committed in connection with the invasion of this so-called New World. Melgarejo did a brisk business, selling these indulgences to the Spanish soldiers he met in Villa Rica and on the road to the highland, and he was a rich man by the time he reached Texcoco. Then Melgarejo ingratiated himself with Cortés and exhibited admirable courage in sticking with the Spaniards while they were on the offensive. Later, when Melgarejo was ready to return to Spain with his fortune, Cortés entrusted him with ten thousand gold pesos to deliver to Cortés's father in Medellín. Some trouble with Cortés's father developed over the delivery of this gold (Martín Cortés quarreled with several of the messengers who brought him money from his son) but Melgarejo continued to maintain a friendly relationship with Cortés and succeeded to a distinguished career in the Church. It was really nothing for the deft Melgarejo to quiet the fracas between Alvarado and Olid.

After a night with little sleep, Alvarado and Olid led their troops on to Tacuba, which they found deserted. While Alvarado and his men occupied the city and the base of the causeway, Olid advanced with his troop along the lakeshore to the hill of Chapultepec, where he and his men fought off an attack from local Indians and smashed the aqueduct through which fresh spring water flowed to the island capital. So Tenochtitlán—the bejeweled city in the lake, surrounded by floating gardens—was deprived of drinking water. (Probably there were some small springs on the island of Tenochtitlán; otherwise, the original settlement would not have been made there; but whatever sources of water initially existed had long since become inadequate for the burgeoning population.) From Chapultepec Olid went farther and occupied Coyoacán, which, like Tacuba, had been abandoned.

When all this was reported to Cortés, he released Sandoval to round the lake on the other side and to occupy Iztapalapa. As yet, the Aztecs, having yielded both Tacuba and Coyoacán and not having mounted a major defense of the aqueduct, gave no evidence of realizing the significance of the stranglehold on Tenochtitlán that Cortés was applying. But Cortés anticipated that they would now comprehend his strategy and would take the offensive over the last siege-point to be occupied, which was at Iztapalapa. And the Aztecs did come in large numbers across the causeway to oppose Sandoval. But Sandoval and his troop cut their way into Iztapalapa and, breaking up the Aztec vanguard, pushed the battle onto the Mexicaltzingo causeway that linked Iztapalapa and Coyoacán. Meanwhile, Cortés, aboard *La Capitana,* was leading the brigantines southward across the lake to aid Sandoval and his men.

From the island of Tenochtitlán massed Aztec warriors watched as the thirteen ships were laboriously rowed along. Though the ships' sails were raised, the wind was light, and the brigantines were able to make only slow headway. In the canals of the capital there were five thousand large canoes filled with Aztec warriors, the strongest paddlers and fiercest fighters, waiting to spearhead an attack.

It was a definite talent of Cortés as a commander that he would instantly adapt to opportunities in battle, that in the confusion of a fight, whether on land or water, he would keep his head, change and rechange his orders. While proceeding toward Iztapalapa, he passed the islet called Peñón de Tepepolco, the royal hunting preserve to which he had taken Montezuma on Montezuma's first ride aboard one of the brigantines that had been burned. Now the rocky islet was crowded with Aztecs, and in the center of the islet was a small peak from which smoke signals were being sent to cities and towns on the lakeside and in the hills. As it always bothered Cortés to bypass unchastised Indians and the smoke signaling worried him, he turned the brigantines about, brought them in close to the islet and landed with one hundred fifty men. He led the Spaniards in hard fighting to the top of the peak, where they put out the signal-fires. Then from the peak they saw that thousands of Aztec canoes were coming out from the canals of Tenochtitlán and were being paddled rapidly toward them. So the Spaniards rushed down from the peak and reboarded the brigantines.

Cortés kept the brigantines just offshore from the islet, facing the approaching Aztec flotilla. The Spaniards were at the oars; the brigantines were nearly becalmed. The Aztecs in their canoes, cautiously confronting these strange ships, stopped when they were a little more than a crossbow shot or a gunshot from the brigantine line—and the Aztecs hesitated while more Aztecs in canoes continued to come up in support of them. Cortés was uncertain whether or not to fire the cannons in the prows of the brigantines while the ships were immobile because he wanted the first use of the ships to be terrifying. The Aztecs tauntingly paddled their canoes from side to side, as if boasting of their own flexibility and daring the Spaniards to shoot at elusive targets.

Then (thanks to St. James) a breeze rose—a land breeze filling the sails of the brigantines and moving them through the water at increasing speed. The oarsmen withdrew their oars, unsheathed their swords. Often in the aftermath of desperate land battles wishful Spaniards said they had seen visions of St. James on horseback, an ephemeral figure of wispy white fighting on their side. Such visions were doubtable, but this breeze was unquestionably real—and the brigantines rammed into the gathering fleet of Aztec canoes, cannons firing from the prows, harquebusiers and cross-bowmen shooting broadsides. Within a few minutes the water was filled with the wreckage of canoes, with sinking canoes, and with floundering, drowning Aztecs. Trimming and tacking, the brigantines went back and forth like waterborne warhorses let loose, smashing the Aztec formation, leaving cleared channels stained with blood.

With the wind holding steady, the Spaniards in their brigantines pursued the Aztecs in their canoes through a segmented dike that was interspersed with wide water lanes. (It is hard to see of what use in flood control this dike with its segments so widely spaced could have been. The likelihood is that it didn't work at all in controlling floods, which was why the Aztecs had not built more such dikes.) The Spaniards chased the frantically pad-dling Aztecs for miles across the lake until the remaining canoes were able to slip back into the canals of the besieged capital.

The breeze was still strong, and threats from the islet and from the first wave of the Aztec canoe fleet had been eliminated, so Cortés led the brigantines southward along the Iztapalapa causeway. The fight on the water had been observed by Olid in Coyoacán and by Sandoval in Iz-tapalapa and, when the Spaniards in the brigantines were clearly winning, both Olid and Sandoval led cavalry and infantry onto the causeways that joined at the battlement, called Xoloc, through which the Spaniards had passed on their first visit to Tenochtitlán. Cortés, seeing that the Spaniards fighting on the causeways were hindered where the bridges had been lifted, brought the brigantines in close and used the guns in the prows to knock down the barricades the Aztecs had erected on the far sides of the lifted bridges, driving back the Aztecs while the Spaniards swam or waded across. As the day waned, the Spaniards were steadily advancing.

Then Cortés foresaw an opportunity to anticipate the advance of the Spaniards fighting on the causeways by seizing the battlement where the two causeways joined. So he sailed ahead and landed men from the ships (now fighting as marines) to capture the battlement. It was a daring move, and the startled Aztecs rushed at the thirty or forty men he was able to land and who established a cordon across the causeway. But Cortés succeeded in lugging onto the causeway one of the three heavy cast-iron cannons from *La Capitana*. He had this large cannon loaded and aimed at the struggling mob; he ordered his own men to disengage and rush back out of the way; he had the cannon fired—and the quaking gunner by mistake ignited not only the powder in the cannon but the supply of powder that had been landed and piled up behind the artillery piece. The result was such an explosion that both sides were stunned. The cannonball crashed into the Aztecs, killing many and terrifying the rest, but the powder that exploded behind the cannon, though killing no one, not even the gunner, blew many Spaniards off the causeway and into the water.

Drenched and shell-shocked, the Spaniards crawled back onto the causeway, while the bewildered Aztecs retreated to Tenochtitlán to regroup and reconsider. Twilight was coming on, and Cortés landed as many men as he could spare, leaving minimal crews aboard the brigantines. The Aztecs being known not to fight at night, Cortés felt that, if he could hold this junction-point, in the morning the columns from Coyoacán and Iztapalapa would join him.

On that night, however, the Aztecs attacked. In the darkness a great horde of them raced down the causeway from Tenochtitlán—screaming, blowing whistles and horns, conches sounding, drums beating, frustration and hysteria propelling them as they were beginning to sense the seriousness of this siege. But from the brigantines the prow-guns were fired, and the harquebusiers and crossbowmen aligned across the causeway alternated with decimating volleys. In the past the Spaniards, while on the causeways, had been exposed to arrows, stones and spears from Aztec warriors in canoes on their flanks and had been hampered by lack of room to maneuver. But now with the water cleared of canoes and with the brigantines cannonading from the flanks and with disciplined fire from the harquebuses and crossbows cutting into the dense column of attacking Aztecs in a narrow confine, the Spaniards could more than hold their own. The brigantines made all the difference.

Cortés held the junction-point through the night, and in the morning, while the Aztecs continued to attack, he was reinforced by Spaniards moving up from Iztapalapa and Coyoacán. Cortés sent a brigantine to Iztapalapa for more powder. When some of Sandoval's men had trouble crossing a gap on the Mexicaltzingo link of the causeway where the Aztecs had lifted a bridge, Cortés found yet another use for the ships. He dispatched two brigantines that were sailed right into the gap to form a pontoon-bridge by which the Spaniards, men and horses both, could cross. When some of Olid's men were bothered by Aztecs in canoes attacking them from the far side of the Iztapalapa causeway where the brigantines could not go, Cortés had a portion of the causeway dismantled and intentionally made a breach through which he sent four brigantines that promptly scattered the Aztec canoes.

For a week fierce fighting continued, both on water and on land. Sandoval was wounded by a javelin run through his foot. On the water the Aztecs committed thousands of canoes that the brigantines pursued, while from Texcoco there came a fleet of several thousand canoes filled with Texcocan warriors eager to fight on the Spanish side. The Texcocan boy-king—Cortés's godson, Don Fernando—was rousing the Texcocans to the Spanish side and, led by Don Fernando's brothers, the Texcocans were responding with mounting spirit. On the other hand, most of the chiefs of the towns and cities that ringed the lake, though many of them had pledged allegiance to Cortés, were reverting to Guatémoc, and the Spaniards from their bases in Iztapalapa, Coyoacán and Tacuba were fighting on two fronts—one along the causeways forcing their way toward Tenochtitlán, the other on the mainland, where the Spaniards had to forage for food as well as fight off warriors from the lakeside cities and towns.

Thus the climactic battle that was developing was a complicated, intermingled clash—with many thousands of Indians on both sides, as more Indians from the hinterlands, foreseeing great booty and the prospect of Spanish success, were coming to the support of Cortés. In fact, there was a broad, large-scale insurrection of Indians against Aztec rule, and this rebellion obscured the more fundamental aspect of a titanic religious and racial collision.

From Tacuba Alvarado was battering his way forward on the causeway which opened upon the road that led to the huge marketplace of the capital. Desperately the Aztecs were opposing him, lifting every bridge and fighting behind barricades that they erected on the far side of each gap. Cortés sent three brigantines to assist Alvarado, and after a barrage from the ships Alvarado and his men would cross a gap, which the Tlascalans then would fill with rubble. At night, however, after Alvarado had retreated to his base camp, the Aztecs would throw the rubble into the water and restore the gap. While this back-and-forth battling was going on, Alvarado sent word to Cortés, who was in or near the battlement at Xoloc, that traffic had built up on the only undisputed causeway which linked Tenochtitlán to Tepeyac on the north shore. Over this causeway Aztec bearers were bringing food and water to the capital, and many canoes were shuttling alongside the causeway, especially at night.

Cortés was of two minds about the Tepeyac causeway. Originally, he had left it open because he hadn't enough men to block it; he felt he had stretched his forces dangerously thin by dividing them into three land troops and the crew for the fleet. Now, after the success of the brigantines on the water and with each of the three land troops established with defensible base-camps, he was tempted to let the Tepeyac causeway remain open as an invitation to Guatémoc and the people of Tenochtitlán to break out and flee by this route to the mainland. Once they were on the mainland, the Spanish cavalry could attack them; the Aztec army could be broken into pieces; and the veil of Aztec suzerainty would be ripped forever. In Cortés's mind, though, the chief attraction, were he to allow the Aztecs to escape from Tenochtitlán, would be that this dream city would endure. This wondrous island, which was also a formidable fortress, was a realized fantasy surpassing the pleasure-palaces the Moors had built in Spain, yet so few people of the Christian world had seen this Indian glory. But Cortés had no assurance that Guatémoc and his people would ever flee, and as long as the causeway to Tepeyac remained open, they could resupply themselves, defy Christ and the king, and kill more Spaniards.

So Cortés reluctantly decided to send Sandoval, despite his wound, around the lake to Tepeyac. With a contingent of Spaniards and Indian allies Sandoval passed through Alvarado's camp at Tacuba, beat his way to Tepeyac and occupied it. Cortés promptly sent across the lake to Sandoval three brigantines for day-and-night patrolling, and all traffic on or near the Tepeyac causeway was shut down.

Now Tenochtitlán was completely isolated—and Cortés began to tighten the noose. Daily the brigantines would invade the capital by sailing directly into the wider canals. The smallest of the brigantines, named *Busca Ruido* ("Looks for a Fight"), had the shallowest draft and could test a canal for depth; some of the canals were too shallow; in others the Aztecs had set stakes in the bottom; but the Spaniards soon came to know which major arteries were open. All around the edges of the huge city they would land and set fire to the houses before returning to their ships and sailing off, but the city as a whole, built largely of stone and adobe, did not burn well.

Advancing from his base camp in Xoloc, Cortés, with Olid second-in-command and reinforced by swarms of fresh Texcocans and Chalcans, had the strongest force and was the first to break into the capital. Cortés had to spend all of a morning and part of the afternoon crossing and filling sluiceways and canals where bridges had been lifted, but finally, when he entered the city, he found the bridges still in place because the Aztecs had not dreamed that he would penetrate so deeply. Then his over-eager Indian allies and the Spanish infantry rushed forward, the infantry hauling with them and firing a light cannon, but they advanced too fast. Cortés and the other horsemen lagged for fear they would lose their horses to Aztec archers and spearmen gathered on the flat roofs of the houses in the city. Seeing that the Spaniards in the van were without cavalry, the Aztecs surged out from the houses and side streets, routing the Spaniards who abandoned their cannon. The Aztecs chased them back to a wide level stretch of the street where the horsemen finally were able to charge and hold the rear guard while the infantry and Indian allies escaped. Later, the Aztecs ceremoniously dumped that cannon into the lake.

Nevertheless, the Spaniards' penetration of the capital was so signal an achievement that to Cortés at his base-camp came chiefs from Xochimilco and from the Otomí tribes in the mountains to beg for his favor and to pledge allegiance. Cortés told these people to bring their troops for the assault on Tenochtitlán, and he gave them three days to comply. He used the three days to treat wounds, to steady his own men after their forced withdrawal, and to reequip.

Then when Cortés returned to the capital, he found that every sluiceway and canal his Indians had filled with rubble had been reopened by the Aztecs, who had built new and stronger ramparts on the far side of each gap so the crossings, even with support from the brigantines, were more difficult than before. This time, when the city was penetrated, Cortés kept his men and the Indian allies in check; he did not allow them to rush ahead. In the plazas and on the wide streets he had the cavalry lead the infantry, the Spaniards protecting the Texcocans, Chalcans, Xochimilcans and Otomís as the Indian allies worked to fill each gap with the intention that the fill should be permanent, tightly packing down the stone and adobe. Cortés could not restrain the Tlascalans, who broke into the houses and attacked the Aztecs on the roofs.

To the Aztec lords Cortés had been sending messengers with pleas for them to give in without surrendering, that this fighting could cease without victory or indignity for either side—by which Cortés meant, of course, a settlement in his favor. But the Aztecs kept their silence. They would not negotiate terms.

During this second incursion into the city Cortés concluded that the Aztecs, fighting so stubbornly, would never give in. They would never agree to return any of the treasure he had lost on the night of the Spaniards' exodus from the capital, which certainly would have been one of the peace terms he would have demanded, prior to the institution of a system of regular tribute. Which left him no choice, he felt, but to continue with the destruction in the hope that eventually either terror or the facing of inevitable defeat would bring forth an overture for peace.

When Cortés returned to his camp, he received chiefs from six of the lakeside towns, who came to switch sides and pledge their allegiance to him. The Xochimilcans were boasting of the booty they would take from the Aztecs, and the other towns were envious; also, the whole lakeside region was being raided by both Spaniards and the Indian allies. (In 1563 the Xochimilcans sued to be repaid for two thousand canoes and twelve thousand men they said they had provided for Cortés. It did not take the Indians long to become familiar with lawsuits and to catch onto the intricacies and opportunities of the Spanish legal system.) So the people of the lakeside towns followed the Xochimilcans and Otomís under the Spanish banner.

Cortés was not in need of more men to help with the war; he had so many Indian allies that they often caused overcrowding on the causeways, and each night the allies were sent to sleep on the mainland, where they would be out of the way. But it was late May or early June and the Spaniards lacked housing to shelter themselves from the rain at night. So laborers from the lakeside towns built on the Iztapalapa causeway makeshift huts the Spaniards called "ranchos." Thousands of lakeside Indians came and did this work efficiently and quickly. Also, food was short in the Spanish camps, so Cortés called upon the lakeside towns for provisions. The Spaniards had been living on tortillas, of which they never ran out but which by now seemed tasteless, and greens the Indian allies collected from the banks of the lake and boiled. Now they were provided with fresh fish in ample quantity and with ripe cherries (in the mild Mexican climate two crops of cherries are produced annually) and, when the cherries ran out, there was cactus fruit which, when fully ripe, is delicious, though seedy.

Day after day, the three Spanish columns from their camps on the causeways would drive as far as they could into the huge city of Tenochtitlán, then withdraw, drive in and withdraw. The Spaniards could not hold their positions in the capital; the Aztec superiority in numbers was too great. Besides, the Spaniards, after each day's fighting at the high altitude, were exhausted. The Aztecs, however, though acclimated, were also becoming exhausted; they were starving and suffering from dehydration and the effects of drinking brackish water; and at night they were able to reopen fewer and fewer of the canals that had been filled with rubble by the Spaniards' Indian allies. So an increasing number of streets in the capital became passable for the Spaniards, who duly noted this fact when each day they returned to invade the city.

A spirit of competition was developing between the three Spanish columns. Alvarado, invading from the west, had seven canals to cross, which were the broadest and most difficult, but the section of the city toward which he thrust—the market neighborhood called Tlatelolco—had wide boulevards, so he was little bothered by Aztec warriors on the roofs. Sandoval, invading from the north, had to fight his way through a neighborhood where houses were closely clustered along the narrow streets and he was constantly in danger from the roofs. Cortés, invading from the south, was battling toward the neighborhoods where the nobles lived and he had to contend with Aztec warriors massed on the roofs and behind the stone walls of palace compounds. After many days of fighting, Cortés finally reached the homes of the reigning Aztecs on the great squares, and he and his men and the Indian allies ransacked and burned the palaces, including the palace of Axayacatl where the Spaniards had first been housed. Near the palaces were some small, exquisite buildings where Montezuma had maintained his aviaries; Cortés knew how proud the Aztecs were of these aviaries; so he burned them, too.

The Aztecs had concentrated most of their regiments in the marketplace area, where, it was clear, they intended to make their stand. Tlatelolco had once been an independent town separated by creeks from the rest of the island on which Tenochtitlán was built, but in the process of urbanization (a phenomenon even in Aztec times) Tlatelolco and Tenochtitlán had merged. Near the huge marketplace, which was bordered by arcades, stood one of the highest pyramids on the island. It was to this great pyramid of Tlatelolco that the people of the valley of Mexico were trained to look for signals from their emperor. And from the top of this pyramid the Aztec generals were directing the course of battle for the survival of their society.

Alvarado, out of patience with having to refill gaps and canals every day and pressured by his men who wanted to be the first to reach the market-place, decided to move his camp from its location on the Tacuba causeway into Tenochtitlán itself. This he did, and the Aztecs who opposed him, feinting, fell back, drawing him onto another causeway within Tlatelolco. On this interior causeway, which led to the marketplace, the Aztecs had made a gap seventy paces across in which the water at its deepest was chest-high and the bottom fairly smooth. With the Aztecs retreating and an apparent victory at hand, Alvarado's men waded across this gap. But when forty or fifty Spaniards without cavalry emerged on the far side, out from hiding in the buildings rushed thousands of Aztec warriors and out from the little canals around each building darted hundreds of canoes filled with warriors. The canoes blocked the water the Spaniards had waded across and forced the retreating Spaniards to take another route where the water was eight or nine feet deep and where the Aztecs had dug holes in the bottom and had set stakes so the Spaniards had no footing. From their canoes the Aztecs snatched Spaniards who were floundering in the water, speared or bashed to death many of them, and captured five Spaniards alive. The Spanish horsemen, including Alvarado, were unable to help because they dared not take their horses into the water. One horseman, newly arrived from Spain, attempted to cross the gap, and both he and his horse promptly were killed.

This successful tactic by the Aztecs was one of their slow adaptations to take advantage of the fact that they were fighting within a city they knew well and which they controlled at night. Also, around this same time the Aztecs invented a new tactic for fighting on the water. Near the shore they drove stakes into the mud bottom of the lake so the points of the stakes were just under the surface. They arranged these stakes in a pattern with a clear channel into the maze and no channel out. Then in early morning they sent forth decoy canoes laden with brush, as if hidden food or water were being brought to the capital. When these canoes were sighted, the Spaniards on the brigantines rowed vigorously in pursuit and were lured by the canoes through the clear channel until the hulls of the brigantines stuck on the stakes. Two brigantines were snared in this way and attacked by Aztecs who in dozens of canoes were lying in wait among the reeds. One of the brigantines was lost; the other was rescued by Juan Jaramillo, captain of another ship, who came in close and pulled the trapped ship loose. But many Spaniards were dragged by the Aztecs from the snared ships and captured alive, and several of the brigantine captains, including Pedro Barba, were killed.

Cortés had made it a cardinal rule not to advance into Tenochtitlán unless the canals that had to be crossed for withdrawal had been filled in. So he was outraged when he learned of Alvarado's rout. Such an Aztec victory would revive Guatémoc's spirit and prolong the resistance; it might even put the Aztecs again on the offensive. Cortés, escorted by a few horsemen, went by land around the lake to see Alvarado where Alvarado and his men had taken refuge in a new campsite, which was in a defensible square within Tenochtitlán near the Tacuba causeway.

As usual, though, with Alvarado, Cortés's anger calmed when he saw how far into the capital his fellow-Estremaduran had driven and the amazing feats he had accomplished, the very difficult canals he had crossed, the ramparts he had knocked down, against tremendous odds. Cortés and Alvarado were both thirty-five or thirty-six; they weren't young men fighting with all the pliancy and buoyancy of youth. Also, Cortés had to sympathize with the pressure put upon Alvarado by his soldiers because among his own men Cortés was experiencing the same kind of pressure.

When Cortés returned to his camp—and riding with a few horsemen around the lakeshore was not without danger—he was again confronted with the same popular demand: His men were keen to strike into the capital and they wanted to be the first to delve into the booty they foresaw in the marketplace. The chief exponent of this aggressive view was Alderete, the royal treasurer, who, now that he had been in Mexico for a few months, considered himself thoroughly seasoned and was impatient to acquire some gold. Because Cortés viewed the enthusiasm of Alderete and all the Spaniards as simply an excess of Spanish spirit, he tolerated the arguments Alderete and his supporters set forth. But Cortés was fearful that, if he were to order the three columns to advance and establish their camps within the capital, then the Spaniards might place themselves in positions in which they could be besieged, as they had been before. Alderete argued that the Aztecs, if the pressure were increased, would collapse and give up. And Alderete harangued the men in camp and won general support. Cortés, pursuing his own line of thought, felt that, after Alvarado's defeat, he had better take the offensive before the Aztecs, flushed with their victory, took the offensive on their own. So Cortés agreed that a coordinated attack to capture the marketplace should be launched.

The plan of attack that Cortés prepared called for Sandoval to leave only a token force on the Tepeyac causeway and to join his main force with

Alvarado's force. Then, with six brigantines in support, Sandoval and Alvarado, with their Indian allies, were to advance into Tlatelolco—and the first thing they were to do was to repair as permanently as possible the torn-up parts of the interior causeway where Alvarado and his men had been trapped. Then they were to drive for the marketplace, which was only a short distance away, but they were not to take any risks that could lead to their defeat. Cortés seemed to trust that Sandoval, though considerably younger than Alvarado, would have a restraining influence on Alvarado's impetuosity.

Cortés had the greatest distance to go within the capital. And he preceded his attack by sending ahead the brigantines. In his letter to the king Cortés reported that he had at his disposal a total of thirteen brigantines, and, if his number is accurate, this would mean that the brigantine that had become stuck on the Aztec stakes had been retrieved. Actually, the Spaniards who manned the brigantines quickly invented a tactic to counter the staked snares of the Aztecs. The Spaniards would identify an area where stakes had been set, then would wait for a good wind and, beginning from a point distant from the snare, would row to accelerate their speed and smash into the stakes, knocking them loose from the soft mud bottom. In this way many of the snares the Aztecs had constructed were eliminated. To aid the brigantines, Cortés sent Indian allies in three thousand canoes.

Then he divided his own land force into three parts, each supported by thousands of Indian allies, each part to advance along the three main roads within Tenochtitlán in the direction of the marketplace. He put Alderete in command of one part, with the mission to advance along the widest road and carefully to fill in all the canals where the bridges had been lifted and to break up the barricades. He assigned to Alderete an additional dozen men with picks to demolish houses to provide rubble for the fill. He assigned two captains to command the second part, with the assignment to proceed along a narrower road, and he allotted two large cannons to them. He commanded the third part himself, to proceed along the narrowest road, which was heavily barricaded, and he brought light field guns to knock down the barricades.

At first, Cortés's three-pronged attack went well. The Aztecs fell back and were driven from the rooftops by the Tlascalans. Cortés with his men tried to break up ambushes from side streets where the Aztecs were hiding. But Alderete's force made the most rapid progress and, when these Spaniards heard sounds of firing from Alvarado's and Sandoval's men near the marketplace, they raced ahead until they came to a breach about twelve paces across on an interior causeway where the water was about eight feet deep. Then they hastily gathered reeds and threw them into the water until the bed of reeds was strong enough to support them as, one man at a time, they skipped across to the other side. Whereupon, the Aztecs fell upon them so furiously and in such numbers that Alderete and his men were running back in terror—when Cortés rode up to check on their progress.

As Alderete's retreating Spaniards, many together, leapt onto the reeds, which were soggy and softening, the men sank into the water. Dismounting, Cortés tried to stop their flight, but the Spaniards on the far side, being chased by the Aztecs, pushed those on the bank into the water until the water was filled with floundering Spaniards. All Cortés could do was pull up drowning Spaniards who then lay on the near bank, puking mud and blood. When the Aztecs came on, as within moments they did, they were crazed with victory and leapt into the water, where they outnumbered and outwrestled the Spaniards. From nearby canals more Aztecs came in canoes to fish floundering Spaniards from the water.

It was worse than Alvarado's rout because there were many more Spaniards involved. When the few who swam across got out on the side where Cortés was, most had lost their weapons and had nothing with which to defend themselves. The Aztecs were also crossing the canal and disembarking from their canoes, and Cortés on foot was fighting with his sword. The street was jammed with struggling Spaniards and Aztecs. Cortés himself was seized by the Aztecs but, as before in Xochimilco, his aide, Olea, fought and freed him—only this time Olea was killed. Fighting with their swords and shields and with a few weapons taken from the Aztecs, Cortés and about fifteen Spaniards tried to retreat. The horsemen Cortés had left as a rear guard could not charge through the mob in the street, in fact, could hardly enter the street. They tried to send a horse for Cortés, whose own horse had been lost, but the rider was speared in the throat before he could reach Cortés. The whole street was slippery with mud, water and blood, and two riders astride mares slid into the canal, where one rider and his mare were quickly killed, the other rider and mare being pulled out by Spaniards on the near side. Another aide who tried to bring a horse for Cortés was killed. The Spaniards were not trying to save Cortés out of sentimental attachment but because they knew that, if the Aztecs were to realize that the Spaniards' captain-general was gone, the whole tide of the conquest would reverse and the Spanish cause would ebb.

Finally scrambling onto a horse, Cortés could not fight and could scarcely move through the crowd but from horseback he directed the Spaniards in their retreat toward the causeway. (He reported in his letter to the king that this was the Tacuba causeway, but he was probably in error.

Cortés and his men must have retreated to their base on the Iztapalapa causeway because, when he later sent riders to seek Alvarado, the riders had to go around the lake by way of Coyoacán and Tacuba.) In the melee Alderete fought to save his own life and brought out some survivors. The Aztecs, wild in their victory, hacked off the heads of several Spaniards and threw the heads after those who retreated. Within the confine of the causeway Cortés was able to set in place a line of horsemen, cannons and guns, and thus held off the Aztecs. It was still morning.

The Spanish losses were heavy: More than sixty Spaniards had been killed or captured; seven or eight horses had been lost, along with several cannons and field guns and many hand-weapons. Cortés's Indian allies had been overwhelmed by the Aztecs and slaughtered. All the Spaniards who survived were wounded; Cortés, battered all over, had a severe wound in his leg and could hardly stand. For a while, it was thought that the brigantines had been lost, too, and that the men with Sandoval and Alvarado had been defeated. So profound despair prevailed in the camp of Cortés.

Meanwhile, Alvarado and his men (Bernal Díaz among them) were fighting near the marketplace; Sandoval and his men were fighting separately but not far from them. Alvarado first became aware of the catastrophe that had befallen Cortés when fresh Aztec troops, displaying new banners, gaily confronted him and held up a bundle of five severed Spanish heads with the hair and beards tied together. The Aztecs screamed that they had killed Cortés and Sandoval and were going to wipe out all the Spaniards. Not knowing what had really happened, Alvarado called off his advance and retreated in good order toward the camp he had set up in the square on the island side of the Tacuba causeway. Alvarado had learned his lesson, and the gaps over which he retreated were all filled in. From his camp in the square, he blasted away with cannons and field guns and with volleys from the harquebusiers and crossbowmen and kept the Aztecs at bay.

Sandoval, likewise, was attacked by Aztecs holding up severed Spanish heads (all these heads were from Cortés's column) and in the fighting Sandoval and his men were mauled and wounded as they backed down the street toward the Tepeyac causeway where they could better defend themselves. But the panicky allied Indians, even the Tlascalans, jammed the Tepeyac causeway and Sandoval had to drive them off. Finally Sandoval's men, with the aid of two brigantines, were able to hold a defense line.

Cortés sent Andrés de Tápia with a squad of horsemen at a gallop around the lakeshore to see what had happened to Alvarado. Sandoval by the same dangerous route came to see Cortés, and, when Sandoval arrived, Cortés in a fury was berating Alderete. Soon it was affirmed that all three columns had endured, though many Spaniards had been killed and almost all were wounded. Cortés was relieved to learn that the brigantines had not been lost.

It was late in the day—toward the end of June 1521—when the Aztecs began to give notice of their triumph to the watching world and to their gods. (In Mexico City summer afternoons, though never really hot, are sultry, and the slanted sunlight, filtering through the haze of the natural inversion layer that overhangs the city, is reddish and suggests a witching hour.) In their camp on the square within Tlatelolco near the Tacuba causeway Alvarado and his men could see clearly what was going on. From the top of the great pyramid beside the marketplace rose a column of yellow smoke from burning copal, and the perfumed smoke wafted over the broad valley as a sign to the people—Aztecs and their subjects—that a great victory had been won and as a sign of thanks to the gods. Staccato blasts were blown on a deep-toned shell-horn, and a huge drum, placed in front of the temple atop the pyramid, was sounded—the bass booming continuing, accompanied by the screechy jingling of bells, whistles and tambourines. This pounding of the drum of the Aztec emperors could be heard all over Tenochtitlán and it called upon all Aztecs to fight for the ultimate victory that the gods promised.

Then, in clear view, a cluster of Aztec priests slowly forced up the steep steps of the pyramid the first victim. The Spaniard had been stripped naked and his white skin shone in the gathering dusk. After the long, slow ascent had been made, the priests turned the Spaniard toward the watching crowd below, set upon the Spaniard's head a feathered headdress and put into each of his hands a plume. And then the Spaniard danced on the terrace before the Aztec idols—Huitzilopochtli and his brother, Tezcatlipoca. Shuffling, stiff from fright, the Spaniard danced, waved the plumes in his hands, bobbed his head to display the radiant colors of his headdress. It is doubtful if mushrooms or *pulque* had been given to the Spaniard to induce his dancing. Fear would have been sufficient.

While the first victim was performing, a second victim, white and naked, was escorted by another knot of Aztec priests, from the base up the steps of the pyramid. The Aztecs were not in a hurry. When the second Spaniard reached the top, he was adorned with a feathered headdress and was given plumes, and he joined the first victim, both of them shuffling and bobbing in front of the Aztec idols.

Torches were lighted to mark a path up the pyramid steps and all around the temple at the top, so that the terrace of the temple became ablaze with light that illuminated the dancing white-skinned men, shamed and pathetic in their nakedness. Then another Spaniard was brought up the temple steps, and another—the Aztecs had plenty—until the terrace before the idols was busy with gyrating victims, bobbing and turning, with the priests at the sides of the terrace serving as a witnessing chorus.

After an hour a high priest signaled and the dancing was terminated, though the beating of the drum and the jangling of the bells and tambourines continued. Aztec priests rushed forward and took back from the dancers their headdresses and plumes. Then the first victim was pulled to the sacrifice-stone, thrown down on his back and held spread-eagled. The high priest came forward, held above his head the flint knife and drove it into the victim's chest, cut across the ribs, and, plunging his hand into the chest cavity, tore loose the beating heart. The priest held aloft the Spaniard's heart, which with its few final spasms gushed blood that fell on the priest's face, while a din of shrieking rose from the people of Tenochtitlán, who—from the rooftops, in the streets and squares of the great city— were watching with a rapture that Europeans could not comprehend.

Then other priests took the heart into the temple and placed it before the idols, while others systematically cut off the victim's head, arms and legs, and disdainfully rolled the split-open torso to the top of the steps and with a few kicks sent it downward. From the top of the high pyramid the bloody, butchered white body rolled, bounced, nearly stopped at several places, falling down the hundred fourteen steep steps.

Then the second victim was sacrificed.

And the third.

And the fourth.

And when all the Spaniards who had danced for the gods' pleasure had been disposed of, the procedure was begun again—with more naked Spaniards taken up the steps, one at a time, to their disgrace and their death. The torches were kept blazing, the drum-beating went on, all through the night. As Cortés reported to his king, "it seemed as if the world was coming to an end," though this was not the end of the world but a fiery fusion of two disparate parts of it.

If there had been any withheld fury on the Spanish side—among Alvarado's men (including Bernal Díaz, who saw the whole spectacle and wrote down his testimony) or among the men with Cortés or the other Spaniards when they were told—no vestige of mercy or restraint remained. Spaniards would have understood and condoned anything that happened in a fight, but this ceremony, which was elaborate, paced, formalized, and thus obviously had been developed over a long period of time, left the Spaniards hardened as they had never been before.

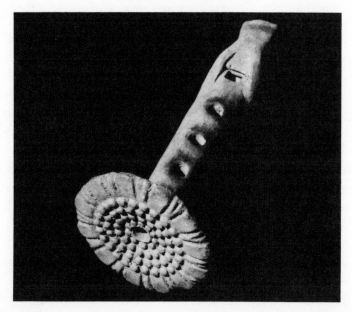

This little Aztec flute, made of clay, has the flare of its horn turned into a flower, which originally was brightly painted. On the flute five notes may be played, four mellow notes and a piercing high note, but the notes can be modulated to make strange-sounding, complicated melodies. It is believed that such a flute was played by a carefully chosen victim who had been indulged for a year; the victim would play several such flutes and break them while he was climbing the steps to be sacrificed to the god Tezcatlipoca.

Within the next few days almost all the Spaniards' Indian allies decamped. Only a few hundred Texcocans, obedient to their Christian boy-king and commanded by one of his brothers, remained with Cortés, and Chichimecatecle with about eighty Tlascalans stayed with Alvarado. On the morning after the sacrifices were begun, Guatémoc issued a proclamation: The gods promised that all Spaniards would be killed within eight days. This news was screamed out by Aztecs in canoes who boldly approached the Spanish camps. The Aztecs even threw at the Spaniards a few cooked arms and legs, the limbs of sacrificed Spaniards, and told the Spaniards to eat if they were hungry because Aztec bellies were full. The allied Indians who decamped, however, did not go back to their homes but waited in the hills to see what would happen within the forecast eight days.

What could not be known by the Spaniards nor appreciated by their allies was how weak the Aztecs in Tenochtitlán really were. The capital had been without decent drinking water for more than forty-five days. The people were sick from drinking bad water. Though in the rainy season it rains every day in Mexico, the rainwater the Aztecs were collecting in earthen pots was not nearly sufficient. Most of the Aztecs were starving; the recent feast on enemy flesh had been shared only by the nobles; the multitude had not participated. Diseases were rampant. The people within Tenochtitlán were emaciated and looked like visions of shades in Hades. The Aztecs had used up the last of their energy in this burst of fighting.

Within the Spanish camps there was rocklike determination. Perimeter defenses were maintained against the faint follow-up forays of the Aztecs, which involved more shouting than fighting. The Spaniards used the days now to treat their wounds and bury their dead; there was not a living Spaniard who was not spangled with bandages. Still, the Spaniards were in place, in accord with Cortés's strategy; the brigantines were afloat; and supply to the Aztecs in Tenochtitlán remained cut off.

Horror was an integral part of the Aztec scheme of living, like a vital pulsing, and Guatémoc—in parallel to Cortés's pressure to make the Aztecs sue for peace—intensified the horror in an attempt to discourage the Spaniards. There were among the Mexican Indians and within the Aztec sphere of domination tribes that were considered barbaric by Aztec and most Indian standards. These were tribes of ancient origin that somehow had not melded into the Indian mass or adopted practices that the other tribes had in common. Most primitive, despised and feared of these barbarians were those who lived in a town called Malinalco, not far from Cuernavaca, and others who lived in and around a town called Matalcingo, near Otomí territory on the way to Tlascala. Guatémoc ordered these barbarian tribes to attack their neighbors who had supported the Spaniards and to hurry to Tenochtitlán to aid him if they wanted to share in the booty he would take from the Spaniards. Aztecs, cruising in their canoes past the Spaniards' camps, warned the Spaniards of the awfulness they could expect from these barbarians.

Consequently, chiefs from Cuernavaca came to Cortés in his camp, chiefs who seemed to be loyal to him, and they asked for help because barbarians from Malinalco were attacking them. Cortés himself needed help; he was not inclined further to reduce the strength of his depleted force, and many of his captains warned him not to do so. Nevertheless, Cortés knew that all the Indians who had been his allies were waiting and watching from the hills; the Spaniards were dependent upon the allied towns for food; and Cortés was stung by the Aztec threats implying that Spaniards should fear the barbarians. So he ordered Andrés de Tápia with a small contingent of Spaniards to go with the chiefs to Cuernavaca.

It was a quick, highly successful expedition. The Spaniards, joined by thousands of local warriors, decisively defeated the simple Malinalcans, who had neither order nor discipline. But two days after Tápia and his men had returned to camp, Otomí chiefs showed up to ask Cortés for help because their towns, which were close by, were being attacked by barbarians from Matalcingo. The Otomí chiefs promised their continued support of the Spaniards. So Cortés dispatched Sandoval with a slightly larger contingent of Spaniards; Otomís came from the hills to serve as auxiliaries; and the combined force of Spaniards and Otomís chased from Otomí territory the barbarians, who fled in fright at the sight of the Spaniards, especially at the sight of the horses.

What Sandoval discovered then, as a measure of the level of these primitive Indians, was that in the sacks of provisions dropped by the fleeing barbarians, in addition to blankets and maize, there were the bodies of roasted babies. This is hard for us now to believe, to imagine: Love and concern for the newborn are such universal characteristics of human beings and of most of the higher forms of animal life. Yet the fact of these roasted babies was twice recorded—and the Spaniards were so fixed in their fury that this appalling discovery brought no further comment from them. Furthermore, when the barbarian chief surrendered and offered his allegiance to the Spaniards, Sandoval in accord with Cortés's policy accepted the pledge. True to their word, the barbarians then marched back with Sandoval to have their pardon confirmed by Cortés, who had them man some barricades where they could be seen by the Aztecs, to the consternation of Guatémoc.

The eight days of Guatémoc's prophecy passed, though on each of the eight days and for a total of thirteen days the Aztecs at the great pyramid of Tlatelolco continued their sacrificial slaughter of the captured Spaniards (about seventy in all). After the eighth day the Indian allies began to move back around the Spanish camps. The Tlascalans particularly were ashamed that they had been put off by the threat of an Aztec attack which had never come. So Chichimecatecle, without coordinating with Alvarado or Cortés, adopted a Spanish tactic and organized four hundred Tlascalan archers to form ranks and to shoot in volleys. Then, without any Spaniards, Chichimecatecle led the Tlascalans across the Tacuba causeway. And on their own, with archers as their spearhead, the Tlascalans fought a fierce daylong battle with the Aztecs, retiring at the end of the day with as many Aztec corpses as they had lost Tlascalans to the Aztecs.

In the course of this battle between the Tlascalans and the Aztecs there was much shouting on both sides. The taunts exchanged were translated for the Spaniards, who in their grimness ignored the Aztecs' gory threats. And when in the evening the Tlascalans butchered, cooked and ate the Aztec corpses—while the Aztecs were eating the Tlascalans who had been lost—the Spaniards spat, went on munching tortillas, watched with little interest, and emotionally revealed nothing. That the Tlascalans by themselves had been able to stand up to the Aztecs was a demonstration for the Spaniards of Aztec weakness and a challenge to the Spaniards to resume the fray.

During the lull following the Spaniards' defeat, while both sides were exhausted, Aztecs on the Iztapalapa causeway called for talks. Malinche and Aguilar duly accompanied Cortés to their side of the first gap—and a dialogue ensued. Cortés once again appealed to the Aztecs to surrender on terms that would not offend their dignity; the tribute system was familiar to them and was, indeed, their own invention; only now they would pay tribute to the king of Spain. The Aztecs' proposal was that the Spaniards could be assured of safe passage out of the country if the Spaniards would agree to leave. The Tlascalans warned Cortés not to believe a word the Aztecs said. Cortés told the Aztecs that he would not strike the Spanish camps, and the brigantines would continue to keep food and water from reaching the capital, and the barbarians Guatémoc had summoned were now fighting on the Spanish side. He implored the Aztecs to cease their defiance, which would lead only to their death. He was wholly unsuccessful, as were the Aztecs, and peace talks were broken off.

Then Cortés decided to raze the capital. No longer would the Spaniards bypass buildings from the roofs of which they could be attacked. The Aztecs had reopened all the canals the Spaniards had filled in and had rebuilt the barricades on their side of all the lifted bridges. Now, when the invasion of the capital was resumed, the Spaniards would slowly and steadily level Tenochtitlán. They would knock down everything they could—the barricades, palaces, houses, huts, temples—and with rubble and mortar cover all the gaps they had to cross. Cortés concocted this strategy regretfully, because he knew he was condemning this dream city to destruction. But he knew how little strength he and his Spaniards had left; they were nearly as exhausted as the Aztecs; and, if they could not succeed soon, their conquest might fail.

So he summoned the chiefs of all the allied tribes and asked them to send from their farmlands laborers with their *coas,* sharpened digging sticks with a crosspiece where pressure can be applied with a foot. As the Spaniards and allied Indians forced their way into Tenochtitlán, the laborers would systematically destroy the place.

The battle and demolition began and went on—day after day after day. The Aztecs had invented a few new defenses; they had placed boulders in the squares and in the wider streets to impede the horses and had built walls to block off some of the streets. But Cortés had sternly cautioned his captains, and the daily advances of the columns were limited. Ample time was allowed for the razing and the filling in of the routes. The Spaniards were not going to be guilty of overeagerness again.

Cortés's empathy with Indians was as critical to his success as his strategy. And it was an *empathy* that he had, not a sympathy; he had no sympathy for people with the practices of the Indians; but he had a profound empathy—an ability to perceive the Indians' feelings, to sense what they wanted and even needed emotionally. This was a vital aspect of Cortés's canniness and genius. He had developed this empathy in the course of all his negotiating sessions with Indian envoys, in the course of his talks with Montezuma and other Indian nobles, probably in his night-time whispering with Malinche, as well as through trekking and fighting and fleeing and fighting again.

Now, as his forces battered their way ahead, Cortés would climb to the top of high pyramids and stand for some while on the terraces, where all the Indians—Aztecs and allies—could see him. Behind Cortés on the skull racks in the burning temples were the heads of sacrificed Spaniards, and he wanted the Indians—all Indians—to see him in the midst of the Aztec capital, avenging his own. He was not gloating, or seeking to present himself as a terror-figure, but Cortés knew, instinctively he knew, that Indians craved personification. They needed to see a figure they could recognize who stood for the tide of conquest that was taking place. The Indian religion did not give them the kind of divine inspiration that filled the minds of Christians. This was why the Indians tended to deify their kings and priests—and this was why Cortés intentionally showed himself. He knew that the Indians needed to see in some particular, recognizable person and would see in him the figure that stood for their destiny, whether retribution or reward. Intuitively Cortés had this aptitude, this knack, for impressing the Indian mind.

The Spaniards found that the famished people of Tenochtitlán were scrounging for edible roots and herbs; at night they were seining the shallows of the lake with their bare hands to catch minnows and to dredge up anything else they might eat; they had torn timber from the houses to use as firewood for what little cooking they could do. They had stripped bark from the trees, and the Tlascalans showed Cortés where the bark had been gnawed.

Crowds of people were milling around in the city, mainly starving women and children. As the Spanish horsemen rode about, the people in the crowd would moan, would make a wailing sound; they were without strength and would not fight, could not fight, yet they did not give up and appeal for mercy. Without direction from the authority-figure they were used to—their monarch, now Guatémoc—they were incapable of action, even submission. On the roofs and on pyramids in the parts of the city that the Aztecs still held, there were armed warriors, but these warriors were unable to put up vigorous resistance; they had few stones, spears or darts to throw; their supply of arrows was low; and gradually they were retreating toward the marketplace. Each day now the Indian allies would swarm into the capital in the wake of the Spaniards; Cortés estimated that more than one hundred fifty thousand Indians were fighting on his side. Still, the Spanish advance was slow because, wherever a bridge had been lifted, the canal had to be thoroughly filled in. Cortés described the leveled city, with flames flickering over the rubble, as "a sad sight."

One morning Cortés was puzzled when he saw smoke coming from the tops of two pyramids near the marketplace, black smoke, not the yellow copal smoke that was Guatémoc's signal. Cortés could not get to the marketplace from where he was; several canals that the Aztecs were defending remained to be filled. But Alvarado, taking advantage of the pressure Cortés was applying, had led his horsemen in a charge and they had broken through to the edge of the marketplace where they had set fire to temples atop the two pyramids; then, before the Aztecs could cut him off, Alvarado had withdrawn. Cortés, when he learned of this, complimented his friend's valor.

While Cortés was filling in the last canal that remained between his column and the marketplace, Alvarado with four horsemen rode up; access had been opened between the vans of the two columns; and within minutes horsemen from both columns rode into the expanse of the marketplace square. The roofs of the buildings around the square were jammed with Aztec warriors, but the Aztecs dared not enter the square where the cavalrymen would spear them, and the roofs were too far away for any of their missiles to do the Spaniards any damage. So these Aztec warriors, still great in number, began to leave the marketplace.

Cortés climbed the high pyramid of Tlatelolco and found on the skull rack of the temple the heads of many Spaniards and hundreds of Tlascalans. Again, Cortés took his stand on the terrace, on this terrace where the Christians had been made to dance, and, as the temple burned, he let the Aztecs and the allies look at him. What he saw in his overview of the

The Aztecs would often decorate the skulls of those who had been sacrificed, using mother-of-pearl for the whites of the eyes, with jet, jade or carnelian pupils, and with noses or tongues indicated by knife-blades of flint or obsidian.

city—the once-magical city, now flattened and smoking—was that seven-eighths of Tenochtitlán was now held by the Spaniards and their allies. Thousands of Aztecs, however, were thronging through narrow streets toward the lakeside of Tlatelolco, where all the houses were built on stilts in the water. There, where the cavalry could not get at them, what remained of the Aztec army would hold out. Cortés could see that in this lakeside district the roofs were already densely crowded with Aztec warriors, even while more were on their way. In the midst of the district was a lagoon in which all the Aztec canoes that were left—many hundreds of them—were gathered. There was no way, Cortés concluded, for the Aztec army to sustain itself, crammed into those houses in the water.

Cortés sent a captured Aztec back to his people with a message: Cortés once again begged them to surrender. But a reply came back from the ruling captains that they would never give in, they would die fighting, and, when attacked, they would throw into deep water whatever they had of value. So Cortés decided not to attack. Because the Spaniards were nearly out of powder, Cortés agreed to the proposal of one of his men, a Spanish carpenter from Seville, that with a little help he could build a catapult that would hurl boulders into the lakeside district.

It took three or four days to build the machine and set it up on a raised stone platform, a kind of stage that was in the center of the marketplace square. While the machine was being assembled, Cortés and his captains, riding about the city, were sickened by the piles of dead, emaciated bodies in the streets. The Aztecs, though starving, would not eat their own. But the Aztecs did not want the Spaniards to be aware of their condition, so they could not throw the bodies into the lake where the brigantines would find them, nor could they leave the bodies in neighborhoods through which the Spaniards were advancing. The retreating Aztecs had carried their dead with them, and only now, without room and with nowhere to go, had they left the corpses to rot in the streets. At night the Spaniards would return to their camps, not to disengage from the Aztecs, but to get away from the stench of the dead. The Indian allies, however, were not so fastidious and, scornful of the Aztecs, camped overnight in the center of Tenochtitlán.

When the catapult was completed, it was wound up and threw one boulder, which fell nearby in the square, and the machine broke. So the Spaniards—without powder and without the catapult—had to proceed with crossbows, pikes and swords. The horses could not be brought into this area where the houses were on stilts. Cortés again appealed to the Aztecs to surrender, again to no avail. Alvarado with all his men on foot attacked one side of the Aztec position, Cortés with his force attacked the other side. The Aztecs, resisting desperately, were overcome—and the Spaniards' Indian allies poured in after the Spaniards and killed the Aztec warriors, women, children, old people, anyone they came upon. Apologetically Cortés reported to the king that more than twelve thousand people were slaughtered on that day. But his reprimand to the Indian allies brought only impassive stares: What did he think the Aztecs had done? How did he think the Aztecs had behaved in victory?

In the morning the Spanish infantry again formed for the attack; the Indian allies who had formerly, even lately, been vassals of the Aztecs were massed behind the Spaniards; and the horsemen formed a rear guard in the square. Then the Aztecs sent a messenger to Cortés, asking for a parley. The Spaniards around Cortés wanted him to parley; though ruthless during a battle, the Spaniards were moved by the women and children they saw suffering and dying. The Spaniards—priests among them—feared for their own souls. Cortés himself acutely wanted the Aztecs to surrender. But Cortés realized that Guatémoc and his highest lords were determined to hold out, and without their capitulation the Aztec mass could not yield. Nevertheless, he parleyed over a barricade with two minor Aztec officials who came to him. And they begged him to slay them all and put an end to their misery. In his turn Cortés begged them to surrender. But without instructions from Guatémoc they could not. So a whole day passed in futile negotiation, with each side repeating itself several times over.

During the night Cortés had a further idea, and in the morning he had brought before him an Aztec noble said to be of good standing who had been captured by a relative of Cortés's godson, Don Fernando, lord of Texcoco. Cortés asked this Aztec noble if he would carry to Guatémoc Cortés's proposal for peace, and the Aztec agreed to do so. A squad of Spaniards escorted the Aztec, who was seriously wounded, to the barricade where he was received respectfully by other Aztecs. As was later reported to Cortés, however, when this man came before Guatémoc and relayed Cortés's message, Guatémoc instantly sent him to be sacrificed. And the answer the Spaniards got was an outcry of Aztec defiance, warriors shrieking from the roofs—darts, stones and spears raining down. Thus passed the second day of negotiation.

On the next day Cortés rode out in front of his army and at the barricade had his message called out, addressed to Aztec lords whom he knew personally, warning them that within an hour he could have them overwhelmed and assuring them that, if Guatémoc would come and talk with him, the Aztecs could have peace and yet keep their dignity. The Aztec lords who knew Cortés came forward and sadly acknowledged his message, which they said they would bear to their emperor. In the afternoon they returned to say that, since it was late in the day, Guatémoc would come to parley with Cortés in the marketplace in the morning. On this note the third day of negotiation ended.

The next morning Cortés had a makeshift banquet table set up on the stone stage in the center of the marketplace square, the pieces of the broken catapult having been cleared away. He posted a minimal guard; Alvarado's men were held back; and the Indian allies, as the Aztecs had requested, were restricted to the causeways. But Guatémoc did not show up. In his place came a delegation of ranking Aztec generals. Cortés gave them food, and while they ate and drank, which they did ravenously like starving men with unslakable thirst, Cortés told them again that Guatémoc would suffer no indignity; Cortés pointed out that he had not punished them, the generals whom he considered responsible for this war; Guatémoc, however, was the only one who could make peace. And Cortés emphasized to them that only through a personal meeting of Guatémoc and himself—the rival power-figures in the Indian mind—was there any hope of avoiding a horror, a crime, a sin. Cortés had the Aztec generals take food and drink with them for Guatémoc when they returned to the Aztec camp. But after two hours they came back to the marketplace and, giving Cortés a few cotton garments, they delivered Guatémoc's reply, which was that he would never come. By then it was late, so Cortés told them to go back and repeat his message to Guatémoc, which they promised to do.

Early the next day the Aztec generals came to announce that Guatémoc at last would parley with Cortés in the marketplace square. So Cortés, increasingly suspicious of Aztec duplicity, deployed his forces as before, and for hours he waited in the square. When neither Guatémoc nor the Aztec generals appeared, Cortés abandoned whatever hope he had had, called up the Indian allies who came running, called up Alvarado's men, and, though it was early afternoon and the Aztecs may have thought they had won for themselves the respite of another day, the Spaniards smashed through their barricades, drove into the Aztec quarter, and the Indian allies went on a binge of killing. At day's end, when the Spaniards and Indian allies withdrew, the Aztec quarter was so littered with dead bodies that the Spaniards and Tlascalans had to walk upon the corpses; no barricades or canals remained behind which the Aztecs could defend themselves.

During the night Cortés refined his plans. Sandoval was in charge of the brigantines, and in the morning at the signal of a harquebus shot Sandoval was to have the brigantines rowed from the lake through a narrow passage into the lagoon where the Aztec canoes were assembled. Alvarado and his men were to wait for Cortés in the marketplace square. Cortés would bring with him all the heavy cannons and, with the remaining powder, the cannons would be used to break up any last-ditch effort by the still-numerous Aztecs. Everyone was to be on the lookout for Guatémoc.

In the morning, while Cortés was on a rooftop on the square appraising the situation, he spoke again with Aztec nobles whom he knew. Again they went to talk to Guatémoc, and a noble who was the greatest of the Aztec generals returned with the emperor's reply. It was the same: that Guatémoc preferred to die where he was, rather than appear before Cortés and bow his head. Cortés had the harquebus fired.

It was a confusing, sickening ending to the stress of the siege. The entire surviving population of Tenochtitlán had been compressed into a very small area; in these houses built on the water people were so closely packed that they were all standing because there was no room to lie down; and they burst out, rushed out into the narrow streets. There were knots of warriors holding out here and there, but they had no stones to throw, no arrows to shoot, and little strength to wield their clubs and spears. In the press women and children toppled into the water. The Spaniards were busier trying to restrain the Indian allies than they were in fighting the Aztecs, but the Indians who had been enemies or even subjects of the Aztecs were merciless.

Sandoval led a few brigantines into the lagoon, and the Aztec warriors in the canoes had neither the desire nor the energy to resist. One canoe bearing a few especially well-dressed Aztecs was being poled away, and a brigantine captain named Garcí Holguín drew alongside and had his crossbowmen take aim. The Aztecs in the canoe signaled their surrender. Spaniards leapt aboard—and Guatémoc was captured. Holguín claimed the prize, but Sandoval outranked him, and Cortés outranked Sandoval. Ultimately it was Cortés who was authorized to include Guatémoc on his escutcheon.

Guatémoc was eighteen years old. Like kings and emperors on both sides of the world, he had been raised to the thought, not that he served his people, but that he served his gods—and those gods that for so long had brought only giddying victories had failed him. Their power was gone, as was his.

When Guatémoc was brought before Cortés, in a dazed mumbled undertone (with Malinche translating) he asked for what he expected: that Cortés should have him killed. Having an instinctive fear of prolonged agony, he pointed to the dagger on Cortés's belt and suggested a quick thrust. Guatémoc was surprised when Cortés, vexed to have had no chance through talk and guile to avoid this destruction and carnage, abruptly turned from him and attended to the direction of the Spaniards and allied Indians who were overrunning Tenochtitlán.

The number of people lost during the siege was and is incalculable. According to a native chronicler educated by Spanish priests in the years immediately following the conquest when recollections were still fresh, 240,000 Aztecs died, including almost all the nobility. Of the 200,000 Texcocans fighting on the Spanish side, more than 30,000 were said to have perished. Gómara wrote what Cortés told him to write, that 100,000 Aztecs were killed, but this did not include those who died of starvation or disease. And none of these figures included women or children.

The siege had lasted seventy-five days, and Tenochtitlán finally fell on August 13, 1521. That date, in the Aztec calendar, was called One Serpent in the year Three House. In the Texcocan calendar, which was a little different from the Aztec, the day was called Five Rabbit. According to the Christian calendar, it was the day of Saint Hippolytus. And it was to Saint Hippolytus that the church built at the site was dedicated.

V
THE DISTORTING MIRROR
OF NATIONALISM

The Mexican Renascence

The social disruptions that threatened the bones of Cortés in their resting place in the Hospital de Jesús in Mexico City (not far from the Church of Saint Hippolytus) were different in nature, one from the other, but were steps in the same direction. Mexican nationalism was aroused early in the nineteenth century when Napoleon put his brother Joseph on the throne of Spain. With Joseph Bonaparte king of Spain, the Spanish colonists in Mexico could make no sense of their allegiance to the mother country, so they fought and effected a political revolution, similar to the revolution that had led to the separation of the United States from England, and many things that stood for Spain—the emblems and rites and the bones of Cortés—were damned. But Spanish law was retained; the Spanish social system was retained; Catholicism was retained; only politically did Mexico become independent. The Mexican revolution a hundred years later, however, was a *social* revolution, a real earthquake—and from the Mexican revolution of the second decade of the twentieth century there emerged modern Mexico, which proclaimed itself socialist, unpledged in religion, and radiantly proud of its Indian heritage. During this social upheaval Cortés's bones were actively searched for, so they might be scorned as a symbol of white racial supremacy.

The point which should not be skipped over lightly, but which usually *is* skipped over lightly, is that the legacy of Cortés in Mexico, as a matter of historical fact, after the dust of the conquest settled, was a period of remarkable stability and peace that lasted for about three hundred years—from the early 1500s to the early 1800s. During these three centuries in Mexico there was little unrest and there were no revolutions or large-scale attempts at revolution. Why? There were inequities and injustices, certainly, and these are the common causes of rebellion. But the answer, curiously, is that the two phases of living imposed by Cortés were the factors that kept the peace: (1) Catholic ritual, and (2) Spanish law. Catholic ritual satisfied the people's longing for spiritual answers. Spanish law assured order. (And order, not social justice, was the aim of *Siete Partidas*.)

This remarkable period of prolonged peace in Mexico and throughout Spanish America was the Pax Hispanica. There are three great periods of relative peace within extensive empires that stand out in the history of human fractiousness—the Pax Hispanica, the Pax Romana, and the Pax Britannica. And without comparing the three, it simply stands to reason that there must be virtue in systems that people tolerated for so long, under which they were increasingly productive and were content.

Another explanation of the Pax Hispanica, however, may be even more fundamental. When the Spaniards came to Mexico, they were already a blended people with strains of Moor, Jew, Visigoth, Roman, Greek and Phoenician mixed into the ancient Iberian. Irresistibly then, copiously, compulsively and convulsively, in accord with their passionate natures, the Spaniards interbred with the Indians. In spite of Spanish snobberies, in spite of the Spaniards' glorification of lineage, in spite of social stratification, the Spanish *siestas* . . . well, panting is the music of the *siesta;* the twanging of a guitar is prelude; and that great, calm, accepting middle span in the emotional nature of the Indian accommodated with affectionate naturalness the impatience of Spanish aggression. Cortés and Malinche were not the only proponents of this blending. Nor, as the years, decades and centuries passed, were only Spanish men involved; Spanish women in the amplitude of their passion equal if not exceed Spanish men. Every Spaniard involved in the conquest—with the possible exception of Sandoval—was as busy blending as he could be. And this was the hope of all the thousands of Indians who had supported Cortés and fought on his side; it was the hope of Mase Escasi and Xicotenga the Elder; it was even the reported intention of Montezuma. It was the hope of the unself-conscious, sexually matter-of-fact Indians that the two races should blend and combine their attributes.

Mexico is a wonder-filled country, blessed with a variety of congenial climates, and in the languor of the tropical lowlands, in the exhilaration of the highlands, on the ocean shores and even in the shade from desert heat (each aspect of the Mexican atmosphere reflecting and accentuating some aspect of Spain), Spaniards and Indians became Mexicans. When the Pax Hispanica came to an end in the early nineteenth century with the war of independence, there were in Mexico two-thirds as many *mestizos* (people of mixed blood) as there were pure Indians.

This Mexican invention—this intermixture of the races—was the assertion of the Mexican Revolution. For fifty years after the revolution it was said in Mexico that "only a brown face could be elected president." And so stubbornly anticlerical were the Mexicans that one brown-faced president stood outside the doors of the church while, inside, his daughter was being married.

But, truly, would anyone have thought that the violence of the conquest would be followed by one of history's longest periods of peace? Or that, from the viewpoint of the many Indians who supported Cortés, from their own revolt against Aztec oppression would eventually come the blending that their paternalistic chiefs had foreseen and desired?

It takes a long time for some of history's snarls to be worked out.

VI
THE VAGARIES OF VICTORY

THE FUSION OF THE WORLDS

When Guatémoc capitulated, a human phenomenon took place that revealed the degree to which the Aztec people had crystallized in the person of their emperor all of their hope, faith and capacity to act: The hitherto-invincible gods to whom Guatémoc spoke, and for whom he spoke to the people, were humbled and silent—and all Aztec resistance suddenly ceased, fell apart, became a shambles. The Aztec people simply gave up; the surviving warriors came down from the roofs, unarmed, and went into the streets; all defenses were abandoned. Men, both those in their prime and the aged, old women and young women with babies on their backs, youths and little children holding onto their mothers, all the Aztecs swarmed from the quarter of Tlatelolco into which they had been compressed, and they spread over the marketplace square, many scurrying away to see what had become of their homes in other parts of the city.

It took the Spaniards a little time to realize that the resistance had so utterly collapsed. Whereupon, a singular thought, like a bolt of lightning, flashed in the Spaniards' minds: Where was their gold, the treasure they had lost on the night of their humiliation, the gold that in sacks and coffers had slipped from their horses' backs or been dropped or wrenched from them? That was *their* gold—gold given to them by Montezuma; it had included their cut from the tribute Montezuma had collected, and had included as well the treasure of Montezuma's father and gifts sent for the Spaniards by subject tribes—and the Spaniards wanted it back! *All* of it, not only the gold bars and the gold grains but the sculptures in gold and silver and the exquisitely worked jewels.

To the Spaniards' dismay, all the Indians who had fought on the Spanish side—the Tlascalans, Texcocans, Cholulans, Xochimilcans, Otomí and others—were enthusiastically ransacking the houses on the water that the Aztecs were leaving. And the allied Indians were forcing the Aztecs—all the Aztecs, men, women and children—to submit to body-searches and were finding on most of them some hidden gold or jade. The Aztec men had the gold in their mouths or under their loincloths and stuffed into their anuses; the women had it hidden there and under their skirts and in their genital cavities. The allied Indians expected this kind of trickery and were pulling out the Aztecs' tongues and holding the tongues while they ran their fingers around the Aztecs' mouths and jabbed into the other orifices. And they were finding gold—bits of it but lots of it. So the Spanish soldiers after a few moments' hesitation did likewise.

Cortés and his captains grasped that, in spite of the best efforts of the allied Indians and the Spanish soldiery, many Aztecs were escaping from the square; others were escaping in canoes; others, hiding in the reeds, were secreting things—and, besides, with so many more allied Indians than Spaniards body-searching the Aztecs to extract gold, the Spanish share was bound to be small. Obviously it would be only slightly productive if the ranking Spaniards were to join in this frantic game of find-the-gold, yet time was of the essence because the Aztecs were quickly dispersing. The ranking Spaniards were in no condition to make detailed, individual body-searches, even had they wanted to. Cortés was hobbled by the leg wound which was still seeping blood under the bandage; Sandoval, whose legs were bandaged in three places, had during the last of the fighting been hit in the face with a rock and one side of his face was swollen black-and-blue; Alvarado was so out of breath he could hardly stand. Cortés and those with him knew they were seeking, not the bits of gold that individual Aztecs might have, but the treasure—the treasure they had lost, which was *theirs!* Most avid of all the Spaniards was Alderete, the royal treasurer who had been appointed by the king's council on Hispaniola. Alderete, who took his own recompense from whatever he acquired for the king, so far had nothing whatever to show for all the risks he had run, the terrors he had undergone, yet, as he loudly proclaimed, he was the one who had the royal sanction.

So Cortés and the Spanish leaders turned upon Guatémoc and a handsomely bedecked Aztec general from the emperor's retinue, with the direct question: Where was the treasure? When the emperor and his general did not reply, the Spaniards tied the general to a stake, gathered together some refuse for a fire, and prepared to burn him. Still, the Aztec emperor and his general kept their silence. So the Spaniards lighted the fire, which burned slowly because there was no decent firewood or even kindling left on the streets of the besieged city. Several times the fire went out or was put out and the Spaniards repeated their question, which was answered with silence, so the Spaniards relighted the fire. And Guatémoc impassively, even with a few contemptuous remarks, watched his general die. Then— when Alderete was beside himself and threatening everyone with the king's displeasure if treasure were not found, and the Spanish captains were seething with frustration—oil or fat was heated and brought to a boil; Guatémoc was put on his back with his feet propped up, his sandals were taken off, and, when the question was repeated and he still did not reply, the soles of his feet were burned. But this torture was little worse than the treatment which the Spaniards applied to their own wounds, so Cortés put a stop to it.

Cortés had further strategy in mind: He intended to use Guatémoc as he had used Montezuma, as a symbol of authority the Aztec people would hesitate to disobey. But Cortés—to his own mortification—had no strategy for finding the lost treasure. When a rumor was reported that the treasure was buried beneath the floor of Guatémoc's palace, he and some of his captains mounted and rode off and had the floor of the palace torn apart—to find nothing. Other rumors were pursued that kept Cortés and his captains wrathfully racing about the wreckage-strewn city, but no substantial hoard was found, no treasure. Guatémoc laconically informed Cortés that the whole treasure had been thrown into the lake.

Then it was demanded of Guatémoc that he point out just where in the lake the treasure had been dumped; Guatémoc pointed to a particular spot; and Bernal Díaz and a number of other Spaniards who were good swimmers promptly dove for it. Though they came up with a few little things, nothing of consequence was recovered. So the typical Spanish backbiting started among the Spanish soldiery—rumors that Cortés and the captains and the official *contadores* and the priests already had the treasure tucked away and were carrying on a charade of searching for what they already possessed.

For at least four days there was confusion among the Spaniards in response to the Aztec surrender. The Spaniards began to brand some of the surrendering Aztecs, especially the good-looking women and the young men who might fight again, but there were too many Aztecs and the Spaniards let them go. The stench from corpses was so awful that the Spaniards, fearful for their health, wanted to leave the city. Yet how could they leave while their Indian allies were still enriching themselves from the houses and from Aztec orifices? So some Spaniards stayed, and others who had left came back. Another rumor began to spread among the Spanish soldiery: that the Spaniards on the brigantines—those who had had to be coerced to serve on the ships in the first place—were finding all sorts of valuables hidden among the reeds and on the lake bottom, and the brigantines now were low in the water from the weight of the gold. Cortés had great bonfires started at streetcorners throughout the razed city, and the Aztecs were allowed to burn their dead to clear some of the stench from the air.

Eventually, as the allied Indians, loaded with booty, left Tenochtitlán, Cortés got his men to return to their camps—Alvarado and his contingent to Tacuba, Sandoval and his to Tepeyac, and Cortés with the largest force to Coyoacán. Thus the island capital of the greatest native empire in North America—the once-magical city now demolished and mostly deserted— was abandoned to the pathetic starvelings who were the Aztec scroungers. At Coyoacán Cortés gave flowery speeches to departing troops of allied Indian warriors, thanking them and promising them favors. The allied Indians had accumulated not only gold but items the Spaniards disdained or overlooked—fine cotton clothing, precious stones and gems, and fea- therwork mantles, especially those with the iridescent tail feathers of the bird called quetzal from the Yucatán and Central America (the name of the god, Quetzal-coatl, combined the name of the bird that supplied royal plumage with the name of the fanged snake). The allied Indians were well satisfied, and satiated, and carried off in their sacks Aztec limbs to give their families at home a taste of revenge.

While the bone-weary Spaniards rested in their camps, as the tension left them and almost to their surprise they could allow themselves to relent and relax, they began, as they always did after a bout of fighting, to behave as if they were drunk—to carouse and revel and quarrel and boast. This time the bout of fighting they had just survived had been climactic, yet they could have only a dry drunk and for feasting they had only the staples the local Indians provided for them, which they were heartily sick of, until a messenger arrived from Villa Rica on the coast and reported that a ship had come into port from Cuba bearing a cargo of wine and live pigs. Cortés sent the messenger right back to the coast with his command that the wine and pigs should be brought to the highland without an instant's delay, along with whatever else the Spaniards had at the port that would make food taste like what Spaniards were used to, especially vinegar and real bread, not tortillas. (The Spaniards at Villa Rica, many of whom were crippled and unable to fight, made handsome profits as traders. They would stock whatever they could obtain from the ships that arrived, then would claim to have paid very high prices, and would overcharge the Spaniards who were working and fighting in the highland. Martín López, while he was building the brigantines at Tlascala, had been forced to pay an exorbi- tant price for a keg of vinegar to keep his shipwrights happy, or, at least, so López alleged when later he sued Cortés.)

Bernal Díaz can be read so that the Spaniards' celebration may seem like an immediate reaction to their ultimate victory, but it takes a long time for a herd of pigs to be driven up the mountains through those gigantic breathtaking swales under the looming snow-capped peaks, past the volcano and down into the valley that was the seat of empire. Besides, when the Spaniards on the coast heard of the final and ultimate Aztec defeat, many of them, including some Spanish women, accompanied the pigs and the bearers carrying the wine on the upward trail.

Cortés loved to be a good host but, although he did the best he could, on the appointed day of the triumphal feast, when all the Spaniards from Tacuba and Tepeyac assembled in Coyoacán, there were only enough tables for half the company. But the Spanish women helped with the cooking, and the smells of the food were the smells of home and filled the heads of the *conquistadores* like fumes from the wine. The Spaniards were emotionally drunk before the feast started and soon, with the taste of a little real wine, as Bernal Díaz reported, "people were jumping over tables who could not walk through the door." Music brought on dancing—grace returning even to bandaged legs, with men who had no clean shirts dancing in their armor—and to many came dreams that had long been held off. Disregarding all the contention and the rumors about treasure which had not been found and all the cantankerous quarreling, crossbowmen imagined they would shoot arrows of gold at the sun and foot-soldiers envisioned themselves astride horses that had golden harnesses.

This party, it was hoped, marked the end of the agony of mortal combat. And the party inaugurated the beginning of Spanish gaiety in Mexico— even though Cortés on the morning after, in spite of or perhaps because of his hangover, discreetly apologized to Father Olmedo and promised that, as soon as everyone sobered up, a solemn Mass would be held at which all Spaniards would seek forgiveness.

Since no great treasure or hoard had been discovered in the ruins of Tenochtitlán, Cortés preferred to put off an accumulation and distribution of gold in the hope that more might be found or acquired. His unruly soldiers, however, wanted to know what was coming to them, so an early assessment was made. All the gold that admittedly had been collected was appraised. The rarities were set apart as gifts for the king. Then the gold was apportioned: one-fifth for the king, one-fifth for Cortés, so much for each of the captains, so much for each of the priests including Melgarejo, so much for the officials, and Cortés had to be repaid for lost horses he said had belonged to him personally—after which there was so little left for the ordinary cavalrymen and foot-soldiers that a terrific Spanish fracas developed with the disgruntled cavalrymen and foot-soldiers (among whom one of the most vociferous was Bernal Díaz) renouncing their paltry shares in favor of "the halt, the deaf, the blind, and those who had been scorched by gunpowder."

Cortés was able to calm things down by directing everyone's attention to this vast country from which the gold was drawn. In all likelihood the Aztecs had dissipated their hoard of gold by having to pay nearby tribes to run the Spanish blockade and bring food and water into Tenochtitlán. Some of the men now had their wives with them; Olid's Portuguese wife had arrived; and the presence of the wives sharpened, if that was possible, the Spaniards' acquisitiveness. But Cortés reminded them that the mines remained, the mines from which had come all the gold and silver, and Spaniards who knew something about mining and who had visited the mines had nothing but scorn for the Indians' mining methods. There was no telling to what extent the yield of these mines could be increased, and from now on the gold would flow straight into the pockets and coffers of Spaniards. Cortés, as captain-general, began to talk about the grants he would make: Each and every Spaniard would be rewarded with a piece of this country as an *encomienda,* in effect, a private fiefdom.

When a delegation of Indians from a province called Michoacán, which lay to the west, came to Cortés and he put on a show for them and they accepted his suzerainty, he was especially pleased because, in addition to including in his territory a reputedly rich area without having to fight for it, he had heard that Michoacán had an outlet on the southern sea. The idea of the southern sea intrigued Cortés and occupied his mind almost as soon as Tenochtitlán was demolished. Cortés had not yet seen this sea, but it had been described to him. Vasco Nuñez de Balboa had seen it from the western shore of Panama, and his sighting had been reported while Cortés lived in Hispaniola. This so-called southern sea—actually it was the western sea, the Pacific Ocean—must lie to the west of Mexico. Thus in Spanish minds, not alone Cortés's, was rising again the vision of Columbus, that by sailing further westward could be found China and the riches of the true Indies.

News of the Spaniards' triumph at Tenochtitlán spread quickly from Villa Rica to Cuba, Hispaniola and the other Caribbean islands, the significance of the victory resounding even in Spain. As a consequence, late in 1521—while Cortés and his Spaniards, still resting in Coyoacán, were wondering what next they would have to deal with—two ships from Hispaniola came into the harbor at Villa Rica. Aboard the more commodious of the two ships was a gentleman named Cristóbal de Tápia (apparently not a relative of Andrés de Tápia, one of Cortés loyal captains). Debarking, Cristóbal de Tápia announced that he was now the governor of New Spain—and he had the papers to prove it.

Pedro de Alvarado happened to be in Villa Rica (because Cortés and the men in the highland were not unaware of the price-gouging being practiced by the Spaniards of the port) and, as ranking captain, he was in command. When Tápia presented to him some of the papers which instructed that Tápia should be received and accepted as governor, Alvarado—for once not rash—read the papers slowly and carefully and told Tápia that he (Alvarado) was unable to pass upon the propriety of papers so momentous; the full council of Villa Rica would have to be summoned and assembled so that the authenticity of the papers might be verified and the manner of transmission approved. Tápia saw no reason for such dillydallying and said so, but Alvarado looked like the kind of man with whom it might be dangerous to argue too much.

While Tápia waited—and the functioning of the Villa Rica government inched forward (needless to say, a horseman at a gallop was on his way to Cortés)—Tápia mingled with all the Spaniards he could find at the port and sought out those who had come with Narváez or who had some connection to Veláquez. Tápia's papers had been prepared in Spain at the direction of the bishop of Burgos. To each Spaniard who Tápia thought might be influenceable, he gave a copy of a letter from Bishop Fonseca promising rewards for those who cooperated with him (Tápia) and threatening terrible punishment for those who opposed him. Tápia had a stack of these letters, which the bishop had signed with a flourish. The Spaniards in Mexico had only a dim notion of what was happening in Spain; they had heard rumors about Bishop Fonseca losing authority to the king's Flemings, yet the bishop did seem still to be president of the Council of the Indies and, hence, controlled commerce with the New World.

Tápia could not immediately proceed to the highland to present his commission to Cortés because Tápia's horses were seasick from the trip, so Tápia wrote a letter to Cortés, which Alvarado sent to the highland, to the effect that Tápia also had in his possession certain sealed letters which he would present personally to Cortés in the highland just as soon as his horses were well. Cortés had known Tápia for years, ever since Cortés and Tápia had both lived on Hispaniola; Tápia had been a *veedor*, specifically assigned to keep his eye on the iron foundries in Hispaniola to make sure that governmental revenue from the ironworks was not excessively siphoned off (for Tápia to siphon off a little for himself was expected). By the time Cortés received and thought over Tápia's letter, Tápia had set out for the highland, so Cortés had him intercepted on the road by Sandoval and a few other redoubtable captains with the talented Fray Melgarejo, who, having sold all his indulgences, was very interested in Tápia's letters. Cortés's men politely but firmly diverted Tápia from his route and led him to Zempoala.

In Zempoala the captains, following Melgarejo's lead, read over, line by line, Tápia's documents, excluding the sealed ones. The captains and Melgarejo, as a sign of submission and respect, placed on their heads the sheet that purported to be a royal commission. But they questioned the king's intentions regarding New Spain; they doubted that Bishop Fonseca had explained to the king the true state of affairs; they questioned the motives of the bishop, who was known to favor Velázquez; and they said that they could not possibly comply until the king's wishes were made clearer. Actually, they so scared Tápia that he became sick (or maybe he became sick from some mainland food he wasn't used to). Then the captains and Melgarejo sent their recommendation to Cortés that he should send down for Tápia a few gold ingots. When these gold ingots arrived, Alvarado gave them to Tápia in exchange for some Negroes Tápia had brought, his three horses, and the smaller cargo ship. Still, Tápia, when he was taken to Villa Rica for embarkation on his remaining ship, became balky and insisted that he should be allowed to present his sealed documents directly to Cortés. It was now nearing year's end, and this whole procedure had dragged on for so long that a few of the councilmen of Villa Rica were leaning toward an accommodation with Tápia and acceptance of him as governor. At this point it was Sandoval who lost patience, visited the wavering councilmen "with fifty of our toughest men," and then went to Tápia and told him to get back on his ship and go home or else they would send him home in a canoe.

In this way Bishop Fonseca's gambit was thwarted. When Tápia reached Hispaniola, the Jeronymite Fathers scolded him severely. They had told him not to go, as they had told Narváez not to go, because dissension would be aroused among the Spaniards, and the natives, if the Spaniards fought among themselves, would rise up, and this conquest, which promised to be a profitable and glorious one for both Spain and the Church, might be jeopardized. But this ruckus never came to the king's attention because the king was in Germany—and Tápia kept the gold.

. . .

In the early part of 1522 Cortés enjoyed a respite. Malinche having borne him a son, Cortés took the birth to be a sign of divine approval and named the boy Martín after his own father. Also, Cortés and his captains in council, after a good deal of thought, decided to rebuild Tenochtitlán. This was not an easy decision to reach because Coyoacán, situated on the shore of the lake, was a healthier place for a capital; the terrain was flat and defensible, less vulnerable to siege. But for many generations Tenochtitlán had been the center, the vortex and apex of life in this part of the world, and the Spaniards wanted for themselves that mantle of Aztec regality. So the rebuilding of Tenochtitlán was set in motion. The surviving Aztecs were put to work, and help was sought from friendly people like the Texcocans. Cortés moved his residence from Coyoacán back onto the island and personally supervised the laying out of the new municipality, in an effort to revive the glory of the fantasy city he had loved and destroyed. But, inevitably, the city he reconstructed was a Spanish city with churches where temples atop pyramids had been. The geometric look of Tenochtitlán was not duplicable; the ritualistic Aztec atmosphere that had kept the flagstone plazas clean and had regulated the activities of the people was replaced by Spanish hurry and jumble.

Early in 1522 Cortés began to write what has been designated his third letter to the king, accounting for his actions from the time he was driven out of Tenochtitlán and found refuge in Tlascala to the present. He described the ordeal he and his Spaniards had been through, yet he did not dwell on the triumph; he carried his narration right into his new resolution, which was to explore the southern sea, perhaps to find a link with the Caribbean, and to sail again westward for the spices and riches of the Orient.

In May Cortés finished this letter to the king and signed it. But Cortés and his captains were reluctant to dispatch it. They knew so little of the true situation in Spain, and nothing of the new king's attitude. Especially after Tápia with his royal commission and all his papers had come and gone, Cortés held many whispered, intimate, confidential conversations with his most trusted and stalwart followers about the danger that others like Tápia, at the instigation of Velázquez and with the support of Bishop Fonseca, might try with the king's approval to take political control of this conquest that Cortés and those with him had won with their blood and their courage. From many captains came hints and suggestions more blunt than hints that Cortés should declare for himself, should confirm the assignment of *encomiendas* without the king's approval, should perhaps even make this great new land independent of political control from Spain; at the least, he might try to limit control from Spain. This was seditious talk, and Cortés and his men knew it.

Backing off from the seditious talk, Cortés continued to maintain that the most certain way to win the king's favor—and to shake off the threats from Velázquez, Bishop Fonseca and others in the islands and in Spain— would be to send to the king another great load of treasure to prove beyond doubt the value of their conquest. Cortés and his captains did not know precisely what had happened to the last load of treasure they had sent. But Cortés was not proud of the amount of treasure now on hand, comparing it in his own mind with the treasure that had been lost on the night of the defeat. So he delayed in preparing a treasure fleet that would take his third letter to the king.

Many Spaniards were coming now to New Spain; they were tumbling into the new country. In harbors all along the eastern coast ships from the various islands and from Spain itself were dropping anchor. One of the best harbors was in the mouth of the Pánuco River (north along the coast from Villa Rica), but Francisco de Garay, the governor of Jamaica, had repeatedly tried to establish a settlement there and repeatedly had been defeated by the local Indians. So Cortés decided to subjugate Pánuco himself. He was advised against doing this by several of the captains who were closest to him in the circle of veteran battlers that still remained intact. They did not want Cortés to risk himself because they knew of the reverence the Indians were developing for him personally. Cortés, however, could stand only so much political machination, and he was tired of puzzling over what he should do with regard to the king and king-sponsored rivals. So, in spite of the captains' objections, he organized a substantial force of Spaniards with forty thousand Indian auxiliaries, went to Pánuco, and in a difficult campaign subdued it and returned to the capital.

It was in August 1522 that yet another ship from the islands came into harbor on the east coast of Mexico. This ship, carried by the current down the coast of Yucatán, had sought the first available haven, which was in Coatzacoalcos; the ship did not persevere to Villa Rica. Sandoval, having put down a rebellion of the Indians in Coatzacoalcos, was on hand to watch the debarkation of this lot, coming like the carpetbaggers of a later day to join in the exploitation. Sitting astride his horse, Sandoval watched the dinghies plying to the shore, bearing many gentlemen who wore lace, as well as some fashionably dressed ladies, and heaps and heaps of baggage. The valuable horses Sandoval could see aboard the ship were yet to be unloaded. Then up to him with a bold stride came one of the elegant women, who announced that she was Catalina Suárez Marcaida de Cortés, wife of the captain-general. With her were her sister, similarly dressed, and her brother, Juan. (Whether this Suárez sister accompanying Catalina was the other sister Cortés had once carried on with is a matter that defies historical research. If this was the sister Cortés had once liked, it would have been reasonable for Catalina to bring her as insurance. On the other hand, it would also be reasonable for any unmarried Suárez sister to come along in hope of marrying a gold-heavy *conquistador.* The brother, Juan, came along because he had once been an equal partner with Cortés in some land Velázquez had granted them, and from this original stake Juan traced his entitlement to half of whatever Cortés was said to have conquered.)

Sandoval was nonplussed. The arrival of La Marcaida was not expected, with or without her relatives. So Sandoval, trying to remember his manners, advised them all to rest from their voyage and settle down as best they could—while he sent a horseman at breakneck speed to inform Cortés.

In the capital Cortés—with his and Malinche's baby on his knee— received the news with the calmness of an experienced commander who had coped with many surprising and unwelcome developments. Cortés did not know to what extent this coming of the Suárez family could be attributed to their patron, Velázquez, but he suspected a good deal. Nevertheless, he ordered that his wife and her retinue should be provided with whatever comforts there were in Coatzacoalcos and that Sandoval, as soon as he could organize a fitting escort, should bring them to the highland.

And so Catalina—of whom her husband once said that she was as loved as if she were the daughter of a duchess—forced her marital reunion. When she reached the capital, Cortés ensconced her in commodious quarters; festivities in her honor were scheduled; and all the *conquistadores* who were in the capital gathered round to watch.

La Marcaida was a boisterous woman who suffered from asthma and she soon began to squabble with many of the captains around Cortés, squabbles that were duly recorded by the chroniclers. To everyone Catalina emphasized that whatever Cortés had she considered hers *("mío"),* completely disregarding the shares due the captains. Four or five days after her arrival, a ball was held for her, at which, after a lot of eating and drinking and swinging about at the high altitude she wasn't used to, she had a furious spat with a captain and Cortés had to terminate it by telling her that he wanted absolutely nothing of hers *("tuyo")*.

After the spat Cortés and his wife went to bed—and she died. By this time in the conquest there were doctors about, and the doctors concluded that Catalina died of asthma during an apoplectic spasm brought on by too much activity and feasting in the rarefied atmosphere of the highland. When Catalina's brother, Juan, subsequently sued Cortés and accused him of murder, Juan testified that there were marks of strangulation on his sister's throat. The doctors testified that these marks were the mottling caused by her spasm. Since the Spanish soldiery doted on gossip and black humor, stories of course spread quickly that Cortés had killed her. But Bernal Díaz thought nothing of these stories, in fact thought reasonably that the idea of uxoricide would never enter the mind of a sixteenth-century Spanish gentleman like Cortés, and the whole matter quieted—though the delicious little whisperings will go on forever.

In October or November Cortés decided that enough or perhaps too much time had passed and he had better send his third letter and the treasure that he had to the king. So there was a final calculation of the melted-down gold, which produced one figure according to Bernal Díaz and a lesser figure according to Gómara, who was supplied his information by Cortés, but the king's share—the royal fifth—which had amounted to twenty-six thousand castellanos after the fall of Tenochtitlán now came to thirty-seven thousand. The king was informed that in his royal name many slaves were being held in Mexico. And the king was sent, in addition to the gold in bulk, an assortment of marvels: Indian shields of wickerwork covered with puma skins, lined with feathers and rimmed in gold; pearls as large as hazelnuts, though the pearls were blackened because the coastal Indians put the oysters into fire to cause the shells to open; an emerald the size of the palm of a hand and pointed like a pyramid; many sculptures that the Spaniards had the Indian goldsmiths prepare, lifelike birds in gold, and fish, antelope, flowers and fruit, and gold plate and goblets for the king's table; and chests full of nose rings and lip pieces of inlaid gold. The collection was priceless and included fantastic, bejeweled mosaic masks and Aztec idols.

In December the whole amassed load was packed into three caravels, filling the holds, and on the largest ship were to sail Cortés's delegates with his letter to the king and another letter from the councilmen of the new capital asking explicitly for the king's approval of the *encomiendas* which had already been granted. (Cortés had previously disfavored the *en-*

comienda system because it set no measurable value on the personal service rendered by the Indians, and Cortés was sensitive to this inequity. Under the *encomienda* system, in Cortés's view, Spaniards were able to overuse their Indians in their rush to extract the riches of the land as quickly as possible, to the detriment and often death of the Indians and to the neglect of long-term development, as had happened on Hispaniola and Cuba. Yet Cortés, under pressure from his captains and his men who had little gold in hand, finally supported the *encomiendas* because he knew of no other arrangement—and no other system existed—that would reward the *conquistadores*, assure production from the land, and yet promise a semblance of Christian comfort for the Indians. Once brought around to this point of view, Cortés, being the keen competitor that he was, assigned to himself the most enormous *encomienda*.) It was also requested that the king should send a learned noble person to see all the wonders that had been found and to confirm the accomplishments of the *conquistadores*, that farmers should be sent with seeds and brood cattle, and devout priests to Christianize the Indians. The king was specifically asked *not* to send those who might add to the confusion and fractiousness: no Moslem or Jewish converts who might slip back into their old religious practices and bewilder the Indians, and, most particularly, *no lawyers*. Many *conquistadores*, including Cortés, sent personal letters and gold to their families at home.

Cortés chose as his chief delegates Alonso de Ávila and Antonio de Quiñones, accompanied by a selection of others from the Spanish army in Mexico, including Fray Melgarejo. Cortés did not go himself because he felt that he had to hold what he had conquered—and this meant warding off intruders like Tápia, keeping the Spaniards from fighting among themselves, and utilizing to the fullest his own personal standing in the eyes of the Indians. Besides, Cortés knew that the real worth of Mexico lay, not in this treasure that was being sent (which was a mere token), but in the future production from this land. So he bade his delegates and the treasure fleet *buen viaje* and good luck.

They did not have it.

East of the Azores, the Spanish fleet was attacked by French privateers who captured the slow treasure-laden caravels. So the treasure intended for the king of Spain ended up, instead, in the hands of the king of France. A month or two before the treasure fleet sailed, however, Cortés had sent another copy of his letter to his king, and this copy of the letter, taken by Cortés's secretary aboard a faster ship, got through to Spain. But this copy of Cortés's third letter with the inventory of the treasure was all that Carlos Quinto would ever see.

THE QUESTION OF SUBMISSION TO THE KING

In the psyche of the *conquistadores* there was undeniably a strong urge to declare themselves independent of the king. Cortés and his men knew that in their invasion of this vast land with its savage, heathen race they essentially had only God and themselves to rely on. Even financially they had supported their own venture. Though in communications to the king they used all the forms of etiquette that were customary in their times—"Most High and Powerful and Catholic Prince," "Most Invincible Emperor, King and Sovereign," "Your Caesarean Majesty Whose humble servants and vassals kiss Your Very Royal Hands and Feet"—beneath this gloss flickered their temptation to thank the king for nothing and to cast off all obligation to the king and his pernicious bureaucrats.

Were the *conquistadores* to raise a banner of their own in this land they had conquered and proceed to organize in the manner they themselves deemed best, they had enough gold and silver on hand and coming in to buy all the supplies they needed—powder, firearms, horses and the like. They could buy from merchants in the Caribbean islands or in Spain or elsewhere in Europe; there would be no shortage of suppliers willing to sell for gold. And more Spaniards would flock to them, were already flocking to them, with or without permission from the king and his official appointees. Knights were coming, soldiers were coming, priests were coming, farmers—both yeomen and peasants—would happily come from Andalucía and other provinces of Spain. In truth, the *conquistadores* had no intention of yielding control of their land. In their own opinion they who were on the ground and familiar with local conditions were best qualified to govern and devise practical solutions. To the king they were paying lip service.

And the irony was that Carlos—or Charles, as the king called himself—couldn't even speak Spanish. Born in Flanders in 1500, he spoke French as his natural language, German as his second language. Raised by his Austrian father's family in a Habsburg court, he thought of himself as the head of the Holy Roman Empire; only to the Spaniards was he primarily king of Spain. The fact was that the Habsburgs had a dream of restoring the Roman empire as it had been for its last eighty years after Christianity became the state religion, and they had intentionally raised the boy to be anti-nationalistic—in stark contrast to the pent-up, hard-won patriotism that was sweeping over Spain and to the sense of nationhood that was awakening in France and England.

This Habsburg scheming went against the grain of the *conquistadores* and was barely comprehended by them. Not one of the battle-scarred Spanish fighters in Mexico had ever seen this sovereign. To be coerced now in the king's name by Velázquez's uncle, Bishop Fonseca, and Fonseca's employees in the Council of the Indies was insufferable. Cortés and his men knew that Fonseca had put a ban on shipments to the New World in order to keep supplies from reaching them—and they resented it. They were eager to rattle a bagful of their newly minted gold coins and put the bishop's ban to the test.

Yet the Spaniards in Mexico, like all Spaniards, were instinctive traditionalists. And, though their king was only half-Spanish and was reported to have brought many Flemings with him to Spain, still the *conquistadores* could not reach a consensus to cast off the tradition of kingship, precarious though the history of kingship had actually been in Spain.

Until Tenochtitlán had fallen, the Spaniards in Mexico were not in a position even to contemplate the degree of their cooperation with the Spanish Crown. Prior to their triumph, they were nothing more than a little band of adventurers hardly worth noticing. By the time Tenochtitlán had fallen, however, and the adventurers had become conquerors and were in possession of Aztec gold, by that time the half-Spanish king and his Flemish advisors were entrenched in Spain, alerted to Spanish resentment, and, like crouching lions, they were poised to leap at the slightest indication of defiance to royal authority. From the Spaniards who were pouring into Mexico now, Cortés and his men heard the details about the town councils in Spain—the *comunidades*—that had rebelled in objection to the exorbitant subsidies demanded of them to further the new king's Holy Roman ambitions, and how the rebellion had been crushed.

On the one hand, the men in Mexico were infused with their own Spanishness, proud of their spirit, exultant in their success. They did not really want to disavow Spain or any aspect of it, and their Catholic faith was for them an essential part of their Spanishness. On the other hand, they were bedeviled by their envious enemies and, specifically, of most importance, Cortés and his men did not know whether they could trust the king himself. They had had absolutely no confirmation from him.

Mexico was like a keg of powder with a wick in it. But the wick had not been lighted.

Proceeding as if he had the king's approval, Cortés sent troops to the west coast to set up shipyards on the southern sea and he ordered that two caravels should be built; he also prepared expeditions to conquer the provinces south of Mexico, with the intention that troops on both coasts should search for a passage which might connect the Pacific and the Caribbean. From time to time Indian feuds had to be put down. Also, occasionally Spaniards would fall out with each other, over gold or *encomiendas,* and Cortés would have to restore order within the town councils, while more and more towns were being founded to legitimize the occupation of this land.

A report was brought to Cortés that there was an island of Amazons off the western shore. This notion probably was stimulated by the exceptionally tall, statuesque Indian women of Tehuantepec on the west coast in the south of Mexico and in all likelihood was embellished by a Spaniard who had read a sequel to *Amadís de Gaula* called *Sergan de Esplandían;* in this romance the ancient legend of huge, domineering warrior-women—a legend told in many versions throughout much of the world, probably dream-material in the minds of all men—was once more repeated. Cortés thought the report important enough that he in turn relayed it to the king. Cortés himself was obsessed with the promise of the Pacific.

But the weak spot that worried Cortés was Pánuco. One of his purposes in subjugating Pánuco had been to occupy the one place on the east coast where Francisco de Garay, the governor of Jamaica, might with royal approval try again to establish a foothold. The Pánuco expedition had left Cortés out of pocket because he had found no gold and, upon his return to the capital, he had sought to reimburse himself for his own outlays from the royal fifth that was accumulating. But the Spaniards responsible for the royal fifth, knowing they would eventually be held accountable, turned him down on the grounds that the purpose of his expedition had not been to advance the Spanish cause but only to preempt Garay.

Then in the mid-summer of 1523 Cortés heard that Garay, Velázquez and Columbus's aging son, Diego Colón, were conspiring in Cuba and preparing again to go to Pánuco. Garay, who was wealthy, had assembled a fleet of eleven vessels and, with Velázquez's assistance, was enlisting an army sworn to support and never abandon him. The fleet was commanded by Velázquez's nephew, Juan de Grijalva, who apparently was back in favor, and the army included one hundred fifty horsemen and four hundred or more foot-soldiers, perhaps as many as eight hundred fifty Spaniards, with ample artillery, firearms and provisions, and many Jamaican Indians. Actually Velázquez was reluctant to cooperate in this venture, having been nearly ruined when Cortés had defeated Narváez. Velázquez did not believe that Garay was equal to the task he was undertaking and feared he would fail, as had Narváez and Tápia. (While Tápia had been in Villa Rica, he had visited Narváez in jail. One-eyed Narváez had told him that, considering Cortés's luck, Tápia should get out of the country as fast as he could and beg help from Bishop Fonseca. When this had been reported to Cortés, he had ordered Narváez brought to him in the highland. Fearing punishment, Narváez on his knees had beseeched Cortés for mercy. And Cortés had lifted him up and assured him that their old friendship would be resumed, after which he kept Narváez with him for a while and then freed him to return to Cuba. Narváez professed to be eternally grateful to Cortés for his release, and Cortés even gave him some money to get back to Cuba, yet Narváez later sued Cortés. Tápia, likewise, sued Cortés.)

When Cortés heard about Garay's invasion fleet, he was confined to his bed in the capital, having broken his arm two months before in a fall from his horse. He was jittery from lack of sleep; the pain from his arm kept him awake. But Cortés got up and ordered that his bedding be packed. He summoned Alvarado, who was about to set out with a substantial force for Guatemala, and sent him instead to Pánuco. Then with another hefty force Cortés took to the trail behind Alvarado.

Around midnight on the first day out from the capital, as Cortés was uncomfortably settling down to try to sleep, two riders from the capital with an escort and guides overtook him. Cortés hadn't seen these two men in many years; they were his cousin, Rodrigo de Paz, and another cousin or brother-in-law, Francisco de las Casas. They had reached Villa Rica on a ship from Spain, had sought Cortés in the capital, and finally followed him on the road to Pánuco. Into Cortés's hands they delivered decrees which the king had signed the previous April, confirming Cortés as governor and captain-general of New Spain, with the power to grant *encomiendas,* and forbidding anyone, especially Francisco de Garay, from intruding upon the lands Cortés had conquered.

These decrees were the first evidence of royal approval that Cortés had ever seen. And he was enormously—to the bottom of his weary soul—relieved. His whole broken, battered body nearly collapsed in contentment. Cortés meant it most sincerely when he later wrote the king that "I kiss the Royal feet of Your Caesarean Majesty *a hundred thousand times.*" So profoundly relieved was Cortés that he had his bedding repacked the next morning (he who used to sleep on the ground) and, leaving Alvarado to deal with Garay, he returned to the capital, where he had the royal decrees read by a crier in the public square.

. . .

What had transpired in Spain over the previous four years was a curious sequence of failures and successes. After the first load of treasure Cortés had sent the king had been impounded by Bishop Fonseca in Seville (even the personal effects of the passengers were impounded), Puertocarrero and Montejo, with nothing but the coins in their purses and the clothes on their backs, had made their way to Medellín, where they replenished themselves and enlisted the help of Cortés's father, Martín Cortés de Monroy. Then the three had set out for Barcelona in search of the king. But when they reached Barcelona—in January 1520—they found that the king had gone to Burgos. In Barcelona, however, they located a Cortés cousin who was involved in the affairs of the Court, and soon they were joined in their cause by a few powerful noblemen, led by the Duke of Bejár; these Spanish noblemen were attracted by the stories of gold and valor. Montejo, Puertocarrero and Martín Cortés pursued the king to Burgos, but he had left Burgos, and they found him at Tordesillas, a small town near Valladolid, where he was visiting his demented mother, who was kept in a convent there. It was in Tordesillas that Carlos Quinto finally granted Montejo and Puertocarrero an audience and heard their petition, which certainly sounded peculiar to him: that someone named Hernán Cortés should be confirmed as head of a newly founded town somewhere in the New World. This had to be translated into French for the king/emperor and, though the link of language between Spanish and French was better than the link from Spanish to Mayan to Nahuatl, still it was a less-than-perfect connection. To make matters more difficult, both Bishop Fonseca and Velázquez's agents in Spain furiously disputed this petition, recommending instead that Cortés be condemned as a traitor and rebel.

Carlos, though young, was by nature strong-willed but cautious and conservative, and he listened patiently to both sides. What interested him was the impounded treasure in the warehouses of the Council of the Indies in Seville. Fonseca's customs officials had not been able to keep themselves from showing off some of the precious oddities to friends in Seville, and the excitement of these friends had echoed at Court. So Carlos ordered that the treasure be brought to him so that he might see it.

When the treasure arrived, Montejo and Puertocarrero, quickly checking against their inventory, noted that many pieces were missing. But there was enough treasure—in fact, a dazzling lot of it—so that Carlos and his Flemish counselors and all the Spanish noblemen at Court were intrigued, by both the gold and the curiosities. In the nearly thirty years since Columbus had discovered the New World, some gold and silver had been brought to Spain, but there was no appreciation as yet of the volume of the outpouring that would come from Mexico, an outpouring that could and would finance the Habsburg dream of resurrecting the Roman empire.

Before Carlos departed from the port of La Coruña—in May 1520— he ordered the officials of the Council of the Indies to surrender or account for every item in the inventory of the treasure and to release to Puertocarrero and Montejo all personal effects, including bags of gold the *conquistadores,* Cortés among them, were sending home to their families. In addition, Carlos refused Fonseca's plea that Cortés should be declared a rebel. But Carlos would not go further. (Bernal Díaz in Mexico eventually heard the story that Puertocarrero was jailed by Bishop Fonseca and died in prison, but this story is doubtful because Fonseca would not have acted so drastically against Puertocarrero alone while not bothering Montejo, who subsequently returned to the New World and conquered much of the Yucatán.)

So Montejo and probably Puertocarrero were left more comfortably off than they had been, though they were not reassured. The regent ruling Spain during the king's absence was Adrian of Utrecht, a remarkably even-tempered cleric who later became Pope. To the regent the partisans of Cortés kept passing whatever bits of news they could gather to supplement Cortés's letters addressed to the king. And the regent came to realize what Cortés was actually doing in Mexico, in contrast to Fonseca's and Velázquez's legalistic caterwauling. Consequently, Adrian ordered that Fonseca should not be permitted to participate in the lawsuit that Velázquez had brought against Cortés.

In July 1522, when Carlos returned to Spain, he generally subscribed to his regent's feeling, yet with habitual carefulness he appointed a board of eminent Spanish nobles to adjudicate all the questions regarding Cortés. In October 1522 the judgment of this board was rendered in favor of Cortés, and it was then that Cortés was named governor, captain-general, chief justice and *distributor* of New Spain. Velázquez's claim was shrunken to a mere civil suit to recover whatever sum the governor of Cuba may have invested in the original fleet that left Cuba with Cortés in command—and Velázquez's claims that the spoils from the conquest belonged to him, along with Fonseca's accusations against Cortés of treason and rebellion, were thrown out.

Still, it took until the following July for word of this thorough exculpation to reach Cortés on the highland of Mexico.

· · ·

What happened then to Garay was pathetic. Garay, who was not a natural leader, came to the Pánuco coast full of fire, landed and sent out his men to inform the Indians that he, not Cortés, was the Spanish governor they should obey and that he was going to chastise Cortés for his wrongdoing. Garay's men in their turn began to ravage the countryside—until Garay's cavalry came into contact with Alvarado. At an arranged meeting Alvarado informed Garay's captain that Cortés had received the king's endorsement and was royal governor; Garay's captain refused to believe it; but Alvarado demanded that Garay's men surrender their arms and horses—and sensibly Garay's captain and men complied. Garay's men were undoubtedly intimidated by Alvarado and his battle-scarred troopers, but the Garay faction also noticed all the gold that Alvarado and his men genially showed off.

Garay himself was marching overland through a swamp, beset by mosquitoes and bats, and he and the men with him were starving because all the Indian villages they came upon had been emptied and were deserted. Grijalva, with most of Garay's fleet, was anchored in the mouth of the Pánuco River about fifteen miles from the upriver town that Cortés had founded and where Cortés maintained a garrison. The commander of this garrison came to the fleet and showed Grijalva a copy of Cortés's decree from the king; as authorization for Garay's venture, Grijalva could show only the old license from Bishop Fonseca. So, although Grijalva remained defiant, two of his shipmasters conceded and prepared to sail their ships upriver to the town, but Grijalva threatened to fire on them. After a tense standoff, Garay's crews sided with Cortés's men; all the ships were sailed upriver to the town; then Cortés's commander arrested Grijalva and others of Velázquez's faction who were ship's officers.

Garay arranged to meet Cortés's captain who had the copy of the royal decree that appointed Cortés governor. They met at a village in the interior of the province, and Garay arrived so sick that he had to be carried in a litter; to an onlooker he appeared to be a prisoner. Garay's own men, despite their oaths, had turned on him. Garay knew that Cortés, in the light of the royal decree, had won. So Garay proposed that, if Cortés's people would help him gather his men together, he would sail away with his army and settle somewhere else. The only trouble with this proposition was that Garay's men would no longer follow him, nor would they obey anyone's orders. The cavalrymen had sold their horses and the foot-soldiers their arms in exchange for gold, at the preposterous prices that were offered in

Mexico. When Cortés's commander in the town had criers read out a summons calling upon all Garay men to reassemble for departure, the men fled to Indian villages in the interior and hid. Six of Garay's vessels had been lost in a storm, the rest were worm-eaten. Garay's men contended that they had fulfilled their contracts and complied with their oaths by coming to Pánuco; they were not obliged to go elsewhere.

Garay asked, begged, to be taken to Cortés. He had lost everything—his fortune, his army, his fleet. Cortés, when notified, agreed to have Garay brought to him. At the same time, under powers granted him by the royal decrees, he ordered Grijalva and the other Velázquez partisans expelled from Mexico.

While Garay was being escorted to the highland, he concocted a truly Spanish plan to solve his troubles: He offered to marry his eldest son, with full inheritance, to an illegitimate daughter Cortés was known to have in Cuba, a girl called Doña Catalina Cortés or Pizarro. The girl's mother, Leonor Pizarro, was a Spanish woman living in Cuba, and, though she must have been only a girl herself when she had borne Cortés's baby, the parentage was not in question. Cortés had acknowledged this daughter—and he liked Garay's proposal.

So the two potential relatives—Cortés and Garay—had a joyous reconciliation in Cortés's new palace in the capital of Mexico. But Garay died. Bernal Díaz warranted that it was a typical case of pneumonia *(dolor de costado)*, a kind of pleurisy peculiar to the country that came on suddenly and from which many had died in precisely the same way in Texcoco and Coyoacán. Cortés had held a banquet in Garay's honor on Christmas Eve 1523, after which Garay vomited all night, and on Christmas Day Cortés and Garay attended church together, but following the service Garay was stricken. Two doctors attended him, and he was bled; he made his will, naming Cortés as executor; and within four days he succumbed.

In the aftermath of these events which culminated in Garay's death, the Indians in the province of Pánuco revolted against all Spaniards. Many hundreds of Garay men hiding in the villages were killed by the Indians and eaten, and the town Cortés had founded was besieged and nearly overrun. Cortés had to send Sandoval with a strong force to put down the rebellion, which Sandoval did. He rounded up three hundred fifty Indian village chiefs and nobles and corraled tens of thousands of common Indians; then he let the common Indians go but had them watch while he burned the chiefs and nobles.

In this way order was again imposed upon Pánuco.

EXPIATION

The king's belated designation of Cortés as governor, captain-general and *distributor* of New Spain and Cortés's grateful acceptance of these offices signaled a crucial shifting of gears within the machinery of the conquest. As long as Cortés, with his hoked-up authority from his newly founded town of Villa Rica, was leading his men into the depths of a hitherto unknown empire, the loyalty of the Spaniards in Mexico to the Crown of Spain could be doubted. But once the king, after the *conquistadores* had rendered homage to him, chose to ignore the questionable nature of the authority under which they had operated and he legitimized their efforts, from that point on the potentially renegade *conquistadores* became—like many others in Spain and throughout the Spanish empire—duty-bound servants of Crown and Church.

So Cortés, now with royal authority, continued to respond to his impulse as explorer as well as conqueror and concentrated upon the southern sea. Spain's great rival, Portugal, dominated the Orient, which the Portuguese reached from Europe by sailing southward to round Africa, then eastward across the Indian Ocean. Cortés, who did not appreciate the breadth of the Pacific, hoped to sail westward from Mexico to the Orient, where Spain would contest the dominion of Portugal. (When the treasure Cortés had sent to the king of Spain was seized by French privateers and brought to the king of France, the French king's comment was that he wanted to be shown where in the will of Adam it said that the rest of the world was to be divided between Portugal and Spain.)

Also, Cortés wanted to acquire Guatemala and Honduras to the south. What Cortés did not know was that there was little gold or silver there; arduous expeditions to these regions would drain the vigor of the *conquistadores;* and the new arrivals weren't up to the rigors of such ventures. A few days before Garay died, Cortés dispatched Alvarado with his strong force to Guatemala; thus Cortés deprived himself of the presence of a resolute friend who personally was one of Cortés's main supports. After Alvarado had gone, Cortés sent to Honduras a substantial force under Olid. Alvarado went overland to Guatemala, but Cortés bought and paid for a fleet to take Olid and his men to Honduras. It was costly to mount these expeditions; horseshoes in Mexico cost more than their weight in silver; and, even with the flood of immigration, Cortés sent out so many exploring parties that he was frequently short of men, which caused some worry in the capital. Twice Cortés had to send troops to quell the Zapotecs and Mixtecs.

As the duly appointed agent of the king, in effect the viceroy of Mexico, Cortés had to function officially in an administrative capacity, which was a relief from fighting but which produced problems that became increasingly annoying. Prior to Cortés's appointment as *distributor,* the Spaniards had not quibbled much when Cortés assigned *encomiendas* because everyone knew the assignments were tentative. Now that Cortés was empowered to make these grants, nearly every *encomendero* objected to the *encomienda* he had been given; disputes arose over boundary lines (always vague), the quality of mines and farms that were included, the number of Indians in the villages, and so on and on. These disputes festered among the Spaniards, who were spread all over Mexico and who as settlers were trying to keep control. At one point Cortés decided that it was no longer necessary to maintain the town of Segura de la Frontera at its location on the road from Tlascala to the capital and he transferred the town to a harbor on the southern sea, only to have the Spaniards (former Narváez men) who were the designated officials of the transplanted town abandon the site on the southern sea and invade the province of Oaxaca, where they set up *encomiendas* of their own choosing. Cortés had to send a captain with a troop to put down this insubordination; the two ringleaders were captured and sentenced by the captain to death by hanging; but Cortés canceled the death sentences and instead exiled the two, one of whom later sued Cortés for 2,000 ducats.

During most of 1524 it was one of Cortés's pleasures to go on with the rebuilding of the capital. He supervised the grand patterning of the central square, the *zócalo,* with avenues running out from it and with junctions where monuments would be; he laid the foundation for the Hospital de Jesús; he assigned separate sections of the city for the Indians. The palace Cortés built for himself was surrounded by an extensive compound that had high defensible walls, and the stone walls of the palace itself were thick enough to withstand a cannon-blast. In the interior of the palace Spanish arches prevailed and created a churchlike vaultiness, unlike low Aztec rooms with their air of repose. Cortés's palaces resembled Spanish castles, except that they were not high-stacked like castles but spread out around patios filled with flowering trees and shrubs; through the grounds Aztec gardeners routed channels of water so everywhere a cascade could be heard. In many sensual, appreciative ways the Spaniards and the Indians enjoyed mutual responses. Cortés, basking in the favor of the king, set up for himself an elaborate household appropriate for his new position, with bailiffs, butlers, guards, lackeys, swarms of servants and maids, and he had Indian silversmiths make for his own table the kind of service he had sent to the king. (Narváez in his lawsuit against Cortés included the accusation that Cortés had too many trees cut down for use in the construction of his palace.)

Some Spaniards detected resentful rumblings among the Indians at work in the capital. But Cortés retained as captives the three Indian monarchs who had been most respected and revered by their people: Guatémoc; and the lord of Texcoco (the one who had abandoned his city and fled to Tenochtitlán and who had been replaced by Cortés's godson); and the lord of Tacuba (who likewise had abandoned his city for the capital). The Spaniards suspected that these three Indian lords were secretly sending messages to the populace urging rebellion. So Cortés began to take the three captives with him through the streets, treating them respectfully but keeping them under heavy guard, and in this way exhibiting to all the Indians their four authority-figures—himself and the three Indian lords— while demonstrating his own primacy. The observant Indians proceeded to work on the reconstruction.

Cortés himself unintentionally exacerbated the *encomienda* problem by issuing a series of regulations which were intended to slow down exploitation and encourage long-term development but which were bitterly resented by many Spaniards. He required that each *encomendero* stay on his land for at least eight years. If an *encomendero* had a wife, he must bring her to Mexico within eighteen months; if he had no wife, he was encouraged to marry. (Although this ordinance regarding marriage was intended to reduce the Spaniards' inclination to indulge themselves with so many Indian women, coming from Cortés, whose sexual enthusiasm was well known and whose reunion with his own wife had been short-lived, the regulation struck many Spaniards as ludicrous.) Cortés even offered to pay for the bringing from Spain as prospective brides young women who were called "Old Christian," by which was meant women among whose grandparents there were no Moors or Jews. This revealed Cortés's provinciality, because some of the most prominent prelates in Spain came from families of converted Jews, and among Cortés's own men there was at least one Jew, a blacksmith in his sixties named Hernando Alonso who had helped build the brigantines, but he was regarded as a good fellow and was Diego de Ordaz's brother-in-law and no special attention was paid to him. Also, Cortés required that every *encomendero* must consent to be tithed to support both proselytizing clergy and the construction of churches and monasteries; in order to accomplish tithing in a businesslike fashion (in what Spaniards thought would be a businesslike fashion), the right to collect tithes was to be auctioned off to the highest bidder, who would then make the collection, reimburse himself for expenses and take his profit, before turning over the remaining proceeds to the Church.

In his fourth letter to the king, Cortés asked for the king's approval of these regulations. As always, he begged the king to send farmers with seeds and draft animals, and urged the king to permit free shipment of goods to New Spain, to forbid officials of the Council of the Indies to impose limitations, and to order Spanish merchants in the islands to permit brood mares to be shipped to Mexico since brood mares were being withheld in order to sustain the outrageous prices of horses in Mexico. The economic picture of post-conquest Mexico—not strangely in the history of such mass developments—was one of unbridled inflation and furious greed.

In two respects, Cortés and the king may be likened, though Cortés was fifteen years older than Carlos, knew little about the king, and had never lived in Spain while Carlos was king. Both of them responded with élan to the lure of the southern sea—as if here was the next God-given challenge, their next, deserved reward. Also, the king and Cortés shared a profound, though markedly different, feeling about God.

Cortés was all-Spanish. He never doubted that it was his faith, not his spiritedness or the strength of his arm, but his faith that had carried him to victory, just as faith had carried Spain to epic triumph. Cortés, though, knew the earthiness of Spanish life; he was part of the earthiness of Spanish life, the sensual enjoyment and release of it, the dissoluteness of it, even the corruption of it. He knew the condition of the Spanish clergy in the early sixteenth century; he knew that priests, in contravention of their vows, kept women, sired children, and would provide for their children through entailed estates. He knew that many of the clergy, perhaps even most, were as venal as the laymen around them. Yet—in spite of all this that he knew, in spite of the requirements of battle, in spite of his own venality and promiscuity—he was pure in his faith and forever steadfast.

Cortés wrote the king begging for chaste clerics to be sent to New Spain to convert the Indians and lead the Spaniards in their worship. He wanted priests who were true to their vows and their principles and warned against sending bishops who might concern themselves with aggrandizement and glorification. Cortés even warned the king that, however awful were the practices of the Indians, still the Indians of New Spain in their own clergy had orders of priests pledged to chastity and honesty, and such purity was expected of these Indian priests that, if they were found transgressing, they were put to death. Accordingly, Catholic priests sent to convert the Indians must be no less true to the principles they espoused, or conversion of the Indians would fail. Neither Cortés nor the king doubted that Christianization of the Indians validated and justified the conquest.

But Carlos varied from Cortés in his sensibility to his religion. Carlos, having been imbued with the idea that his personal destiny was to create the greatest Christian empire the world had ever seen, felt that his cause was so transcendent that all the bribing and conniving needed for its achievement and the ruthlessness occasionally called for were incidental. In his eyes the ineradicable human nature of the clergy, the nobility and himself was not part of a natural and enveloping atmosphere that he could accept. Carlos was not unworldly; he had a few extra-marital affairs and sired a bastard son whose existence he kept secret for many years; yet the degree of his promiscuity, of his deviation from his own ideal, was by the standards of his time and in his own estimation limited and excusable as evidence of his own, not excessive humanness. Carlos was reclusive by nature, internalized, under the constant strain of his responsibility, and he was undoubtedly fearful that he had inherited his mother's tendency toward insanity. The Flemish clerics who surrounded Carlos all his life were demanding and dedicated moralists determined to improve Church practices in all the nations and lands they would come upon. It was, in part, the antiseptic attitude of these Flemish clerics that had caused considerable resentment when the Flemings accompanied Carlos to Spain.

The purity of Carlos's piety was most dramatically proved at the end of his life. Having in the course of half a century spent his life's strength endeavoring to reestablish Catholic Rome, Carlos abdicated while still in good health, leaving the throne to his pious son, and retired to a small monastery in the Gredos mountains of Spain. It is a tiny, inconspicuous place, neither grand nor glorified nor elegant. There he spent his last few years in meditation and, when he sensed that he was weakening, he chose his deathbed with care. Beside his cot he had a hole cut in the wall, providing a window through which he could observe the bare feet of the monks as they went to the altar and prayed for him. And thus he died, watching the procession of worship which he viewed as the connection of humanity and divinity.

In our cynical modern age we are inclined to doubt everything and to find piety suspect. But it is difficult to question, almost impossible not to accept, the piousness of a man who thoughtfully chose such a view from his deathbed. Personally, I accept that both Hernán Cortés and Carlos Quinto were true believers to the bottoms of their souls.

In the fall of 1523 the first two clerics sent from Spain by the king reached Mexico. They were Flemings and members of the Franciscan order; their names were Johann van den Auwera and Johann Dekkers. That Dekkers had been chosen was a particular compliment to the *conquistadores*, though they probably did not appreciate it, since Father Dekkers had been the king's confessor. Unable to pronounce the Flemish names, the Spaniards of Mexico took the phonetically easy way out and called them Juan de Ayora and Juan de Tecto. Dutifully Cortés welcomed them into his household. In the following spring a larger delegation arrived, consisting of ten Spanish Franciscans, including Motolinía, and two lay brothers; they were called "the Twelve Apostles." Cortés, after studying the calculated penury of these Franciscans, decided that he liked what he saw, so he set the example all Spaniards in Mexico were to follow: Approaching the monks with cap in hand, he knelt and kissed the hems of their ragged cassocks. The watching Indians were amazed by such obeisance. Then the Indians emulated the Spaniards. This was typical of Cortés's style. Soon the Franciscans were working among the Indians effectively and on a grand scale.

Along with the incoming tides of men and women who wanted to join in the exploitation of the conquest and devout clerics who wanted spiritually to substantiate the conquest, inevitably there arrived enemies of Cortés, four in particular—a royal treasurer, a royal accountant, a royal *veedor*, and a royal *factor*. These men appeared to be routine appointees of Spanish officialdom sent in the normal process of integrating the empire. The four, however, were sub rosa agents of the Council of the Indies, which was still dominated by Bishop Fonseca, and one of these agents was equipped with a secret code he was to use to report his findings to the Council, where the mind-set was so anti-Cortés that everything done in Mexico was predetermined to be evidence of both illegality and disloyalty. In Mexico the four new arrivals were not provocative; they quietly moved themselves into positions from which they could observe. But their presence made Cortés more self-conscious and uncomfortable because he knew that eventually he would be held accountable in minute detail for every one of his actions.

What the royal officials observed, and what was going on in the capital in 1524, was that Cortés was heavily fortifying it. He erected a large fort that had attached defensible sheds over the water where the brigantines were moored, and in the fort and in his palace he was accumulating artillery. Tin had been discovered near Taxco in an area which previously had produced only silver, so Cortés now had tin to mix with copper to make bronze, and he was casting bronze field guns. Also, a vein of iron was found; at long last, the Mexican Indian civilization under Spanish leadership was propelled into the iron age; and Cortés was forging iron cannons. Cortés was assembling this fire power for protection against a possible Indian uprising or, even more likely, insurrection by Spaniards, but to the royal officials this looked like a threat to royal rule and they reported accordingly. (As a gift for the king, Cortés had a cannon cast of pure silver, but to the men in the Council of the Indies in Spain the dedicatory verse on the barrel reflected too well on Cortés, so the cannon was melted down, and the silver minted and pocketed.)

Cortés's administrative difficulties compounded. In Spain Fray Bartolomé de las Casas was carrying on yet another of his campaigns denouncing all Spaniards in the New World, and the king, in accommodation of Las Casas, sent to Cortés a decree revoking *encomiendas*. Cortés himself, having originally been against the *encomienda* system and having endorsed it only because he had no alternative, now had to take issue with the king by pointing out the practical impossibility of abolishing the *encomiendas*. The king yielded to him, but the courtiers who had prepared the decree never forgave Cortés for causing this reversal—and the king, meanwhile, had gone off again to Germany.

So by the fall of 1524 Cortés was pestered and irritable—when riders from Villa Rica came galloping into the capital and reported that Olid had revolted in Honduras. Olid had not been heard from in eight months. Cortés had equipped him with a powerful force; Cortés had purchased five ships and a brigantine and had enlisted four hundred men; an advance agent had been sent to Cuba to buy horses and to enlist more men. When Olid sailed from Villa Rica, he was to proceed to Cuba, load the additional horses and men, then sail past the cape of the Yucatán and down to Honduras, which was at the base of the Yucatán peninsula on the east.

What had happened, according to the riders, men who had been with Olid, was that, while in Cuba, Olid had been won over by Velázquez, and they had hatched a plot. If Honduras looked promising, Olid should declare himself independent of Cortés and allied with Velázquez, and Velázquez would continue to supply him and reinforce him from Cuba; if Honduras looked unpromising, Olid was not to declare his independence, and would remain a costly appendage of Cortés. It was a subtle scheme. And Olid, after landing in Honduras, founded a town as Cortés had instructed him to do and named as officials the men Cortés had recommended. Only after surveying the place and deciding that it *was* worthwhile did Olid retract his allegiance to Cortés, whereupon some men loyal to Cortés broke away, seized one of the ships and returned to Villa Rica to disclose the mutiny.

Beneath his fury, Cortés was hurt. Everyone, including Cortés, respected Olid. There was not a grittier, more staunch comrade to have in battle than Olid; Cortés knew there were many times when he had owed his life to Olid. But Olid was influenceable when Velázquez men, Garay men or Narváez men had his ear. As Bernal Díaz regretfully said of Olid, he was "a very brave man but of no foresight."

Responding, Cortés dispatched Francisco de las Casas (Cortés's relative, unrelated to the monk) with two ships and about a hundred men to go to Honduras and arrest Olid. In sending such a small force under an inexperienced officer, Cortés was depending that, when an arrest warrant was presented, most of Olid's men would side with Cortés and turn upon Olid. After Las Casas left, however, Cortés changed his mind and determined to go after Olid himself. All the Spaniards in the capital opposed him and urged him to send Sandoval. Even the royal officials who were spying on him begged him not to go. But Cortés stubbornly dissembled and said he would go only as far as Coatzacoalcos on the way to Honduras, though it was his firm intention to go farther. He was fed up with the nagging problems in the capital and, as he later wrote to the king, he felt that, although his arm was not completely healed, for too long he had not personally done any great service for the empire. Many years later, Cortés told Gómara that he feared Olid would set an example for Spaniards in the New World and rebellions would spread. The most likely reason for Cortés's decision to go to Honduras was that the king had promised him one-twelfth of all that he could win for Spain in the southern sea or in these southern provinces. Maybe he was stung by the intrusion once again of his old enemy, Velázquez.

To administer the capital in his absence, Cortés appointed two of the royal officials, and he took the other two with him. He also took with him the three captive Indian kings and their retinues. The two Flemish Franciscans decided to accompany the expedition to acquaint themselves with the country. According to Bernal Díaz, Aguilar had died, so only Malinche came as interpreter, but her Spanish was now fluent and she herself could make the connection between Nahuatl, Mayan and Spanish. Cortés brought Sandoval as second-in-command.

And so Cortés went—in his new mode, escorted by part of his household including two falconers, five musicians, a stage dancer, a juggler, and a puppet player (he intended to be as amused as Montezuma). He had a less than formidable contingent of cavalry and infantry, and a few thousand Indian auxiliaries. And trundling after him was a large herd of pigs. Cortés did not try to purchase another fleet of ships to take him to Honduras because he lacked the funds and had already borrowed heavily from the royal fifth. But he hit the trail in good spirits, passing sung verses back and forth with the two royal officials as they rode along. The two officials, who were younger than Cortés, called him "uncle." Cortés was about thirty-nine years old.

At Spanish settlements along the way Cortés and his people were feted; in the villages triumphal arches were erected under which they passed; and there were fireworks celebrating the victories of the Spaniards over the Moors. (All Indians adored fireworks and quickly became adept at making them of powder-filled bamboo; the Indians didn't care what the fireworks were supposed to commemorate.) About fifty Spaniards, recently arrived from Spain and on their way to the capital to make their fortunes, unexpectedly encountered Cortés and his contingent and happily joined up.

In this self-congratulatory, festive spirit, while staying at a town near Orizaba, not far from the capital, Cortés instigated the marriage of Malinche and Juan Jaramillo. Gómara reported that for this marriage Jaramillo was drunk, but this was what Cortés years later told Gómara. Bernal Díaz, who attended the wedding, reported nothing of the kind. And it is incredible that, in the presence of the two severe Flemish Franciscans, a drunken parody of the marriage rite could have been performed. It is far more likely that Cortés was shamefaced when he told his secretary of the wedding, and made light of it by saying that Jaramillo was drunk. Jaramillo had to be sober, and Malinche accepted him for her husband, as she accepted everything she was allotted by Cortés. For his part, Cortés, though Malinche had borne him a son, was in his own mind already planning ahead and contemplating his entry into the highest echelon of Spanish nobility. In Mexico, Spaniards who had some claim to noble blood were marrying Indian princesses and boasting of their wives' lineage, so well entrenched in the Spanish mind was the concept of social hierarchy, but it was known that Malinche had been given to the Spaniards as a slave girl and had belonged to Puertocarrero before Cortés. Surely Cortés envisioned for himself an eventual marriage that would distinguish him. So he married off Malinche to Jaramillo, who had been a daring brigantine captain during the siege of Tenochtitlán. Jaramillo was younger than Cortés and probably liked Malinche, who was sweet-natured as well as quick-minded. Nor is there any reason to think that Malinche did not like Jaramillo; she may well have appreciated his mildness in contrast to Cortés. The overriding consideration for her, however, was that the marriage was Cortés's wish, to which she consented, and she continued to be dauntless in Cortés's service as his interpreter.

. . .

Nothing went right. And the whole expedition was needless. Francisco de las Casas, searching along the east coast of the Yucatán, discovered Olid in a town on the Gulf of Honduras. Sailing toward the mouth of a river where Olid's ships were anchored, Las Casas ran up a signal flag indicating peaceable intent, but Olid, realizing these ships were sent by Cortés, fired on Las Casas, who fired back. Las Casas wanted to go ashore to read aloud his arrest warrant and let it take effect on Olid's men, but Olid blocked his landing (Olid's own ships were anchored in the river). During a tense standoff a sudden storm blew up, the wind catching Las Casas's ships in the gulf and driving them aground. For several days Las Casas and his surviving men hid out, soaked and starving, and finally all were captured by Olid, who had some other Spanish prisoners. A land party had come northward from the Spanish settlement in Panama looking for the strait they all were seeking, and Olid, having disarmed the advance guard of this party, went on to capture the rest, including the leader, Gil González, at a town in the interior called Naco. So Olid held as prisoners at Naco both Las Casas and González, and self-confidently allowed them, since he was armed and they were not, to dine with him at his table. One evening, after the cloths had been removed and while Olid's guards and servants were away eating their own dinners, Las Casas and González attacked Olid with fruit knives. Slashed about the face, throat and hands, Olid escaped into the woods, but when his guards and servants came running, Las Casas called upon them to stand loyal to the king and Cortés—and he was obeyed. Olid was caught, and Las Casas and González had his head chopped off in the muddy open space that served as the central square of the jungle town.

(Spaniards were comparatively unimaginative in their methods of execution: Either they hanged, or they burned at the stake, or they beheaded. But—a century of humanitarian progress after the Spanish conquest—the English, when they executed Sir Walter Raleigh because he was suspected of being a renegade, depended for the style of the execution upon speed. Raleigh was first hanged but not with a hangman's knot, just throttled to take whatever fight there might be out of him, then was cut down while alive and conscious, quickly split open from throat to crotch, his heart and bowels pulled out as his genitals were being cut off, and his penis and scrotum were thrown into a fire while his eyes were still open and seeing. Only then was his head hacked off and his body quartered. To the Aztecs, who always cloaked human sacrifice and cannibalism with religious rites, all the European methods of execution may with some justification have seemed inexcusably barbaric.)

But when Olid was executed, Cortés was on the other side of the Yucatán peninsula along the southern shore of the Gulf of Mexico in the province of Coatzacoalcos, and Cortés did not know that Olid's mutiny would be put down. What Cortés did know, because he had received reports while on the road, was that the administration he had left in place in the capital was not functioning smoothly. As soon as he was out of sight, the two royal officials began fighting with each other. Spaniards and Indians alike were distressed. So Cortés sent back the two officials who were with him and authorized them to assume control if necessary. Cortés also wrote to his cousin, Rodrigo de Paz, whom he had left in charge of his household and personal affairs, asking for money, at least five or six thousand *pesos de oro*, because Cortés wanted to be able to pay cash for supplies from Villa Rica. Cortés even wrote to ask for another loan from the king's fifth.

After the departure of the royal officials, Cortés rather belatedly took count of the force that he had: about two hundred fifty Spaniards in total, ninety-three cavalrymen, with about one hundred fifty horses to serve as mounts and spares, and about three thousand well-armed highland Indians. A supply ship from Villa Rica was in harbor, and Cortés put much of his artillery and equipment aboard and instructed the captain of the ship to sail along the coast and meet him at the next harbor, which was in Tabasco. The chiefs of Tabasco, who had come to Cortés in Coatzacoalcos, prepared for him a map, drawn on cloth, of the overland route to Honduras. None of these chiefs had ever been to Honduras but their traders had been there, and the map they produced was based on the traders' reports. In answer to Cortés's questions, these chiefs confirmed that they had heard about Spaniards (presumably Olid and his men) being on the far side of the Yucatán peninsula, and what they had heard was that these Spaniards had robbed Indian traders of their goods and had disrupted a pattern of trade that had existed for many years, so now there was no trade with Honduras.

Cortés—with this much information—set out with his Spaniards and the highland Indians on the most disastrous trek of his life. The part of the province of Tabasco through which they went was delta-like and they had to cross more than fifty rivers. Few of these rivers were bridged, so trees had to be cut down and bridges or rafts constructed, and the local Indians disappeared into the forest when work was to be done. The horses swam the rivers, which were swollen from frequent downpours; Spaniards in canoes would pull the swimming horses by the bridle-straps. When a raft carrying precious iron tools overturned, the tools could not be retrieved and the men had to scramble quickly ashore because alligators on the banks were slipping into the water. The expedition could not connect with the supply ship on the coast because a huge marsh intervened; only a few supplies were brought from the ship by canoe.

While Cortés went doggedly eastward in accord with his map, he would send ahead a squad of Spaniards to alert the local Indians and the men would take with them and show off the Aztec lords. Several times this was effective and the local Indians, duly impressed, delivered food and sometimes canoes. But soon the local Indians, deep within the Yucatán, didn't recognize either the Spaniards or the Aztecs and fled, leaving their villages cleared of all provisions.

Cortés and his people slogged through a tropical rain forest, in perpetual mist and gloom. As they went farther inland, away from the sea, the sickening effect of the jungle worsened. (Even today it is treacherous to travel across the base of the Yucatán in a jeep with four-wheel drive. Rain continually washes out the bridges and the dirt roads. Driving over the gravel of the stream beds after the water has run off, which is often the most efficacious way to go, is tooth-rattling and backbreaking.) Cortés found no roads in the trackless flatland, and the few Indians he encountered, those the Spaniards could catch before they ran away, told him that everyone who inhabited this region traveled by canoe. So the local Indians didn't know how men with horses and on foot, carrying equipment and supplies, could get from one place to another, no matter what was shown on Cortés's map. In the swamps the horses sank up to their girths and in the rivers often fell into holes and went up to their ears, and the horses became so exhausted that they could not stand. How the pigs endured, Gómara wrote, was "a miracle," which was not a statement the lay priest made easily. (The mountain pigs of the Yucatán today are almost surely descended, at least in part, from Cortés's pigs. And these modern-day Yucatán pigs—bristly muscular runts, very energetic, with big heads and sharp tusks—are among the hardiest pigs in the world.)

The Spaniards became so lost they didn't know the direction to the coast and the sea. Cortés produced a ship's compass from his baggage so that on overcast days they could keep to the eastward course the map prescribed. The Spaniards and the highland Indians weakened from lack of food; they had only dried maize and an occasional pig to eat; they began to suffer even from thirst because the marsh water was undrinkable and they couldn't collect enough rainwater before it disappeared into the porous limestone. And this slow plodding went on for month after month after month— while the Aztec lords silently watched the fiasco. Guatémoc and the lord of Texcoco and the lord of Tacuba stoically observed the Spaniards (their conquerors) trying to take their horses through water where the horses could not go, trying to cross rivers without boats, exhausting themselves building bridges, starving and floundering, nearly helpless.

In a village where the Spaniards caught a few Indians and found some cassava, green maize and peppers, Cortés came upon one of his highland Indians eating the corpse of a local Indian he had killed. So Cortés had Father Dekkers preach a sermon to all the assembled Indians—a sermon that Malinche meticulously translated into Nahuatl and Mayan—to the effect that it was a sin to eat one's fellow-man, a theme on which the fastidious Flemish Franciscan had never in his life sermonized before. Then Cortés had the guilty highland Indian burned at the stake to prove to the local Indians that Christians forbade cannibalism. But this lesson, which seemed clear to Cortés and his men, confounded the jungle Indians, who comprehended only that these white men would roast a fellow-man but not eat him.

It was the end of February 1525 when Cortés and his party came to a town of friendly Indians who gave them food and even gifts of small pieces of gold. So the Spaniards and highland Indians rested for a while. It was already Lent—and the Franciscan friars led the Spaniards in holy services.

But at night a highland Indian—one who had been baptized and named Cristóbal—came to Cortés and reported that Guatémoc and the lords of Tacuba and Texcoco were plotting to kill Cortés; they were urging the highland Indians to fall upon all Spaniards in the expedition, while they as chiefs would rouse the local Indians to kill any other Spaniards, such as Olid and his men, who might be in this region; then the Aztec lords would return to Tenochtitlán and call upon the people there to wipe out the Spaniards living in the capital. The Aztec plot even extended to harbors on the eastern shore, where Indian garrisons would be stationed to kill the Spaniards from any ships that might arrive. When this information was reported to Cortés, he and his men had only a pittance of energy with which to maintain their control of the highland Indians.

So Cortés behaved as he had before when mortally threatened: He took decisive action to reinstill fear. He interrogated the three Aztec chieftains, confirmed that they were plotting, and had them hanged. (There are variations of this story, but the essentials are all the same. Though Bernal Díaz liked Guatémoc, as he had liked Montezuma, and mourned Guatémoc's passing as that of a monarch who had known greatness, still Bernal Díaz could not deny the fact of the plotting, which was admitted by the Aztec lords, though they denied they had approved of the plot. From the

Aztec point of view, this was obviously an opportune moment to strike, when the Spaniards were so little able to resist. Had the Aztec chieftains— or other highland Indians who were plotting—waited just a little longer, or had their secret been kept a little longer, they might have had better luck.)

As it was, the executions served as an exemplary show of strength and worked for Cortés. The situation had been very dangerous: There were only about two hundred Spanish survivors facing about twenty-five hundred armed highland Indians, with an uncounted number of armed local Indians watching. Cortés's personal aura was the decisive factor that prevented an outbreak by the highlanders. After the executions, whatever rebelliousness there had been among them quieted. And Cortés's firmness impressed the local Indians, who continued to assist him.

Yet Cortés reacted to the killing of the Aztec lords as if again he had demolished Tenochtitlán. He could not sleep at night; sleeplessness periodically beset him; and he would wander about the Spanish camp. The local Indian priests had extracted his promise not to destroy their idols. One night he went to the temple where the idols were kept, and on his way in the darkness he fell twelve feet from an embankment and hurt himself. He never revealed his intention, which most likely was to try to topple the idols with his own hands, in spite of his promise, in spite of the risk; the senselessness of his situation and the marked absence of divine approval so depressed him.

The Spaniards struggled on through the mire, then over jagged, fractured mountains (the low coastal mountains) until Easter—this agony had lasted half a year—when they captured an Indian trader who told them that Spaniards were in the town of Nito, another ten days of difficult traveling from wherever they were. This trader was one of those robbed by the Spaniards. So at last it was learned with some sureness that Spaniards were nearby. But when Cortés came upon these Spaniards, they weren't Olid's people but Gil González's people, about sixty men and twenty women, starving, living in a deserted Indian town, most of them sick with yellow fever and dysentery, without horses and with few arms. Stumbling out to greet Cortés as their savior, the feeble Spaniards informed Cortés of Olid's execution and of the return of Las Casas and González to Mexico. And they poured out to Cortés all their troubles—when Cortés himself was in desperate need of help.

They told Cortés that González and Las Casas, with Olid's men merged into their own forces, had solicited volunteers to settle in Honduras where the settlers could expect to be granted extensive *encomiendas*. The two captains had equipped the settlers as best they could and had set out overland for Guatemala en route to Mexico, where they were to arrange for more people and supplies to be sent to Honduras. As the result of many mishaps, the settlers—and there were several groups of them—had lost their equipment, even most of their arms; their horses had died; no reinforcements had yet arrived; they were afraid to go far from their villages; and they were destitute.

On the banks of the river at Nito were a damaged caravel, a wrecked brigantine, and the remnants of a few other ships that had been left for the settlers' use. Cortés set his men to repairing and rebuilding the ships. The pressure of hunger was worse than ever because there were more mouths to feed, so Cortés sent squads in all directions to search for villages where there might be food or planted fields that could be harvested. Cortés himself contracted what was probably yellow fever from the swarming mosquitoes. And the rain fell with a tropical heaviness Cortés and his men had never known before. The rainy season in Central America, in the neighborhood of the Río Dulce, was different from the rainy season in the Mexican highland, even different from that of the Mexican shore. Here along the river the soggy land lay in low hummocks and, as soon as the rain started, the tepid rivers, already full, would overflow their banks and turn into raging gushers of water, rushing into bays and ponds that became churning lagoons. (The animals in the jungle are diseased; the black spider monkeys in the towering trees have yellow fever; cats in the scrub woods are rabid. Yet when the rain stops, it is all enchanting, a tropical paradise, especially at sunset when the languid river becomes a stream of light curving lasciviously through the darkening, perfumy land.) Cortés, partially incapacitated and with a high fever, took to going about without his helmet and, while on a raft bringing back green corn, he was hit in the head by stones Indians threw from the riverbank (which in all likelihood accounts for another crack in Cortés's extant skull).

A ray of divine approval shone through when a ship from Cuba made its way into the Gulf of Honduras and happened upon the desperate Spaniards at Nito. The ship's captain, having heard that Cortés was en route to Honduras, was looking to sell his goods for the best prices, and Cortés paid him four thousand *pesos de oro* for the ship and the whole shipload, which included thirteen horses, thirty soldiers who wanted to join up, sailors who came along with the ship, seventy pigs, twelve casks of salted meat, thirty bundles of tortillas. Through all his travail Cortés apparently had kept his coffers, which is not hard to believe because the Spaniards also still had in their possession some heavy cannons, as well as a few pigs.

There were other groups of settlers at Naco in the interior and at a place to the north on Ascension Bay, all in sorry shape, and from them Cortés learned that several attempts had been made to establish bases in Central America; not only had Gil González been sent northward by the governor of Panama, who wanted to expand his domain, but a merciless lawyer in a well-armed, well-stocked ship had come from Hispaniola and had refused to help the settlers. To Cortés these feelers from Panama and Hispaniola were invasions of his own holding, and he wanted to extend his sway to include all the territory south of Mexico to the inter-ocean passage he dreamed of finding. He was a man of endless dreaming.

When four ships were readied, Cortés sent them separately to Mexico, Cuba, Jamaica and Hispaniola to announce his whereabouts and to bring back supplies, but all four ships missed their destinations and were blown about the islands. The worst tragedy was that the ship bound for Mexico, on which the two Flemish Franciscans chose to travel, was wrecked on an island off the western tip of Cuba—and the ascetic Flemings drowned, dying as martyrs in their crusade to Christianize the Indians. The ship bound for Cuba missed its port, and the two ships bound for Jamaica and Hispaniola had to take refuge on the south coast of Cuba. In Cuba it was learned that there was chaos in Mexico, especially in the capital; the two royal officials Cortés had sent back had displaced the other two but were even more tyrannical; they had set themselves up with great pomp, had spread the word that Cortés was dead, and they had ransacked Cortés's palace in search of treasure and had tortured and hanged Cortés's cousin Rodrigo de Paz when he had refused to show them the hiding place. A letter with this information was prepared and sent on a fast sailing ship to Cortés in Honduras.

Upon receipt of the news, Cortés tried to leave Honduras for Mexico. Several times the weather was against him. Finally he did leave on April 25, 1526—nearly a year and a half after he had left Mexico for Honduras on what had turned out to be an aggravating, debilitating, costly wild goose chase.

RETURN OF THE DEAD

Cortés's destination was the newly founded port town north of San Juan de Ulúa, named Medellín after his own hometown, but his ship leaked and was brought into harbor in Cuba, where Cortés might have expected a confrontation with Velázquez—more fuming, blustering, maybe fighting.

His old enemy Velázquez, however, was dead, as Bernal Díaz commented, "of despair." Also, Juan de Fonseca, bishop of Burgos, who had impeded Cortés and all the men of valor who had opened up the New World, had died in Spain, after having been removed as head of the Council of the Indies. But Cortés, though surviving his ancient enemies, was now so yellow, wan and wasted that some who had known him when he lived in Cuba did not recognize him. Cortés himself felt so close to death that for some time he had been carrying with him a brown Franciscan cassock in which he wanted his corpse to be wrapped.

For ten days Cortés remained in Cuba, while his ship was careened and found to be unseaworthy, so he had to buy another ship. Then he crossed to the Mexican coast—to the land he had proudly named New Spain of the Ocean Sea—and his ship hove to at dusk. He had a boat lowered to take him with only Sandoval and a few others ashore. They had to walk two or three miles from the beach to the town where, unnoticed, Cortés went to the church to kneel humbly, to acknowledge God. He was too tired to be thankful for his survival and unsure he would endure.

At midnight the townspeople found him in the church. Candles were lighted; criers with torches ran through the streets. And an outpouring of emotion began from the Spaniards in Mexico who regarded his return as if the night sky had turned bright. Messengers galloped off in all directions to alert the people that Cortés had returned, that he was alive. Food was brought for him and his few men. Indians came from hundreds of miles around and brought presents. Cortés stayed and rested for nearly two weeks and then began a slow ascent to the highland. On his way up, he was feted as he had been on his way down. Again, Spaniards in towns along the route had arches built and held displays of fireworks. Swarms of Indians came to Cortés, sprinkling flower petals in his path, repledging their allegiance, venerating him as the only sovereign figure they had left, and in whispers to him bemoaning the bad things that had happened while he was gone. It took Cortés and his entourage two weeks to reach the ridge of the mountains from which they descended into the valley of Mexico.

By this time Cortés was well informed. In the capital a wild faction-fight was in progress. In the wake of the conquest there had come a backwash of opportunists, including the four spying royal officials. The population of Spaniards in the capital had been greatly increased by men who had not been tempered in battle. The royal officials, each of whom led a faction, had repeatedly announced that Cortés was dead. And when a Spanish peasant woman—a typical, strong-bodied, passionate Spanish woman named Juana de Mansilla, whose husband was with Cortés—refused to believe that she was widowed, the officials had her whipped through the streets. When Las Casas and González reached the capital, they were arrested for the murder of Olid and would have been executed had not the veterans in the town council strenuously objected, so they were sent in chains to Spain, along with another load of gold that the royal officials sent to the king. Now, fearing Cortés's approach, the royal official currently in charge in the capital, having occupied Cortés's palace with two hundred men, rolled out all of Cortés's artillery. Within the capital Cortés's cohorts reassembled, and in a face-off at the palace the men who supported the royal official gave up.

When ultimately Cortés made his triumphant entry into the capital before a cheering crowd, he reined in his mount and held out his hand for Juana de Mansilla. She was promptly assisted by a page in Cortés's entourage who made a hand-stirrup for her—and with a flare of her skirt she swung up her white legs, common dusty *alpargatas* on her feet, and rode behind Cortés on his horse.

While Cortés was staying with Motolonía in the monastery of St. Francis and was confessing, a blow which no one had foreseen was relayed by a messenger from the coast: A judge who bore a royal commission had arrived to conduct a *residencia* of Cortés's entire time as governor. A *residencia* was the medieval Spanish equivalent of an audit by the Internal Revenue Service but it was even stricter in that the investigating official, called a judge *(juez de residencia),* actually took over all the public and private positions and possessions of the person being audited, received all income, paid just debts, examined all contracts, and after a period of many months and frequently years reported to the king and, if no gross misconduct had been discovered, turned back all sums and positions to the one who had been investigated. The people appointed to conduct *residencias* were above reproach, and this one was Luis Ponce de León, a relative of Juan Ponce de León, the sexually aging nobleman who had lost his life while searching for a Fountain of Youth.

When Cortés heard this news, he was devastated and ready to ask for final absolution, so little expected was this assault, and he had so little strength with which to resist it. What had happened in Spain while Cortés was in Honduras was that Pánfilo de Narváez had been wildly and furiously denouncing Cortés before the Council of the Indies, where he was being defended by Fray Melgarejo and by the Duke of Béjar, the nobleman who had long been his supporter. Eventually the quarrel was put before the king, and Carlos as ever was cautious; he had received many reports critical of Cortés from the royal officials in Mexico as well as a considerable amount of gold; so the king's compromise was this *residencia*, which was to be a fact-finding exercise.

Luis Ponce, who was a young man, arrived in Mexico forewarned by members of Fonseca's old set who still dominated the Council of the Indies. Hence, Ponce was wary and suspicious in the extreme, and he was haughty and determined not to make a mistake. With him he brought a large number of Dominican friars, for the Dominicans, alerted by Fray Bartolomé de las Casas, envied the position the Franciscans had established for themselves in Mexico. When Cortés sent a letter to Ponce on the coast offering accommodations and assistance, Ponce refused all help and replied that he would remain encamped until rested, then would come to the capital. Ponce, however, immediately set out for the capital; it had been whispered to him that he might be assassinated en route, so he intentionally began his journey without notice. There were two main roads leading to the highland, and Cortés, not knowing by which road Ponce would come, sent parties to welcome the judge on both roads. One of these parties intercepted Ponce and his group only about fifty miles from Mexico City, but Ponce refused an escort. He said he would march to within a few miles of the capital the next day; Cortés should not send a committee to him; and he would enter the capital after lunch on the day following. Then Ponce hastened his advance and entered the capital unexpectedly.

To the assembled town council, Ponce read out his royal commission and presented his papers. Cortés and all the councilmen kissed the papers and held them over their heads in token of submission. Then the papers were publicly proclaimed in the town square. The councilmen surrendered to Ponce their staves of authority, which he returned to all except Cortés, in accord with the protocol of a *residencia*. Ponce would neither stay in Cortés's palace nor in any other place designated by Cortés, nor would he eat anything that Cortés provided. Ponce had brought his own cooks, two brothers who prepared all his food.

This was a time of celebration in Mexico City, celebrating the return of Cortés, which for the citizens promised both safety and peace, and the advent of the *juez de residencia* could not dampen the festive spirit. Banquets and displays of fireworks were going on, and there were daring exhibitions of riding round and round long-horned bulls; to all of these events Ponce and his party were invited. But there had been sickness aboard Ponce's ship, and some of the judge's followers had become ill on the way to the highland. It was after a feast provided by Cortés in Iztapalapa that many of the newly arrived party began vomiting violently and then developed diarrhea and high fevers. Within ten days Ponce and thirty others, including two Dominicans, were dead.

Rumors flew. Some blamed the sickness on the flan and cheesecake, but Ponce hadn't eaten any. Others blamed cold water, the altitude and overeating. A physician who attended the stricken men initially said they had all died of a fever, but after being threatened with excommunication by the Dominicans he changed his testimony and said they might have been poisoned. There was the usual Spanish overabundance of black humor and dirty jokes. But sudden death was not uncommon in Mexico in the early sixteenth century; men and horses would nibble a plant that appeared to be edible and would drop dead; six dead horses were found at one spot. In spite of all the rumors, Cortés was never accused of Ponce's death; there was no incriminating evidence, only insinuating circumstance. So Ponce's power devolved on his second-in-command, Marcos de Aguilar (no relative of the translator/priest; Aguilar is a place-name). This Aguilar was old and ailing; he may also have been scared nearly to death. He would take only goat's milk and, when the supply of goat's milk ran out, according to Bernal Díaz, Cortés, always a good host, found a woman from Castile who was fresh—and she suckled the old man.

In view of Aguilar's incompetence, the councilmen of Mexico City wanted Cortés to resume full control of the government, but Cortés had to refuse. As captain-general, he was in military control, to everyone's relief, but Cortés knew the law and knew that, while he was the subject of a *residencia*, he was barred from functioning as governor. And so the faction-fighting resumed with a fury.

During this time Alvarado and his men from Guatemala arrived, as did Cortés's men from Honduras. Cortés was deeply moved when he rode out and greeted Alvarado and noticed, after Alvarado dismounted, that one of his legs, shot full of arrows in Guatemala, was now shorter than the other by several inches and that Alvarado, the dandy, walked with a decided limp. Subsequently, petitions for *encomiendas* for the Guatemala veterans were prepared but no one in Mexico City was authorized to approve them. So Alvarado left Mexico for Spain to place before the king his petition to rule Guatemala.

Civil order degenerated. After Aguilar died of syphilis, it was uncertain who had the power of the *juez de residencia*, and the four royal officials, who had been caged and then jailed, managed their release and rallied their followers, and men fought to the death in the streets and taverns. When the come-lately faction seized Hernando Alonso, the Jew to whom Cortés had awarded a generous *encomienda*, they burned him at the stake for being a heretic.

It was ironic that Cortés, who at the outset of the conquest had so cleverly utilized Spanish legalities for his own advantage, was now hobbled by the Spanish legal system. He simply could not bring to bear all his power while he was under the constraints of a *residencia*. The royal officials had published their accusation against him, that he had taken 60,000 *pesos de oro* from the treasury (it was later proved that Cortés was owed from the treasury 150,000 *pesos de oro* for the fleets and armies he had equipped and sent out), and as usual Cortés was short of ready cash. But when he tried to recover many of his properties, he found they had been sold at auction on the presumption of his death.

The faction-fighting reached a pitch when in a brawl a Cortés man killed an anti-Cortés man, and the anti-Cortés faction, at that moment in control of the town council, had the right hand of the Cortés man cut off as punishment. Then the anti-Cortés faction, afraid Cortés, who was at his estate in Cuernavaca, would come storming back, declared him exiled from Mexico City. And Cortés chose to respect the council's declaration. He could have contested it; he could have defied it; many of the old *conquistadores* begged him to do so. But Cortés saw no legal way he could quell this rioting unless he had a royal ruling in his favor. So, like Alvarado, he decided to return to Spain to plead his own case before the king.

From Coyoacán outside Mexico City, Cortés tried to put his personal affairs in order. He had vast holdings of land and Indians, and he had to systematize his collection of tribute. To the east coast he sent an agent to purchase, equip and provision two ships, inviting all veterans who wanted to accompany him to Spain to come at no cost. And he assembled a grand entourage, befitting the conqueror of Mexico. He was escorted by Sandoval, Andrés de Tápia and a score of renowned *conquistadores*, and he brought a delegation of noble Mexican Indians. He loaded the ships with gold, silver and jewels, featherwork, all kinds of Indian artifacts, and he brought caged animals unknown in Europe—armadillos, albatrosses, pumas, jaguars, opossums. Cortés brought Indian albinos and dwarfs; he brought the acrobats who twirled logs with their feet, a ball team, and others who, spinning, flew through the air on ropes from high poles. With this treasureload of riches and wonders, Cortés sailed for Spain in the autumn of 1528.

VII
THE KALEIDOSCOPE OF
MODERN MEXICO

DOS MUNDOS

The Hospital de Jesús, founded by Cortés in 1524, is the oldest hospital in the western world, and, amazingly, it is functioning today, admirably and wonderfully, in the service of humanity and the Mexican people. It is located in the heart of downtown Mexico City, the old center of the city, amid noise, clutter and bustle. On both sides of the narrow street where the hospital is situated are little disheveled shops selling everything from *alpargatas* to souvenirs. The entranceway of the hospital is through a short arcade as if one were entering an office building, and on the street side the entrance is marked only by the arc of a sign with art deco letters reminiscent of the nineteen twenties. But this short passage leads to the ancient hospital which fills the inside of the entire block. There, within the crust of the shops, are the sixteenth-century structures—broad staircases of worn stones, wide hallways under vaulted or beamed ceilings, Spanish arches revealing the patio gardens designed for meditation. And in this atmosphere of lovely antiquity patients on gurneys are being pushed by quick-stepping, white-capped nurses, white-coated doctors in attendance, many of whom have brown faces accentuated by white hair.

The unbroken lifeline of the Hospital de Jesús—extending from 1524 to the present day—seems to echo the life of Cortés, whose lifetime was an explosion of vitality. After Mexico's social revolution of 1920, Cortés, as a reminder of imperial Spain, was more furiously damned by those who championed the nobility of Indian forebears than he had been damned during the preceding century by the Spanish colonists-turned-nationalists who asserted Mexico's independence. Yet now, in this hospital, both worlds are extolled in ceremonies and speeches—*dos mundos*—the distinctive, unique, majestic world of ancient Indians and the civilization of late medieval and early modern Spain. There is an acknowledgment that Mexico is a hybrid with graces, virtues, vices and energies stemming from each of the progenitive worlds. Broadly, however, this admission of Mexico's parentage is still made reluctantly—whispered, not trumpeted.

Near the altar in the little church that adjoins the hospital Cortés's bones repose within a thick, cemented wall on which there is a small plaque. In the rear on a vaulted part of the ceiling under a layer of grime is a mural by José Clemente Orozco, who was famed as a nationalist (contradictions in Mexico never end). But this church has had its interruptions; after being ransacked during the revolution of 1920, it was a place where junk was stored. Then people of the neighborhood brought pressure for the reestablishment of this humble church because they wanted their own church, as distinct from the cathedral a few blocks away. Probably the people associated in their minds the unpretentious church, which they regarded as their own, with the adjoining hospital, which has never ceased to serve them.

A priest in vestments in the church of the Hospital de Jesús says in a confidential tone, "It is still not understood that the mission of Cortés was to bring Christ to the people and the people to Christ." This is true—and the religiosity of the sixteenth century, especially in Spain, must be granted if modern Mexico is to be comprehended. Only now, little by little, are some of history's snarls untangling.

In 1978, a few blocks away from the Hospital de Jesús—in fact, alongside the central plaza of downtown Mexico City—workers digging an extension of the subway came upon the base of the great pyramid of Tenochtitlán. The *conquistadores*, as a battle tactic, had become good at making rubble of Aztec structures in order to fill canals, and the base of the pyramid up to a height of perhaps twenty feet had become so thoroughly covered up and obscured that it had never been exhumed and restored. So, since 1978, Mexican archaeologists have been at work, carefully revealing Aztec objects never seen before—the flagstone paving, the battened walls that formed the base of the pyramid, a *chac-mool* with the paint still on (a formalized reclining figure with its belly flattened to receive offerings), horrific masks, and a wall made of human skulls. But archaeologists working at this site, called the *templo mayor*, found themselves in conflict with preceding Mexican archaeologists. The current generation wanted to expose Tenochtitlán as it was when Cortés saw it, as it had looked to the Spaniards. This had never, since 1920, been the aim of Mexican archaeology. All the major artifacts found throughout Mexico had been shipped to the wondrous Museum of Anthropology in Mexico City (out in Chapultepec Park in the affluent neighborhood of Polanco, far removed from the bones of Cortés) where the presentation emphasized the worthiness of Indian cultures and downplayed many realities. The Mexican archaeologists at the *templo mayor* dared to leave the skull-wall on view, with the bones whitening in the sun, just as this skull-wall had been viewed by the populace of Tenochtitlán, symbolizing the awe-inspiring death-power of the gods whom the Aztecs served and who served the Aztecs. The upshot was that a new museum has been erected beside the excavation of the *templo mayor* in downtown Mexico City, and in the new museum, which is only partially filled so far, artifacts are displayed with the aim, not of extolling Indian culture, but of presenting a fully rounded view of it.

Yet what is most surprising and stupendous is that on huge engraved tablets on the outside of the new museum of the *templo mayor* are quotations from Cortés's second letter to the king, from Bernal Díaz, and from Motolinía. Never before in recent Mexican history have these voices been heard. And they are being proclaimed now in an effort to allow us, even encourage us, to see Tenochtitlán as it was, with both the Aztecs and the Spaniards presented truly.

Hanging on the wall in the board room of the Hospital de Jesús is one of the few portraits of Cortés painted from life, the work of an unidentified artist in Toledo in 1530, after Cortés returned to Spain. It is a formalistic portrait of a knight in armor; it makes Cortés look older than he was; and it certainly does not capture his spirit. This portrait, however, is relegated to an obscure place, a windowless interior chamber where few people and not the general public will see it, so firmly fixed in Mexico is the resentment of a proudly part-Indian nation toward Cortés. The influence of the Black Legend and the influence of successive waves of nationalism, if no longer mounting, have only begun, perhaps, to recede.

Along the Paseo de la Reforma, the grand boulevard that rivals the Champs Élysées, the old mind-set of Mexico remains clear. Statues line the walks—mostly busts of stiff-faced authorities, occasional upstanding figures, a few *caballeros*. Due respect is paid to the presidents and generals who ruled during the first century of Mexican independence. The heroes of Mexico's social revolution, of course, are accorded prominent places. Near the Reforma there is even a statue of Christopher Columbus. Yet nowhere in Mexico—neither in the thrumming capital nor in the provincial cities nor in the towns and villages nor in the countryside—is there a single sculpture of Cortés. The spirit of the *gran conquistador* may be seen, if it can be seen, only in the specks of light that glitter from pierced tin lampshades in dim saloons, or perhaps it may be seen in the grainy Mexican light of late afternoon.

After Cortés conquered Mexico, the first task at which the Indians were

A portion of the floor of the *templo mayor* recently excavated in downtown Mexico City, showing the flagstone paving, the bases of two staircases that led to the dual temples atop the original pyramid, with an eagle's head adorning the near staircase.

This wall of skulls stood, and now stands once more, at the base of the *templo mayor*, the great Aztec pyramid in downtown Mexico City, which was the formal center of Tenochtitlán (the center was not in the marketplace of Tlatelolco). These skulls of sacrificial victims were covered with a light layer of stucco to bind them to the wall—the skull-wall serving notice of the awesome power of the Aztec gods.

put to work was the building of churches, and it was credibly chronicled that the Indians would embed in bases for the Cross remnants of their idols that the Spaniards had smashed. Then, when the Indians—with the approval of the Spaniards—passed by the Cross and made gestures of devotion, the Indians would know that they were respecting both the old gods and the new. Correspondingly, there is now in Mexico City on the Reforma, about halfway between the *templo mayor* and the Museum of Anthropology, a traffic circle where in the central grassy plot stands a memorial to Cuauhtémoc (the Mexicans prefer the phonetic spelling of Guatémoc), and the story may be true that in the grass beside the memorial someone has buried a statuette of Cortés. Such a minor infraction of municipal ordinance wouldn't be hard to accomplish, secretively, at about five o'clock in the morning, when the traffic lets up and after the policeman on the beat has passed by: to dig a little hole, insert a figurine of Cortés, cover it up. And if this story is true, then in the vortex of this spinning automotive circus in the blue air of exhaust fumes, homage is being paid today both to the indomitable Indian emperor who epitomized native America and to Hernán Cortés who, more than anyone else, tied the two worlds together.

VIII
THE REWARDS OF LIFE

HOMECOMING

The ocean crossing for Cortés and his comrades was an easy one of only forty-two days. The passengers aboard the ships did not eat all the banquet foods that had been put aboard for them; even when the ocean was calm, Spaniards at sea seldom had much appetite. But when the ships finally came into harbor at Palos in Spain, Cortés, Sandoval and many others were seriously ill, not from the voyage, but from all the fevers and ailments they had in their blood, and, debarking, they staggered ashore to disperse and to creep into convenient havens—these men who had conquered Mexico, each of them with a few bars of Aztec gold to provide ready money. Cortés, with his entourage supporting and following him, went to the Franciscan monastery of La Rábida. Sandoval, however, was so sick that in the port town of Palos he had to be taken into the home of a ropemaker—and he died there, this most youthful, loyal and intrepid of the *conquistadores*. Further, it is likely that the ropemaker robbed Sandoval while he was dying, because when Cortés went to find out what had happened, both the ropemaker and Sandoval's gold had disappeared.

Cortés was heartsick over Sandoval's death and longed to go after the ropemaker, who had fled to Portugal. Sandoval was less than thirty when he died, and his life had been so wholly devoted to valor and conquest that he left no wife or concubine or illegitimate children. Cortés, who took down Sandoval's last wishes, recorded as beneficiary of Sandoval's estate his sister in Medellín, a sister whom he had not seen for many years and who later, with her endowment, married a bastard son of the Count of Medellín. The returning veterans of Mexico were saddened, so soon after their arrival in Spain, to forgather for Sandoval's burial. They were nervous and restless, as men are when from the tension of danger they come back to a homeland that is complacent and peaceful and only dimly aware of the other world where the veterans have been. In the monastery outside Palos, Cortés, distraught and depressed by Sandoval's untimely death and by the absence of his own father who had recently died, suffered another bout of fever and could not travel.

While Cortés was incapacitated, news of his arrival spread. His coming

Portrait of Cortés that hangs in the Hospital de Jesús in Mexico City; it was painted in 1530 in Toledo by an anonymous artist.

Inset: Portrait of Carlos Quinto (detail), painted in 1548 by Titian.

had not been heralded and probably had been intentionally played down by his detractors in the Council of the Indies. Now, though, talk ran rapidly from Palos to Seville and across southwestern Spain, reaching the Court, which was then in Toledo. Everywhere, people were gabbling about the fantastic curiosities Cortés had brought from the New World, about the great wealth he had won for the empire; they were calling him the *gran conquistador*.

Cortés and his men had been unsure of their reception in Spain, after having been bedeviled by the Council of the Indies and by the Spanish officials sent to Mexico, and they were surprised by this rise of cheerful chattering. Spain, as a nation, was in the mood to hail a hero; the moment was propitious, with blessings seeming continuously to flutter down like blossoms from a tree upon the shoulders of the nation, first Spain's triumph over the Moors, now the promise of a steady flow of gold and silver from the New World.

Although Cortés calculatedly had returned in the grandest style he could arrange, he and his veterans among themselves retained the casual intimacy of comrades-in-arms. In Mexico it had been suggested to Cortés that he should devise for himself some honorific way by which he should be addressed, but Cortés by his men was always called simply "Cortés," and all the captains maintained the same informality.

From La Rábida Cortés dispatched a letter to the king, informing the sovereign of Sandoval's tragic death and of Cortés's own indisposition. Then the king commanded all towns along Cortés's way to Toledo to build archways of triumph and to prepare appropriate ceremonies of welcome. Carlos himself was in a jubilant mood, with his coronation as Holy Roman Emperor in the offing, and he was happy to suspend his usual caution and join in the popular acclaim. From the king's viewpoint, Cortés had come home to ask for royal favors, and he was in fragile health; he expected to be elevated into the Spanish hierarchy; and this was the kind of reward for a *conquistador* that the king could very easily manage.

Buoyed by indications of royal approval, Cortés got up from his sickbed, organized his procession, which was really a treasure train, and progressed from town to town on the way to Toledo, along a route lined with celebrating people. Nearly a quarter-century had passed since Cortés had last been in Spain, and the closeness of his own people revived him—the sight of boys in the streets, boys such as he had once been, *señoritas* on the balconies, the gaiety, flowers, bravado, the music and dancing, smells of Spanish food and wine. When Cortés reached Toledo, he was put up in accommodations the king had arranged for him. He suffered a relapse of his fever, and the king himself, attended by nobles from the most respected and ancient families of Spain, came to greet him.

When Cortés was sufficiently recovered to make his appearance at Court, the king was ready with favors, which he promptly and generously bestowed: Cortés was named Marqués del Valle de Oaxaca (a title not delimited to the province of Oaxaca, because Cortés held the largest *encomienda* in Mexico); he was confirmed in his *encomienda* and as captain-general of New Spain and of the provinces bordering on the southern sea; he was guaranteed an enormous income from these territories. Only in two respects did Cortés overreach. The king offered him the knighthood of St. James, but Cortés desired to be a commander of the order, and in the flurry of proclamations he was not so nominated. Also, Cortés asked to be named governor of New Spain, but the cautious king had in mind limits on the bounty he would bestow, and he did not want to overblow the expectations of future conquerors, nor did he want Cortés to be able to return to Mexico and resume his dominance. So, all in all, Cortés was magnificently rewarded, accorded a station high in the hierarchy of the nobility, assured of being very, very rich. (In Mexico, over the ensuing years, as Cortés's *residencia* ground on and on, the auditors caught Cortés's concession to himself of one-fifth, the same as the king's share, so they penalized him and reduced it; they also reduced the shares he had given himself as a "natural lord," and made a few other changes; but Cortés remained one of the wealthiest noblemen in the empire.)

In his face-to-face contacts with Cortés, what the king responded to with most eagerness was news about the southern sea. The king knew that Magellan's fleet, having passed from east to west through the strait at the southern tip of South America, had crossed the Pacific to the spice islands; all the ships except one had been lost; but that single ship had continued on to return to Spain loaded with spices. So it was established beyond doubt that the spice islands could be reached by sailing westward, and the king also knew that the Portuguese in the spice islands had jailed many of Magellan's men. Now the king's aims were further exploration, acquisition, and vengeance against the Portuguese. Cortés was able to tell the king that the three ships Cortés had ordered built at Zihuatanejo on the southern sea—after the first set of hulls at Zacatula had burned—had been completed. At his own expense Cortés had fitted the ships out handsomely with armaments and provisions and had put aboard crews under the command of a kinsman of his; then the fleet had set sail. This fleet, Cortés assured the king, would be able to maintain itself against both savages and Portuguese. The king was very pleased.

(Zihuatanejo is on a nearly landlocked bay on the west coast of Mexico, a bay almost completely ringed by cliffs and hills; it is like a smaller version of Acapulco and even safer as a storm shelter because it is connected to the sea by a serpentine channel, so the bay is little affected by the ocean swells. The narrow channel has a big black rock in the middle of it and is difficult to sail through at night, yet passage can be managed in the dark if there is constant reference to a good chart and attention to a clifftop lighthouse which serves as a fixed point. Within the haven of the bay windstorms occasionally whip up a powerful surf, and landing then from a dinghy can be dangerous. For shipbuilding the Spaniards first used Zacatula at the mouth of the Río Balsas but then shifted about fifty miles south to Zihuatanejo, which they preferred because it was better sheltered. Cortés naturally would be optimistic about a fleet sailing from this pleasant tropical cove. But the fact was that his fleet sailed into the expanse of the Pacific and had to go over five thousand miles to reach the spice islands. All Cortés's ships were lost, and the few Spaniards who survived in small boats and reached the East Indies were captured and imprisoned by the Portuguese, a few hapless Spaniards being taken by Filipinos to China and sold into slavery there. This venture, organized and financed by Cortés, ended in dismal failure, although none of this was known or expected when Cortés reported to the king.)

So aroused was Cortés by the adulation he was receiving in Spain that an aspect of his personality, long neglected, an aspect which had nearly atrophied, came quickly into play again. In Seville and at other stops along the way to Toledo, Cortés would call upon the duchesses who were in the vicinity. At the salons of the noblewomen he would appear, escorted by his retinue of valiant captains, and he gave openhandedly to the causes for which the noble ladies held solemn Masses. To these duchesses and their friends Cortés gave presents both costly and exotic—fans of green feathers with handles of gold, emeralds set in gold. He held his own entertainments to which he invited the noblewomen, and he had the Indian acrobats perform. To his gratification Cortés found that he was as good at gallantry as he had ever been, perhaps a little better, considering his present resources. And the duchesses began to bring forward their as-yet-unwed female relatives. Though Cortés was still a bit yellow and thin from his fever, and his body from his head to his feet was covered with scars and welts, most of which fortunately did not show, he was, as a widower in his mid-forties, a dazzling candidate for an attractive match. The blue-blooded wife of Don Francisco de los Cobos wrote to her noble husband that she "was much taken with the politeness and generosity of Cortés" and "the fame of Cortés and his heroic actions was far short of the judgment which must be formed of him by those who had the good fortune of his acquaintance." This lady, Doña Maria, had her own unmarried sister in mind.

All of which coincided with what Cortés had in mind. Having attained the status of high noble rank, he intended to found a legitimate line—and, ever since Cuba, his ambition had been to have a nice, naked duchess. (This is a dream that is perhaps universal among Spanish men. Every Spaniard wants a nice, naked duchess. Goya painted his duchess twice, once naked and once richly and intimately dressed. In bars in Madrid around the Prado, the great museum where paintings of many duchesses are hung, among artists and art students nowadays it is frequently bemoaned that there simply are not enough duchesses to go around.)

It was the niece of the Duke of Bejár who won out. For years the duke, Don Alvaro de Zúñiga, had staunchly defended Cortés, and he had three times before the king pledged his life as surety for Cortés. Maybe the duke, while making those pledges, had had the future of his favorite niece in mind. The girl, whose name was Doña Juana Ramirez de Arellano y Zúñiga (her father was Don Carlos Arellano, Count of Aguilar), had been alerted in advance to her prospective fate, which she viewed as her good fortune. Soon after the king departed for Italy, where a Spanish army was fighting the French over Milan, Cortés married Doña Juana, who was good-looking, good-natured, and fertile.

Spain and all the world then was unabashedly jewel-crazy—as were the Indians of Mexico and Central America—and Cortés had brought with him to Spain five emeralds that were talked about by everybody. These jewels, which no longer endure, were described in detail by Gómara, and they were huge emeralds of exceptional clarity: one carved into the shape of a rose, another into the shape of a cornucopia, another into the shape of a fish replete with scales and with eyes of gold; another was carved into the shape of a bell set in gold with a perfect pearl for a clapper and engraved in the gold in Spanish, as a compliment to whoever would receive the jewel, "Blessed be He who made thee!" And the finest and largest emerald was carved into the shape of a cup with a gold base and a spout of gold, connected by four gold chains to an oblong pearl, and on the gold engraved in Latin, "Among those born of women, no one grander has come forth." To this day Spaniards are uninhibited when it comes to investigating the value of anything. Specialists in jewelry were summoned with their diamond glasses; lines formed to scrutinize the jewels. Some Genoese merchants at La Rábida offered Cortés forty thousand ducats for the bell, intending to resell it to the Sultan of Turkey, but Cortés in lordly

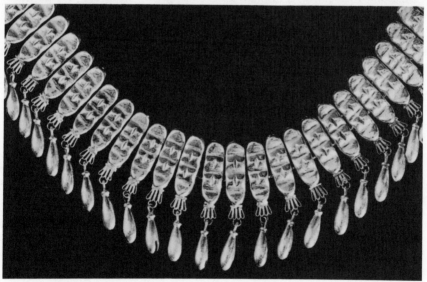

Exquisitely made art objects like these, of gold inlaid with emeralds and pearls, were presented by Cortés to receptive noble dowagers in Spain.

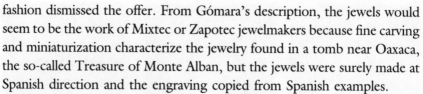

fashion dismissed the offer. From Gómara's description, the jewels would seem to be the work of Mixtec or Zapotec jewelmakers because fine carving and miniaturization characterize the jewelry found in a tomb near Oaxaca, the so-called Treasure of Monte Alban, but the jewels were surely made at Spanish direction and the engraving copied from Spanish examples.

The queen—who was the infanta of Portugal and, as the result of her marriage with Carlos, had brought Portugal under the Habsburg sway— was supposed to have intimated that she would be pleased if Cortés would make presents of these jewels to her. Cortés, however, sent the queen many fine gifts but not the five rarities, which he gave to his betrothed, Doña Juana.

THE GAMBLE OF THE SOUTHERN SEA

Cortés had a very good time in Spain but, after more than a year, he had enough, and he wanted to show Doña Juana the land he had conquered. So in the middle of 1531 Cortés, accompanied by a large escort and with his wife and widowed mother, set sail again for the New World (it's worth remarking that Cortés and many of the *conquistadores* were very good to their parents).

In Mexico, while Cortés had been away, the bureaucracy had taken over again. As a normal step in the extension of Spanish administrative apparatus, the Council of the Indies had set up a department for Mexico, called an *Audiencia,* with a president and four lawyers as sitting judges, the purpose being to regularize the hearing of lawsuits and the impartial administration of justice, including the continuation of Cortés's *residencia* and the management of governmental affairs. Two of the lawyers in the *Audiencia* had died of pleurisy soon after arriving in Mexico, which caused Bernal Díaz to comment that it was a good thing Cortés was in Spain at the time because otherwise he would certainly have been blamed for their deaths. The first appointed president of the *Audiencia* was a Narváez man who had acted unrestrainedly and was fired by the king. A new *Audiencia,* consisting only of four lawyers (for a year there was no president), had assumed control and had to some extent restored decent administration in the capital. But the Indians throughout Mexico were on the verge of revolt.

This was the situation when Cortés reached Veracruz, and it was not dissimilar from the situation when Cortés had returned from Honduras. Whenever he was away from Mexico, the Indians felt the lack of the empathy he had for them, and the Spaniards likewise suffered from the absence of a natural leader. Now there came flocking to Cortés on the coast more than a thousand Spaniards and many Indians complaining of mal-treatment by the *Audiencia,* mainly while it had been led by the Narváez man. But the current members of the *Audiencia* in Mexico City were alarmed by this congregating around Cortés and ordered all residents of the capital to return immediately, threatening to order Cortés himself to leave Mexico as a disrupter of the peace. This was not the kind of reception he had led Doña Juana to expect. So Cortés, whose own force num-bered several hundred well-armed men with plenty of horses, put himself at the head of the Spaniards and Indians who came to him, had a public crier read out his royal appointment as Captain-General of New Spain, sent a copy of the royal appointment by a messenger on a fast horse to the capital, and then began a forced march upward into the mountains. The *Audiencia,* urging him to stop at Texcoco, changed its mind when a widespread Indian rebellion actually broke out, a rebellion that had been carefully planned by chiefs of many tribes to take advantage of dissension among the Spaniards. The Indians seized and killed more than two hun-dred Spaniards in outlying towns and on the roads. Then the *Audiencia* begged Cortés to enter the capital and assume military command. He did so—and Doña Juana had the pleasure of seeing her husband welcomed by the scared citizens. Cortés moved back into his fortress, organized and equipped troops for punitive expeditions under his veteran captains, and he quickly, harshly put down the uprising.

With safety and order restored, relations between Cortés and the *Au-diencia* became more cordial, and Cortés agreed to go to the west coast to visit his shipyards at Zihuatanejo, Acapulco and Tehuantepec, from these harbors to pursue his exploration of the southern sea in accord with his agreement with the king. Cortés did not really want to become embroiled again in the political fracas of the capital, and the *Audiencia* feared that his presence would endanger the system of regulations that the lawyers were trying to impose upon the fiercely individualistic Spanish settlers. On the pleasant side, Cortés knew that in fall, winter and spring the climate on the west coast of Mexico was heavenly—flowers everywhere, palms shading the shore. He wanted his young wife to see and enjoy this paradise.

Cortés ensconced Doña Juana at Acapulco, where she promptly became pregnant for the third time. She had already borne two children, a boy and a girl, both of whom died in infancy, and this third child, delivered in Cuernavaca, was a boy, after whom she bore three more girls. With the boy, though, a slight embarrassment arose because Doña Juana wanted to name the child for his paternal grandfather, Martín. The trouble was that, probably unknown to Doña Juana, there already existed a child named Martín Cortés, a bouncing little brown boy who was Cortés's illegitimate offspring with Malinche. The other Martín lived with his mother around Coatzacoalcos; Cortés had assigned to Malinche several good tribute-paying towns. Now he analyzed the problem and came up with a simple solution: Let there be two Martín Corteses. By this time Solomonic decisions were easy for Cortés.

Traveling from one of his shipyards to the other, Cortés supervised the ship construction. Ocean-going ships had to be more stoutly built than brigantines for the inland lakes. Actually these ocean-going ships, handfitted, both nailed and doweled, were extremely strong, once the wood was swollen by the water. But fittings and supplies were hard to obtain and sometimes had to be brought from Spain to the east coast of Mexico, then transported overland to the west coast, so progress was slow.

By the middle of 1532 two ships were ready at Acapulco, and later other ships were completed at Zihuatanejo and Tehuantepec, and Cortés sent them up and down the coast and outward—searching for a strait connecting the Pacific and the Caribbean and seeking out a sea-trail to the Indies. Nothing had ever been heard from the fleet Cortés had sent westward from Zihuatanejo before he had returned to Spain. And nothing of consequence came of these new voyages. So Cortés decided to become personally involved.

Sending a well-equipped fleet of three vessels from Tehuantepec to an appointed meeting-place at a bay on the coast of Jalisco, he himself led a force by land to Jalisco where he recovered the stripped hulk of one of his ships (the ship had cost him fifteen thousand ducats). When the fleet from Tehuantepec joined him, he boarded the men, horses and weapons and sailed northward all the way to Baja California. But Baja California is a desert; the Indians there did not even raise maize but gathered and hunted for their sustenance, depending upon berries, game and fish. The Spaniards soon began to starve. So Cortés sailed back across the mouth of the sea which separated the peninsula of Baja California from the mainland of Mexico—from Cabo San Lucas to Puerto Vallarta, not a difficult sail— in search of provisions. In the bay of Puerto Vallarta he found another of his ships but ran aground trying to reach it, then had to haul out his own damaged ship for repair. A few Spanish settlers came from the interior and sold him pigs, sheep and maize at exorbitant prices. When he set sail again, a yardarm fell and killed the pilot, who was sleeping at the foot of the mast. Serving as pilot himself, Cortés took his ship first northward, then south-

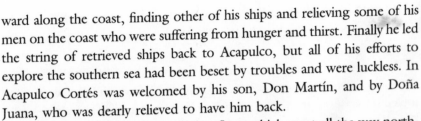

ward along the coast, finding other of his ships and relieving some of his men on the coast who were suffering from hunger and thirst. Finally he led the string of retrieved ships back to Acapulco, but all of his efforts to explore the southern sea had been beset by troubles and were luckless. In Acapulco Cortés was welcomed by his son, Don Martín, and by Doña Juana, who was dearly relieved to have him back.

In 1539 he dispatched yet another fleet, which went all the way north-ward between Baja California and the mainland of Mexico to the head of the gulf where the Colorado River discharges, and Cortés named this gulf for himself, the Sea of Cortés, which was little enough return for his efforts. In all, Cortés spent two hundred to three hundred thousand ducats, an enormous sum, on these explorations.

In Mexico City, gradually but steadily, the conservative, stabilizing influ-ence of tradition-bound Spain was taking hold; the system of laws and habits that was to be maintained for three hundred years was catching on. The president of the *Audiencia,* a bishop, was doing his work honestly and well. And a viceroy had been sent from Spain to govern Mexico, Don Antonio de Mendoza, a distinguished nobleman whom Cortés both liked and respected. Nevertheless, when Cortés returned to Mexico City, he and Don Antonio began to argue over the recompense due Cortés from the treasury for his explorations. Cortés based his claim on the risks he had run, financial and otherwise; once more, he had come close to starving or dying of thirst or being shipwrecked, not to mention the ever-present threat of hostile Indians. But the viceroy, rebutting him, wanted to know what profit there would be for the Crown—very little, as it seemed. Cortés and Don Antonio quarreled and, despite their liking for each other, fell out and became estranged.

Cortés was by nature genial with both men and women, though this did not always work well for him. For example, in his own household Cortés insisted that Doña Juana should be treated with elaborate respect, which she was, but Cortés was free and flippant with other men's wives and women. This so angered one of the captains that he called Cortés to his face a *"putañero,"* usually translated as a libertine, but the sense of *putañero,* which in modern Spanish usage would be *putero,* is "a guy whose manners were learned in a whorehouse." This was a typical Spanish spat climaxed by an insult, but Cortés never responded to such provocations. Always with his men he maintained an easy barracks-room familiarity: The men felt free to insult him, which they did; he was free to insult them back, which he did; and Cortés, unless discipline was affected, would answer an insult with a laugh.

Wrangling between Cortés and the viceroy led eventually to litigation. An auditor, who had been working for years on Cortés's *residencia*, disallowed some of his privileges. The viceroy ordered a recount to be made of Cortés's vassals, which was a step Cortés felt was unjustified, so he sued. And, since the court of first and last resort for a high-ranking nobleman was the king, Cortés, taking his son with him, returned to Spain in 1540.

REQUIEM MASS WITH A *LEITMOTIF*

Again, Cortés returned to Spain in style, but not with the ebullience of his previous return. Doña Juana did not accompany him. She preferred to stay with her daughters in Mexico; the sea-trip was an unpleasant prospect; and Cortés knew that his family would be safe in Mexico, with Don Antonio in control. Cortés was now fifty-five years old, and the eight or nine vexing years on the west coast of Mexico, years of only familial accomplishment, had aged him. In spite of nearly starving on the exploratory voyage he had made, he—who had always been lithe and lean—now had a paunch. And people in Spain, he found, were no longer talking about Mexico; the talk now was about Peru.

After Cortés had set the pattern of conquest in Mexico, Spaniards throughout the New World, both north and south of the equator, tried to duplicate his success. But, no matter how valiant their efforts, success of the magnitude Cortés had achieved depended upon finding another mighty lode of gold and silver. Peru in the southern hemisphere was the only other place in the Americas where such a lode existed. It had never occurred to Cortés to explore southward from Panama along the western edge of South America; he had never been near the region. Once, he had encountered the grizzled, scarcely literate soldier-adventurer, Francisco Pizarro, who in 1533 had conquered Peru. When Cortés had been in La Rábida near Seville in 1528, Pizarro had been there, and probably Cortés had seen Pizarro later at the Court; Pizarro then was seeking the king's help and approval, but he was indistinguishable from many hopeful Spaniards with similar plans, and Cortés did not remember him. Pizarro may even have been a distant relative because Cortés's mother's maiden name was Pizarro, though that was a common family name (Francisco Pizarro came from the city of Trujillo in Estremadura). Years later, while Cortés was in Acapulco, he had

Portrait of Cortés that hangs in the Museo Naval in Madrid, by an anonymous artist. Judging by the whitening beard, probably painted during Cortés's final years in Spain. It was the style when sitting for one's portrait to project *dignidad,* so Cortés was constrained not to wink or smile. According to Bernal Díaz, Cortés was a great winker.

received a copy of a letter Pizarro had sent from Peru to all Spanish governors asking for their aid, and Cortés had tried to send a shipment of some weapons. In the wake of the Peruvian discovery, Mexico was old news.

In Spain Cortés encountered the same problem that had confronted Montejo and Puertocarrero many years before: He couldn't catch up with the king, who was forever on the move. Carlos with an army of invincible Spanish infantry had left Spain for France en route to Flanders to put down a rebellion in the city of Ghent, where the king had been born. The citizens of Ghent felt they were being overtaxed, but their rebellion was mercilessly suppressed. When the king/emperor returned to Spain in 1541, he had no time to listen to the details of a dispute in Mexico because he was on his way to attack the Muslim stronghold in North Africa. Habsburg scheming had not worked out as well as was hoped. Adrian of Utrecht, as Pope, had died after a very short time in office; Carlos's relations with subsequent Popes had been less than harmonious. Now, to identify himself as the indisputable champion of Christianity, Carlos was going to North Africa to tighten the siege of Algiers and to capture the Arab stronghold.

So Cortés at his own expense raised a troop of cavalry and, along with many other Spanish noblemen, each of whom led his own troop, followed the king to the coast, where they all were taken aboard a huge fleet—a combined supply and troop-carrying operation. The fleet made the short voyage across the Mediterranean and reached the bay of Algiers, only to be caught there by a storm that drove most of the ships aground on the rocky shore. Cortés was nearly killed—as he had been countless times before. His ship broke up on the rocks and he was carried along by the swirling water, half-swimming, half-drowning. (It is impossible for a swimmer to keep control during a grounding; the waves, already whipped up by the storm, crest and break on the underwater shelf of the land and, regardless of how strong a swimmer might be, he is either tossed like driftwood onto the beach or pulled under and buried in the subsurface muck, and whether his fate is one or the other is simply a matter of luck.) Cortés was washed up on the sand, spitting water. When he crawled a bit farther to a place where he could sit splay-legged while the wind and rain continued to lash him, *he realized the worst:* His five great jewels, the five carved emeralds prized by Doña Juana, which were perhaps the finest jewels in the world, he had been carrying in a leather pouch tied around his neck—and they were gone! Somewhere in the salty surf of Africa amid the waving plants on the floor of the sea, being covered by the sand, lay the rarest jewels of Indian America.

Drenched, with most of their supplies and horses lost, the survivors assembled ashore. (Spaniards really had terrible luck at sea. Their subsequent Armada against England was defeated mainly by a storm. The English, on the other hand, had wonderful luck. When a Spanish troop stationed along the Strait of Magellan lay in wait for Francis Drake, Drake and his squadron were blown southward around Cape Horn and bypassed the ambush completely, leaving the Spanish troopers to starve at a place duly named Port Famine.) The king/emperor endured, as did Cortés's son. The soaked Spaniards were met by members of the composite Christian force that already had Algiers under partial siege.

The tactical problem was that there weren't enough Christians—Spaniards, Italians, Germans—to encircle the Arab citadel completely. The new arrivals had been intended to provide the needed reinforcement, but most of them had drowned. Now it was concluded, when the straggling survivors joined those on duty under the shelter of their tents, that this siege should be abandoned. Cortés objected. He begged the captains, he went among the soldiers and tried to rally them, urging them not to accept defeat. If they would follow him for one week, he vowed he would take this infidel city. It is doubtful if Carlos Quinto ever heard him. And the younger commanders, especially those who had been sitting for a while outside Algiers, were sick of this engagement and, without hope of further reinforcement, wanted to go home. So they held a war council, to which Cortés was not invited, and voted their minds.

Then home they all went—Christians accepting defeat, and Cortés without his jewels, which made him financially second only to the king/ emperor in being the biggest loser on the whole expedition. The only good that came out of it was that Cortés met Gómara and hired him to be his secretary.

Back in Spain, the two men went over Cortés's papers. He had lots of lawsuits—and the points at issue were complicated. In the case of the recount of his vassals, for instance, the quibble was over the word *vecino* (neighbor). Cortés's vassals were limited to so many *vecinos*. The question was: Did *vecinos* refer to landholders who were in control and could pay tribute (Cortés thought so) or did it mean everyone who lived on the landholdings, all the servants, workers, every human head (as the viceroy maintained)? Cortés had ancient lawsuits that had been brought against him by people like Narváez (even after Narváez's disappearance and pre-

sumed death by drowning, Narváez's heirs carried on their suit; Velázquez's heirs, however, never claimed anything from Cortés).

For years Cortés stubbornly trailed after the Court. He was attended by
a large retinue, as suited his rank, and was comfortably put up in monasteries and castles, sometimes in inns. But he missed Sandoval. Alvarado had
been killed during a fight with Indians in Jalisco. After Alvarado had
returned with a fleet from Guatemala, intending, like Cortés, to explore the
southern sea, he had been called ashore to help in a skirmish with some
Indians, and the horse of a Spaniard above Alvarado on a steep slope had
slipped on shale and fallen, both horse and rider tumbling onto Alvarado
and both men and both horses falling down the mountainside. Cortés
missed his old captains.

Cortés was never able to gain the king/emperor's attention, nor would
Carlos appoint a tribunal to weigh Cortés's cases. Quarrels involving eminent noblemen always related to large amounts of money so the cases could
not be taken lightly, and the consequences were sure to disappoint one
group or the other. Carlos Quinto thought he had done more than enough
to reward and elevate Cortés, and his attitude toward him grew colder. The
king/emperor, naturally austere, introverted and moody, had his own
distractions and preoccupations, and sometimes would even fail to recognize Cortés, who in his early sixties no longer looked like the conqueror he
had once been, nor was his conquest fresh in the king's mind. A story was
told that, after Carlos had passed through a crowd that included Cortés,
the king was heard to ask his coachman who that was by the coach door.
And Cortés shouted through the window, "It's the one who gave you
more kingdoms than you used to have towns!"

Cortés had troubles besides litigation. His children, both legitimate and
illegitimate, were growing up, and in the manner of the times he was trying
to arrange enviable marriages for them. He had betrothed his eldest legitimate daughter, Doña María, to the eldest son of the Marqués de Astorga,
and had promised a dowry of a hundred thousand ducats and an elegant
wardrobe. But somehow the engagement had fallen through, some of
Cortés's children being as headstrong as their father.

Finally, in disgust, Cortés, curbing the stubbornness that was such a
strong element in his character, decided to give up pursuit of the king and
prepared to return to Mexico, where, in spite of all the lawsuits and the
residencia, his income had never been garnished or substantially reduced.
In Seville, however, he took sick—another bout of fever, pleurisy, dysentery. Sensing that this might be his last illness, Cortés executed the will that
for some time he and Gómara had been drafting, various versions of which

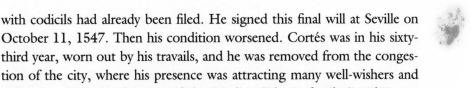

with codicils had already been filed. He signed this final will at Seville on October 11, 1547. Then his condition worsened. Cortés was in his sixty-third year, worn out by his travails, and he was removed from the congestion of the city, where his presence was attracting many well-wishers and callers, to the palatial home of the Medina-Sidonia family in what was considered the more salubrious atmosphere of the nearby country town of Castilleja de la Cuesta. There, after confessing his sins and receiving final absolution, Hernán Cortés died on December 2, 1547.

In his will, Cortés, after making lifelong provision for his wife, left most of his property to his legitimate heir who was with him, Don Martín, then fifteen years old, with full income to be delivered when Don Martín was twenty and full control turned over when he was twenty-five. Cortés recommended to his son the bailiffs and agents who had rendered good service. To his other children, including the illegitimate ones, Cortés left ample amounts, dowries for all the girls, and he specified generous allowances for the retainers of his household. He endowed three institutions — the Hospital de Jesús in Mexico City as the repository of his remains, a bilingual training school in Coyoacán for missionaries who would work in the conversion of the Indians (and where many Christian Indians were taught to work among their own people), and a nunnery in Coyoacán.

In the naming of his executors to function in Spain, Cortés put his trust in the nobility and named three distinguished noblemen, including the Marqués de Astorga, who, in conjunction with Cortés, had tried without success to arrange the marriage of their children. To act as executors of his estate in Mexico, Cortés named three prelates — because they were the most honest men he knew — and his wife.

In his will, Cortés expressed the troubling thoughts that persisted in his mind. He insisted that the Indians for whom he was responsible, those who were included in the *encomienda* he was passing to his son, should never pay more in tribute than they had paid to their own Indian sovereigns. If Don Martín were ever to find that more was being exacted from the Indians than had been exacted by Indian kings, the excess was to be restored to the Indians.

Also, Cortés questioned whether it was right that personal service, like labor in the mines, should properly be regarded as tribute. He cautioned his heir that a fair valuation must be placed on all personal labor, and fair compensation must be allowed for it.

Lastly, and on the point most troubling to him, Cortés expressed doubt that, in good conscience, any Indians at all should ever be regarded as slaves. This was a question Spain had been grappling with for many years,

ever since the Portuguese had begun the importation into Europe of black
Africans as slaves. Cortés knew that for the American Indians themselves
within their own societies before the advent of the Spaniards slavery was an
established social condition, and the Indians had never questioned its
legitimacy. Likewise, slavery was established and accepted among the black
Africans, as it was among the Arabs. But that slavery had its precedents in
heathen societies did not relieve Cortés of the perplexity he felt. There were
Christian advocates on both sides—Christian philosophers who argued
from the Aristotelian premise that natural differences existed between
peoples which made slavery inevitable and proper, and fiery Christian
clerics, both Dominicans and Franciscans, who argued that each and every
human being, and particularly each Indian innocent in limbo, had a soul
that was precious and priceless and that no one could own. The upcoming
buccaneering nations—England, France, Holland, Denmark—were accepting and endorsing slavery with gusto. But Cortés held to his doubts.
He would not take it upon himself to solve this conundrum; the best he
could do was to refer the problem to his son.

These were the thoughts in the mind of the conqueror of Mexico, the
thoughts that bridged his life into eternity—not recollections of the rigors
or rewards of his spectacular career, but concerns for his children and
speculations on the propriety of his conduct in the eyes of God.

BIBLIOGRAPHY

This bibliography does not purport to be complete. This story of ancient glories has been in my mind for many years, and bits and pieces of it have come from all sorts of sources, including many personal investigations. The books listed are among the most substantial written sources. The sources that have not been translated from Spanish into English are marked with an asterisk.

Anonymous Conqueror (The). *Narrative of Some Things of New Spain and of the Great City of Temestitan, Mexico.* Translated and edited by Marshall H. Saville. Cortés Society, New York, 1917.

Bancroft, Hubert Howe. *History of Mexico.* Vols. 1 and 2 (of 6). San Francisco: A. L. Bancroft & Co., 1883–1888.

Bandelier, A. F. *Art of Warfare and Mode of Warfare of the Ancient Mexicans.* Pages 95–161. Reports of the Peabody Museum of American Archaeology and Ethnology, 1877.

Bourne, Edward Gaylord. *Spain in America 1450–1580.* New York: Barnes & Noble, 1962.

Butterfield, Marvin E. *Jerónimo de Aguilar, Conquistador.* University of Alabama Press, 1955.

*Casas, Bartolomé de las. *Historia de las Indias.* Mexico: Fondo de Cultura Económica, 1951.

————. *A Relation of the First Voyages and Discoveries Made by the Spaniards in America, with an Account of their Unparallel'd Cruelties on the Indians in the Destruction of Above Forty Millions of People.* Printed for Daniel Brown and Andrew Bell, London, 1699.

Cervantes de Salazar, Francisco. *Life in the Imperial and Loyal City of Mexico in New Spain*. Translated by Lee Barrett Shepard. Edited by Carlos Eduardo Castañeda. Facsimile ed. Austin: University of Texas Press, 1953.

Conway, George Robert Graham. "Hernando Alonso, A Jewish Conquistador with Cortés in Mexico." *Publications of the American Jewish Historical Society* XXXI (1928): 9–31.

————. *Last Will and Testament of Cortés, Marqués del Valle*. Mexico, 1939.

Cortés, Hernán. *Letters from Mexico*. Translated and edited by A. R. Pagden. New York: Orion Press, 1971.

Crow, John A. *Spain: The Root and the Flower*. New York: Harper & Row, 1963.

Díaz del Castillo, Bernal. *The Conquest of New Spain*. Translated and edited by J. M. Cohen. Penguin Books, 1965.

————. *The Discovery and Conquest of Mexico, 1517–1521*. Translated and edited by Alfred Percival Maudslay. New York: Farrar, Strauss, 1956.

————. *The True History of the Conquest of Mexico*. Translated by Maurice Keatinge. London, 1800; Ann Arbor, Michigan: University Microfilms, 1966.

————. *The True Story of the Conquest of New Spain*. 5 vols. Translated by Alfred Percival Maudslay from the only exact copy of the original manuscript written in 1568 and later edited and published in Mexico by Genaro García. London: Hakluyt Society, 1908–1916.

Durán, Fray Diego. *Aztecs: The History of the Indies of New Spain*. Translated by Doris Heyden and Fernando Horcasita from the copy made in 1854 by José Fernando Ramírez of the Spanish version published in Madrid from the original manuscript in 1586. New York: Orion Press, 1964.

Elliott, John Huxtable. *The Mental World of Hernán Cortés*. Transactions of the Royal Historical Society. 5th series (1967): 41–58.

Gardiner, C. Harvey. *The Constant Captain: Gonzalo de Sandoval*. Carbondale: Southern Illinois University Press, 1961.

————. *Martín López: Conquistador Citizen of Mexico*. Lexington: University of Kentucky Press, 1958.

————. *Naval Power in the Conquest of Mexico*. New York: Greenwood Press, 1956.

*Glass, J. *Lienzo de Tlaxcala*. Mexico City: Museum of Anthropology, unpublished.

Gómara, Francisco López de. *The Life of the Conqueror by His Secretary.* Translated and edited by Leslie Byrd Simpson from the Spanish version published in Zaragoza in 1552. Berkeley and Los Angeles: University of California Press, 1965.

――――. *The Pleasent Historie of the Conquest of Weast India.* Translated by Thomas Nicholas. London, 1578. Ann Arbor, Michigan: University Microfilms, 1966.

Gurría Lacroix, Jorge. *Itinerary of Hernán Cortés.* Translated by Paul Cannady with captions by Sheila Prieto. Mexico: Ediciones EuroAmericanos, 1973.

Hanke, Lewis. "Conquest and the Cross" and "Art as Propaganda: The Black Legend." *American Heritage,* February 1963: 4–19, 107–111.

――――. *The Spanish Struggle for Justice in the Conquest of America.* Philadelphia: University of Pennsylvania Press, 1949.

*Herrera y Tordesillas, Antonio de. *Historia General de los Hechos de los Castellanos en las Islas y Tierra Firme del Mar Oceano.* Spain, 1728–1730.

Kehoe, Alice B. *North American Indians.* New Jersey: Prentice-Hall, 1981.

Kelly, John Eoghan. *Pedro de Alvarado, Conquistador.* Princeton University Press, 1932.

López, Enrique Hank. "Mexico." *American Heritage,* April 1969: 4–37.

MacNutt, Francis Augustus. *The Sepulture of Fernando Cortés.* Letter to Mrs. Zelia Nuttall, privately printed. New York, 1910.

――――. *Fernando Cortés and the Conquest of Mexico.* G. P. Putnam's Sons, New York and London, 1909.

――――. *Bartolomé de las Casas: His Life, His Apostolate, and His Writings.* G. P. Putnam's Sons, New York and London, 1909.

――――. *De Orbe Novo: the Eight Decades of Peter Martyr D'Anghera.* G. P. Putnam's Sons, New York and London, 1912.

Madariaga, Salvador de. *Hernán Cortés: Conqueror of Mexico.* Coral Gables, Florida: University of Miami Press, 1942.

Motolinía (Fray Toribio de Benavente). *Motolinía's History of the Indians of New Spain.* Translated by Elizabeth Andros Foster. Berkeley: University of California Press, 1950.

Padden, R. C. *The Hummingbird and the Hawk: Conquest and Sovereignty in the Valley of Mexico, 1503–1541.* New York: Harper & Row, 1970.

Prescott, William Hickling. *History of the Conquest of Mexico*. New York: Harper Bros., 1843.

Sahagún, Fray Bernardino de. *Florentine Codex: General History of the Things of New Spain*. Translated by Charles E. Dibble and Arthur J. O. Anderson. Salt Lake City: University of Utah Press, 1982.

Sedgwick, Henry Dwight. *Cortés, the Conqueror*. Bobbs-Merrill Co., Indianapolis, 1926 (for unpublished letter from Cortés to Carlos Quinto, see the Appendix).

Smith, Bradley. *Mexico: A History in Art*. Garden City, New York: Doubleday & Co., 1968.

———. *Spain: A History in Art*. Garden City, New York: Doubleday & Co., 1966.

Solís y Rivadeneyra, Antonio de. *The History of the Conquest of Mexico by the Spaniards*. Translated by Thomas Townsend. London, 1753.

Soustelle, Jacques. *Daily Life of the Aztecs*. New York: MacMillan, 1962.

Tannenbaum, Frank. *Slave and Citizen*. New York: Alfred A. Knopf, 1947.

*Toro, Alfonso. *Un Crimen de Hernán Cortés*. Mexico, 1922.

*Torquemada, Fray Juan de. *Monarquía Indiana*. Madrid: Chávez Hayhoe, 1723; Facsimile ed., Mexico, 1944.

Vaillant, George C. *Aztecs of Mexico*. New York: Doubleday, Doran, 1941.

*Vázquez de Tápia, Bernardina. *Relación del conquistador Bernardino Vázquez de Tápia*. Edited by Manuel Romero de Terreros. Mexico, 1939.

Wagner, Henry R. *The Rise of Fernando Cortés*. Berkeley and Los Angeles: Cortés Society, 1944.

Wauchope, R., ed. *Handbook of Middle American Indians*. Austin: University of Texas Press, 1967.

INDEX

Italicized page numbers refer to illustrations.

A NOTE ON THE TYPE

This book was set in ITC Galliard, a typeface drawn by Matthew Carter for the Mergenthaler Linotype Company in 1978.

Carter, one of the foremost type designers of the twentieth century, studied and worked with historic hand-cut punches before designing type-faces for Linotype, film and digital composition. He based his Galliard design on sixteenth-century types by Robert Granjon. Galliard has the classic look of the old Granjon types, as well as a vibrant, dashing quality which gives it a contemporary feel.

Composed by ComCom, a division of The Haddon Craftsmen, Allentown, Pennsylvania.

Printed and bound by Courier Book Company, Westford, Massachusetts.

Designed by Robert C. Olsson

Maps by Claudia Carlson

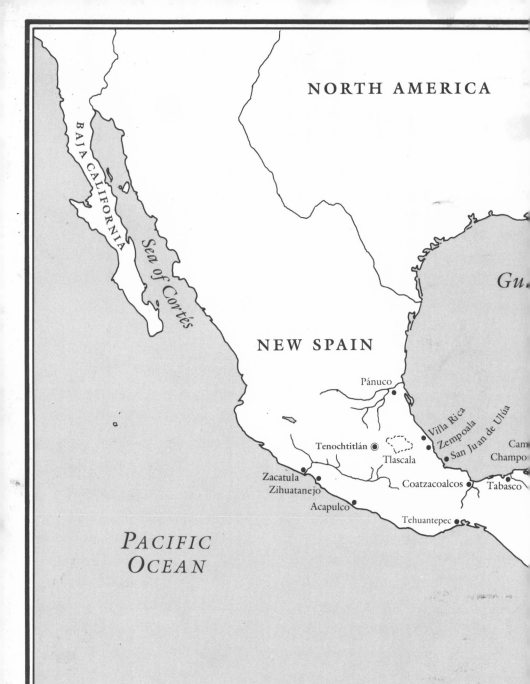

NORTH AMERICA

BAJA CALIFORNIA

Sea of Cortés

NEW SPAIN

Gu.

Pánuco

Villa Rica
Zempoala
San Juan de Ulúa

Tenochtitlán

Cam
Champo

Tlascala

Zacatula
Zihuatanejo

Coatzacoalcos

Tabasco

Acapulco

Tehuantepec

PACIFIC
OCEAN

SCALE OF MILES

0   125   250